The Business Word Book

A Spelling, Usage, and Vocabulary Guide

The Business Word Book

A Spelling, Usage, and Vocabulary Guide

Sheila B. Sloane

John L. Dusseau

Scott, Foresman and Company
Glenview, Illinois   London, England

Copyright © 1984 Scott, Foresman and Company.
All Rights Reserved.
Printed in the United States of America.
ISBN 0-673-15962-0

Library of Congress Cataloging in Publication Data
Sloane, Shiela B.
   The business word book; a spelling, usage, and vocabulary guide.

   1. English language—Business English.   2. English
language—Usage.   3. Spellers.   4. Vocabulary.
I. Dusseau, John L.   II. Title.
PE1115.S585   1984   428.1'02465   84-10331

1 2 3 4 5 6-MPC-89 88 87 86 85 84

Dedicated to
Melvin and Ruth
Beloved Brother and Sister
and Affectionate Sharers of Our Lives

Contents

Preface

"When I use a word," Humpty Dumpty said in a rather scornful tone, "it means just what I choose it to mean—neither more nor less."

"The question is," said Alice, "whether you can make words mean so many different things."

"The question is," said Humpty Dumpty, "which is to be master—that's all."

Lewis Carroll

The meanings of words do indeed vary, and one might even say with Humpty that mastery of language does imply a free-swinging attitude toward words. But, alas, the spelling of words does not vary, save in a few ambiguous instances. That Thoreau said, "I distrust a man who can spell a word only one way" is a pleasant thought, not a license to misspell, for consistently correct spelling is the basis on which the meaning of words rests. To write "principle" instead of "principal" is to defeat the purpose of language.

These days technical terms are in every letter and on every tongue. Attend a cocktail party with a sprinkling of bankers and stockbrokers and you will find, mixed with the Parmesan and Perrier, a blend of terms like "monetarism," "interpolation," and "cybernetics"; visit the home of an engineer and you will hear about "hydrology," "electro-osmosis," and "deaeration."

The Business Word Book, however, is not a dictionary, but simply what its subtitle suggests—a spelling and vocabulary guide. It was written in the hope that not only secretaries and transcriptionists but business people as well would profit from a sure and solid guide to orthography. It is, therefore, its purpose to provide a simple method of locating a sought-after word or phrase with ease and speed. The attempt here is to give the reader a listing of common and uncommon business terms and phrases to ease the burden of searching many books for what can now be found in a single volume. The special needs of the secretary have guided the organization and treatment of its content.

Part 2 of the work is divided into seven sections arranged in a single alphabetical listing. The users will find terms where they would expect them, i.e., in each major category of business. Through the method of keeping each such section complete within itself, the time spent in seeking out a word is greatly reduced. If the term or phrase applies to several categories, it will be listed in each appropriate section, thus relieving the user of guesswork.

When a listed entry appears as the first word of one or more compound terms, it is spelled out only the first time. For example, the reader will find such entries as follow:

tenancy —	or	sintered —
t. in common		s. carbides
		s. clay
		s. fly-ash

Also the system of subentries gives the user a "double check" on garbled or unfamiliar terms. In this system, many compound terms appear both as regular entries and as subentries. For example, "dynamic allocation" appears as an entry under D and as a subentry under "allocation", "digital integrator" appears as an entry under D and as a subentry under "integrator" and so on. This enables the user to check the subentries under the appropriate entry if there is uncertainty about the first word in any such compound term. With the alphabetical arrangement of chapters, any section can be easily found by flipping through the pages and noting the section title at the top of each page.

We believe we have been consistent in the use of these and other devices to ensure the reader's ready access to the best use of this book. But if, as Emerson said, consistency be the hobgoblin of little minds, then our minds are large indeed, for we have been scarcely consistent in restricting content of the work to spelling only. But there has been some method in our inconstancy. The very first chapter on "Difficult Words and Phrases" provides definitions, for the distinction between *misfortune* and *calamity* cannot be drawn without giving their meanings. Throughout this chapter we have also included examples of use from literature. In the instance of *misfortune,* it is a pleasure to quote Disraeli on his arch political rival: "Were Gladstone to fall into the Thames, that would be a *misfortune.* Were someone to pull him out, that would be a *calamity.*" Further, even in the business vocabularies we have not hesitated to define words whose common meaning is quite different from their special meaning. For example, in engineering a kid is not a young boy or a young goat, but a bundle of brushwood used as a protective facing on sea walls or river banks.

It has been the observation of one of the authors as editor that even the most stalwart friendships may not survive the rigors of coauthorship. In the instance of *The Business Word Book* the authors are wife and husband, and their marriage has been strengthened by work together. "Marriage," said Johnson, "has many pains; but celibacy has no pleasures." One of the pleasures of marriage is exchanging the thoughts and ideas that make writing a shared and exciting adventure.

Finally, we should like to express our debt of gratitude to the skilled staff of Scott, Foresman and Company and our hope that the book will be a valuable reference tool to all those concerned with proper use of business terms. We should even dare to think that here and there in the book the reader will find small examples of the wit and wisdom that made writing *The Business Word Book* fun and challenge for its authors.

SHEILA B. SLOANE

JOHN L. DUSSEAU

Adjunctive Vocabulary

Difficult Words and Phrases

In the use of difficult words and phrases reliance is put upon teaching by example rather than by precept, for the canons of rhetoric and good usage may often be wisely disregarded. ''Rules and models,'' said Hazlitt, ''destroy genius and art.'' E. B. White, too, was a gentle breaker of rules and especially distrusted the notion that sentences should not end with prepositions. Hence he liked the story of the father of a little boy going upstairs to read to his son but accidentally bringing along the wrong book. ''What,'' the boy asks, ''did you bring the book that I don't want to be read to out of up for?'' Few indeed are sentences that end in five prepositions, but it is said that Don Juan ended almost every sentence with a proposition. A good example of the importance of a single letter in some of the look-alike and sound-alike words to follow is *forbear* and *forebear*.

It is hoped that the quotations here used to illuminate principles of correct usage are apt and in themselves interesting and sometimes amusing. The examples, when not credited, are inventions of the authors. Occasionally, too, they have sprung from memories capacious but not infallible. We shall hope that, if we have not always been precise in quotation, we have never been unjust.

Ability (n); **Capacity** (n).
These words should not be used interchangeably. *Ability*: Competence, faculty, skill, dexterity, talent. ''To every man according to his *ability*'' (St. Matthew). ''From each according to his *ability*'' (Communist Manifesto). *Capacity*: The power to receive, hold or contain. ''A small bucket of slight *capacity*.'' ''He had a certain *capacity* for instruction in violin playing but only slight *ability* to perform.''

Abjure (v); **Adjure** (v).
The two words are often confused; but their Latin prefixes are a guide to their separate meanings (Ab-, away from; Ad-, toward). *Abjure*: To renounce, repudiate, avoid, shun. ''And other pleasures all *abjure*'' (Milton). *Adjure*: To charge or command solemnly—often under oath—to entreat or request. ''His friends *adjured* him to take care of a life so valuable to his country'' (Macaulay).

Absorb (v), **Absorption** (n); **Adsorb** (v), **Adsorption** (n).
Absorb: To suck up, to swallow, to engross or engage wholly, to take in without recoil or other reaction. ''I have nothing to do today. My practice is never very *absorbing*'' (Dr. Watson to Sherlock Holmes). *Adsorb*: An essentially chemical term meaning to condense and hold by *adsorption* as when charcoal *adsorbs* gases. *Adsorption* is the adhesion in thin layers of the molecules of gases or liquids or dissolved substances to the surface of solids with which they are in contact, so that *adsorption* is a technical antonym for *absorption*.

Accelerate (v); **Exhilirate** (v).
This would scarcely seem a necessary distinction—*Accelerate* meaning to quicken; *Exhilirate* to gladden. Nevertheless, one does hear the *accelerator* of an automobile sometimes called its *exhilirator*. How this must gladden the heart of the car and sadden the heart of the purist.

Accept (v); **Except** (v & prep).
It seems unlikely that these words should ever be confused; but they sometimes are. *Accept* (v): To take or receive, to agree or consent to, to respond affirmatively or acknowledge formally. "Margaret Fuller: 'I *accept* the universe.' Carlyle: 'Gad! she'd better' " (Oxford Dictionary of Quotations). *Except* (v): To exclude or omit. "You should always *except* the present company" (O'Keefe). *Except* (prep) "All a little daft *except* thee and me and I'm not so sure about thee" (Anon.)

Accident (n); **Mishap** (n).
Accident: Any event occuring unexpectedly or without plan or purpose. Hence an *accident* may be either fortunate or unfortunate. "What a lucky *accident* that we met when I needed money." "What an unlucky *accident* that you left home without your wallet." *Mishap*: Any *unfortunate* accident. "Alas for unforeseen *mishaps*" (Cowper).

Accidentally (adv); **Accidently** (adv).
Accidentally: Unexpectedly, by chance, without conscious purpose. "*Accidentally* is often mispronounced and misspelled. It has five syllables: ac-ci-den-tal-ly" (Dictionary of Problem Words and Expressions). *Accidently*: There is no such word.

Adapt (v); **Adept** (adj); **Adopt** (v).
Adapt (v): To make suitable, to adjust or modify. "A farmhouse *adapted*, I suppose, from the old ruin" (Hawthorne). "A three-act comedy *adapted* from a French novel" (The Saturday Review). *Adept* (adj): Skilled, proficient. "Whoever is *adept* at the speaking trade will *adapt* himself to inconvenience" (Macaulay). *Adopt* (v): (1) To choose for oneself, to make one's own by selection, specifically to take as one's own child. (2) To vote upon affirmatively, to accept. (1) "Friends not *adopted* with a schoolboy's haste,/But chosen with a nice discerning taste" (Cowper). (2) "The House *adopted* the resolution because time and truth were running out." In general: "A jeweler *adept* at *adapting* designs from abroad will find the customers here *adopt* them eagerly."

Addendum (n); **Addenda** (n).
Addendum is a singular noun meaning anything added, and takes a singular verb. "After I had gone over the instructions, I wrote an *addendum*" (Holmes). *Addenda* is its plural; but because of a falling-off in the study of Latin, even literate writers now use *addendums*.

Adduce (v); **Deduce** (v).
Adduce: To cite evidence conclusive or persuasive. "All that I have *adduced* is sufficient to convince any reasonable person" (Holmes). *Deduce*: To reach a conclusion from something known or assumed. "Poirot *deduced* from scanty evidence that the butler did it." Also see *Deduce*.

Adept: See **Adapt.**

Adjacent (adj); **Contiguous** (adj).
The distinction between the words is observed more in law than in common parlance. *Adjacent*: Lying near or close, neighboring. "We furnished ourselves with provisions at the *adjacent* inn" (Tyndall). *Contiguous*: Touching, in contact. "When Mrs. Malaprop referred to the contagious countries, she undoubtedly meant *contiguous*. A touching rather than infective example."

Adjure: See **Abjure.**

Adopt: See **Adapt.**

Adversary (n); **Antagonist** (n); **Opponent** (n).
An *Opponent* is anyone on the other side of a contest, whether a bridge game, lawsuit, or battle of wits. An *Antagonist* is an opponent of determined, hostile opposition, one who seeks with personal antagonism to win the stake at issue. An *Adversary* may be either an opponent or an antagonist; but his opposition is implied to be of long standing: "My desire is that mine *adversary* had written a book" (Job).

Adverse (adj); **Averse** (adj).
Adverse: Antagonistic, opposing, hostile. "*Adverse* circumstances delayed completion of the Panama Canal." *Averse*: Having distaste or dislike for, reluctant, unwilling. "What female heart can gold despise?/What cat's *averse* to fish?" (Gray).

Advice (n); **Advise** (v).
Advice is a noun only, meaning opinion, recommendation, counsel. "*Advice* is seldom welcome; and those who need it the most always like it the least" (Lord Chesterfield). *Advise* is a verb only, meaning to offer suggestion or guidance as worth following. "It's my old girl that *advises*. She has the head. But I never own to it before her" (Dickens). It is a word greatly overused in business correspondence as a genteel substitute for tell or say.

Affect (v); **Effect** (n & v).
These are words of different meaning and pronunciation. *Affect* (v): To act on, to create a response in. *Effect* (v): To bring about, to cause, to accomplish. *Effect* (n): (1) Result, consequence, influence. (2) A mental impression as produced by poetry or painting. (3) *Effects*: Goods or property. "Hot toddy will not *affect* the course of the common cold, but it will *effect* a pleasant sense of well-being." (1) "I don't know what *effect* these men will have upon the enemy, but, by God, they terrify me" (Duke of Wellington). (2) "That is the bitterness of arts; you see a good *effect*, and some nonsense about sense intervenes" (Stevenson). (3) "Unwillingly he willed his *effects* to charity."

Affective (adj); **Effective** (adj).
Affective: Caused by or causing emotion, emotional. "He was a judicious preacher, more instructive than *affective*" (Burnet). *Effective*: Adequate to a purpose, producing the intended result. "A more *affective* preacher would no doubt be more *effective*."

Afflict: See **Inflict.**

Aggravate (v); **Annoy** (v); **Irritate** (v).
There is a genuine distinction among these words. *Aggravate/aggravation* (n) is the strongest, meaning to intensify or make worse anything evil, disorderly or troublesome. "Such threats only serve to *aggravate* hostility" (Thackeray). "I think it's liquid *aggravation* that circulates through his veins, not regular blood" (Dickens). *Annoy/annoyance* (n) is less strong, meaning to pester or disturb. "Speak roughly to your little boy,/And beat him when he sneezes;/He only does it to *annoy*,/Because he knows it teases" (Lewis Carroll). *Irritate/irritation* (n) has the more specific meaning of arousing impatience or exciting a bodily response or reaction. "Any new taxation may *irritate*" (Ranken). "We come now to those motions which depend on *irritation*" (Darwin).

Alien (adj & n): **Alienist** (n); **Alienate** (v).
Alien as an adjective means simply foreign but by extension strange or even hostile. "She stood in tears amid the *alien* corn" (Keats). "A system of confusion remains which is *alien* to all economy" (Burke). *Alien* as a noun means one born in a country other than that in which he resides but of which he has not become a naturalized citizen or subject. "Obsolete statutes prohibiting *aliens* from working in the kingdom" (Macaulay). An *Alienist* is specifically a psychiatrist who specializes in the legal aspects of sanity and insanity. "Opposing *alienists* confused the jury and the issue." *Alienate* means to turn away, to make apathetic or averse. "No difference of political opinion can *alienate* Cicero" (Macaulay).

All Ready (adj); **Already** (adv).
All Ready (adj): Completely ready or prepared. *Already* (adv): Previously or earlier. "He was *all ready* to go; but the train had *already* gone."

Allude (v), **Allusion** (n); **Elude** (v), **Elusive** (adj), **Elusion** (n); **Illusory** (adj).
These words are not often confused, but they are sometimes misused. *Allude* means to refer to a person or thing indirectly or by implication—not by name. "Though he never uses your name, the *allusion* to you is obvious" (Fowler's Modern English Usage). But it is incorrect to say: "When the speaker *alluded* to President Lincoln, his words were received with loud cheers" (New York Times). *Elude* means simply to evade and its adjective *elusive* means evasive. "Is he in heaven?— Is he in hell?/That demmed *elusive* Pimpernel?" (Baroness Orczy). The *illusory* is that which appears to be of greater real or solid value than is so: "The *elusive* mocks its pursuer, the *illusory* its possessor" (Fowler's Modern English Usage).

Alright; All Right.
There is no such word as *Alright*; it is a common misspelling for *all right*, meaning satisfactory or acceptable. "I'm *all right*; you're *all right*."

Alternate (adj, v. & n); **Alternately** (adv); **Alternative** (adj & n); **Alternatively** (adv).
Alternate (adj): In a state of constant succession. "This battered Caravanserai whose Doorways are *alternate* Night and Day" (Fitzgerald). *Alternate* (v): To change back and forth between conditions and states, to rotate, to occur successively. "We should *alternate* hot compresses with cold" (Beeson-McDermott Textbook of Medicine). *Alternately* (adv): Successively or in rotation. "The laughing hyena may *alternately* laugh and weep." *Alternative* (adj): Affording an option or preference. "The *alternative* courses before us are war or temporary compromise." *Alternative* (n): A choice. "An unhappy *alternative* is before you, Elizabeth. Your mother will never see you again if you do *not* marry Mr. Collins, and I will never see you again if you *do*" (Jane Austen). *Alternatively* (adv): In a way that offers a selection. "Roast chicken is *alternatively* offered with roast duck." In general, the distinction between *alternate* and *alternative* is that the former implies one thing *after* the other, the latter one thing *or* the other.

Alumnus, Alumni, Alumna, Alumnae (n's).
A male graduate of a specific school or university or (by extension) any institution is an *alumnus*— plural, *alumni*. Such a female graduate is an *alumna*—plural *alumnae*. When referring to male and female graduates together, the masculine plural *alumni* is used. "The poorer and less steady *alumni* of the school" (Lytton).

Amaze (v); **Astonish** (v); **Surprise** (n & v).
Amaze (v): To astound, stun, overwhelm with surprise. "Ye gods, it doth *amaze* me" (Shakespeare). *Astonish* (v): To strike with sudden wonder, to daze or silence, literally to turn to stone. "One of these days I'll loore him on to skittles and *astonish* him" (Byron). *Surprise* (v): To take unawares. Lord Chesterfield caught by his wife in a compromising situation: "Madam, I am *surprised*; you are *astonished*." *Surprise* (n): An unexpected occurrence or circumstance. "Two lovely black eyes,/Oh! what a *surprise*!" (Coborn).

Amend (v), **Amendment** (n); **Amends** (n); **Emend** (v), **Emendation** (n).
Amend (v): To alter, modify, correct. "Patiently adjust, *amend* and heal" (Hardy). *Amendment* (n): The act of amending or improving but, specifically, alteration in or addition to a legislative act or resolution. "Let us hastily amend the *amendment*." *Amends* (n): Reparation or compensation for loss or damage. "And doth not a meeting like this make *amends*,/For all the long years I've been wand'ring away?" (Thomas Moore). *Emend* (v): Although the word was once simply an alternative spelling to *amend*, it has come to mean specifically to edit a manuscript by correcting its flaws and errors; and *Emendation* (n) is the act of manuscript editing. "God save me from busybody *emendation*."

Among (prep); **Between** (prep).
Correct usage presumably requires that *among* be used to indicate a relationship of more than two objects or persons; and *between* a relationship of only two objects or persons. "*Between* the Devil

and the deep blue sea." But this is a distinction now as much honored in the breach as in the observance.

Amoral (adj), **Immoral** (adj), **Unmoral** (adj).
Amoral means without moral quality—neither moral nor immoral. "Birds and animals may justly be considered *amoral.*" *Immoral* means wicked, depraved, consciously sinful. "There is no such thing as a moral or *immoral* book. Books are well written, or badly written" (Wilde). *Unmoral* means having no relationship to morality, unable to distinguish between right and wrong. "The homicidal maniac may be considered *unmoral* and hence not consciously vicious."

Angry (adj); **Mad** (adj).
These words should never be confused. *Angry*: Wrathful, indignant, resentful. "Do no sinful action,/speak no *angry* word" (Alexander). *Mad*: Insane, abnormal, frenzied. "For Allah created the English *mad*—the maddest of all mankind!" (Kipling).

Annoy: See **Aggravate.**

Antagonist: See **Adversary.**

Apologize (v), **Apology** (n); **Excuse** (n & v); **Pardon** (n & v).
Apologize (v): To admit, with regret, error or wrongdoing. "I never *apologize*" (Shaw). *Apology* (n): Written or spoken regret or remorse for a wrong or insulting act or a malicious deed. "An *apology* for the Devil: It must be remembered that we have heard only one side of the case. God has written all the books" (Byron). *Excuse* (n & v): Both noun and verb have the same essential meaning. An excuse shifts rather than admits blame; it offers extenuation for a fault. "Let my obedience then *excuse*/My disobedience now" (Cowper). *Pardon* (n & v): Both forms signify forgiveness of an offense, wrong, or discourtesy. "Dr Mudd's heirs and defenders believe that his *pardon* implied guilt and that he should be exonerated" (Dusseau). From the foregoing it is clear that "Pardon me" is too strong an expression for use in the instance of a trivial discourtesy. "*Excuse* me" is generally preferable.

Apposite (adj); **Opposite** (adj).
Apposite: Suitable, well-adapted, relevant. *Opposite*: Opposed, contrary, radically different. "His statement though *opposite* to accepted ideas, was *apposite.*"

Appraise (v), **Appraisal** (n); **Apprise** (v), **Apprize** (var).
Appraise (v): To assess. To estimate the size, quantity, worth or monetary value of anything. *Appraisal* (n): The act of appraising and, specifically, item-by-item evaluation of property for insurance or tax purposes. *Apprise* (v): To inform or disclose (often followed by of). *Apprize* is a seldom-used variant of *apprise*. "When *apprised* of the *appraisal*, he was astonished at the value of his legacy."

Apprehend (v), **Apprehension** (n), **Apprehensive** (adj); **Comprehend** (v), **Comprehension** (n), **Comprehensive** (adj).
These words all signify understanding, but they have subtle differences of meaning and of extension as shown in their roots, for *ap-* forms denote *getting* hold or grasping and the *com-* forms *having* hold or possession of. What is beyond one's *apprehension* is beyond perception; what is beyond *comprehension* is not fully understood. *Apprehend* (v): (1) To grasp the meaning of, to perceive. (2) To take into custody, arrest, catch. (3) To be suspicious or fearful of. (1) "He that can *apprehend* and consider vice with all her baits and seeming pleasures" (Milton). (2) "The sheriff *apprehended* the cattle thieves in the midst of their dastardly attempt." (3) "The sense of death is most in *apprehension*" (Shakespeare). *Comprehend* (v): To understand the nature, meaning or significance of. (2) To include or comprise. (1) "Our souls, whose faculties can *comprehend*/The wondrous Architecture of the world" (Marlowe). (2) "Such tricks hath strong imagination/That, if it would but apprehend some joy,/It *comprehends* some bringer of that joy" (Shakespeare).

Assay (n & v); **Essay** (n & v).

Assay means, as a verb, to analyze or to test; as a noun test or trial. "The *assay* disclosed that all that glitters is not gold." *Essay* as verb or noun means attempt or effort; but the noun has also the specific meaning of a short literary composition built upon a central theme. Hence Lord Bacon: "My *essays* come home to men's business and bosoms."

Assure (v); **Ensure** (v); **Insure** (v), **Insurance** (n): **Reassure** (v), **Reassurance** (n).

Assure: To declare earnestly, to convince, to state confidently, to be certain of. "Drest in a little brief authority,/Most ignorant of what he's most *assur'd*" (Shakespeare). *Ensure*: To make sure or certain. "This letter will *ensure* your admission but hasten your departure." *Insure*: To guarantee or indemnify against loss or harm. "Down went the owners—greedy men whom hope of gain allured;/ Oh, dry the starting tear, for they were heavily *insured*" (Gilbert). *Insurance* has the more particular meaning of the act or business of insuring property or person against loss or harm by providing indemnification therefor. *Reassure*: To assure again or repeatedly but with the connotation of bringing encouragement or comfort or confidence to. "His praise *reassured* me and restored my courage."

Astonish: See **Amaze.**

Aural: See **Oral.**

Average: See **Median.**

Averse: See **Adverse.**

Avert (v), **Aversion** (n); **Divert** (v), **Diversion** (n); **Evert** (v), **Eversion** (n).

The words have the same Latin root (to turn) but different meanings. *Avert*: To turn aside or ward off. "Use any expedient which might *avert* the danger" (Macauley). *Divert*: To deflect, to distract, or, more broadly, to entertain. "An avocation to *divert* her thoughts, fill her time, and divide her interests" (Bronte). *Evert*: To turn outward or inside out, to overturn. "It is a very simple and easy thing to *evert* the eyelids" (Harlan).

Backward (adj & adv); **Backwards** (adv).

As an adverb either form may be used. "It is a poor sort of memory that only works *backwards*" (Carroll). But as an adjective, only *backward* may be used. "But I by *backward* steps would move" (Vaughan).

Bad (adj); **Badly** (adv).

Bad is a curious word with its comparative *worse* and superlative *worst* and its wide range of meanings from wicked and evil, through faulty and rotten, to inadequate, naughty and ill. It is also scorned as an adjective in the prevalent misuse, "I feel *badly*." If this means anything, it is that one's sense of touch is operating poorly. However, the error is now so common that the grammatical distinction between adjective and adverb is breaking down; but resist this temptation and say, instead, "I feel *bad*." Disraeli has one of his characters say, "I rather like *bad* wine; one gets so bored with good wine." Hence it was said of Disraeli that his inverted snobbery was but *badly* disguised.

Bail out; Bale out.

In securing a person's release from custody by guaranteeing his reappearance for trial, the spelling is always *bail out*; and the Oxford English Dictionary stoutly maintains that for emptying a boat of water we should use the same spelling, for the verb derives from the French *baille*, bucket. But the OED might as well save its breath, for public usage prefers, indeed insists upon, *bale* both for the boat and for making a parachute descent, and reserves *bail* for prisoners. Perhaps a mania for differentiation has caused this strange distinction, or perhaps the boat balers and descending parachutists are thought to be *baleful* in its archaic sense, full of woe.

Barbaric (adj); **Barbarous** (adj).
The two words are close in meaning, each referring to the customs and ways of barbarians. However, *barbaric* is sometimes used in a favorable sense to mean vigorous, strong or splendid. "Where the gorgeous east with richest hand/Showers on her kings *barbaric* pearl and gold" (Milton). But *barbarous* always means uncivilized, fierce, cruel, savage. " 'Twas a *barbarous* deed" (Shelley).

Bear (v); **Bore, Born, Borne** (pp).
Bear as a verb has various but distinct meanings. To give birth to, to produce by natural growth, to support, to endure, to take. However, in the use of its past participle curious distinctions are preserved, *borne* being correct in all senses except that of birth. "*Borne*, like thy bubbles, onward" (Byron). But: "All men were naturally *born* free" (Milton). However, and unfortunately, *borne* is also used in its active sense to refer to birth: "She has *borne* no children"; and in the passive sense when *by* follows: "Several children *borne* by her survive." But in the passive sense without *by*, *born* is correct: "A *born* fool." This is confusing enough without bringing four-legged Carnivora into the picture. "*Bears born* in hibernation are known to have *borne* subzero temperatures nicely."

Because of, Due to, Owing to, On account of (prep's).
Because of and *on account of* are clearly adverbial prepositions in good and standard use: "He fell *because of* the slippery ice." But *due to* and *owing to* present a curious problem. *Due* and *owing* are both adjectives and seemingly should hence only modify nouns, so that "His fall was *due to* the slippery ice" is correct; but "He fell *due to* the slippery ice" is incorrect. However, long usage has sanctioned *owing to* in an adverbial character: "He fell from His Grace's grace *owing to* his gracelessness." But this privilege has not yet been accorded *due to*. "The preposition *due to*, is not more incorrect than the preposition *owing to*, but it is not yet so thoroughly established in the language" (Curme). The only present satisfactory answer to this grammarian's dilemma is to avoid *due to*.

Beside (prep), **Besides** (adv & prep).
Beside is a preposition only, meaning by the side of; whereas *besides* is an adverb meaning in addition to, but it does have use as a preposition in the sense of except. Hence "I sat *besides* the stream" is incorrect. The old song title has it right: "I Do Like To Be *Beside* The Seaside" (Glover-Kind). "Indeed I too would like to be *beside* the sea; but I have things to do *besides* lolling on the beach."

Between: See **Among.**

Biannual (adj); **Biennial** (adj).
There is not a great deal to be said for use of either word, and what little there is is complicated by the fact that *bi* (two or twice) is used ambiguously in these as in other similar hybrids (*biweekly, bimonthly*, and *biquarterly*). Nevertheless, *biannual* means twice a year, whereas *biennial* means once every two years. Even the Bulletin of the International Association of Professors of English fails to keep the distinction in mind: "An annual bulletin is our aim; but *biennial* issues may become necessary if the Association enlarges." Since *semi* means half, we might gain by replacing *biannual* with "semiannual" or even "twice a year." And for all we know, the professors of English do hope to publish once every two years instead of annually.

Billion (n); **Bullion** (n); **Bouillon** (n); **Million** (n).
It should be kept in mind that *billion* for many nations (e.g., United States and France) means a *thousand million* (1,000,000,000), whereas for the British it means a *million million* (1,000,000,000,000). The English stubbornly persist in calling our *billion* a *milliard*. "*Billions* for defense" must have meant to the British an overwhelming commitment. *Bullion* simply means gold or silver in mass and has no connotation of value. Hence there is no such thing as a bullionaire. For those who can't spell, the word is sometimes confused with *bouillon,* a clear broth.

Blatant (adj); **Flagrant** (adj).
Blatant means obtrusive, brazenly obvious, offensively noisy, clamorous; whereas *flagrant* means glaringly evident or notorious. "Maledictions, *blatant* tongues, and viperous hisses" (Southey). But "Many individuals were cut off on account of their *flagrant* wickedness" (Fletcher).

Bloc (n); **Block** (n & v).
Bloc (n): A French word meaning specifically a coalition or political group, i.e., the farm *bloc*. *Block* (n): A word of numerous meanings—a mass of wood, metal or stone, a cube-shaped toy, a hollow masonry building unit (i.e., a concrete *block*), a pattern used in the making of woodcuts, and a part of a city or town enclosed by four adjoining streets. In its basic meaning, "Awaiting the sensation of a short, sharp shock/From a cheap and chippy chopper on a big black *block*" (Gilbert). *Block* (v): Also a word of many meanings, but its most common is to hinder or obstruct. "No visible political force can *block* the power of the labor *bloc*."

Boat (n); **Ship** (n).
The difference is simply put. A *boat* is a small vessel, a *ship* a large vessel. The height of misuse would be calling the Queen Elizabeth II a *boat*; and yet "slow boat to China" does not suggest a small craft.

Born and **Borne**: See **Bear.**

Brake (n): **Break** (n & v)
The words signifying bracken, thicket, harrowing implement, or decelerating device are all spelt *brake*. "The heath, with withering *brake* grown o'er" (Crabbe). *Break* as a verb has innumerable meanings but they all involve the idea of splitting, smashing, dividing and, by extension, of violating, infringing, dissolving, interrupting, or fleeing from. *Break* as a noun has similar meanings but a few not inherent in the verb (i.e., a lucky stroke of fortune or a blank line between paragraphs). In its usual meaning, "Thou wast up by *break* of day" (Herbert).

Breach (n); **Breech** (n).
Breach: A break, rupture, or gap. An infraction or violation of law, trust or promise. A severance in relationships, as of friendship. "Once more unto the *breach*, dear friends; once more;/Or close up the wall with our English dead!" (Shakespeare). *Breech:* The rear or lower part of anything. Hence *breeches* become trousers. "Sir, it is no matter what leg you shall put into your *breeches* first" (Johnson).

Breath (n); **Breadth** (n); **Breathe** (v).
Breath (n): Air inhaled and exhaled in respiration. Hence, figuratively, life or vitality: "Poetry is the *breath* and finer spirit of all knowledge" (Wordsworth). *Breadth* (n): Width but, more specifically, the second largest dimension of a plane or solid figure. Hence, figuratively, freedom from restraint or from narrowness of view. "Simplicity, harmony and *breadth* combine in these pictures with a restfulness which is truly admirable" (Ruskin). *Breathe* (v): To inhale and exhale in respiration. Hence, figuratively, to inject as if by breathing, to infuse. "She can *breathe* life into any dull party." These words are seldom confused in meaning but occasionally in spelling.

Broach (v); **Brooch** (n).
Broach (v): To mention or suggest for the first time. "*Broach* me no broaches, and I'll but you no buts" (Anon.) *Brooch* (n): A jewel or clasp having a pin at the back for securing the ornament to cloth. "I will make you *brooches* for your delight" (Stevenson).

Bur (n); **Burr** (n).
The words are often used interchangeably; but they do have distinct meanings. *Bur:* (1) The spiky rough outer case around seeds. "Grand rough old Martin Luther,/better the uncouther:/Do roses stick like *burs?*" (Browning). (2) Anything that adheres like a *bur.* (3) A rotary cutting tool used in

dentistry and surgery. *Burr:* (1) A guttural pronunciation of the "R" sound. (2) A rough or irregular protuberance as on a tree or on a ragged metal edge after punching or cutting. Nevertheless, no one really faults two r's when one is meant: "I am a kind of *burr;* I shall stick" (Shakespeare).

Bust (v); **Burst** (v).
Burst is a verb in good repute. "Let me not *burst* in ignorance" (Shakespeare). But *bust* (as verb only, not as noun) is in ill repute, is in fact an illiteracy, but who will gainsay "spring is *busting* out all over" or even "block-*buster*"? However, slang does condone *bust* (to fail an examination or to demote a military person in rank) and *bust up* (to disagree or break up) and to *go bust* (to become bankrupt).

Cache (n & v); **Hide** (n & v); **Stash** (v).
Cache as a noun means hiding place; as a verb to conceal: "He accordingly *cached* enough provisions to last them back" (Kane). *Hide* as a verb also means to conceal; but as a noun it has the unrelated meanings of the skin of larger animals or trace of something: "The police were unable to find *hide* nor hair of the murder weapon." *Stash* is a word of unknown origin—perhaps a corruption of *cache*—for it shares its meanings: "The squirrel *stashes* away nuts for winter."

Caid: See **Qaid.**

Calamity: See **Misfortune.**

Can (v); **May** (v); **Might** (v or n); **Must** (v).
Can suggests the ability to be or do something: "Malt does more than Milton *can*/To justify God's ways to man" (Housman). Whereas *may* implies being or doing something with sanction or approval. "It is not what a lawyer tells me I *may* do; but what humanity, reason and justice tell me I ought to do" (Burke). *May* also expresses contingency and possibility: "There *may* be heaven; there must be hell:/Meantime there is our earth here — well!" (Browning). *Might* is a form of *may* in its sense of possibility: "If it was so, it *might* be: and if it were so, it would be; but as it isn't, it ain't" (Carroll). *Might* as a noun has no sense of the contingent; it is a word meaning absolute strength: "Ev'n that same Lord, that great in *might* and strong in battle is" (Scottish Metrical Psalm). *Must* means to be obliged or required to do or be something by force of duty, law, custom, conscience or circumstance: "Genius does what it *must* and talent does what it can" (Lytton).

Canvas (n); **Canvass** (v or n).
Canvas is a rough cloth, often used in the making of sails and hence the sails themselves: "Thou comest, much wept for: such a breeze/Compell'd thy *canvas*" (Tennyson). *Canvass* (v): To solicit funds, votes, opinions, etc. *Canvass* (n): A solicitation for funds or orders; a campaign for election to office: "In short, their success in the *canvass* quite astonished them" (Lord Sheffield).

Capacity: See **Ability.**

Capital (n or adj); **Capitol** (n).
The first of these words has a wide variety of meanings, the latter only one. *Capital:* A city or town that is an official seat of government. An uppercase letter as in capital C. An accumulation of stock or other wealth. Wealth employed in productive facility or in the earning of more wealth. As an adjective *capital* also has various meanings: Pertaining or relating to investments or assets; principal or important; excellent or first-rate; and, from its Latin root, fatal or serious or punishable by death as in *capital* error or a *capital* crime. *Capitol*, on the other hand, has only the meaning of a specific building. Capitalized it means either the meeting place of the United States Congress or the Temple of Jupiter in Rome. In lowercase it means specifically a building used for the meetings of state legislatures or the statehouse. "The state capital boasted a Neo-Grecian *capitol* of marble columns."

Carat (n); **Caret** (n); **Carrot** (n); **Karat** (n); **Karate** (n).

A *carat* is a unit of weight used in the appraisal and evaluation of jewelry, as in a diamond solitaire of three *carats*. A *caret* is a printer's or proofreader's mark used to indicate an omission. It arises from the Latin *carere*—to be without or lacking. *Carrot* is a vegetable considered edible by all rabbits and some people. *Karat* is simply a variation of *carat*: but for obscure reasons it is preferred as the unit for measuring the fineness of gold. *Karate* is a system of defense developed in Japan in which an opponent is rendered powerless without use of weapons but by striking sensitive areas of an attacker's body.

Carton (n); **Cartoon** (n)

A *carton* is a box or other container made of corrugated craft paper. It is also the small white disk within the bull's-eye of a target. *Cartoon* also has two somewhat different meanings. The first is of a drawing usually in caricature and meant to be humorous or satirical. The second is of a drawing on heavy paper meant to be reproduced and completed in same size as a tapestry or fresco. "How fine the *cartoons* of the tapestries for the Sistine Chapel" (Jameson).

Casual (adj); **Causal** (adj).

Words often confused, mispronounced and misused. *Casual*: Accidental, occuring by chance, indifferent, occasional, not serious, informal, relaxed: "And we, light half-believers in our *casual* creeds" (Arnold). *Causal*: Implying or constituting a sufficient cause. "A *casual* approach to duty can be the *causal* force in downright dereliction."

Celebrant (n); **Celebrator** or **Celebrater** (n).

A *celebrant* is a person participating in public religious rites or other ceremonies and, specifically, the officiating priest in celebration of the Eucharist: "There cannot be more than one *celebrant* or one chief consecrator" (London Times). One who celebrates festive occasions by merrymaking or one who praises effusively and widely is a *celebrator:* "I am really more a well-wisher to your felicity than a *celebrator* of your beauty" (Pope).

Censer (n); **Censor** (n); **Censorship** (n); **Censure** (n or v).

Censer: An incense burner. *Censor:* A person, usually but not necessarily official, who examines plays, books, motion pictures, television programs, in order to suppress parts objectionable on moral, military or legal grounds. Hence any supervisor of public customs and morals and, in Freudian analysis, the force that represses ideas or impulses in their undisguised forms. "Assassination is the extreme form of *censorship*" (Shaw). *Censure* as noun or verb means blame, reproach, rebuke. "Those who durst not *censure* scare could praise" (Johnson).

Ceremonial (n & adj); **Ceremonious** (adj).

Both words as adjectives mean characterized by formal ceremony or ritual; but *ceremonial* is applied to events, whereas *ceremonious* describes people or human character and means carefully observant of ceremony or elaborately courteous: "Entered the room with a most *ceremonious* bow" (Cowper).

Childish (adj); **Childlike** (adj).

These words illustrate the difference in connotation between the suffixes -ish and -like, the former unfavorable or disparaging and the latter favorable or neutral: "The wife was pretty, trifling, *childish*, weak;/She could not think but would not cease to speak" (Crabbe). "Newton, *childlike*, sage! sagacious reader of the works of God" (Cowper).

Chord (n); **Cord** (n)

Perhaps only inadvertent misspelling confuses these words. A *chord* is various things: (1) In music a combination of two or more notes struck simultaneously. (2) In geometry the line between two points on a curve. (3) In life an emotion or feeling: "His story struck a *chord* of pity in his listeners." (4) In aeronautics the straight line between the edges of an airfoil section. *Cord* too has various meanings: (1) In practice a string or thin rope made of several strands. (2) In anatomy a cordlike structure as in spinal *cord* or umbilical *cord*. (3) In life a restraining influence: "Marriage is a civil contract and a binding *cord*." (4) In winter a unit of measurement of firewood.

Circumlocution: See Locution.

Cite (v); **Site** (n).
The words sound alike and should not be confused but sometimes are. To *cite* is to quote from, to refer to as support or authority, to use as an example. "As proof of this I may *cite* such a town as New York" (Helps). Whereas *site* means the position or location of anything, especially with reference to its environment. "How shines your tower, the only one / Of that especial *site* and stone" (Blake).

Claque (n); **Clique** (n); **Coterie** (n).
Claque derives from the French verb to applaud and means specifically a group of persons hired to applaud a public performance, as in a theater, night club or symphony hall: "He organized in 1820 the first Parisian *claque*" (Brewer). *Clique* is a small group of self-selected people, and so is a *coterie*. But *clique* has a derisive connotation of persons self-appointed as authorities or banded together for selfish purposes: "Choose well your set; our feeble nature seeks / The aid of Clubs, the countenance of *Cliques*" (Holmes). *Coterie* is not so contemptuous a term and usually applies to small groups interested in specific aspects of art or literature: "Fame is but a lottery / Drawn by the blue-coat misses of a *coterie*" (Lord Byron).

Classic (n & adj); **Classical** (adj).
Classical means pertaining to or typical of the art, literature, and culture of the ancient Greeks and Romans. "*Classical* quotation is the parole of literary men all over the world" (Johnson). *Classic* means of the highest or preeminent excellence: "Homer's Iliad is a *classic*, but World Series homers should not be called such." In short, *classic* is a word to be used somewhat sparingly.

Clench (v); **Clinch** (v).
These words are sometimes confused, because they both refer to holding or securing. But *clench* means to close tightly or grind together, as in *clenching* one's hands or teeth. *Clinch* means to secure or fasten down as in *clinching* an argument, contest or contract or in *clinching* nails: "He drove in the nails and *clinched* them flat." *Clinch* also has the meaning in boxing of body entwinement and its extended slangy meaning of passionate embrace.

Climacteric (n); **Climactic** (adj); **Climatic** (adj).
Climacteric and *climactic* refer to climax; whereas *climatic* refes to climate. *Climacteric:* Any critical period, hence the time of decrease in reproductive capacity of men and women and the specific year in which such change is likely to occur—usually called the grand *climacteric*. *Climactic:* Pertaining to or forming a climax in an ascending series: "Give the history of development a *climactic* form" (Whitney). *Climatic:* Of or pertaining to weather: "No *climatic* action has significantly changed the hues of the lava" (Reid). *Climatic* arises from the Greek *klima* (zone); whereas *climactic* has its root in the Greek *klimax* (a ladder), and hence implies gradual ascent to a peak or culmination.

Collaborate (v), **Collaborator** (n); **Corroborate** (v), **Corroborative** (adj).
Collaborate is a useful word meaning to assist in the doing of something, to cooperate; but the subtle sense of words does change with time, and history has given *collaborate* and especially *collaborator* a bad name. However, just as time wounds all heels, it also heals all wounds, and perhaps *collaborate* will soon be restored to innocent use. "Composers who *collaborated* with Metastasio in the opera of the eighteenth century" (Lee). *Corroborate* means to verify, to confirm, and *corroborative* means validating, authenticating. "Merely *corroborative* detail, intended to give artistic verisimilitude to an otherwise bald and unconvincing narrative" (Gilbert).

Collusion (n); **Connivance** (n).
Collusion means furtive agreement for the carrying out of some deceitful or fraudulent act: "The *collusion* of the false Templars with the infidels" (Fuller). *Connivance,* from its Latin root, means winking at—hence intentionally averting one's eyes from wrongdoing and so assisting it. "And what was this but his *connivance* at wicked and licentious people?" (Sandys).

Compare (v), **Comparison** (n), **Comparable** (adj); **Contrast** (v), **Contrasting** (adj).
The two verbs are sometimes confused, although they have quite different meanings. To *compare* things or ideas or people is to examine them for similarities: "I have been studying how I may *compare*/this prison where I live unto the world" (Shakespeare). *Contrast* means to compare in order to note unlikenesses or differences or opposing characteristics: "Perpetually *contrasting* it with systems with which it has nothing in common but the name" (Whately).

Compendium or **Compend** (n); **Compendious** (adj).
It is curious that *compend* is generally used correctly as a brief account of an extensive subject—a summary or epitome, whereas *compendium* and *compendious* are often used incorrectly. *Compendium* is the same word as *compend* and shares its meaning: A concise treatment of some subject or an abridgement. Nevertheless, both *compendium* and especially *compendious* are often mistakenly used to mean extensive or exhaustive. Matthew Arnold had it right: "A cheap and *compendious* help to study."

Complacent (adj); **Complaisant** (adj).
The latter adjective is no longer in great use; but when it is used it is often confused with the former. *Complacent:* Pleased with one's self or circumstances or surroundings. Contented; self-satisfied. "Whenever Gibbon was going to say a good thing, he announced it by a *complacent* tap on his snuff-box" (Hunt). *Complaisant:* Obliging, eager to please. "The most affable, *complaisant,* and cheerful creature in the world" (Charleton).

Complement (n & v); **Compliment** (n & v).
Complement (n): Anything that completes or improves as an addition to: "Information from other documents will *complement* these" (Stubbs). *Compliment* (n): An expression of praise, admiration or approbation. "You're exceedingly polite,/And I think it only right/To return the *compliment*" (Gilbert).

Compose (v); **Comprehend** (v); **Comprise** or **Comprize** (n); **Constitute** (v).
Each of the words involves the concept of containment; but each has a distinctive meaning. *Compose:* To make, form or create by combining things or elements. Hence to create a literary or musical work and to settle an argument or quarrel. Also to induce calmness or quiet and, specifically, to set type (i.e., to create something by combining discrete elements): "Were it a Caske *compos'd* by Vulcan's skill/My Sword should bite it" (Shakespeare). *Comprehend:* To understand the nature of something but also to include. "Such tricks hath strong imagination,/That, if it would but apprehend some joy,/It *comprehends* some bringer of that joy" (Shakespeare). *Comprise:* To comprehend in its sense of containing: "The People's Republic of China *comprises* several separate republics"; but it has also the meaning of consisting of: "Water is *comprised* of oxygen and hydrogen." *Constitute:* To compose in the sense of creating, to form, to establish: "Ordained and *constituted* the Services of Angels and men in wonderful order" (Book of Common Prayer). But *constitute* also means to form a constituent element, as "Vivacity *constitutes* her greatest charm."

Comprehend: See **Apprehend** and **Compose.**

Comprehensible or **Comprehendible** (adj); **Comprehensive** (adj).
Comprehensible means simply capable of being comprehended or understood: "For reasons not easily *comprehensible*" (Wilson). But *comprehensive* means of large scope, inclusive: "He was the

man who of all modern and perhaps ancient poets had the largest and most *comprehensive* soul''
(Dryden).

Concave (adj); **Convex** (adj).
Words sometimes confused, although they have opposite meanings. *Concave:* Curved inward.
Convex: Curved outward. A cave turns inward toward the earth; a vexation sticks out.

Confidant (n); **Confident** (adj); **Confidential** (adj).
Sources of mild confusion. *Confidant* (n): A person with whom secrets or intimate thoughts are
shared. The word *confidant* is, however, not much used, for its female form is *confidante*.
Confident (adj): Assured, certain, bold. "She was unwisely *confident* that her *confidante* was
trustworthy and discreet." *Confident* also means sure of oneself or assured of some thing or idea:
"There is not so impudent a thing in Nature, as the saucy look of an assured man, *confident* of
success" (Congreve). *Confidential* means spoken or written in secret or entrusted with hidden or
private matters, as in a *confidential* secretary: "I am desirous of beginning a *confidential* correspondence with you" (Lord Chesterfield).

Congenial (adj); **Congenital** (adj); **Genial** (adj).
Congenial: Of similar nature, compatible, suited in character or temperament, agreeable. "Poetry
and music are *congenial* companions" (Wharton). *Congenital:* Existing from birth or hereditary as
in *congenital* defect. *Genial:* Cheerful, cordial. "No lily-handed Baronet he,/A great broad-
shoulder'd *genial* Englishman" (Tennyson).

Connote (v), **Connotation** (n); **Denote** (v), **Denotation** (n).
Connote: To suggest meanings or implications beyond a primary meaning: "The word 'fireplace'
connotes hospitality and good fellowship." *Denote:* To indicate, to be a sign or mark of something:
"This line shall be the Equinoctial line and serve to *denote* the hour distances" (Maxon).

Consequent, Consequential: See Subsequent.

Contemptible (adj); **Contemptuous** (adj).
It is curious that these words are sometimes confused, for *contemptible* means deserving of
contempt or despicable. "A little group of wilful men have rendered the great Government of the
United States helpless and *contemptible*" (Wilson). But *contemptuous* means having or showing
contempt, scornful, disdainful. "Sometimes she was hard and cold and *contemptuous*" (Garrett).

Contiguous: See Adjacent.

Core (n); **Corps** (n).
They sound alike, but their distinctive meanings arise from their Latin roots—*cor* (heart) and *corpus*
(body). *Core:* the central or essential part of anything, especially that of a fleshy fruit containing its
seeds or of a magnet or induction coil. "Sweet as the rind was, the *core* is" (Swinburne). *Corps:* a
military unit or a group of any persons associated together in a common cause, as in signal *corps* or
diplomatic *corps*.

Corroborate, Corroborative: See Collaborate.

Coterie: See Claque.

Council (n), **Councilor** (agt), **Counsel** (n or v); **Counselor** (agt), **Consul** (n).
A *council* is a group of persons formed or convened for consultation or deliberation in some issue of
common concern and a *councilor* is a member of such a body: "The *Council* of Trent convoked to
meet the crisis of the Protestant Reformation" (Columbia Encyclopedia). *Counsel* is advice or
opinion and to *counsel* is to offer advice, opinion or recommendation. "Take my *counsel*, happy
man;/Act upon it, if you can" (Gilbert). A *counselor* is any adviser but the word also has the
specific meaning of attorney, as in the phrase "*counselor*-at-law." *Consul* is an official appointed
by a government to look after commercial affairs of its citizens in a foreign country, as in the phrase
"*consul* general."

Covert (adj); **Overt** (adj).
Although these words are sometimes confused, they have opposite meanings. *Covert* means secret, hidden, disguised; whereas *overt* means open to view or inspection, acknowledged. "The beaver has *covert* ways beneath the ice" (Steele). "Wage thy war *overtly*" (Cowper).

Credible (adj); **Creditable** (adj).
Credible: Worthy of confidence, believable: "He had the fate to be disbelieved in every *credible* assertion" (Sterne). But *creditable* means deserving credit or esteem or praise, although the word sometimes has the connotation of just barely deserving honor. The phrase "*creditable* performance" does not suggest the highest excellence. Incredible is the opposite of *credible*, and discreditable that of *creditable*.

Criterion (n), **Criteria** (n).
The latter is simply the plural of the former. *Criterion* means a standard of judgment or a measure by which anything is rated: "The only infallible *criterion* of wisdom to vulgar judgments—success" (Burke).

Cue (n & v); **Queue** (n & v).
The words are sometimes used interchangeably; but they shouldn't be. A *cue* is anything said or done in the theater that is to be followed by a specific passage or action and hence a hint, intimation, or suggestion: " '*Cue* for the soldier's entrance,' shouted the prompter" (Edwards). *Cue* is also the playing rod used in billiards and pool. "On a cloth untrue/With a twisted *cue*/ And elliptical billiard balls" (Gilbert). A *queue* is a line or a file of people awaiting their turn for anything from tickets to thingamajigs. It is also a braid of hair: "The Chinaman's *queue* was once the *cue* to his station in life, you see./But gone is the *queue* and so is the clue to what he might or mightn't be" (Tang).

Deadly (adj); **Deathly** (adj & adv).
Deadly means causing or tending to cause death, as in a *deadly* poison. It also means implacable—a *deadly* enemy—extremely accurate—*deadly* aim—and excruciatingly boring as well—*deadly* dull. Here Mark Twain in one use manages both its first and second meanings: Soap and education are not as sudden as a massacre, but they are more *deadly* in the long run." *Deathly* (adj) means resembling death as in *deathly* pallor. "Let no night seal thy sense in *deathly* slumber" (de la Mare). As an adverb it means extremely as in *deathly* afraid.

Debar (v); **Disbar** (v).
Debar means to exclude or prohibit. "The love which Fate so enviously *debars*" (Marvell). *Disbar* has the specific significance of excluding from the practice of law or from the bar of a particular court. "*Disbarring* a barrister from the bar, a power vested in the benches of the four inns of the court" (Wharton).

Deduce (v), **Deduction** (n); **Deduct** (v), **Deduction** (n); **Induce** (v), **Induction** (n).
Deduce is to reason from the general to the particular but, more loosely, also to arrive at a conclusion from known facts. Hence *deduce* and *deduction* are favorite words in detective fiction: "When a fact appears opposed to a long train of *deductions*, it invariably proves to be capable of some other interpretation" (Conan Doyle). *Deduct* means simply to subtract: "His Master might buy him bow and arrows and *deduct* the price out of his wages" (Gouge). In logic a *deduction* is a conclusion following inevitably from its premises so that the conclusion cannot be false if its premise is true. If we know that all red fruits are edible, then the *deduction* may be made that the tomato is edible, but we cannot *deduce* that the orange is *inedible*. This we could *deduce* only from the premise that all edible fruits are red. *Induction*, on the contrary, is reasoning from the particular to the general and hence secures conclusions not absolutely certain but of highly probable certainty. If seen planets are observed to revolve around suns, then the *induction* may be made that all planets

revolve around suns whether visible or not. *"Induction* from experience may provide us convenience, not science" (Locke). To *induce* also is to persuade; but *induction* into the armed services has been on occasion something more than persuasive. In general, *induction* starts from observed instances and derives generalizations therefrom or exercises the principle of applying to new or unseen instances what has been confirmed in old, seen instances; whereas *deduction* starts from a general principle, whether established or assumed, and arrives at some less general principle or some individual fact that inherently follows from the broader principle. (See also *Adduce.*)

Deference (n), **Deferential** (adj); **Differential** (n & adj).
To *defer* is to yield to, and *deference* and *deferential* carry the connotations of respectfulness and courtesy: "Though trunkless, yet / It couldn't forget / The *deference* due to me" (Gilbert). *Differential* arises from *difference* and means diverse, distinctive, constituting a difference, as in *differential* diagnosis. Hence a *differential* is also a set of gears designed to allow two or more shafts to revolve at differing speeds.

Deficient (adj); **Defective** (adj).
The first of these words is related to *deficit,* the second to *defect.* Hence *deficient* means lacking or insufficient or inadequate. "Every man of any education would rather be called a rascal than accused of being *deficient* in the graces" (Johnson). *Defective* means faulty or imperfect, as in *defective* wiring.

Definite (adj); **Definitive** (adj).
Definite: Clearly defined or determined, precise, exact. "Even the serfs had now acquired *definite* rights" (Tyndall). *Definitive:* Exhaustive, reliable, complete, as in a *definitive* biography.

Delimit: See **Limit.**

Denote: See **Connote.**

Deny: See **Refute.**

Deprecate (v); **Depreciate** (v).
Deprecate means literally to pray against and hence to urge reasons against or to protest; but it also commonly means to express strong disapproval of. Something of both meanings is apparent in: "To persist in such a *deprecated* and odious innovation" (Shaw). *Depreciate:* To belittle, to represent as of small value or merit: "Our architectural reputation, never high, is still more *depreciated* by the building at South Kensington" (Fraser's Magazine). And of course, *depreciate* also means to claim depreciation (lessening of value) on a property for tax purposes.

Desert (n & v); **Deserts** (n); **Dessert** (n).
Desert (n): An arid region supporting sparse or no vegetation: "Wherein of antres vast and *deserts* idle / It was my hint to speak" (Shakespeare). *Desert* (v): To leave, abandon, forsake: "*Deserted* at his utmost need / By those his former bounty fed" (Dryden). *Dessert* (n): Any sweet as the final course of a meal: "The pastry cook is very useful. He supplies such *dessert* as an ordinary cook could not be expected to make" (Scribner's Magazine). But *deserts* has nothing to do with confections or defections. It arises from the same root as *deserves* and means either rewards or punishments, as in just *deserts.* It is also, in the sense of deserving, used in singular form: "Use every man after his *desert*, and who should 'scape whipping?" (Shakespeare)

Different from, Different than, Different to.
Different than is not the illiteracy it is commonly supposed to be and is defended by the Oxford English Dictionary; but *different from* has somehow become accepted usage: "Miss Buss and Miss Beale / Cupid's darts do not feel. / How *different from* us, / Miss Beale and Miss Buss" (Anon., describing the Headmistress of the North London Collegiate School and the Principal of the Cheltenham Ladies College). *Different to* is in more common use in Great Britain than elsewhere: "It is quite a *different* thing within *to* what it is without" (Fielding).

Disability: See **Inability.**

Disassemble (v); **Dissemble** (v).
To *disassemble* is to take apart; but it may also mean by extension to separate or disburse. Its antonym is *assemble:* "He who *disassembles* a motor may well so scatter its parts that he cannot *assemble* it again." To *dissemble* is to conceal, hide or feign: "Perhaps it was right to *dissemble* your love,/But—why did you kick me downstairs?" (Bickerstaff).

Disburse (v); **Disperse** (v).
Disburse: To pay out, to distribute, to expend. "They had *disbursed* money largely, and had *disbursed* it with the certainty that they should never be reimbursed" (Macaulay). *Disperse:* To scatter, to send or drive off in different directions. "And thus the ashes of Wickliff are the emblem of his doctrine, which now is *dispersed* all the world over" (Fuller).

Discomfit (v), **Discomfiture** (n); **Discomfort** (n & v); **Discompose** (v), **Discomposure** (n);
   Disconcert (v), **Disconcertion** (n).
Discomfit is commonly misused. It means defeat completely, to rout or to thwart: "Kings with their armies did flee, and were *discomfited*" (Book of Common Prayer). *Discomfiture* means not the act but the result of *discomfiting*—defeat, rout, frustration. *Discomfort* means anything that disturbs comfort—uneasiness or mild pain: "Does the want of the cushion *discomfort* you?" (Couch). *Discompose* means to dissarange, unsettle, disturb, agitate: "It were better that Passion never *discomposed* the mind" (Walpole). *Discomposure*, like *discomfiture* means not the act but the state of being *discomposed*, i.e., agitation or perturbation. *Disconcert* means to disturb self-possession, to ruffle: "'Tis part of the Devil's business to *disconcert* our minds" (Collier). *Disconcertion* may mean either the act of *disconcerting* or the state of being *disconcerted*. "To his still greater *disconcertion*, he was asked to make a speech" (Thompson).

Discreet (adj), **Discretion** (n); **Discrete** (adj).
These sound-alike words have completely different meanings. *Discreet*: Prudent, cautious, circumspect: "The better part of valour is *discretion*" (Shakespeare). *Discrete*: Separate, distinct, particulate: "To hold together, and keep *discrete*, simultaneous phenomena" (Barratt).

Disinterested (adj); **Uninterested** (adj).
Disinterested means impartial, not influenced by selfish or partisan motives: "A nation of shopkeepers are very seldon so *disinterested*" (Adams). But *uninterested* simply means having no interest in and *uninteresting* creating no interest. "A Republic is a government in which attention is divided among the *uninterested* many, who are all doing *uninteresting* things" (Bagehot).

Disorganized: See **Unorganized.**

Disqualified: See **Unqualified.**

Dissatisfied: See **Unsatisfied.**

Dissemble: See **Disassemble.**

Dissimilate (v), **Dissimilar** (adj), **Dissimilarity** (n); **Dissimulate** (v), **Dissimulation** (n);
   Simulate (v), **Simulation** (n).
Dissimilate is not a frequently used word. It means to make unlike or to become unlike. Its meaning is clearly conveyed in the more frequently used words *dissimilar* and *dissimilarity*. "It is far easier for distinct languages grouped and used together to assimilate than to *dissimilate*" (Catlin). *Dissimulate* means to disguise under a false appearance, to dissemble. It too is more frequently used in its noun form, *dissimulation*. "Let love be without *dissimulation*" (St. Paul's Epistles to the Romans). *Simulate* means to make a pretense of or to assume the character or appearance of: "He *simulated* the manners and mannerisms of the aristocracy."

Distinct (adj); **Distinctive** (adj), **Distinguished** (adj).
These words similar in root and connotation do have separate meanings. *Distinct*: Clear, separate, unmistakable in identity: "Not more *distinct* from harmony divine,/The constant creaking of a country sign" (Cowper). *Distinctive*: Characteristic, individual: "Progress, man's *distinctive* mark alone" (Browning). *Distinguished*: Preeminent by reason of excellence or renown as in *distinguished* guests or *distinguished* scholar.

Divert: See **Avert.**

Divulge (v): **Disclose** (v).
These words have essentially the same meaning: To make known or reveal. But *divulge* has the connotation of private revelation; *disclose* that of public revelation: "No farther seek his merits to *disclose./*Or draw his frailties from their dread abode" (Gray). But: "Cease your obstreperous clamors and *divulging* slanders" (Adams). "The Commission sought means to *disclose* the secrets *divulged* to its members."

Dominate (v), **Domination** (n); **Domineer** (v).
Dominate: To rule or govern, to tower over: "Until the military *domination* of Prussia is wholly destroyed" (Lord Asquith). *Domineer*: To rule arbitrarily or despotically: "With a certain conscious despotism he rules, nay *domineers*, over us" (Oliphant).

Draft (n & v); **Draught** (v), **Drought** (n).
Draft: (1) A drawing or sketch. (2) A preliminary piece of writing subject to revision. (3) A current of air. (4) A device to regulate the flow of air. (5) The force required to pull a load or the team of animals to pull it. (6) A levy or conscription. (7) A selection of persons for military or other purpose. (8) An order directing the payment of money. (9) Anything drawn. "It is not *drafting* a bill, but passing it that is the difficulty" (Seeley). *Draught* is an older spelling of *draft* and is now regarded as archaic except in Great Britain, where one often feels a cold *draught*. *Drought* is an extended, often injurious, period of dry weather or any extensive shortage, as in a *drought* of good writing.

Due to: See **Because of.**

Effect: See **Affect.**

Effective: See **Affective.**

Egoism & Egoist (n), **Egoistic** (adj); **Egotism & Egotist** (n), **Egotistical** (adj.)
These words have similar meanings, for they all derive from Latin *ego* (the "I" or self). But there is preserved a distinction between *egosim* and *egotism*, the former meaning the practice of valuing things only in reference to one's personal interest (as opposed to *altruism*), the latter meaning preoccupation with one's self, hence self-conceit, boastfulness, excessive reference to one's status and accomplishment. "The mature man, hardened into skeptical *egoism*, knows no monition but that of his own frigid caution and interest" (Carlyle). But "His absorbing *egotism* was deadly to all other men" (Emerson on Napoleon).

Elapse (v); **Lapse** (n).
Elapse was once used as a noun to mean the duration or termination of a period of time; but it is now commonly used only as a verb meaning to slip or glide away, to pass, as in the passage of time: "Twenty-seven years had *elapsed* since the Restoration" (Macaulay). But *lapse* has a broader meaning than the obsolete noun *elapse*. It not only signifies an interval of time, it also has a great variety of extended meanings: (1) An accidental or temporary decline from an expected standard. (2) A fall from rectitude. (3) A decline into a lower grade or condition. (4) A falling into disuse. (5) In law the termination of a right through failure to exercise it. (6) In insurance the discontinuance of coverage of a policy either through its termination or failure to pay premium thereon. Perhaps the

most common example of these extended meanings is in "*lapse* of memory." A more severe connotation is apparent in "Evil is represented to have been brought upon the human race by the *lapse* of Adam" (Tucker).

Elder, Eldest, Older, Oldest (adj's).
These words have obvious enough meanings; but correct use is not always observed, because *elder* and *eldest* apply only to persons, whereas *older* and *oldest* apply to both persons and things. A brother may be either *older* or *elder* but his house may only become *older*.

Elemental (adj); **Elementary** (adj).
Although the words share a common root, they have different meanings. *Elemental.* Pertaining to ultimate constituents; simple, uncompounded; basic or primitive. "For the *elemental* creatures go/ About my table to and fro" (Yeats). *Elementary*: Simple, easy, introductory, plain. " 'Excellent'; I cried. '*Elementary*,' said Holmes" (Conan Doyle).

Elicit: See Illicit.

Eloquence (n), **Eloquent** (adj); **Grandiloquence** (n), **Grandiloquent** (adj).
These words are rarely confused; but it is not always realized that *grandiloquent* has a pejorative connotation. *Eloquence* is the art of using language, especially verbally, with fluency and power. "The beauty of the mind is *eloquence*" (Cicero). But *grandiloquence* is speech so lofty in tone as to become bombastic or foolish. "One cannot help smiling sometimes at his affected *grandiloquence*" (Boswell).

Elude: See Allude.

Emanate (v); **Emerge** (v); **Emerse** (v); **Immerge** (v); **Immerse** (v).
Emanate: To flow forth, to issue from a source, to emit. *Emanate* is usually used in reference to immaterial things or intangible forces. "The feudal idea views all rights as *emanating* from a head landlord" (Mill). *Emerge*: To rise or come forth (as from water or other liquid); to come into view from obscurity; to arise or appear as a problem or difficulty. "Strong against tide, th' enormous whale *emerges*" (Smart). *Emerse*: The verb no longer is used except as the past participle *emersed*. Standing out from a medium into which something has been plunged or from which it naturally *emerges*. A water lily standing out of surrounding water is *emersed*. *Immerge:* To plunge into, as in water or other liquid, to disappear by entering into a different medium. "They pour not water upon the heads of infants, but *immerge* them in the Font" (Fuller). *Immerse*: To plunge into a liquid; to become deeply absorbed. "A youth *immersed* in Mathematics" (Cowper).

Emend: See Amend.

Emigrate (v), **Emigrant** (n); **Immigrate** (v), **Immigrant** (n).
To *emigrate* is simply to leave one's country or region for another, and whoever does so is an *emigrant*. "The mountaineers *emigrate* during the summer to the Tuscan coast" (Spalding). To *immigrate* is to enter a new country or region as residence or temporary abode. "The *immigrants* to Australia *emigrated* mostly from the British Isles."

Eminent (adj); **Imminent** (adj).
Spelling similarity often confuses two words of entirely different meanings. *Eminent* means distinguished, famous, outstanding, of high rank or repute. "He above the rest/ In shape and gesture proudly *eminent*/ Stood like a tower" (Milton). Whereas *imminent* means impending; likely to occur soon; or overhanging, often in a threatening sense. "Oppose, first of all, the nearest and most *imminent* danger" (Robertson).

Enclose (v); **Endorse** (v).
The two words have nothing to do with each other except that both are ill-used in business jargon. "Enclosed, please find" is an essentially silly expression; say, instead, "I am enclosing." Equally absurd is "Endorse on the back," for *dorse* means back. Say, instead, "Endorse the check".

Endemic (n & adj); **Epidemic** (n & adj); **Pandemic** (n & adj).
Endemic: Peculiar to a region or people, indigenous. Often used to describe disease but by no means confined to such use. "An unreflecting habit of routine that seems *endemic* among official men in our country" (Blackie). *Epidemic*: Affecting simultaneously a large number of people in a given locality by spreading from person to person. Usually said of disease, but one may speak of an *epidemic* of fads or even of riots. "The *epidemic* and *endemic* diseases in Scotland fall chiefly, as is usual, on the poor" (Malthus). *Pandemic*: Prevalent throughout an entire country, continent, or the world. Used principally in medicine but appearing also in its general sense of universal as in "the *pandemic* fear of nuclear war" (New York Times).

Ensure: See **Assure.**

Enviable (adj); **Envious** (adj); **Invidious** (adj).
Enviable is a quality in the thing beheld, meaning highly desirable or to be envied. "Unlike the *enviable* ostrich, I cannot shut my eyes to danger when it is near" (Tyndall). *Envious* is a quality in the beholder, meaning full of envy often of a spiteful or malicious kind. "*Envious* Displeasure against an Harmless, Suffering People" (William Penn). *Invidious* means causing resentment or animosity, but it often has the connotation of arousing *envious* dislike. "I must speak what wisdom would conceal/And truths, *invidious* to the great, reveal" (Pope).

Epitaph (n); **Epigraph** (n); **Epithet** (n).
Both *epitaph* and *epigraph* mean an inscription on a tomb or elsewhere memorializing the dead. However, *epigraph* has the additional meaning of a quotation introducing any piece of writing, e.g. a book or chapter in a book. "I must say, I don't care for any of the *epigraphs* you have suggested for your essay" (Core). However, *epithet* means a word or phrase describing succinctly any person or thing; but it often has a censorious or vindictive connotation. "The frog is justly sensitive/To *epithets* like these" (Belloc).

Equable (adj); **Equitable** (adj).
Equable: free from variation, uniform, calm, undisturbed. "Thus the *equable* climates of Western Europe are accounted for" (Maury). *Equitable*: Just, right, fair, reasonable. In law pertaining to or valid in equity as distinguished from validity in common law. "Their punishment, if tyrannical in form, was *equitable* in substance" (Froude).

Erotic (adj); **Esoteric** (adj); **Exoteric** (adj); **Exotic** (adj).
Erotic: Pertaining to or arousing sexual desire or activity, the word deriving from the god Eros. "The *Erotic* passion is allowed by all learned men to be a species of Melancholy" (Charleton). *Esoteric*: Recondite; understood by or meant for a select few or elite; secret, confidential. "Walls covered with mythological representations and *esoteric* texts, explanatory of the old religion" (Birch). *Exoteric*: Suitable to the general public, not confined to a select group. "His *exoteric* teaching admitted fable and falsehood; the *esoteric* only what he believed to be true" (Warburton). *Exotic*: Of foreign origin, strange, unusual, glamorous; of remarkable appearance or effect. "The Italian opera, an *exotic* and irrational entertainment" (Johnson).

Eruption (n), **Eruptive** (adj); **Irruption** (n); **Irruptive** (adj).
An *eruption* is a forceful breaking *out*—an *irruption* a forceful breaking *in*. "This bodes some strange *eruption* in our state" (Shakespeare); but "The Goths made *irruptions* into Gaul" (Humphrey).

Essay: See **Assay.**

Evert: See **Avert.**

Exceedingly (adv); **Excessively** (adv).
Similarity of sound obscures the altogether different meanings of these words. The former means extremely or very much; the latter too much or unduly. One can be *exceedingly* or even *excessively*

generous and one can be *exceedingly* talented but scarcely *excessively* so. "I like *exceedingly* your Parthian dame" (Hood); but "The scenery seemed *excessively* rudimentary" (Lady Brassey). However, it may be worth note that this distinction, however sound and useful, is new, *excessively* having once had both meanings. "I am *excessively* obliged to you" is not now good usage, but was a popular phrase of the eighteenth century.

Except: See **Accept.**

Excite (v), **Excitement** (n); **Incite** (v), **Incitation or Incitement** (n).
To *excite* is to rouse or stir up emotions or feelings, to stimulate—"I'll come no more behind your scenes, David, for the silk stockings and white bosoms of your actresses *excite* my amorous propensities" (Johnson to Garrick). *Incite* is to urge on or to exhort to action. "The Pope *incited* the King of Spain to make war upon the Republick" (Bramhill).

Excuse: See **Apologize.**

Exercise (n & v); **Exorcism** (n), **Exorcise** (v).
The words are rarely confused; and, when they are, the confusion is probably due to misspelling rather than misunderstanding. Nevertheless, to *exercise* is to train or condition faculties either mental or physical. It is also to make use of privileges or powers, and to discharge duties or functions. "The sad, mechanic *exercise*" (Tennyson). *Exorcise* is to expel evil spirits or demons by prescribed ceremony and, by extension, to drive out any malign person, thing, or influence. "The spirit which devised it, is not *exorcised* either from the priesthood or the population" (Gladstone).

Exhausting (adj); **Exhaustive** (adj).
These look-alikes are misused with some frequency. Whatever is *exhausting* drains off energy, wears out, uses up, or fatigues. "The misfortune of coming after this *exhausting* generalizer" (Emerson). Whatever is *exhaustive* is complete, comprehensive, thorough, detailed, and if it be an *exhaustive* twenty-volume treatise may well also be *exhausting*.

Exhilirate: See **Accelerate.**

Explicit (adj); **Implicit** (adj).
Explicit: Clearly expressed, leaving nothing implied, hidden or obscured. "How impossible it is to have a clear and *explicit* notion of that which is infinite" (South). *Implicit*: Implied rather than specifically stated; also absolute, unreserved, as in *implicit* trust. As opposed to *explicit*: "Yet, because it is but *implicit*, I send again to know more clearly" (Harington).

Extant (adj); **Extent** (n).
Extant means still in existence, not destroyed. "The story is *extant*, and writ in very choice Italian" (Shakespeare). *Extent* means the space anything occupies or the degree which anything achieves; hence scope, volume, range, length, area. "The English Bible, if everything else in our language should perish, would alone suffice to show the whole *extent* of its beauty and power" (Edinburgh Review).

Extemporize: See **Temporize.**

Extern (n); **Intern or Interne** (n).
Extern: Anyone associated with an institution (usually of learning) but not residing in it. "The matter affecting the congregation alone, he puts to the good sense of *externs*" (Clerical Journal). *Intern*: A resident member of the staff of a medical school or hospital and, more broadly, any resident trainee or student. "How can the *intern* cope with the bewildering complexities of clinical medicine?" (Beeson).

Extraneous (adj); **Intrinsic** (adj).
These are near antonyms, *extraneous* meaning irrelevant, not pertinent, coming from without; and *Intrinsic* meaning innate, indigenous, proper to the very nature of something. "Hastings attributed

the weaknesses of his government to *extraneous* interferences'' (Burke). But ''Then came out the *intrinsic* rottenness of the whole system'' (Kingsley).

Facility (n); **Faculty** (n).
These words are near synonyms in the sense of ability; but there is also a difference between their separate connotations. *Facility* has the extended meanings of anything designed to serve a specific function, as in ''educational *facilities*,'' or anything that permits readier performance of an act, as in ''providing every *facility* for accomplishing our purpose,'' or ability due to skill and practice, as in ''writing with great *facility*.'' But *faculty* is more restricted in its basic meaning of ability. ''Though old, he is in full possession of his *faculties*.'' It also has the extended meaning of the teaching staff of any educational institution. ''The *faculty* of the Sorbonne was acknowledged to be the first in Europe'' (Simmonds).

Factitious (adj); **Fictitious** (adj).
Factitious: Artificial or contrived. ''The acquisition was invested with a *factitious* value'' (Mill). *Fictitious*: False, not genuine, pertaining to fiction. ''It has come, I know not how, to be taken for granted that Christianity is *fictitious*'' (Butler).

Faker (n); **Fakir** (n).
A *faker* is anyone who fakes anything, hence a fraud or swindler. ''We never call them thieves here, but prigs and *fakers*'' (Borrow). Whereas a *fakir* is a Muslim or Hindu religious devotee, often one who dedicates his life to contemplation and self-denial. ''A *fakir* would hardly be an estimable figure in our society'' (Morley).

Fancy (n); **Fantasy** (n).
Fancy is the product of imagination and implies also an artistic ability to create whimsical ideas or decoration. It is also a capricious image, preference or inclination. ''The soldier of today is not a romantic animal, dashing at forlorn hopes, full of *fancies* as to a love-lady or a sovereign'' (Bagehot). Whereas *fantasy* is the product of unrestrained, unreal or extravagant imagination. ''Yea, faileth now even dream;/Even the linked *fantasies*, in whose blossomy twist/I swung the earth a trinket at my wrist'' (Thompson).

Farther (adj); **Further** (adj).
Although the distinction between the two words is gradually breaking down, the purist will still insist that *farther* refers only to a measurable space or distance. ''O my brave soul!/O *farther*, *farther* sail!'' (Whitman); but that *further* means only greater in degree or in additon to. ''Without *further* Preface, I am going to look into some of our most applauded Plays'' (Addison).

Fatal (adj); **Fateful** (adj).
The two words both deriving from ''fate'' have, nevertheless, distinct meanings. *Fatal*: causing death, destruction or misfortune. ''It was that *fatal* and perfidious bark/That sunk so low that sacred head of thine'' (Milton); whereas *fateful* primarily means momentous or decisively significant. ''That *fateful* inability to review their position'' (Pall Mall Gazette).

Fatuous (adj), **Fatuity** or **Fatuousness** (n); **Foolish** (adj), **Foolishness** (n).
Both adjectives mean lacking in judgment or common sense, stupid, asinine, silly; but *fatuous* implies also a sense of complacency about one's *foolishness*. ''The moment the very name of Ireland is mentioned, the English bid adieu to common feeling, common prudence, and common sense and act with the *fatuity* of idiots'' (Smith). ''The veteran courtier, *fatuous* as he was, was not duped by professions of regard'' (Morley).

Faze (v); **Phase** (n & v).
These sound-alikes are rarely confused, because they have completely different meanings. *Faze*: To disconcert or to disturb. ''This blow, altho' a fearful one, did not *faze* me'' (Columbia Dispatch). *Phase*: Any of the various major aspects in which a thing of varying appearances manifests itself or

a stage in the process of growth or development. "He saw her in the most attractive *phase* of her character" (Lytton). However, the verb *phase* has meanings somewhat unrelated to the noun: (1) To schedule so that a product will be available when needed. (2) To synchronize. (3) *Phase in*: To incorporate or put in use gradually. (4) *Phase out*: To withdraw slowly out of use or service. "*Phase out*" has become something of a fad phrase. Nothing is any longer gradually reduced—it is *phased out*.

Feasible (adj); **Possible** (adj); **Probable** (adj).
Feasible means capable of being done or suitable to being done. "To an infinite power all things are equally *feasible*" (Ward). But *possible* means capable of happening, and *probable* means likely to happen. "The Prohibition amendment can be revoked only by the same methods as secured its adoption. I met no one in America who deemed this *probable,* few who thought it even *possible*" (Fowler). *Possible* is often misused, as in "Our thanks go to the committee for making this affair *possible.*" Nonsense—the affair was always *possible;* the committee transformed possibility into reality.

Feign (v); **Fain** (adj); **Feint** (n); **Faint** (v & adj).
Feign: To put on the appearance of, to imitate deceptively, to pretend. "*Feigned* necessities, imaginary necessities, are the greatest cozenage that men can put upon the Providence of God" (Cromwell). *Fain*: Willing, eager, content, also obliged, to do or be something. "The wills above be done! but I would *fain* die a dry death" (Shakespeare). *Feint*: Any movement made to deceive or distract an adversary. "*Feint* him—use your legs" (Hughes). *Faint*: As a verb, to grow weak or lose consciousness. "Oh lift me from the grass!/I die! I *faint!* I fail!" (Shelley). As an adjective, lacking strength or brightness, feeling weak, or lacking courage. "*Faint* heart never won fair lady!/ Nothing venture, nothing win—/ Blood is thick but water's thin—/ In for a penny, in for a pound—/ It's love that makes the world go round!" (Gilbert).

Felicitous (adj); **Fortuitous** (adj); **Fortunate** (adj).
The words have somewhat similar but nevertheless distinctive meanings. *Felicitous*: Apt, appropriate, well suited to the occasion or circumstance. "This striking essay abounds in *felicitous* comparisons" (Felton). *Fortuitous*: Happening by chance. "Accidental and *fortuitous* concurrence of atoms" (Viscount Palmerston). *Fortunate*: Resulting favorably, receiving a good or benefaction from an unexpected source, lucky, auspicious. "Of all axioms this shall win the prize/'Tis better to be *fortunate* than wise" (Webster).

Ferment (v); **Foment** (v).
The two verbs in extended meaning may both signify to cause trouble; but *ferment* literally means to cause or undergo fermentation, whereas *foment* means to instigate or encourage anything, especially discord or rebellion. "All love at first, like generous wine,/*Ferments* and frets until 'tis fine" (Butler). But "These evil commotions were constantly *fomented* by the monarchs of Blefuscu" (Swift).

Fictitious: See **Factitious.**

Flagrant: See **Blatant.**

Flair (n); **Flare** (n & v).
Flair: The word originally meant keen scent, the capacity to get on the scent of something desired, and has so come to mean also a sense of discernment or a natural inclination, talent or ability. "I see you have the true *flair*" (Braddon). *Flare* means to burn with an unsteady flame or to blaze forth with a sudden flash. As a noun, it means the flame or flash itself. "Forth John's soul *flared* into the dark" (Browning).

Flammable (adj); **Inflammable** (adj); **Inflammatory** (adj).
Inflammable, from *inflame*, is a sensible and useful word meaning capable of being set on fire, combustible, or capable of being aroused or excited. "This is the gas which was formerly known as *inflammable* air, and is now called hydrogen" (Huxley). Some presumed ambiguity in *inflammable* must have led to the coining of *flammable*—a word that has no philologic justification and is little used except for the signs on gasoline tank trucks. However, if people believe *inflammable* to mean incapable of being set afire, then *flammable* becomes a life-saving, if senseless, alternative. *Inflammatory* is somehow more fortunate in its meaning of tending to arouse hostility, anger or passion and no one seems to feel the need for *flammatory* as its replacement. "People read poisonous and *inflammatory* libels" (Junius).

Flaunt (v); **Flout** (v).
Words often confused but of distinctly different meanings. *Flaunt*: To show off, to display ostentatiously. "Here's to the maiden of bashful fifteen;/Here's to the widow of fifty;/Here's to the *flaunting*, extravagant queen;/And here's to the housewife that's thrifty" (Sheridan). *Flout*: To scorn, scoff at, disregard, show disrespect to. "*Flout* 'em and scout 'em; and scout 'em and *flout* 'em;/Thought is free" (Shakespeare).

Flotsam (n); **Jetsam** (n).
Although the words have become almost inseparable, they do have different meanings. *Flotsam* (from Old English float) is that part of a wreck or wreckage floating on the water surface, whereas *jetsam* (same root as jettison—from Latin throw) means cargo or gear thrown overboard to lighten a ship and then found on shore. Under the old laws of salvage *flotsam* belonged to the king of subjects who reclaimed it and *jetsam* to the lord of the manor on whose land it was found. In modern times the words used together have taken on the meaning of useless trifles or junk and, figuratively, of human down-and-outs.

Flout: See **Flaunt.**

Fluctuate (v); **Vacillate** (v).
Each of these verbs means to change back and forth, to be irregular or unstable; but *fluctuate* can be applied to actions, persons and objects, whereas *vacillate* usually applies only to persons. "Mr. Nickleby's income *fluctuated* between sixty and eighty pounds per annum" (Dickens). "He may pause and tremble—but he must not *vacillate*" (Ruskin).

Foment: See **Ferment.**

Foolish: See **Fatuous.**

Forbear (v); **Forebear** (n).
Forbear: To abstain or desist from, to refrain, to be patient with. "A fair region round the traveller lies,/Which he *forbears* to look upon" (Wordsworth). *Forebear* (but usually *forebears*): Ancestors, forefathers. "A yoeman whose *forebears* had once owned the land" (Murray).

Forcible (adj); **Forceful** (adj).
Forcible describes that which is achieved by force or violence. "Compel, by *forcible* means, submission to authority" (Wilson). But *forceful* means powerful, vigorous, effective. "Melodious and *forceful* verse" (Ruskin).

Foreword (n); **Forward** (adj); **Forwards** (adv).
There is no possible reason except phonetic untidiness for these words to be misused, but they are still often confused. A *foreword* is a word that goes before—hence a preface or introduction. "The translator has felt no hesitation in placing his *Foreword* at the end of the volume" (Dasent). But *forward* means onward, in front, ahead. "They carried them out of the world with their feet *forward*" (Browning). But *forwards* is an adverb and should only be used as such. "Swings backwards and *forwards*,/And tilts up his chair" (Holmes).

Former (adj); **Latter** (adj).
The *former* is the first of two; the *latter* the second of two. The *former* should never be used as the first of three or the *latter* as the last of three.

Fortuitous: See **Felicitous.**

Fortunate: See **Felicitous.**

Frequent: See **Recur.**

Funeral (n & adj); **Funereal** (adj).
Funeral means the ceremonies attending burial of the dead and, as an adjective, pertaining to such services, as in *funeral* director; but *funereal* means mournful, gloomy, dismal, doleful. "Man in portions can forsee/His own *funereal* destiny" (Byron).

Funny (adj); **Peculiar** (adj); **Strange** (adj).
Funny is often used incorrectly to mean odd or strange. It should be used only to mean witty, droll, humorous. "He became very sociable and *funny*" (DeQuincey). *Peculiar* means uncommon, odd, eccentric. "Mr. Weller's knowledge of London was extensive and *peculiar*" (Dickens). But it also means (followed by *to*) characteristic of, as in "an expression *peculiar* to Canadians." *Strange* means abnormal, bizarre, foreign, extraordinary, unfamiliar. "But Lord! to see the absurd nature of Englishmen, that cannot forbear laughing and jeering at everything that looks *strange*" (Pepys).

Further: See **Farther.**

Gage (n); **Gauge** (n).
In the sense of measurement these words are interchangeable, as in a narrow-*gauge* railway; but *gage* can also mean a greengage plum or a pledge or challenge. "A gauntlet flung down is a *gage* of knightly battle" (Scott).

Gantlet (n); **Gauntlet** (n); **Gamut** (n).
A *gantlet* is an old and cruel form of military punishment in which an offender was made to run between two rows of men who struck at him with swords. *Gamut* is the entire musical scale—hence any range, as in the *gamut* of emotion from gaiety to grief. Thus one may run either a *gantlet* or a *gamut* but not a *gauntlet*, for the last is a medieval metal glove and, by extension, a challenge. "Civic independence flings/The *gauntlet* down to senates, courts and kings" (Campbell).

Garnish (v); **Garnishment** (n), **Garniture** (n).
To *garnish* is to decorate or supply something ornamental. But it is also to summon to litigation or to attach property belonging to a debtor that is in the hands of a third party. "It will be a miracle if no one finds out who the trustee is; and as soon as his name is known, he will be *garnished* to a certainty" (Pall Mall Gazette). But it is curious that the noun *garnishment* carries both meanings of the verb, whereas *garniture* means only a decoration or adornment. "Stomachers, Caps, Facings of my Waistcoat Sleeves and other *Garnitures* suitable to my Age and Quality" (Addison).

Genial: See **Congenial.**

Gild (v); **Gilt** (v & n); **Guild** (n).
To *gild* something is to overlay it with gold or gold leaf; and *gilt* is the past tense and past participle of *gild*, but as a noun it means anything gold or golden, as in *gilt*-edged securities. A *guild* is a union of workers or a trade, professional or business association. "There were at least as early as the twelfth century *guilds* of weavers in London" (Prescott).

Glutton (n), **Gluttonous** (adj); **Gourmand** (n), **Gormandize** (v); **Gourmet** (n).
A *glutton* is anyone who eats excessively or who has an excessive capacity or desire for something. "Of praise a mere *glutton*, he swallow'd what came" (Shakespeare). A *gourmand* is a person

overly fond of good eating; whereas a *gourmet* is a connoisseur of fine and delicate foods, an epicure. "Greedy *gourmands* that cannot eat moderately" (Prescott). But "the most finished *gourmet* of my acquaintance" (Thackeray).

Grandiloquence: See **Eloquence.**

Grateful (adj); **Gratify** (v); **Gratuitous** (adj).
These words are sometimes misused. *Grateful* means appreciative or thankful; but we are *grateful to* other persons and *grateful for* benefits. "I came to be *grateful* at last for a little thing" (Tennyson). *Gratify* is to give pleasure, to indulge one's self, or to humor the whims of someone else. Hence its past participle, *gratified*, does not mean thankful but rather pleased or indulged. "The lineaments of *gratified* desire" (Blake). *Gratuitous* has nothing to do with gratitude. It means either given or bestowed without charge or occurring without sufficient reason, as in *gratuitous* insult. "Prophecy is the most *gratuitous* form of error" (Eliot).

Guild: See **Gild.**

Habitat (n); **Habitant** (n); **Habitans** (pl).
The *habitat* is the natural environment for anything from man to mango. "All things are good for nothing out of their natural *habitat*" (Lowell). A *habitant* is anyone who inhabits any place. "The little city of which he was now an *habitant*" (Disraeli). But the word also has the curiously specific meaning of a French settler in Canada or Louisiana or the descendant of such a settler. "A hamlet of cottages, occupied by Acadians, or what the planters call *habitans*, French Creoles" (Olmsted).

Hang (v), **Hanged, Hung.**
The meaning of *hang* is clear enough, but there is an odd distinction preserved in use of its past participle. *Hung* applies to everything except a victim of the gallows. Pictures are hung, but felons are *hanged*. "Men are not *hanged* for stealing horses, but that horses may not be stolen" (Lord Halifax).

Harbor: See **Port.**

Healthful (adj); **Healthy** (adj).
Healthful means conducive to health or wholesome; *healthy* means possessing or enjoying good health. "No warmth, no cheerfulness, no *healthful* ease" (Hood). But "Everybody saw with joy/ The plump and hearty, *healthy* boy" (Hoffman).

Helpmate (n); **Helpmeet** (n).
King James's bishops in their precise sonorous way, referring to Adam's need for a wife-companion, have the Lord say "I will make him an *help meet* for him." A perfectly good sentence in which *help* means someone who provides assistance or comfort and *meet* means suitable or appropriate. Somehow lexicographers did not perceive the meaning of the two words and made them one, *helpmeet*. Still later lexicographers deciding that *helpmeet* doesn't make much sense— which it doesn't—changed it to *helpmate*, which doesn't make a great deal of sense either in respect to the original *help meet*. Of the two corrupted words *helpmate* is more common and sounds as if it meant something. "A waiting woman was generally considered the most suitable *helpmate* for a parson" (Macaulay).

Heterodox (adj), **Heterodoxy** (n); **Orthodox** (adj), **Orthodoxy** (n).
Heterodox means differing from or not in accord with established doctrine or currently held ideas. *Orthodox* means conforming to established theological doctrine or other widely held beliefs. "Admissions which recommended him to neither the *orthodox* nor the *heterodox*" (Stubbs).

Hide: See **Cache.**

Historic (adj); **Historical** (adj); **Histrionic** (adj).
The first words overlap in meaning but not in connotation, for *historic* means broadly known, important, or significant in history, as in the *historic* meeting between Livingstone and Stanley; whereas *historical* means simply pertaining to or characteristic of history. "In such tales as *Kenilworth*, Scott created the *historical* novel" (Brooks). *Histrionic* means pertaining to actors or acting and hence unreal or artificial. "He loved the theatre and everything which savoured of *histrionics*" (Ward on Dickens).

Hoard (n); **Horde** (n).
A *hoard* is a supply or a store of materials for future use carefully guarded and usually hidden. "Our *hoard* is little, but our hearts are great" (Tennyson). A *horde* is any large multitude but especially a tribe or troop of nomads. "Can history offer a more terrifying prospect than that of a *horde* of ruffians led by a fanatic? Yes, that of a band of Presbyterians rising from their knees to do the Will of God" (Gregg).

Homesickness: See **Nostalgia.**

Human (adj. & n); **Humane** (adj).
Human means characteristic of man or consisting of men and women, as in the *human* race. "All *human* things are subject to decay,/And, when fate summons, monarchs must obey" (Dryden). *Humane* means characterized by tenderness, compassion or sympathy. "The *humane* spirit of the law which supposes every man innocent till proved guilty" (Edgeworth).

Humbleness (n); **Humility** (n).
Humbleness suggests a state of feeling or being inferior or insignificant. "All *humbleness*, all patience, and impatience;/All purity, all trial, all obeisance" (Shakespeare). Whereas *humility* suggests not only a modest sense of one's place and importance but also an acceptance of low station or rank. "And the Devil did grin, for his darling sin/Is pride that apes *humility.*" (Coleridge).

Hurdle (v); **Hurtle** (v).
Hurdle: To leap over, to overcome. "To *hurdle* this obstacle, we must exert our utmost force" (Gladstone). *Hurtle*: To move speedily or rush violently. "An avalanche *hurtled* down the mountainside" (New York Times).

Hypothecate (v); **Hypothetical** (adj); **Hypothesize** (v).
The first two words might appear to be related in meaning but are not. *Hypothecate* means to mortgage or pledge. "The assembly adopted a system of paper money secured and *hypothecated* upon the public lands" (Scott). *Hypothetical* means assumed or supposed. "It would be impossible to declare what would be our conduct upon any *hypothetical* case" (Wellington). *Hypothesize* has a kind of pretentiousness about it. "If an allied verb is really necessary, *hypothesize* is the right form, though it is to be hoped we may generally content ourselves with *assume*" (Fowler).

If (conj); **Whether** (conj).
If introduces a single condition; *whether* introduces alternate conditions and is usually followed by *or not*, either implied or expressed. "*If* you can keep your head when all about you/Are losing theirs and blaming it on you" (Kipling). But "*Whether* 'tis nobler in the mind to suffer/The slings and arrows of outrageous fortune/Or to take arms against a sea of troubles" (Shakespeare).

Illicit (adj); **Licit** (adj); **Elicit** (v).
Illicit: Unauthorized, unlawful, unlicensed. "A more profitable but *illicit* trade was carried on with the Spanish settlements" (Yeats). *Licit*: A word meaning the opposite of *illicit* but little used— lawful, permitted, proper. "To obtain the recognition of Christianity as a *licit* religion of the empire" (Baring-Gould). But the verb *elicit* means to draw out or bring forth, to evoke. "A corrupt heart *elicits* in an hour all that is bad in us" (Robertson).

Illusory: See **Allude.**

Immanent (adj); **Imminent** (adj).
Immanent: In-dwelling, inherent. A word not often used and usually within the context of theology or philosophy. "What of the *Immanent* Will and its designs?—/It works unconsciously" (Hardy). *Imminent*: Likely to occur soon, impending. "Presaging their intended and *imminent* destruction" (Fuller). (See also *Eminent*.)

Immerge, Immerse: See **Emanate.**

Immigrate: See **Emigrate.**

Immoral: See **Amoral.**

Immune (adj), **Immunity** (n), **Immunize** (v); **Impugn** (v), **Impunity** (n), **Impunitive** (adj).
The meanings of the first three words all derive from *immune*: Protected from disease, especially by inoculation; or exempt from. "We are never altogether *immune* from contagion" (Cobbs). However, the last three words are not related in meaning. *Impugn*: To assail the truth of, to challenge veracity of, to call into question. "The *impugned* department will send down a cohort of witnesses" (Saturday Review). *Impunity*: Exemption from punishment or freedom from legal restraint and, by extension, from unpleasant consequences. "Any nose/May ravage with *impunity* a rose" (Browning). *Impunitive* has a meaning, special to psychology, of not condemning oneself or others and of justifying actions as the reflection of inner feelings.

Immured (pp); **Inured** (pp).
Immured from its basic root "wall" means confined, imprisoned, enclosed, "Love . . . lives not alone *immured* in the brain, but . . . courses as swift as thought in every power" (Shakespeare). Whereas *inured* means accustomed to or habituated to by exercise or convention. "Why should not the habit of youth be that of middle age, and the wont of middle age be the *inured* custom of advanced age?" (Pusey).

Imperial (adj); **Imperious** (adj).
Imperial: Of or pertaining to an empire or emperor, hence also grand, magnificent, domineering. "There is nothing so bad or so good that you will not find Englishmen doing it. They do everything on principle. They fight you on patriotic principles; they rob you on business principles; they enslave you on *imperial* principles" (Shelley). But *imperious*, from the same root and once meaning befitting an emperor, has in modern times come to mean imperative or urgent "The laws of honour make it an *imperious* duty to succour the weak" (Bentham).

Implicit: See **Explicit.**

Impudent (adj); **Impertinent** (adj).
Impudent: Bold, rude, arrogant, shameless. "There is not so *impudent* a thing in Nature, as the saucy look of an assured man, confident of success" (Congreve). But *impertinent*—not pertinent—has the connotation of rudeness inappropriate, uncalled for, intrusive, or presumptuous. "I'm privileged to be very *impertinent*, being an Oxonian" (Farquhar).

Inability (n); **Disability** (n).
Inability means lack of ability or of power or means. "My distressing *inability* to sleep at night" (Dickens). Whereas *disability* means incapacity due to physical weakness, flaw or handicap. "The author labours under many *disabilities* for making a good book" (Westminster Review).

Incidentally (adv); **Incidently** (adv).
Incidentally: Happening by chance in connection with something else or in additon to the main point or circumstance. "The supreme object of learning should be truth, and *incidentally* self-improvement" (Douglas). *Incidently* no longer exists as a word and is now considered an illiteracy although it was once in good use.

Incite: See **Excite.**

Incredible (adj); **Incredulous** (adj).
Incredible: Unbelievable, seemingly impossible, not credible. "The *incredible* sums paid in one year by the great booksellers for puffing" (Emerson). *Incredulous*: Not believing, skeptical, disposed to doubt. "Thou hast, in truth, a most *incredulous* mind" (Cowper).

Incriminate (v), **Incrimination** (n); **Recriminate** (v), **Recrimination** (n).
Incriminate: To charge with a crime or fault, to implicate. "Evidence which *incriminates* others while it clears themselves" (Manchester Examiner). *Recriminate*: To bring a countercharge, to accuse an accuser. "Athanasius had the charge of Heresy *recriminated* also upon him" (Ashwell).

Indict (v), **Indictment** (n); **Indite** (v).
Indict means to charge with an offense or crime. "I do not know the method of drawing up an *indictment* against an whole people" (Burke). *Indite* means simply to write or compose. "Men far too well acquainted with their subject to *indite* such tales of the Philistines as these" (Disraeli).

Induce, Induction: See **Deduce.**

Inflammable, Inflammatory: See **Flammable.**

Inflict (v); **Afflict** (v).
Inflict means to lay on or impose and has the connotation of imposing something burdensome, unwelcome or grievous. "It is almost a definition of a gentleman to say that he is one who never *inflicts* pain" (Newman). *Afflict* means to trouble or to distress. "The mind is free, whate'er *afflict* the man,/A king's a King do Fortune what she can" (Drayton).

Informer (n); **Informant** (n).
The distinction between these words is gradually disappearing. An *informer* is anyone who provides information but is also a person who informs against another for money or other reward, as in the great cinema classic *The Informer*. An *informant* is also one who informs but in law is a person who provides information to civil authorities in order to lead to successful prosecution of those guilty of wrongdoing or criminal acts. "The matter of such information shall be substantiated by the oath or affirmation of the *informant*" (Blackstone).

Ingenious (adj); **Ingenuous** (adj).
Ingenious: Cleverly inventive, resourceful, original in creation. "I like you and your book, *ingenious* Hone!" (Lamb to the editor of the Every-Day Book). *Ingenuous*: Artless, innocent, free from ordinary reserve or dissimulation. "These were fine notions to have got into the head of an *ingenuous* country maiden" (Black).

Insure: See **Assure.**

Intelligent (adj); **Intellectual** (adj & n).
Intelligent: Having strong mental capacity and quickness of comprehension. "Politics we bar,/They are not our bent;/On the whole we are/Not *intelligent*" (Gilbert). *Intellectual*: Pertaining to the intellect and hence characterizing any highly rational pursuit or a person who studies the more complex and rigorous fields of knowledge, especially on an abstract or philosophical level. "Oxford! Beautiful city! So venerable, so lovely, so unravaged by the fierce *intellectual* life of our century" (Arnold).

Intense (adj), **Intensive** (adj).
Intense: Existing in an extreme degree, acute, strong, vehement. "Love thy country, wish it well,/Not with too *intense* a care" (Baron Melcombe). *Intensive* has much the same meaning as *intense* except that it adds the element of great concentration or compression or strenuous direction. "*Intensive* thinking is tedious and tiresome" (Woodhead).

Intern: See **Extern.**

Intrinsic: See **Extraneous.**

Inured: See **Immured.**

Invidious: See **Enviable.**

Irrefutable: See **Refute.**

Irregardless (adj).
There is no such word. Use *regardless* instead, usually followed by *of*. "In gallant trim the gilded vessel goes,/*Regardless* of the sweeping whirlwind's sway" (Gray).

Irritate: See **Aggravate.**

Irruption: See **Eruption.**

Jealous (adj), **Jealousy** (n); **Zealous** (adj), **Zeal** (n), **Zealot** (n).
The two adjectives are in fact rarely confused; but "rarely" is enough to merit their distinction. *Jealous*: Characterized by resentment of a rival or animosity at another's success. "Who wit with *jealous* eyes surveys,/And sickens at another's praise" (Churchill). *Zealous*: Ardently active, devoted or diligent, full of zeal. "One always *zealous* for his country's good" (Gray). However, the noun *zealot* has the distinct connotation of excessive zeal, of fanaticism. "I do not aspire to the glory of being a *zealot* for any particular national Church" (Burke).

Jetsam: See **Flotsam.**

Judge (n), **Jurist** (n).
These words are not synonyms. A *jurist* is anyone learned in the law. "The doctrines of the Mohammedan *jurists* are somewhat at variance in this matter" (Wilson). Whereas a *judge* is a public officer authorized to hear causes and actions in a court of law. He may well be a lawyer but may not be a *jurist*. " 'I'll be *judge*, I'll be jury,' said cunning old Fury;/'I'll try the whole cause and condemn you to death' " (Carroll).

Judicial (adj); **Judicious** (adj), **Judiciously,** (adv).
The words have a common base but distinctive meanings. *Judicial* characterizes only judges or courts of law and the judgments of either. "A *judicial* rent was a rent fixed by a *judicial* body, a dispassionate and impartial body" (Gladstone). Whereas *judicious* means characterized by good judgment, prudence or wise understanding. "The art of reading is to skip *judiciously*" (Hamerton).

Karat and **Karate:** See **Carat.**

Kind of, Sort of
The two phrases are interchangeable; and, if not whole volumes, at least lengthy disquisitions have been written about their proper use. In vernacular employment both phrases may be used quite loosely; but by any standards "He is *kind of* stupid" is an illiteracy. In writing, use should be restricted to the literal sense of the words. "Amber is a *kind of* fossil resin" (Strunk). In general *kind of a* should be avoided and we should think of *kind* or *sort* as meaning a species or class or category or division of a category. "All the world is divided into two *kinds of* people. Those who divide the world into two *kinds of* people and those who don't" (James).

Kith (n); **Kin** (n).
The words are not synonymous. *Kith*: An acquaintance, friend, neighbor or the like. *Kin*: A relative or, collectively, a group of persons descended from a common ancestor. "Of all the words of tongue or pen/The most overused are '*kith* and *kin*' " Almost as bad as "kith and tell."

Knot (n).
Knot in nautical use, unlike mile, is not a measure of distance but is a unit of speed: one nautical mile an hour. Hence "The carrier Wasp is limping home at eight *knots* an hour" is incorrect. The words *an hour* or *per hour* should never follow *knot*. "A torpedo-boat destroyer has made a record speed of 35 *knots*, almost exactly equal to 41 miles an hour" (Daily News).

Know: See Realize.

Lapse: See Elapse.

Laudable (adj); **Laudatory** (adj), **Laudative** (adj).
Laudable: Worthy of praise, commendable. "He who would not be frustrate of his hope to write well hereafter in *laudable* things ought himself to be a true poem" (Milton). *Laudatory* and *laudative* mean the same thing: Full of praise or expressing praise. "An artist is not apt to speak in a very *laudatory* style of a brother artist" (Hawthorne).

Lead (v), **Led** (pt).
Confusion here arises almost entirely from a problem of pronunciation, for the verb *lead* is pronounced "leed"; but its past tense *led* is sounded like the metal *lead*. "Education makes a people easy to *lead*, but difficult to drive; easy to govern, but impossible to enslave" (Baron Brougham). "I have *led* my ragamuffins where they are peppered; there's not three of my hundred and fifty left alive" (Shakespeare).

Learn (v); **Teach** (v).
It should scarcely be necessary to distinguish between the two. However, to *learn* is to acquire knowledge or skill by study or practice; whereas to *teach* is to impart knowledge or skill. "*Learn* to write well or not to write at all" (Dryden). "Sir, it is no matter what you *teach* children first, any more than what leg you shall put into your breeches first" (Johnson).

Least (adj); **Less** (adj); **Lest** (conj).
Least is the superlative degree of *little*, and *less* its comparative degree; whereas *lest* is a conjunction meaning for fear that. "For I am the *least* of the apostles" (Paul to the Corinthians). "There is now *less* flogging in our great schools than formerly, but then *less* is learned there; so that what the boys get at one end they lose at the other" (Johnson). "There are five reasons we should drink;/Good wine—a friend—or being dry—/Or *lest* we should be by and by—/Or any other reason why" (Aldrich). We shall not confuse the basic issue by introducing the circumstance that, of course, *littler* and *littlest* can also be the comparative and superlative degrees of *little* and that *less* and *least* can also be adverbs. Perhaps one example of the last-named use is justified by its truth. "Whatever we anticipate seldom occurs; what we *least* expect generally happens" (Dryden).

Leave (v & n); **Let** (v & n).
Leave (v): To depart from, to quit a person, place or thing. "This very night I am going to *leave* off tobacco!" (Lamb). *Let* (v): To allow or permit. "Rob me, but bind me not and *let* me go" (Donne). Confusion between the verbs may arise from the fact that the noun *leave* means permission to do something, as in "by your *leave*"; while *let* as a noun means an obstruction or impediment, although this use is becoming rare. "At last all *let* and hindrance ceased for the merry lady upon the sudden death of her husband" (Lover).

Legible: See Readable.

Liable (adj): **Libel** (n & v).
Liable: Likely or subject or exposed to something—especially something unpleasant. In law, under legal responsibility or obligation. "Difficulties, I am sensible, may be *liable* to occur" (Ruskin). And "Every one of the partners is *liable* to the full extent of his fortune for all the debts incurred by the partnership" (Pearson). *Libel* as a noun and verb means technically defamation by or to defame

by written or printed words or pictures—but not by spoken words or gestures. Loosely, however, it means any damaging misrepresentation. "Convey a *libel* in a frown, / And wink a reputation down" (Swift).

Licit: See Illicit.

Lie (v), **Lay** (pt), **Lain** (pp); **Lie** (v), **Lied** (pt); **Lay** (v), **Laid** (pt & pp); **Lay** (adj), **Lay** (n).
Confusions surround the proper use of these words, most of them arising from the fact that *lay* and *lain* are the past tense and past participle of the intransitive verb *lie*, while *laid* is both past tense and past participle of the transitive verb *lay*. *Lie* means (1) to be in a recumbent position and (2) to make a false statement. Its past tense is illustrated in "And his lifeless body *lay* / A worn-out fetter" (Longfellow); its past participle in the fine verses from the Book of Kings: "For now should I have *lain* still and been quiet, I should have slept: then had I been at rest, / With kings and counsellors of the earth, which built desolate places for themselves." A small confusion at once arises in the circumstance that the past tense of *lie*—to utter falsehood—is *lied*. "I said to Heart, 'How goes it?' Heart replied: / 'Right as Ribstone Pippin!' But it *lied*" (Belloc). *Lay* means to put in place, usually in a horizontal position or a position of rest, as in *lay* the book on the table. Its past tense and past participle is *laid*. Hence "The best *laid* schemes o' mice and men / Gang oft a–gley" (Burns). *Lay* in its adjectival and noun forms is alone in not going readily a–gley. As an adjective: Of or belonging to the laity as opposed to the clergy; as in a *lay* sermon. As a noun: A short narrative poem, especially one that is sung—"He touch'd the tender stops of various quills, / With eager thought warbling his Doric *lay*" (Milton). We shall not mention the colloquial *lay*.

Lifelong (adj); **Livelong** (adj).
Lifelong means continuing through life; but *livelong* means whole or entire, especially when tediously slow. "Plato . . . in his *lifelong* effort to work out the great intellectual puzzle of his age" (Jowett). And "For though it seems so little a time . . . it hath been a whole *livelong* night" (Marvell).

Lightening (pres p); **Lightning** (n).
Lightening is the present participle of *lighten*: to brighten or become less dark or to make lighter in weight. "*Lightening* the steamer Amaryllis ashore at Savannah will enable her to get off" (Daily News); but *lightning* (a noun) is a luminous electrical discharge in the sky. "When I'm playful . . . I scratch my head with the *lightning* and purr myself to sleep with the thunder" (Mark Twain).

Like (prep)
Propriety is gradually giving way; but *like* used as conjunction, is still slovenly. The fact that Darwin wrote, "Unfortunately few have observed *like* you have done" does not excuse misuse. *Like* should be used only as a preposition " 'There's nothing *like* eating hay when you're faint.' . . . 'I didn't say there was nothing better,' the King replied, 'I said there was nothing *like* it' " (Carroll).

Limit (n & v); **Delimit** (v).
To *limit* is to restrict or contain and the noun *limit* is the farthest point of extent, amount, procedure and the like. "There is, however, a *limit* at which forbearance ceases to be a virtue" (Burke). To *delimit* is to set boundaries or to mark the *limits* of. "The question of *delimiting* the Russo-Afghan frontier" (The Times).

Linage (n); **Lineage** (n).
Linage is simply the number of printed lines contained in a newspaper or magazine article or advertisement. "One of the terms of the reporter's engagement was that he should have half the *linage*" (Mercury). *Lineage* means line of ancestry or descent. "We Poets of the proud old *lineage* / Who sing to find your hearts, we know not why" (Flecker).

Liquor (n); **Liqueur** (n).
Liquor is any liquid but especially a distilled or spiritous beverage as opposed to a fermented drink like beer. "Candy's dandy, but *liquor*'s quicker" (Parker). *Liqueur* designates a special class of alcoholic liquors, usually sweet, highly flavored and aromatic and often served after dinner. "At dinner we had different sorts of wine and a *liqueur*" (Boswell). You bet they did.

Litany (n); **Liturgy** (n).
A *litany* is a ceremonial form of prayer consisting of invocations or supplications with responses that are repeated, and hence any continuous repetition resembling a litany. "The *Litany* of the Saints is chanted on the feast of St. Mark and on the three Rogation days" (Catholic Dictionary). *Liturgy* is a form of public worship or ritual and hence also a compendium of formularies for worship. "We have a Calvinistic creed, a Popish *liturgy*, and an Arminian clergy" (William Pitt).

Livid (adj); **Vivid** (adj).
The words are scarcely ever confused; but *livid* is frequently misused. It means having the discolored bluish appearance of a congestion of blood vessels or it means deathly pale. It does not mean suffused with red. Hence *livid* with rage and *livid* with fear demonstrate its two meanings. Whereas *vivid* means strikingly bright or intense. "Trusty, dusky, *vivid*, true,/With eyes of gold and bramble-dew" (Stevenson).

Loath (adj); **Loathe** (v).
Loath means reluctant, disinclined, unwilling. "His relations being *loath* to part with the estate they had gotten by his supposed death" (Bargrave). *Loathe* means to abhor, detest. "We fix our eyes upon his graces and turn them from his deformities, and endure in him what we should in another *loathe* or despise" (Johnson on Shakespeare).

Locution (n); **Circumlocution** (n).
Locution is a style of speech or phraseology or a particular form of phrase or expression. "A permanent Philological Board to watch over the introduction of new words or *locutions*" (Illustrated London News). *Circumlocution* could be described simply as run-about *locution* or use of excessive words. "After much *circumlocution* and many efforts to give an air of importance to what he had to communicate" (Scott).

Longshoreman (n); **Stevedore** (n).
For no very good reason, these words are often used interchangeably. But, in fact, "to waterfront people a *longshoreman* is a laborer and a *stevedore* is an employer of *longshoremen*" (Bernstein).

Lustful (adj); **Lusty** (adj).
Lustful means greedy or lecherous, whereas *lusty* means vigorous, robust, hearty. "There are also *lustful* and chaste fishes, of which I shall give you examples" (Walton). But "Though I look old, I am strong and *lusty*" (Shakespeare).

Luxuriant (adj); **Luxurious** (adj).
Luxuriant: Abundant, exuberant in growth, flourishing vigorously. "Wit's like a *luxuriant* vine" (Cowley). *Luxurious*: Characterized by, conducive to, or having intense liking for luxury. "Men are conservatives when they are least vigorous, or when they are most *luxurious*. They are conservative after dinner" (Emerson).

Mad: See **Angry.**

Manifold (adj); **Multiform** (adj); **Multiple** (adj & n).
Manifold: Of many kinds; numerous, varied; suggesting also complexity. "*Manifold* stories, I know, are told not to thy credit" (Byron). *Multiform*: Having many forms. "The variations so common and *multiform* in organic beings under domestication" (Darwin). *Multiple*: Consisting of or having many parts or elements or individual components. "Why should not solvent thieves and cheats be rather punished with *multiple* restitutions than death, pillory and whipping?" (Petty).

Multiple as a noun has a purely mathematical significance: Any number divisible by another number without remainder. Twelve is a *multiple* of 2,3,4, and 6.

Manner born (usually preceded by *to the*)
The phrase means accustomed by birth to high position or having a lifelong acquaintance with certain customs or conditions. It is frequently misspelled as *manor born* under the mistaken notion that the meaning is born to feudal aristocracy, whereas the idea intended is that of habituation or practice. Indeed in its broadest meaning the phrase signifies destined by birth to be subject to a specific custom. ''But to my mind, though I am native here / And to the *manner born*, it is a custom / More honor'd in the breach than the observance'' (Shakespeare).

Marital (adj); **Martial** (adj).
With good reason the words are sometimes confused. *Marital* means pertaining to marriage. ''What a deal of *marital* discomfort might have been avoided'' (Thackeray). Whereas *martial* means pertaining to war or warfare. ''All the delusive seduction of *martial* music'' (Burney).

Martyr (n); **Victim** (n).
A martyr is anyone who willingly suffers torture or death because of his faith or beliefs or one who endures hardship in defense of a principle, cause, ideal or conviction. ''And the bitter groan of the martyr's woe / Is an arrow from the Almighty's bow'' (Blake). A *victim* is the unwilling or unknowing sufferer of wrong or injury or one cheated or deceived by others. ''The *wictim* o' connubiality, as Blue Beard's domestic chaplain said ven he buried him'' (Sam Weller in Pickwick Papers).

Masterful (adj); **Masterly** (adj).
Masterful: Having the qualities of a master, hence authoritative, arbitrary, imperious, forceful. ''Some children are very *masterful* and disobedient'' (Whateley). *Masterly*: This word also derives from master but in the restricted sense of mastery of a skill or art. ''The Commons, faithful to their system, remained in a wise and *masterly* inactivity'' (Mackintosh).

May: See Can.

Mean (adj; v & n); **Meant** (pt & pp); **Mien** (n).
Mean as an adjective signifies inferior, unimposing, ignoble, vicious, malevolent. As a verb *mean* denotes intention or signification. The noun *mien* signifies countenance, aspect or bearing. ''He *meant* to be *mean*; but his kindly *mien* belied the intent.'' The noun *mean* is, in its technical sense, an average. ''The *mean* of Buenaventura's elevated temperature is *mean* indeed.'' But in plural form it has the specific meaning of an agency or method to attain an end or of available resources, especially monetary. ''Increased *means* and increased leisure are the two civilizers of man'' (Disraeli).

Median (adj); **Average** (adj & n); **Medium** (n).
Median as adjective means being in the middle, hence pertaining to a plane dividing something (especially the animal or human body) into two equal parts. ''His physician does still let blood in the *median* vein of the heart'' (Hall). Hence also in statistics describing a point in a series at which half the individuals in the series are on one side of it and half on the other, as distinguished from *average*. To illustrate: If five persons have respective hourly wages of $3, $4, $5, $7, and $11, the *average* hourly wage is $6; the *median* wage is $5. *Medium*, whose plural may be either *mediums* or *media*, has a wide variety of meanings: (1) A middle state or condition. (2) An intervening substance through which a force acts. (3) An element that is the natural habitat of an organism. (4) Surrounding objects, conditions or influences. (5) A means, agency or instrument. (6) In biology the substance in which specimens survive or are preserved. (7) A person serving as an agent through whom a deceased person or supernatural force manifests itself. (8) In photography, the middle distance. Of these varied significations, one of the most common is that of an agency or instrument, well exemplified in Wilde's famous critical dictum: ''Meredith is a prose Browning, and so is Browning. He used poetry as a *medium* for writing in prose.''

Meet (adj & v); **Met** (pt); **Meet with**; **Mete** (v).
Meet as an adjective (see also *Helpmate*) is now somewhat sparingly used but is still a useful word meaning suitable or appropriate. "The Eye is very proper and *meet* for seeing" (Bentley). The verb *meet* has various meanings that are essentially related. (1) To encounter. (2) To notice in passing. (3) To become acquainted with. (4) To join at an expected place of arrival or at an appointed time. (5) To come into the company of a person or group of persons. (6) To confront directly. (7) To come into physical contact with. (8) To encounter in opposition or conflict; to oppose. (9) To form a junction, as with lines, planes, or areas. (10) To cope with effectively. (11) To come together face to face. (12) To assemble for conference or action. Of these varied meanings the most common is seen in the phrase from the Book of Common Prayer: "When we assemble and *meet* together." *Meet with*, however, has the more restricted meanings of encounter, join the company of, and undergo. "Continually we *met with* many things worthy of Observation and Relation" (Bacon). *Mete* is a verb no longer much in use. It means to distribute, to measure out, to allot. "I *mete* and dole unequal laws unto a savage race" (Tennyson).

Metaphor: See **Simile.**

Meticulous (adj); **Scrupulous** (adj); **Scrupulosity** (n).
The adjectives are not true synonyms. *Meticulous* means extremely careful about small details, finicky, precise. "The decadence of Italian prose composition into laboured mannerisms and *meticulous* propriety" (Symonds). *Scrupulous* means having scruples or showing a strict regard for the principles of right and honesty. However, *scrupulous* may also mean minutely careful, with the implication of excessive zeal. "He washed himself with oriental *scrupulosity*" (Johnson).

Mien: See **Mean.**

Might: See **Can.**

Militate (v); **Mitigate** (v).
These words are needlessly confused. *Militate* means to exert effect on or to influence; to act either against or in favor of, but more often in the negative sense of in opposition to. "To incur the displeasure of his father and Sir David by disobeying the one and *militating* against the peace of the other was what he could not bear" (DuBois). *Mitigate* means to make less severe, to lessen the force or intensity of. "The envoys interposed to *mitigate* the king's anger" (Prescott).

Million: See **Billion.**

Misfortune (n); **Calamity** (n).
Misfortune has the connotation of mischance whereas *calamity* that of grievous affliction or very serious misfortune. Asked to distinguish between the two, Disraeli replied: "Were Gladstone to fall into the Thames, that would be a *misfortune*. Were someone to pull him out, that would be a *calamity*."

Mishap: See **Accident.**

Moral (adj & n); **Morale** (n).
Moral as adjective means pertaining to right conduct or to the distinction between right and wrong. Hence also conforming to the rules of good conduct, virtuous. "An Englishman thinks he is *moral* when he is only uncomfortable" (Shaw). As a noun *moral* means the ethical teaching or practical lesson contained in a fable, maxim or experience. "He left the name, at which the world grew pale, / To point a *moral*, or adorn a tale" (Johnson). *Morale* refers to the state of mind or spirit of a person or group of persons, usually with the connotation of cheerfulness or zeal or high intention. "The *morale* of the troops is excellent" (Times).

Moslem (n); **Muslim** (n).
Both words mean a believer in Islam, a religious faith founded by the prophet Mohammed and taught through the Koran. For obscure reasons *Moslem* is the spelling most common in ordinary use and in newspaper and magazine publication. However, students of religion and adherents to the faith prefer the spelling *Muslim*. "The mosque of the Sultan Hassan, perhaps the most beautiful in the *Moslem* world" (Edwards). But "All the *Muslim* wants is a courtyard with a tank for ablution" (Forrest).

Motive (n); **Motif** (n).
The words are not often confused. A *motive* is anything that prompts a person to act in a certain way; an incentive or, by extension, a goal. "Our country has undertaken a great social and economic experiment, noble in *motive* and far-reaching in purpose" (Hoover on the Prohibition Amendment). *Motif* is a recurrent feature, theme or idea or a recurring form or figure in a design or the basic theme of a musical composition. "I feel original. I have got hold of a *motif*! Oh, if we had a sheet of scored paper!" (Mrs. A. Edwardes).

Multiform and **Multiple:** See **Manifold.**

Musical (adj); **Musicale** (n).
Musical: Of or pertaining to music; hence also harmonious, melodious; fond of or skilled in music. "We were none of us *musical*" (Gaskell). A *musicale* is a program of music forming part of a social occasion. The word has something of an emphasis on the sociability of such occasions. "The ladies' receptions are of a different character. Some are *musicales*" (Cosmopolitan).

Must: See **Can.**

Nauseate (v); **Nauseated** (pp); **Nauseous** (adj).
The distinction to be preserved is between *nauseated* (affected with nausea, feeling sick or queasy) and *nauseous* (causing nausea or queasiness). One may be *nauseated* by a *nauseous* odor—not the other way around.

Naval (adj); **Navel** (n).
Another easy distinction. *Naval* means pertaining to warships or to affairs of a navy. " 'It was a maxim of Captain Swosser's,' said Mrs. Badger, 'speaking in his figurative *naval* manner, that when you make pitch hot, you cannot make it too hot' " (Dickens). But the *navel* is the depression in the middle of the abdomen marking the point of attachment of the umbilicus and thus, by extension, meaning also the middle of anything. "Thy *navel* is like a round goblet" (Song of Solomon).

Noisome (adj); **Noxious** (adj); **Obnoxious** (adj).
Noisome has nothing to do with noise. It means offensive, disgusting or sickening and is often applied to odors. "For he shall deliver thee from the snare of the hunter, and from the *noisome* pestilence" (Book of Common Prayer). *Noxious* means harmful, injurious or pernicious. "It blows over the whole island steadily—a cold, *noxious* wind" (Haughton). *Obnoxious* means objectionable, giving offense or annoyance. "I know of no method to secure the repeal of bad or *obnoxious* laws so effective as their stringent execution" (Grant).

Nostalgia (n), **Nostalgic** (adj); **Homesickness** (n), **Homesick** (adj).
From its Greek root *nostalgia* originally meant a desire to return home; but it has come to mean the desire to return to a former period of one's life or to some other past circumstance or time. "The terror, the agony, the *nostalgia* for the heathen past were a constant torture to her mind" (Lawrence). *Homesickness* is specifically a longing for home so intense as to become an illness. "I am *homesick*. I am not accustomed to be away from mamma for so long" (Trollope).

Not only . . . but also
The principal care in good use of these correlative conjunctions concerns their proper placement; and this is purely a matter of parallelism, for the part of speech or grammatical construction following *not only* must be paralleled by the part of speech or construction following *but*. To illustrate: "They hope to discover *not only* how the antibiotic attacks pathogenic microorganisms *but also* to learn how it produces its other remarkable effects." This is incorrect; it should be recast thus: "They hope to discover *not only* how the antibiotic attacks pathogenic microorganisms *but also* how it produces its other remarkable effects."

Notable (adj); **Noted** (adj).
Notable means worthy of note or attention, especially on account of excellence or distinction. "David obtained *notable* victories" (Golding). Whereas *noted* means celebrated, eminent, famous, renowned. "That evening Clarendon and several other *noted* Jacobites were lodged in the Tower" (Macaulay). Usually, if not necessarily, *notable* is applied to objects or things and *noted* to persons. "Dr. Tompkins is a *noted* scientist whose practical inventions have had *notable* success."

Obnoxious: See **Noisome.**

Observance (n); **Observation** (n).
Observance is the act of following or conforming to customs, laws, creeds. More specifically, it also means the celebration of ceremonies or rites. "Dublin-born Maureen O'Hara joins Andy Williams in *observance* of St. Patrick's Day Thursday night on Channel 4" (New York Times). *Observation* is the act of noticing or perceiving and also whatever is learned in such perception. "To *observations* which ourselves we make,/We grow more partial for th' observer's sake" (Pope).

Obsolete (adj); **Obsolescent** (adj).
What is *obsolete* is no longer in use. What is *obsolescent* is passing out of use. "Such olde and *obsolete* words are most used of country folke" (Spenser). "In another generation the *obsolescent* will have become *obsolete*" (Wright).

Official (n & adj); **Officious** (adj).
An *official* is anyone elected or appointed to a position charged with certain duties and responsibilities, and the adjective *official* describes an office or position of trust and authority. "The heavy footfall of the *official* watcher of the night" (Dickens). Whereas *officious* means objectionably forward in offering services or advice; meddlesome; overeager to oblige. "One of those *officious*, noisy, little men who are always anxious to give you unasked information" (Disraeli).

Older, Oldest: See **Elder, Eldest.**

On account of: See **Because of.**

Opaque (adj); **Transparent** (adj); **Translucent** (adj).
These words are of different meanings that are not always carefully distinguished in use. *Opaque* means impenetrable to light, not transparent, and, by extension, hard to understand, obscure. "The lions . . . having the advantage of thick and *opaque* jungle" (Baker). *Transparent*: Admitting the passage of light; easily seen through; hence also obvious or open. *Translucent*: Permitting the passage of light but diffusing it so that objects cannot be seen readily through it. The Oxford English Dictionary quotes this passage from the Times: "The windows of this classroom were once *transparent*; they are now *translucent*, and if not cleaned very soon will be *opaque*."

Opponent: See **Adversary.**

Opposite: See **Apposite.**

Optimistic (adj); **Sanguine** (adj), **Sanguinary** (adj).
An *optimistic* person (or *optimist*) is one who takes a favorable view of life in general and expects things to turn out favorably. "The *optimist* proclaims that we live in the best of all possible worlds;

and the pessimist fears this is true'' (Cabell). A *sanguine* person is cheerful and hopeful; but he may or may not be *optimistic*. *Sanguine* from its Latin root means bloody; and in ancient physiology blood as a predominating humor was the cause of both ruddy countenance and cheerful disposition. However, *sanguinary* retains its basic meaning of bloody, even of eagerness to shed blood, and is often applied to warfare, as in a *sanguinary* conflict.

Oral (adj); **Verbal** (adj); **Verbosity** (n); **Aural** (adj).
Oral means of or pertaining to the mouth and hence spoken rather than written. ''Temptations to petulance . . . which occur in *oral* conferences'' (Johnson). Whereas *verbal* means of or pertaining to words and so can refer either to what is written or to what is spoken and hence is the root of *verbosity*: excessive wordiness. ''A sophistical rhetorician, inebriated with the exuberance of his own *verbosity*'' (Disraeli on Gladstone). *Aural*, on the other hand, means primarily of or pertaining to the ear and is used mostly in medicine; but *aural* can also be the adjectival form of *aura* and so means characterized by a distinctive or pervasive quality. ''Magnetic power of personality depends upon an *aural* impression'' (Hook).

Ordinance (n); **Ordnance** (n).
An *ordinance* is a law or regulation or a public decree. ''Wilt thou have this woman to thy wedded wife, to live together after God's *ordinance* in the holy estate of matrimony?'' (Book of Common Prayer). But *ordnance* means artillery or military weapons of any kind and, specifically, the branch of an army that procures and distributes military supplies, including munitions. ''Armor, weapons, and all other *ordnance* expedient for war'' (Hall).

Ornate (adj); **Ornamental** (adj).
Orante: Elaborately or excessively adorned. ''But who is this, what thing of sea or land?/Female of sex it seems,/That so bedeck'd, *ornate* and gay,/Comes this way sailing'' (Milton). *Ornamental* has no implication of excess and means simply of or pertaining to ornament, decorative. ''The male dress of the time is more or less *ornamental*'' (Saunders).

Orthodox: See **Herterodox.**

Oscillate (v); **Osculate** (v).
Oscillate: To swing back and forth as a pendulum does or to fluctuate between differing views or opinions. ''The language *oscillates* between bombast and bathos'' (Hazlitt). *Osculate*: To come into close contact and, in archaic use, to kiss. 'Professedly prudish . . . they mutter, nod, *osculate*'' (St. Paul's Magazine).

Overlook (v); **Oversee** (v).
Overlook: (1) To fail to notice. (2) To disregard. (3) To look over from a higher position. (4) To rise above. (5) To excuse or pardon. (6) To inspect or peruse. These varied meanings all derive from the basic idea of looking over. But *oversee* has a more restricted meaning: To observe unintentionally or to supervise. ''He *oversees* all and *overlooks* none'' (Spurgeon).

Overt: See **Covert.**

Owing to: See **Because of.**

Paid (v); **Payed** (v).
Paid is the past tense and past participle of *pay* in all its usual and various meanings. ''Till Noah said: 'There's wan av us that hasn't *paid* his fare!' '' (Kipling). But *payed* is the past tense and past participle of *pay* only in the sense of releasing slowly, or uncoiling. ''We *payed* out the hawser by which we were riding'' (Smeaton).

Pandemic: See **Endemic.**

Pardon: See **Apologize.**

Partial (adj); **Partially** (adv); **Partly** (adv).
Partial is an adjective of two quite different meanings. (1) Of or pertaining to or affecting a part only; incomplete; as in a *partial* eclipse. (2) Inclined to favor one party or thing or faction more than another; biased; foolishly fond. "I do hope I shall enjoy myself with you . . . I am *partial* to ladies if they are nice" (Ashford). *Partly* as an adverb is near synonymous with *partially* in the meaning of incompletely and is preferred to *partially* in this sense by purists; but it should not be overlooked that *partially* alone has the meaning of to a limited degree, as in his *partially* restored health.

Peculiar: See **Funny.**

Pendant (n); **Pendent** (adj); **Pennant** (n).
A *pendant* is any hanging ornament. "Stoles and maniples all with *pendants* of gold and gems" (Chalmers). *Pendent* is an adjective describing something hanging or suspended. "The *Pendent* Barometer is a machine rather pretty, and curious, than useful" (Chambers). Whereas a *pennant* is any tapering flag, especially those used aboard naval or other vessels for signalling and those used to designate college football teams. "A squire's mark was a long *pennant* similar to the coach-whip *pennant* of modern ships of war." (Preble).

Percept (n), **Perceptive** (adj); **Precept** (n), **Preceptive** (adj).
Percept: The mental result or effect of perceiving. "Word-images as integral components of *percepts* and concepts" (System of Medicine). *Precept*: A commandment or direction for action or conduct; hence also a maxim or guide. "Example is always more efficacious than *precept*" (Johnson). Hence *perceptive* means having the faculty of perception, or the character of intuitive understanding. "Our active and *perceptive* powers are improved and perfected by use and exercise" (Reid). And *preceptive* means instructive, mandatory, or didactic. "The whole treatise is *preceptive* and hortatory" (Friend).

Perpetrate (v), **Perpetration** (n); **Perpetuate** (v), **Perpetuity** (n), **Perpetuation** (n).
Perpetrate: To perform or do; to commit (often as an offense). "The auspicious hour to *perpetrate* the deed" (Smollett). *Perpetration*: The act of doing or performing. "A man whose passions might impel him to the *perpetration* of almost any crime" (Radcliffe). *Perpetuate*: To make long-lasting or to preserve from extinction. *Perpetuity* (often preceded by *in*) is the state of indefinitely long duration. "But the inquity of oblivion blindly scattereth her poppy, and deals with the memory of men without distinction to merit of *perpetuity*" (Browne). *Perpetuation* is the act of securing long or indefinite life. "This invention [printing] contained within itself a self-preserving power which assured its *perpetuation*" (Smilee).

Persecute (v); **Prosecute** (v).
These verbs are sometimes confused; but each has a distinctive meaning. To *persecute* is to harass persistently or to oppress with punishment, especially for belief in unpopular creeds or principles. "Princes have *persecuted* me without a cause" (Book of Common Prayer). Whereas *prosecute* means either to take legal action against or to carry forward (usually to its completion) anything begun. "If you lodge this charge, you will be bound over to *prosecute* this gang" (Scott). "The Dutch war commenced without necessity and *prosecuted* with ill-judged parsimony" (Coleridge).

Personal (adj); **Personnel** (n).
Personal: Pertaining to or coming from a particular person; hence also individual or private. "No *personal* considerations should stand in the way of performing a public duty" (Grant). *Personal* is one of the considerably overused words of our language, and is unnecessary in such phrases as "*personal* friend." How many of us have impersonal friends? The adverb *personally* is also overused in such phrases as *Personally*, I think or believe. How else can one think except *personally*. Personally, I feel the word could be spared altogether from our use. *Personnel*: The body of persons jointly engaged in any work or undertaking. "He knew the *personnel* of the University" (Thackeray).

Perspective (n); **Prospective** (adj).
Perspective is the technique of depicting spatial relationships on a flat surface so they appear three-dimensional; hence also a picture or a scene having this quality. *Perspective* is also the faculty for seeing all the data of a specific problem or situation in their relationship to the whole; hence also insight. "We need a new *perspective* in the matter of unilateral disarmament" (New York Times). But *prospective* means likely, potential, expected. "Not only a large *prospective* but even a large immediate profit would be returned" (Fawcett).

Perspicacity (n), **Perspicacious** (adj); **Perspicuity** (n), **Perspicuous** (adj).
These words are often confused but shouldn't be, for the first two concern the ability to see through, the second two the capacity to be seen through. *Perspicacity*: Keenness of mental perception; acute intelligence or discernment. "She showed the same *perspicacity* in the selection of her agents" (Prescott). *Perspicuity*: Clearness, lucidity, intelligibility. "There is nothing more desirable in composition than *perspicuity*; and in *perspicuity* precison is included" (Southey). "His *perspicuous* philosophy" (Johnson); that is, philosophy penetrable or understandable.

Phase: See Faze.

Pitiable (adj); **Piteous** (adj); **Pitiful** (adj).
Pitiable means deserving of pity or compassion. "The champion of injured and *pitiable* women" (Milman). *Piteous* means evoking pity by reason of suffering or misery. "Behold, a silly tender Babe / In freezing winter night. / Alas, a *piteous* sight!" (Southwell). Whereas *pitiful* means such as to excite pity but also such as to evoke contempt by its mean or inferior quality. "It is no more than a *pitiful* village" (Lovell). But *pitiful* also means characterized by pity, compassion, tenderness. "For the Lord is full of compassion and mercy, long-suffering and very *pitiful*, and forgiveth sins, and saveth in time of affliction" (Ecclesiastes).

Policy (n); **Polity** (n).
A *policy* is a formulated course of action calculated to assure some end or to conform to principles of prudence or practical wisdom. "Honesty is the best *policy*; but he who is governed by that maxim is not an honest man" (Whately). A *policy* is also a contract of insurance, whose originators must have adopted the word because of its connotation of prudence, just as they thought of the unlikely euphemism of calling a bill a premium. *Polity* is a broader term signifying either a particular form of government, as in ecclesiastical *polity*, or governmental or administrative regulation. "The original constitution of the American Colonies possessing their assemblies with the sole right of directing their internal *polity*" (Jefferson).

Popular (adj); **Vulgar** (adj).
These words once meant the same thing; but *popular* has come to have a favorable connotation: Regarded with approval or affection by people in general. "He had but one eye and the *popular* prejudice runs in favour of two" (Dickens). Whereas *vulgar* has taken on the implication of poor taste, low breeding, or coarse ignorance. "'Father' is rather *vulgar*, my dear. The word Papa besides, gives a pretty form to the lips. Papa, potatoes, poultry, prunes and prism are all very good words for the lips; especially prunes and prism" (Mrs. General in Little Dorrit).

Population (n); **Populace** (n); **Populous** (adj).
Population: The total number of persons within a specific area; also the number or body of inhabitants belonging to a particular class, race or creed, as in working-class *population*. "*Population*, when unchecked, increases in a geometrical ratio. Subsistence only increases in an arithmetical ratio" (Malthus). *Populace:* The common people of a nation or community, as distinguished from the more elevated classes. "Where the *populace* rise at once against the never-ending audacity of elected persons" (Whitman). *Populous:* Full of residents or inhabitants. "As one who long in *populous* city pent, / Where houses thick and sewers annoy the air" (Milton).

Port (n); **Harbor** (n).
A _port_ is a place where ships load or unload. "In every _port_ he finds a wife" (Bickerstaff). But a _harbor_ is a safe body of water deep enough for the passage and anchorage of ships and usually providing access to a _port_. "A ship is floating in the _harbour_ now,/A wind is hovering o'er the mountain's brow;/There is a path on the sea's azure floor,/No keel has ever ploughed that path before" (Shelley).

Possible: See **Feasible.**

Practical (adj), **Practically** (adv); **Practicable** (adj).
The two adjectives are not identical in meaning. _Practical_ means adapted to actual use or engaged or experienced in actual practice of a trade, profession, or calling; hence also both efficient and sensible. "Out of the range of _practical_ politics" (Gladstone). The adverb _practically_ has the natural meaning of in a _practical_ manner; but it also means virtually or in effect. "The application was supported by _practically_ all the creditors" (Law Times). _Practicable_ means capable of being done or used or put into effect. "The only _practicable_ pass through these mountains to the upper settlements on Connecticut River" (Belknap).

Precede (v); **Proceed** (v).
Precede means to go before in order, rank, place or time. "All the sons of viscounts and barons are allowed to _precede_ baronets" (Rees). _Proceed_ means to go forward or onward, especially after an interruption; or to carry on any course of action or intention. "We will _proceed_ no further in this business" (Shakespeare).

Precedence or **Precedency** (n); **Precedent** (n).
Precedence is the act or fact of going before; priority in rank or importance. "Sir, there is no settling the point of _precedency_ between a louse and a flea" (Johnson). _Precedent:_ A preceding instance or case that serves as an example or, in law, acts as an authoritative rule. "Every public action which is not customary, either is wrong or, if it is right, is a dangerous _precedent_. It follows that nothing should ever be done for the first time" (Cornford).

Precept and **Preceptive:** See **Percept.**

Precious (adj); **Preciousness** (n), **Preciosity** (n).
Precious deserves an entry all its own because it is a word of varied meanings, is apt to be overused and is sometimes misused. It has the primary meaning of highly valuable and describes jewels or other costly ornament. "This _precious_ stone set in the silver sea" (Shakespeare). By extension it takes on the natural meanings of highly esteemed or deeply cherished. "All that's _precious_ in our joys, or costly in our sorrows" (Sterne). And, "I often wonder what the Vintners buy/Half so _precious_ as the Goods they sell" (Fitzgerald). But then things begin to go downhill, _precious_ meaning, half sardonically, wonderful or exquisite: "Her little house is just _precious_." Also it takes on the meaning of flagrant or gross, as in a _precious_ fool. Finally, it becomes excessively delicate or refined "An apparent desire of Admiration, . . . a _precious_ Behaviour in their general Conduct are almost inseparable Accidents in Beauties" (Steele). It is difficult to explain its meaning of very or extremely, as in _precious_ few. In any event it does not here mean the few that are deeply cherished, simply the exceedingly few. And, ultimately, it takes on the ironic meaning of worthless. "'Well, Sir Peter, I have seen both my nephews. A _precious_ couple they are!'" (Sheridan). It is curious that the noun _preciosity_ has almost the sole meaning of affected refinement in language or taste. "'Circle' he pronounced 'circul' with a certain affected _preciosity_ which was noticeable in the other parts of his behaviour" (Carlyle).

Precipitate (v, adj & n); **Precipitous** (adj).
Precipitate as a verb means to hasten the occurrence of. "Men will not bide their time, but will insist on _precipitating_ the march of affairs" (Buckle). It also means to plunge headlong. Hence the adjective _precipitate_ means either rushing headlong and without deliberation or proceeding with a

great haste. "She set my heart into a palpitation, like a *precipitate* pendulum in a clock case" (Richardson). The noun *precipitate* has entirely the technical meanings of a substance *precipitated* from a solution or the fall of rain, snow or hail on the earth's surface. But *precipitous* means extremely steep. "Down the *precipitous* rocks they sprung" (Moore). In general, *precipitous* is usually reserved for physical characteristics, as in a *precipitous* cliff, and *precipitate* for actions, as in his *precipitate* departure.

Predicate (v); **Predict** (v), **Prediction** (n).
Predicate means to proclaim or affirm or to assert as an attribute or quality of something or to imply, as in snow *predicates* whiteness. "Your mentality, too, is bully, as we all *predicate*" (Beerbohm). To *predict* is simply to foretell or prophesy. "Dreams and *predictions* ought to serve but for winter talk by the fireside" (Bacon).

Prescribe (v), **Prescription** (n); **Proscribe** (v), **Proscription** (n).
Prescribe: To set down in writing or otherwise as a rule or guide; to enjoin. "It is silliness to live when to live is torment; and then have we a *prescription* to die when death is our physician" (Shakespeare). See also *Receipt*. *Proscribe:* To prohibit or denounce or condemn; to banish or exile; to publicly announce the name of someone condemned to death. "A declaration was signed by all the Powers, which *proscribed* Napoleon as a public enemy, with whom neither peace nor truce could be concluded" (Alison).

Presentiment (n); **Presentment** (n).
A *presentiment* is a foreboding or a sense of something about to happen. "Some *Presentiment* told me this agreeable Gentleman would certainly succeed" (Manley). *Presentment* is now a fairly rare word, though occasionally mistaken for *presentiment;* and means simply the act of presenting. "Such *presentments* are now usually made once a year at the archdeacon's or bishop's visitation" (Church Law).

Presumptuous (adj); **Presumptive** (adj).
Both words spring from the same Latin root but have different meanings. *Presumptuous* means impertinently bold or arrogant. "Man only—rash, refined, *presumptuous* man / Starts from his rank and mars creation's plan" (Canning). Whereas *presumptive* means assumed or based on inference, as in *presumptive* heir to the throne.

Preventative (n & adj); **Preventive** (n & adj).
There is nothing actually wrong with *preventative* and both words mean serving to prevent or hinder, but the law of economy in language forbids use of long when short will do, so that now some dictionaries fail even to list *preventative*, and *preventive* holds undisputed sway. "A *preventive* war, grounded on a just fear of invasion, is lawful" (Fuller).

Primeval (adj); **Primitive** (adj).
Primeval means pertaining to or characterized by the first age or ages of anything, especially the world. "He sleeps with the *primeval* giants" (Carlyle). But *primitive* means not only early or earliest but also unaffected by civilizing influences and, by extension, simple, old-fashioned, unsophisticated, crude. "But he shaved with a shell when he chose—/ 'Twas the manner of *Primitive* Man" (Lang).

Principal (n & adj); **Principle** (n).
Perhaps not the substance but the spelling of these words is often confused. The noun *principal* means a chief person or party and also, specifically, the director or head of a school. It also means either the main body of an estate, as distinguished from income, or a capital sum, as distinguished from interest or profit. As an adjective it means chief, foremost, highest in rank or authority. "Wisdom is the *principal* thing; therefore get wisdom: and with all thy getting get understanding" (Proverbs). *Principle* means a rule of ethical conduct or a general law or truth from which others spring. "Damn your *principles!* Stick to your party" (Disraeli).

Probable: See **Feasible.**

Proceed: See **Precede.**

Propose (v); **Purpose** (n & v), **Purposive** or **Purposeful** (adj); **Purport** (n & v).
Propose: To offer a matter or idea for consideration or action. To nominate a person to some position. To propound a question or riddle. To make an offer of marriage. To intend. "Man *proposes*, but God disposes" (Thomas à Kempis). *Purpose:* To set as an aim or design for oneself. To plan with deliberate intent. "What can be avoided/Whose end is *purpos'd* by the mighty gods?" (Shakespeare). The noun *purpose* has similar meanings: Design, intention, determination. "The Englishman never enjoys himself except for a noble *purpose*" (Herbert). *Purport:* To profess or claim, often falsely; to imply. "Jack Downing . . . who *purported* to accompany the presidential party and chronicle its doings" (Quincy). But the noun *purport* signifies the import or meaning or sense of something. "I endeavoured to give the general *purport* of what was actually said" (Jowett).

Proscribe: See **Prescribe.**

Prosecute: See **Persecute.**

Prospective: See **Perspective.**

Prostrate (adj); **Prone** (adj); **Supine** (adj), **Supinely** (adv).
These words have a common general meaning: Lying flat. But each has its individual signification. *Prostrate:* Physically weak or exhausted; submissive; overcome or overthrown. "The violent reaction which had laid the Whig party *prostrate*" (Macaulay). *Prone:* Lying face downward but also having a natural inclination or tendency to some act or state. "I hope you do not think me *prone* to any iteration of nuptials" (Congreve). *Supine:* Lying with the face upward; but *supine* has also the connotative meanings of submissive or passive "Decent, easy men, who *supinely* enjoyed the gifts of the founder" (Gibbon).

Prudent (adj), **Prudently** (adv); **Prudential** (adj).
Prudent: Wisely judicious or cautious, provident, especially in financial or practical affairs. "A *prudent* man will avoid sinning against the stranger" (Jowett). *Prudential* means characterized by prudence or having discretionary authority in business or financial matters. But *prudential* is not used to describe acts of prudence or persons acting *prudently*. Rather, it describes motives or considerations leading to a *prudent* act or resulting from prudence. "To this I might add many other religious, as well as many *prudential* considerations" (Addison).

Purpose and **Purport:** See **Propose.**

Purposely (adv); **Purposefully** (adv).
Purposely: Intentionally, deliberately. "A fine new yacht . . . built *purposely* for his majestie" (Luttrell). But *purposefully* has the connotation of intention accompanied by resolute determination. "Her feet pattering most *purposefully* along the flagged passages" (Crockett).

Purview (n).
This is a word not so much misused as loosely used. Its meanings are specific and precise. *Purview:* (1) The range of operation or authority. (2) The range of vision or understanding. (3) In law that which is provided or enacted in the body of a statute or the purpose and scope of a statute. (4) The full scope of a document, statement or pronouncement. "We will assume then that the statute intended to include in its *purview* all the circumstances of the consecration" (Gladstone).

Qaid (n) or **Caid** (n).
This entry is solely for Scrabble players, for *qaid* is one of the very few words in actual use in which q does not have its customary trailer u. A *qaid* is a minor Muslim muncipal officer, celebrated in a limerick:

An aide with a Muslim master
Is a *qaid* more incensed than myrrh.
Said the aide with a sneer
To his base overseer,
"You're nought but an alabaster."

Queue: See **Cue.**

Railroad (n & v); **Railway** (n).
The distinction between the two words is rarely observed; but, in fact, *railroad* means a complete system of rail transportation, including rolling stock, rail beds, ticket offices and the like. "There was a rocky valley between Buxton and Bakewell, divine as the valley of Tempe. . . . You enterprised a *railroad* and blasted its rocks away. . . . Now every fool in Buxton can be at Bakewell in half-an-hour, and every fool in Bakewell at Buxton" (Ruskin). The verb *railroad* means to supply a system of rails and also to push forward with undue haste. "The way men are *railroaded* to the gallows in that country" (American Law Review). But *railway* means simply a track providing runway for wheeled equipment. "On his nose there was a Cricket,/In his hat a *Railway* Ticket" (Lear).

Raise (n & v); **Rear** (n & v); **Rise** (n & v); **Raze** (v).
Raise (n): An increase in the amount of something or the specific quantity of such increase. "By continued *raises* Potlatch had everything he possessed at stake" (Welcker). *Raise* (v): To move to a higher position, to lift up, to elevate; also to build or to activate. "Plots, true or false, are necessary things,/To *raise* up commonwealths and ruin kings" (Drydren). *Rear* (n): The back of anything. "My desires only are, and I shall be happy therein, to be but the last man, and bring up the *rear* in heaven" (Browne). *Rear* (v): To take care of and support up to maturity or to build or erect. There was a time when one could *rear* children but not *raise* them; one *raised* only corn or Cain. But that somewhat artificial distinction has fallen into oblivion. "Our Polly is a sad slut! nor heeds what we have taught her./I wonder any man alive will ever *rear* a daughter!" (Gay). *Rise* (v—pt, rose; pp risen): To get up from a reclining or supine position; to become active in opposition; to spring up or grow. "This man is freed from servile bands,/Of hope to *rise*, or fear to fall" (Wotton). *Rise* (n): The act of rising, an incline or elevation; coming into existence, notice or power, as in The *Rise* and Fall of the Roman Empire. This last is often misused as the title of Edward Gibbon's great classic, whose actual title is The Decline and Fall of the Roman Empire. *Raze* (v): To tear down or demolish—an antonym of *raise*. "Canst thou not minister to a mind diseas'd,/Pluck from the memory a rooted sorrow,/*Raze* out the written troubles of the brain?" (Shakespeare).

Rational (adj); **Rationale** (n).
Rational means reasonable or sensible; exercising reason, judgment, or good sense—sometimes used in distinction to emotional. "With men he can be *rational* and unaffected; but when he has ladies to please, every feature works" (Austen). The noun *rationale* means the fundamental reason for or logical basis of an act, principle or belief. "This gives us the true *Rationale* of the Mosaick Law" (Parker).

Readable (adj); **Legible** (adj).
Readable means capable of being read—but, by extension, it also means easy or interesting to read. "The second and third volumes are by far the most *readable*" (Marryat on the Life of Dickens). But *legible* means only capable of being read or discerned and is thus often applied to handwriting. "I trow that countenance cannot lie/Whose thoughts are *legible* in the eye" (Roydon).

Realize (v), **Realization** (n); **Know** (v), **Knowledge** (n).
Realize means to understand clearly; also to give reality to or to bring vividly to mind. "He thought he saw an Elephant,/That practised on a fife;/He looked again, and found it was/A letter from his wife,/'At length I *realize*,' he said,/'The bitterness of life!'" (Carroll). *Know* also means to

perceive or understand; but it does not suggest the completeness and thoroughness of *realize*. "When I say that I *know* women, I mean I *know* that I don't *know* them" (Thackeray).

Reassure: See **Assure.**

Rebound (v); **Redound** (v).
Rebound: To spring back from force of impact or to recoil or recover. "I never think I have hit hard, unless it *rebounds*" (Johnson). *Redound:* To have an effect upon a person or thing, the effect being one either of advantage or of disadvantage, either of credit or discredit. "Which could not but mightily *redound* to the good of the Nation" (Milton).

Receipt (n); **Recipe** (n); **Prescription** (n).
In the sense of a formula for preparing food or medicine, either *receipt* or *recipe* is as good as the other; but in actual practice *prescription* has replaced both of them as a medical formula; and *recipe* has become the usual word for a set of directions for preparing food, while *receipt* has returned to its meaning of receiving or acknowledging payment. Thus "Fit to be entrusted with the *receipt* and expenditure of large sums of money" (Mill); and "The man must have a rare *recipe* for melancholy, who can be dull in Fleet Street" (Lamb). Of course, *prescription* has a wider meaning than that of its medical use, signifying anything prescribed. "Conservatism discards *Prescription*, shrinks from Principle, disavows Progress; having rejected all respect for antiquity, it offers no redress for the present, and makes no preparation for the future" (Disraeli).

Recourse (n); **Resource** (n).
These words are but infrequently confused; nevertheless the distinction between them should be noted. *Recourse:* Access to a person or thing or means for support or protection. "If threats and persuasions proved ineffectual, he had often *recourse* to violence" (Gibbon). *Resource:* A source of supply or support. Its plural form usually means either the collective wealth or natural wealth of a nation or property that can be converted into money—assets. "Alexander Hamilton smote the rock of national *resources*, and abundant streams of revenue gushed forth. He touched the dead corpse of Public Credit, and it sprung upon its feet" (Webster).

Recriminate: See **Incriminate.**

Recur (v), **Recurring** (pres p); **Reoccur** (v), **Reoccurrence** (n); **Frequent** (adj & v), **Frequency** (n), **Frequently** (adv).
These are words of similar meaning; but there are distinctions among them that should be observed. To *recur* is to occur again, but with the implication of repetition more than once of an experience or event. "In every part of the book two thoughts are continually *recurring*" (Saturday Review); whereas *reoccur* suggests a single repetition; "Whenever it is applied in such measure to these several subjects, they will *reoccur*" (Atwater). Hence *recurring* describes anything that happens repeatedly as does *frequent*; but the latter implies occurring at short intervals or habitually. "The auld wife sat at her ivied door,/A thing she had *frequently* done before" (Calverley). The verb *frequent* means to visit often or to be often in some site or place. "Myself when young did eagerly *frequent*/Doctor and Saint, and heard great argument" (Fitzgerald).

Referee: See **Umpire.**

Refute (v); **Deny** (v); **Refutable** (adj); **Irrefutable** (adj)
Refute is in its primary sense a stronger word than *deny*. To *refute* is to prove by fact or evidence that an opinion or charge is either erroneous or false. "Who can *refute* a sneer?" (Paley). To *deny* is to state that something believed to be true is not true. It is also to withhold, to refuse access to, to disallow agreement or approval, to gainsay. "I must go down to the seas again, for the call of the running tide/Is a wild call and a clear call that may not be *denied*" (Masefield). *Refutable* and *Irrefutable* are antonyms. *Refutable* describing charges or statements that can be disputed or disproved, and *irrefutable* describing statements or charges that are incontestable or incontrovert-

ible. "It is not in the abstract, but in the concrete that it is *refutable*" (Godwin). And "Though our Argumentations for an Immaterial Soul in the Body of man be solid and *irrefutable*" (More).

Regretful (adj); **Regrettable** (adj).
Regretful means filled with sorrow or regret or anguish because of something done or lost. "They soon forgot the *regretful* impressions of the day" (Du Maurier). But *regrettable* means deserving of or arousing regret or sorrow. "These raids are very *regrettable*" (Times). See also *Repent*.

Repel (v); **Repulse** (v).
Because both words in origin mean to drive back, they are mistakenly used as synonyms. To *repel* is to drive or force back or to resist effectively. "It remains that we retard what we cannot *repel*, that we palliate what we cannot cure" (Johnson). But *repel* has also the connotation of arousing distaste or aversion. "Such extravagances *repel* minds that have a sense of truth" (Hare). Whereas *repulse* means only to turn away, to refuse or reject, and is essentially without the implication of arousing revulsion. "Hope may vanish, but can die not;/Truth be veiled, but still it burneth;/Love *repulsed*—but it returneth" (Shelley).

Repent (v); **Regret** (v).
The two words are near synonyms. But to *repent* is to feel self-reproach or contrition because of a past act, with an implication of atonement in addition to remorse. "Let this hour be but/A year, a month, a week, a natural day,/That Faustus may *repent* and save his soul" (Marlowe). Whereas, *regret* is not so powerful a word. It too means to feel remorse or sorrow but without the implication of redress. It may even mean simply to feel disappointment or to express polite refusal. "He *regretted* that he was not a bird" (Roche).

Reputed (pp); **Reported** (pp); **Reportedly** (adv).
Reputed means supposed or held to be such. "He had no opinion of *reputed* felicities below" (Browne). Whereas *reported* means simply related or made known. "Cases *reported* with too great prolixity" (Caxton). However, *reportedly* has the connotation of by rumor as well as by report. "The picture of those *reportedly* gownless backs had depressed him abominably" (Malet).

Required (pp); **Prescribed** (pp).
Whatever is *required* is obligatory or necessary, demanded. "To whom nothing is given, of him can nothing be *required*" (Fielding). That which is *prescribed* is recommended or laid down as a course to be followed or designated for use or other purpose. "On the *prescribed* day the Sheriff's officers ventured to cross the boundary" (Macaulay).

Resolution (n); **Motion** (n).
In parliamentary procedure both these words mean a formal expression of opinion or a formal proposition; but a *motion* is a proposal made to a deliberative or governing body requiring a vote thereon or other action. "Then they all with one consent said to this Bramble, do thou Reign over us. So he accepted this *motion* and became the King of the Town of Mansoul" (Bunyan). A *resolution* may be no more than an expression of the opinion that something is true or desirable and hence need not result in action. Of course, *resolution* has the less formal meaning of a resolve. "Great actions are not always true sons/Of great and mighty *resolutions*" (Butler).

Resource: See **Recourse.**

Respectful (adj), **Respectfully** (adv); **Respectable** (adj), **Respectably** (adv); **Respective** (adj), **Respectively** (adv).
The first two of these three pairs of words mean with respect; but *respectful* means showing respect or deference, while *respectable* means worthy of respect or esteem. "For I *respectfully* decline/To dignify the Serpentine/and make hors-d'oeuvres for fishes" (Dobson). And "In the bosom of her *respectable* family resided Camilla" (Burney). But *respective* means pertaining individually to each of a number of persons or things or to each person or thing in the order named. "The Waters under the heavens were now gathered together into their *respective* and distinct places" (Whiston).

Restive (adj); **Restless** (adj).
Restive: Uneasy, impatient of control or restraint. "He proved as ready a scholar as he had been indocile and *restive* to the pedant who held the office of his tutor" (Godwin). *Restless:* Never at rest, agitated, unceasingly active. "For something in its depths doth glow / Too strange, too *restless*, too untamed" (Arnold).

Resume (v), **Resumption** (n); **Continue** (v), **Continuance** or **Continuation** (n).
To *resume* is to take up again after interruption; whereas to *continue* is to engage in the same activity without interruption. "The way to *resumption* is to *resume*" (Chase). But "A man ought warily to begin charges which once begun will *continue*" (Bacon). And "Patient *continuance* in well doing" (Acts of the Apostles).

Reticent (adj), **Reticence** (n); **Taciturn** (adj), **Taciturnity** (n).
Both terms signify a reluctance to speak; but *reticence* implies shyness or withdrawal, whereas *taciturnity* implies sullenness or severity. "Mr. Glegg was extremely *reticent* about his will" (Eliot). But "After which brief reply John relapsed into *taciturnity*" (Mulock).

Reverend (adj); **Reverent** (adj).
Reverend: Worthy to be revered, deserving of reverence. "What is buzzing in my ears? / Now that I come to die, / Do I view the world as a vale of tears? / Ah, *reverend* sir, not I!" (Browning). *Reverent:* Feeling or characterized by reverence or deeply pious or respectful. "Shall I, the gnat which dances in thy ray, / Dare to be *reverent?*" (Patmore).

Rout (n & v); **Route** (n & v).
Both words have several meanings; but the primary meaning of the noun *rout* is a defeat attended by disorderly retreat. "The only difference after all their *rout*, / Is that the one is in, the other out" (Churchill). The verb *rout* means to search or rummage or to turn over or dig up with the snout. "If you find pigs *routing* in your enclosure, you may kill one" (Kingsley). The noun *route* means a course or road or passage. "The Mariners . . . to be the better assured of their *routes* and courses on the sea do divide every quarter of the Horizon into 8 severall windes" (Blundevil). And the verb *route* means to send or forward by a fixed course. "Goods *routed* this way are taken by rail to Duluth" (Pall Mall).

Row (n & v).
A word ill-used more by reporters than by correspondents. The noun *row* has two distinct pronunciations (ro and rou) and meanings. The first that of a number of persons or objects arranged in a straight line. "The soldier-saints, who *row* on *row*, / Burn upward each to his point of bliss" (Browning). The second that of a noisy dispute or quarrel. "You can do no good to yourself or anyone else by making a *row*" (Anstey). But because of its convenient three-letter length *row* is frequently misused in headlines to mean a serious international dispute or even strife. In fact, it means a noisy but casual commotion. The verb *row* means to propel a boat by the leverage of oars. " 'Ha! Ha!' quoth he, 'full plain I see, / The Devil knows how to *row*' " (Coleridge). But it too can mean to dispute raucously—by words rather than deeds.

Sacred (adj); **Sacrosanct** (adj).
Sacred means devoted to a deity or to some religious purpose and also entitled to veneration or reverence. "Poet and Saint! to thee alone are given / The two most *sacred* names of earth and Heaven" (Cowley). But *sacrosanct* means superlatively sacred and carries with it the sense of inviolability. "Truth, which alone of words is essentially divine and *sacrosanct*" (Morley).

Salon (n); **Saloon** (n).
These words were once indistinguishable; but a difference between them is now carefully preserved. *Salon:* A drawing room or reception hall or a gallery in which works of art are exhibited. "Ambassadors and other Great Visitors are usually received in the *Salon*" (Chambers). But a

saloon is a place where alcoholic beverages are sold and consumed. "A rather first-class *saloon*, bar and restaurant on Broadway" (Leland). But the word still also means a large room for public use, as in a ship's dining *saloon*. "Solomon of *saloons*/And philosophic diner-out" (Browning).

Sanguine and **Sanguinary:** See **Optimistic.**

Script (n); **Scrip** (n).
Script is handwriting and hence, by extension, any manuscript or document. "Mrs. Campbell has had the *script* of 'Tess' on her hands for quite a while" (Western Gazette). But *scrip* is paper money, usually of small denomination, issued for temporary use and redeemable at some later date for actual currency. "You find a dying railway, you say to it, Live, blossom anew with *scrip*" (Carlyle).

Seasonable (adj); **Seasonal** (adj).
Seasonable: Timely, opportune, or appropriate to the season, as in *seasonable* rains. "Are not these times *seasonable* for such a subject as is here handled?" (Gouge). *Seasonal*: Associated with or accompanying the various seasons of the year. "The regular *seasonal* lack of work is no dire calamity" (Forum).

Sense (n); **Sensitivity** (n); **Sensibility** (n).
Sense is a noun of varied meanings. Primarily any of the faculties (sight, hearing, taste, touch and smell) by which man perceives the external world. By extension it takes on such meanings as a faculty of the mind, as in the moral *sense*; or a special capacity for perception, as in a *sense* of humor; or an undefined impression or feeling, as in a *sense* of security; or recognition of something incumbent, as in a *sense* of duty; or an opinion or judgment, as in the *sense* of the meeting. Finally it takes on the meaning of practical intelligence. " 'The woman had a bottom of good *sense*.' The word *bottom* thus introduced was so ludicrous, that most of us could not forbear tittering. . .'Where's the merriment? I say the *woman* was *fundamentally* sensible' " (Boswell on Johnson). *Sensitivity* implies the state or quality of sensing or of being sensitive to, often in unusual degree. "An eloquent exuberance characterizes the style of our author, and a *sensitivity* of imagination which makes even the minutest phaenomenon important to his attention" (Taylor). *Sensibility* is the capacity for sensation or feeling; responsiveness often of an emotional or unduly heightened kind. "Experience is never limited, and it is never complete; it is an immense *sensibility*, a kind of huge spider-web suspended in the chamber of consciousness, and catching every air-borne particle in its tissue" (James).

Sensual (adj); **Sensuous** (adj).
These words are frequently confused but have quite different meanings. *Sensual*: Inclined to or preoccupied with gratification of the senses; carnal, voluptuous. "Of music Dr. Johnson used to say that it was the only *sensual* pleasure without vice" (Seward). Whereas *sensuous* means perceived by or affecting the senses, especially those involved in appreciation of poetry, music or nature. "The external or *sensuous* qualities of art" (Gullick).

Sewage (n); **Sewerage** (n).
Sewage is the wastematter that passes through sewers; while *sewerage* is either a system of sewers or the process of removing refuse through drains and underground watercourses. Examples of their proper use would be odious.

Shall (v); **Will** (v).
Although one cannot deplore that this distinction has broken down, careful writers still use *shall* in the first person and *will* in the second and third persons to express futurity. "When I was a little boy, I had but little wit,/'Tis a long time ago and I have no more yet;/Nor ever *shall* until that I die,/For the longer I live the more fool am I" (Wit and Mirth). But "Where is the man who has the power and skill/To stem the torrent of a woman's will?/For if she *will*, she *will*, you may depend

on't;/And if she won't, she won't; so there's an end on't'' (Anon). In general, *should* and *would* follow the same principle of usage, except in their special meanings of *should* in the sense of obligation and *would* in the sense of habituation.

Ship: See **Boat.**

Sight (n); **Spectacle** (n).
A *sight* is anything seen; but a *spectacle* is something seen of unusually interesting, attractive, or puzzling character. ''Prepost'rous *sight*! the legs without the man'' (Cowper). But ''This great *spectacle* of human happiness'' (Smith). Both words may be used in a derogatory sense, as in ''you are a *sight*,'' or ''you have made a *spectacle* of yourself.''

Simile (n); **Metaphor** (n).
Simile: A figure of speech in which two unlike things are compared through use of ''like'' or ''as.'' ''Making it momentary as a sound,/Swift as a shadow, short as any dream;/Brief as the lightning in the coiled night'' (Shakespeare). But a *metaphor* is a figure of speech in which comparison is made through identification of one thing with another. ''Roses are her cheeks,/And a rose her mouth'' (Tennyson). ''How infinite,'' wrote Churchill, ''is the debt owed to *metaphors* by politicians who want to speak strongly but are not sure what they are going to say.'' In any event, public servants are unabashed users of *mixed metaphors*. ''The Rt. Hon. Gentleman is leading the people over the precipice with his head in the sand'' (Fowler). A strange confusion of identity between Gadarene swine and ostriches.

Simple (adj); **Simplified** (pp); **Simplistic** (adj).
Each of these words means uncomplicated or plain. But *simple* means naturally plain or easy to understand or unadorned. ''I sought the *simple* life that Nature yields'' (Crabbe). Whereas *simplified* means made simple or easy to comprehend. ''It furnishes a *simplified* account of other countries'' (Morse). And *simplistic* means overly simple. ''The facts of nature and of life are more apt to be complex than simple. *Simplistic* theories are usually one-sided and partial'' (Clarke). No doubt because of the nature of the times *simplistic* has become a vogue word and everyone from abecedarians to zealots is accused of *simplisticity*, to coin a word that is now needed.

Simulate (v); **Stimulate** (v).
The words have no relationship except that occasionally one is written for the other. *Simulate*: To make a pretense of or to assume the appearance of. ''Many caterpillars, bettles, moths, butterflies *simulate* the objects by which they are commonly surrounded'' (Spencer). See also *Dissimilate*. *Stimulate*: To rouse to action or effort; to act as a stimulus. ''You have *stimulated* my curiosity'' (Lever).

Single out; Signal out.
The first is fine; the latter does not exist but is in frequent use, no doubt because of confusion with the verb signalize. To *single out* is to pick or choose one from many as an example, model, or the like. ''*Singling out* from the entire body of the Clergy a man under suspicion of heresy'' (Burgon).

Site: See **Cite.**

Slack (adj, n & v); **Slake** (v).
These words are often confused in both spelling and use. *Slack* in all its parts of speech shares the meaning of not tight, negligent, remiss, dull, careless. ''In marriage, a man becomes *slack* and selfish, and undergoes a fatty degeneration of his moral being'' (Stevenson). Whereas the verb *slake* means to allay thirst, to cool or refresh. ''A crystal draught/Pure from the lees, which often more enhanc'd/The thirst than *slak'd* it'' (Cowper). *Slake* can also mean to diminish in intensity. ''The indignation against them will shortly *slake* of it selfe'' (Stafford).

Solid (adj); **Stolid** (adj).
Solid: Having three dimensions; firm hard or compact; without break; and, by extension, real or genuine, sound or good. "A *solid* man of Boston, / A comfortable man, with dividends, / And the first salmon, and the first green peas" (Longfellow). *Stolid*: Not easily stirred, unemotional, impassive. Perhaps with justice *stolid* could be substituted for *solid* in the verse from Longfellow.

Sometime (adv & adj); **Sometimes** (adv).
Sometime as adverb means at some indefinite or indeterminate time. "His Holiness will arrive *sometime* next week" (N. Y. Times). As adjective it means former. "Therefore our *sometime* sister, now our queen" (Shakespeare). *Sometimes* means on some occasions, now and then, at times. "I do love I know not what; / *Sometimes* this, and *sometimes* that" (Herrick).

Sort of: See **Kind of.**

Specie (n); **Species** (n); **Specious** (adj).
Specie is coin or minted currency. "Whether we send our Coin in *Specie* or melt it down here and send it in Bullion" (Locke). *Species*: A class of individuals having characteristics or traits in common. "I describe not men, but manners; not an individual but a *species*" (Fielding). *Specious* has nothing to do with either *specie* or *species* and means superficially pleasing or plausible, though without real merit. "What are these *specious* gifts, these paltry gains?" (Crabbe).

Spectacle: See **Sight.**

Spiritual (adj & n). **Spiritous** (adj).
The adjective *spiritual* means pertaining to or characterized by the spirit or soul, as distinguished from the physical body or world. "An outward and visible sign of an inward and *spiritual* grace" (Book of Common Prayer). A *spiritual* is a religious hymn or song, especially one sung by slaves. "I had for many years heard of this class of songs under the name of 'Negro Spirituals'" (Higginson). But in contemporary use, *spiritous* means containing alcohol produced by distillation. "Not allowing me to take anything *spiritous*" (Smith).

Sprain (n); **Strain** (n); **Stress** (n).
Sprain: Wrenching or tearing of the ligaments around a joint, but without dislocation. "The treatment to be adopted for *sprains* is the immediate application of leeches" (Penny Cyclopedia). *Strain*: Injury to a muscle or tendon due to excessive use or tension. A severe demand on physical or emotional resources. "*Strains* are often attended with worse consequences than broken bones" (Buchan). *Stress*: Physical, mental or emotional tension. "Pious virgins, under *stress* of these things, swoon" (Hewlett).

Stalactite (n); **Stalagmite** (n).
Both are deposits, usually conical, of calcium carbonate formed by the dripping of water. A *stalactite* is a column that hangs down; a *stalagmite* is one that builds up from the floor. "Some calcereous *stalactites* pendent from the roof" (Mills). "The rich *stalagmites* that grew up from the bottom reflected a golden light through the water" (Catlin).

Stanza: See **Verse.**

Stash: See **Cache.**

Stationary (adj); **Stationery** (n).
Stationary: Having a fixed position; not movable. "A field hospital is a very different affair from a *stationary* base hospital" (Daily News). *Stationery*: Writing paper and, less commonly, writing materials. "A rush was generally made to the desk where the *stationery* was kept" (Russell).

Stevedore: See **Longshoreman.**

Stimulate: See **Simulate.**

Straight (adj & adv); **Strait** (n & adj).
Straight (adj): Without a bend or curve, direct. "The voice of one crying in the wilderness, Prepare ye the way of the Lord, make his paths straight" (St. Matthew). *Straight* (adv): In a *straight* course; directly to or from a place. "This piece of eloquence moved me so much that I went *straight* to his Excellency" (Herbert). *Strait* (n): A narrow passage of water. "They may return through the *strait* of Magellan" (Hakluyt). Hence the adjective *strait* means narrow, confined and, by extension strict. "*Strait* is the gate, and narrow is the way, which leadeth unto life, and few there be that find it" (St. Matthew). *Footnote*: The correct spelling is *straitjacket,* not *straightjacket.* In short, a confining rather than a straight jacket.

Strain, Stress: See **Sprain.**

Strange: See **Funny.**

Strategy (n), **Stratagem** (n), **Strategic** (adj), **Strategist** (agt); **Tactics** (n), **Tactic** (n),
    Tactical (adj); **Tactician** (agt).
Strategy: Specifically, planning and direction of large military operations. More generally, any plan or method for obtaining a desired goal or result. But a *stratagem* is a specific trick or scheme used to surprise or deceive an enemy and, by extension, any artifice or ruse used to secure a result or an advantage over an adversary. "For her own breakfast she'll project a scheme,/ Nor take her tea without a *stratagem*" (Young). *Tactics*: The art of disposing and maneuvering military or naval forces in battle in accordance with a *strategic* plan. A *tactic*, like a *stratagem*, is a specific maneuver or expedient. "The soldier—that is, the great soldier—of today is . . . a quiet, grave man, busied in charts, exact in sums, master of the art of *tactics*, occupied in trivial detail" (Bagehot).

Subsequent (adj); **Consequent** (adj), **Consequential** (adj).
For obscure reasons these words are often misused. *Subsequent* means occurring or coming later, following in order or succession. "And he smiled a kind of sickly smile, and curled up on the floor, / And the *subsequent* proceedings interested him no more" (Harte). But *consequent* means following as a result or effect or following as a logical conclusion. "The satisfaction or dissatisfaction, *consequent* to a man's acting suitably or unsuitably to conscience" (South). However, the word *consequential* has departed from *consequent* and in modern idiom means only something of consequence or importance, sometimes used ironically to mean self-important. "Mr. C. bustled about . . . feeling himself the most *consequential* man in the town" (Martineau).

Sufficient (adj), **Sufficiency** (n); **Superfluous** (adj), **Superfluity** (n).
Sufficient and *sufficiency* mean enough. *Superfluous* and *superfluity* more than enough. "I have had an elegant *sufficiency*. Anything more would be a *superfluous* superabundancy" (Anon).

Supine: See **Prostrate.**

Surpise: See **Amaze.**

Syzygy: See **Zyzzyva.**

Taciturn: See **Reticent.**

Tactics: See **Strategy.**

Tactile (adj); **Tactual** (adj); **Textile** (n & adj).
Tactile: Endowed with or affecting the sense of touch. "The *tactile* sensation is a symbol to us of some external event" (Foster). *Tactual* is a less common word than *tactile* and is a near synonym for it; but it also has a somewhat different, more precise meaning: Arising from or due to the sense of touch. "Thy existence is wholly an Illusion and optical and *tactual* Phantasm" (Carlyle). *Textile* is any woven material and, as adjective, it describes anything in general pertaining to weaving. "The *textile* mills lie near the links,/ At noon of every day/ The working children may look out/ And see the men at play" (19th century anonymous workmen's ballad).

Tasteful (adj); **Tasty** (adj).
Tasteful means having or displaying good taste; whereas *tasty* means having a pleasing flavor. "The *tasteful* publisher of the Aldine Poets" (Singer); but "A famous pie or pilau, with rice and a *tasty* sauce" (Curzon).

Teach: See **Learn.**

Temporal (adj); **Temporary** (adj).
Both words refer, of course, to time; but *temporal* has the extended meaning of concern with present life, and hence wordly or secular, as distinguished from ecclesiastical. "His Scepter shows the force of *temporal* power" (Shakespeare). *Temporary* means existing or effective for only a short time. "The use of force alone is but *temporary*. It may subdue for a moment; but it does not remove the necessity of subduing again" (Burke).

Temporize (v); **Extemporize** (v).
Temporize means to gain time by delay, hence to compromise temporarily. "I have behaved like a fool; I ought to have *temporized* with this singular being, learned the motives of its interference, and availed myself of its succour" (Scott). To *extemporize* is to speak with no or slight preparation. "Preachers are prone either to *extemporize* always or to write always" (Phelps).

Textile: See **Tactile.**

That (pron); **Which** (pron).
Perhaps millions of editiorial blue pencils have been used to the nub to enforce the distinction between *that* and *which*; but usage continues to pay scant attention to editorial preference. Nevertheless, the distinction is both real and simple. *That* is restrictive and defining; *which* is simply descriptive. "This is the house *that* Longfellow built." Here *that* defines the house. "This is Longfellow's house, *which* was built in 1837." Here the house is already defined and *which* simply describes it. One should also note that nonrestrictive clauses beginning with *which* are set off by commas.

Their (pron); **There** (adv & pron); **They're** (Contrac).
Their is a possessive, attributive pronoun. "Mine and all *their* free and sovereign king" (Swinburne). *There* is an adverb meaning in or at that place and a pronoun used to introduce a sentence or clause in which the verb precedes its subject. "As I was going up the stair / I met a man who wasn't *there*. He wasn't *there* again today. / I wish, I wish he'd stay away" (Mearns). And "From all these things *there* resulted consequences of vast importance" (Buckle). *They're* is a contraction for they are. "*They're* Rogues as sure as Light's in Heaven" (Ward).

Therefore (adv); **Therefor** (adv).
Therefore means in consequence of, as a result of. "I think, *therefore* I am" (Descartes). *Therefor* means in exchange for or in place of something. "Argument being at an end, recourse was then had to the common substitute *therefor*, ridicule" (Hall).

Timber (n): **Timbre** (n).
Timber: The wood of growing trees suitable for structural use, or a stand of such trees. "It is the love of the people; it is their attachment to their government, . . . which gives you your army and your navy, and infuses into both that liberal obedience, without which your army would be a base rabble, and your navy nothing but rotten *timber*" (Burke). *Timbre*: The quality or character of a sound distinguishing it from other sounds of similar pitch and intensity. "There are scarely any two individuals who have exactly the same *timbre* of voice" (Blaserna).

Titillate (v); **Titivate** (v).
These words are rarely confused, for the good reason that the second is rarely used. *Titillate*: To excite agreeably, to tickle the fancy. "Not to *titillate* his palate, but to keep up his character for hospitality" (Macaulay). *Titivate*: To make smart or spruce up. "It was drawn through the Fair by eight oxen *titivated* with ribbons and flowers" (Daily News). Somehow an unlikely picture.

Tortuous (adj), **Tortuosity** (n); **Torturous** (adj).
Tortuous: Full of twists and turns, bending, winding, and hence, by extension, deceitfully indirect. "The unscrupulous cunning with which he assisted in the execution of the schemes of his master's *tortuous* policy" (Scott). *Torturous*: Characterized by excruciating pain or by torture. "Outworn with sorrow, with hours of *torturous* anguish" (Ellis).

Transcendent (adj); **Transcendental** (adj).
The words are, of course, related, and both mean surpassing usual standards, going beyond ordinary limits. "Such *transcendent* goodness of heart" (Richardson). But *transcendental* has the further meaning of abstract, mystic, metaphysical; beyond the accidental knowledge of human experience; describing what, in fact, Carlyle called "*transcendental* moonshine."

Translucent and **Transparent:** See **Opaque.**

Treachery (n); **Treason** (n).
Both words mean the deliberate, conscious betrayal of trust or confidence; but *treason* means only betrayal of one's country, faithlessness of allegiance to one's land. "I am justly kill'd with my own *treachery*" (Shakespeare). But "If this be *treason*, make the most of it" (Patrick Henry).

Triumphal (n & adj); **Triumphant** (adj).
Triumphal and *triumphant* both mean exulting in victory or success; but *triumphal* usually denotes official celebration of victory or achievement. "O come, all ye faithful,/Joyful and *triumphant*" (translation of Adeste Fideles). "So strook with dread and anguish fell the Fiend;/And to his crew, that sat consulting, brought/Joyless *triumphals* of his hop't success,/Ruin, and desperation, and dismay" (Milton).

Turgid (adj); **Turbid** (adj).
Turgid: Swollen, distended and, hence, overblown, bombastic. "The advocates, who filled the Forum with the sound of their *turgid* and loquacious rhetoric" (Gibbon). *Turbid*: Not clear, opaque, obscured, confused, muddied. "Clear writers, like fountains, do not seem so deep as they are; the *turbid* look the most profound" (Landor).

Typography (n), **Typographical** (adj); **Typology** (n), **Typological** (adj).
Typography is the art of printing from type and the practice of its related processes and is also the appearance or character of printed matter. "The *typography* of both editions does honour to the press" (Boswell). But *typology* is the study of symbolic representations, especially those of religious literature; the classification of types and symbols. "The *Typology* of Scripture has been one of the most neglected departments of theological science" (Fairbairn). However, the adjective *typological* can also mean pertaining to the art of printing. "Future writers on the Invention of Printing should treat the question from a purely historical and *typological* point of view" (Trubner).

Umpire (n): **Referee** (n).
Both words mean a person to whom something is referred for decision—one who adjudicates, as a *referee* in bankruptcy. However in some sports a *referee* decides, but in others an *umpire* does. There is no rational basis for the difference. "Britton claimed the fight on a foul, but the *referee* disallowed the claim" (Sportsman). Or "And in case they can't Decide such Differences, then they shall be referr'd solely to the Decison of the said Sir Thomas Parkyns as *Umpire*" (Wrestling).

Un- (Prefix)
Un is a useful and engagingly simple prefix. It means not. What is not likely is unlikely. Whoever is not distrubed is undisturbed. Robert Lynd tells in a long-ago essay of some Dutch sailors in Portsmouth who became rollicking drunk and then belligerent, eventually punching and even biting some respectable British subjects. At the conclusion of their trial the magistrate addressed the Dutch sea captain gravely: "It is very Unenglish to bite people, and I should like you to impress this on

your men.'' To which the captain replied with equal gravity: "It is very Undutch too, your worship.'' Here we see that *Un-* before national designations has a limited and chauvinistic use. The Oxford English Dictionary gives un-American a fairly ancient lineage. Under the date of 1818 it supplies this example: "Ninety marble capitals have been imported at vast cost from Italy and shew how *un*-American is the whole plan." The sentence illustrates that delicate use of *un-* in its connotation that anything not customary to or practiced by one's own people is either wrong or wrongheaded. Lynd asked a Scotchman if he had ever heard anyone use the adjective Unscotch, and he said he could not imagine it except in reference to Irish whiskey.

Uninterested: See **Disinterested.**

Unique (adj).
Unique means single or solitary in type or character; it is applicable only to what is in some respect the only existing specimen, the precise like of which cannot be found. Hence *unique* is an adjective without comparative or superlative degrees. No *unique* things is more or less *unique* than another. Of course one does not often see uniquer or uniquest; but one does see the misuse of *more unique* and *most unique*. Here we see the word in its sense of singularity: "A thing so totally *unique*/the great collectors would go far to seek" (Taylor).

Unmoral: See **Amoral.**

Unorganized (pp); **Disorganized** (pp).
Both words mean lacking order or unity; but *disorganized* also implies upsetting or overturning an existing orderliness. And, of course, *unorganized* also means not unionized. "A succession of revolutions; a *disorganized* administration" (Macaulay). "The sustained fire threw their dense and *unorganized* masses into rapid confusion" (Froude).

Unqualified (pp); **Disqualify** (v), **Disqualified** (pp).
Unqualified: Lacking the required qualifications. "It is no use sueing a quack. Why did you employ him? You know he is *unqualified*" (Kingslake). *Disqualified*: Deprived of qualifications. From *Disqualify*: To divest of credentials or privileges; to render *unqualified*. "Strong passions and keen sensibilities may easily *disqualify* a man for domestic tranquility" (Stephen).

Unsatisfied (pp); **Dissatisfied** (pp).
Unsatisfied: Feeling that expectations have not been met; discontent. "He seemed a good deal *unsatisfied* that the Spanish Ambassador had received the Advice from England" (Temple). *Unsatisfied* also means unpaid. "He was deeply in debt and had a number of *unsatisfied* judgments out against him" (Hitchman). *Dissatisfied*: Displeased, offended, disappointed. "I think I could turn and live with animals, they are so placid and self-contain'd;/. . . Not one is *dissatisfied*, not one is demented with the mania of owning things" (Whitman).

Urban (adj); **Urbane** (adj), **Urbanity** (n).
Urban means pertaining to or characteristic of a city or city life. "For Cambridge people rarely smile,/Being *urban*, squat, and packed with guile" (Brooke). But *urbane* means having the polish and sophistication that are presumed to be characteristic of the social life of great cities. "A man remarkable for his talents and *urbane* manners" (Tooke).

Vacillate: See **Fluctuate.**

Valuable (adj); **Valued** (pp).
Anything *valuable* is of great worth or merit. "We present you with this Book, the most *valuable* thing that this world affords. Here is Wisdom; this is the royal Law; these are the lively Oracles of God" (The English Coronation Service). But what is *valued* is esteemed, highly regarded, cherished—but it may or may not be *valuable*. "Secrets with girls, like loaded guns with boys, /Are never *valued* till they make a noise" (Crabbe).

Varied (adj); **Various** (adj).
Varied: Characterized by variety; diverse, changed, altered; made different. "No man hath walked along our roads with step/So active, so inquiring eye, or tongue/So *varied* in discourse" (Landor on Browning). *Various*: Of different kinds, distinct, differing. "Unlike the hard, the selfish, and the proud,/They fly not sullen from the suppliant crowd,/Nor tell to *various* people *various* things,/But show to subjects what they show to kings" (Crabbe on books).

Venal (adj); **Venial** (adj).
These look-alikes have entirely different meanings. *Venal*: Willing to betray a trust; open to bribery; corruptible. "As the Senate is smaller . . . the vote of each member is of more consequence, and fetches, when *venal*, a higher price" (Bryce). *Venial*: Pardonable, excusable, not seriously wrong, trifling. "Our own laws not long ago punished forgery and even more *venial* crimes with death." (Yeats). Hence a *venial sin* is for Catholics a transgression against God's law committed without full awareness of its seriousness and so not depriving the soul of divine grace.

Verbose and **Verbosity**: See **Oral.**

Verse (n); **Stanza** (n).
The word *verse* has many meanings, but technically it signifies one line of a poem and is often confused with *stanza*, which means an arrangement of consecutive lines of poetry unified by a pattern of rhyme or meter and making up one of several like divisions that, together, constitute a complete poem. "For rhyme the rudder is of *verses*,/With which like ships they steer their courses" (Butler). "I have adopted the *stanza* of Spenser—a measure inexpressibly beautiful" (Shelley).

Victim: See **Martyr.**

Vivid: See **Livid.**

Vulgar: See **Popular.**

Warp (n); **Woof** (n).
These words are no longer in common use; but together they mean the underlying basis upon which something is built, as in "English common law is the *warp and woof* of our judicial system" However, the words separately have distinctive meanings. The *warp* is a set of parallel threads running vertically on a loom; the threads running horizontally between these are the *woof* or *weft*. The fabric that results is the *web*. "Weave the *warp* and weave the *woof*,/The winding sheet of Edward's race./Give ample room, and verge enough/The characters of hell to trace" (Gray).

Wax (v); **Wane** (v).
Because these words are now rarely used, they are sometimes misused. *Wax* means to grow larger, to increase in strength or power; whereas *wane* means to decline in strength or power, to decrease or diminish. "Yon rising moon that looks for us again./How oft hereafter will she *wax* and *wane*;/How oft hereafter rising look for us/Through this same garden—and for *one* in vain!" (Fitzgerald).

Way (n); **Ways** (n); **Weigh** (v).
The word *way* has many meanings: Manner or mode; characteristic or habitual practice; a method for attaining a goal; a respect or particular; a path or course. However, *way* is in colloquial usage misused to mean away and to mean situation, as in "he is in a bad *way*." *Ways* is simply the plural of *way*; but, despite congressional precedent, the phrase *ways and means* is redundant, for both words mean the same thing. "Seated upon the convex mound/Of one vast kidney, Jonah prays/And sings his canticles and hymns,/making the hollow vault resound/God's goodness and mysterious *ways*,/Till the great fish spouts music as he swims" (Huxley). *Weigh* has nothing to do with the foregoing words, except that in nautical use it is sometimes confused with *way*. A ship, in short, gets under *way* only when its anchor is *aweigh*—that is free from the bottom or *weighed*. "I found about sixty of the convoy had lost their anchors in attempting to *weigh*" (Wellington).

Whence (adv); **Whither** (adv).
Whence means from what place or what position, whereas *whither* means to what place or position. "Drink! for you know not *whence* you came, nor why:/Drink! for you know not why you go nor where" (Fitzgerald). "*Whither*, O splendid ship, thy white sails crowding,/Leaning across the bosom of the urgent West,/That fearest nor sea rising, nor sky clouding,/*Whither* away, fair rover, and what thy quest?" (Bridges).

Whether: See **If.**

Which: See **That.**

Who's (contraction); **Whose** (poss pron).
Who's is a contraction of who is, and *whose* is the possessive form of the pronoun who. Confusion between them arises because *who's* seems to have the possessive form of apostrophe s. "*Who's* the Potter, pray, and who the Pot?" (Fitzgerald). "Yes, lad, I lie easy,/I lie as lads would choose;/I cheer a dead man's sweetheart,/Never ask me *whose*" (Housman).

Will: See **Shall.**

-wise (suffix).
It all began with *clockwise*; but suddenly there was an unlikely rage for use of the suffix *wise* to denote reference to, or manner, direction, or position of, in every conceivable and inconceivable way. Fortunately, a counterclockwise movement set in and the fever abated; but one can still admire the owl anxiously inquiring of his wife how their little owlet is doing wise*wise*.

Won't (contraction); **Wont** (n & adj).
Won't is a contraction of will not. "Will you, *won't* you, will you, *won't* you, will you join the dance?" (Carroll). *Wont* as noun means custom and as adjective accustomed. "Her lodger gave her, contrary to his *wont*, a signal to leave the room" (Scott). And "He might have more good qualities than she was *wont* to suppose" (Austen).

Woof: See **Warp.**

Would: See **Shall.**

Xanthate (n): **Xanthein** (n); **Xanthene** (n); **Xanthin** (n); **Xanthone** (n).
These words do not appear in everyday speech; but both their meanings and spellings are frequently confused. *Xanthate*: An ester of xanthic acid. *Xanthein*: The water-soluble part of the coloring matter in yellow flowers. *Xanthene*: A chemical compound. *Xanthin*: The part of the coloring matter of yellow flowers that is not water-soluble. *Xanthone*: A nitrogenous compound. Examples of usage would make tedious an otherwise instructive lesson.

Yarborough (n).
A term beloved of complaining bridge players, and most bridge players are chronic complainers. Named after the Second Earl of Yarborough, born to nobility and losing, it means a hand at whist or bridge in which no card is higher than the nine spot. "I have held *Yarboroughs* and been doubled and roughed all the evening" (Blackwell's Magazine).

Yester- (prefix).
For some reason other combinations than *yesterday* seem incongruous except in poetry. It is obvious that *yestereve* is shorter than yesterday evening; but what the word gains in economy it loses in a kind of false elegance. But perhaps yesteryear is also acceptable. "Where are the snows of *yesteryear?*" (Villon).

Zeal, Zealous, Zealot: See **Jealous.**

Zyzzyva (n): **Syzygy** (n).

These words are scarcely on every tongue and are mostly for crossworders, double crosticians, and scrabblers. But they are real, sometimes confused, and often misspelled. *Zyzzyva*: A tropical weevil; *Syzygy*: The configuration of the earth, moon and sun lying in a straight line. "Said a termite with sardonic leer, / 'May I ask is the bar tender here? / I'll have a sweet *syzygy* / Or maybe a *zyzzyva*.' / Said the bar, 'Have instead a small bier.' "

Legal Terminology

A

a aver et tener
abaction
abactor
ab agendo
abaissement
abalienate
abandon
abandonee
abandonment
  a. for torts
abandonum
abandum
abandun
ab ante
ab antecedente
ab antiquo
abarticular
abatable
  a. nuisance
abatare
abate
abatement
abater
abator
abavus
abbacy
abbreviate
abbreviation
abbreviator
abbroach
abbroachment
abbrochment
abdicate
abdication
abditorium
abduct
abduction
abductor
abearance
aberemurder
aberrant
aberration

abet
abettator
abettor
ab extra
abeyance
abide
abiding
  a. conviction
  a. faith
ability
ab inconvenienti
ab initio
ab intestat
ab intestato
ab invito
ab irato
abishering
abishersing
abjudicate
ab judicatio
abjudicatio
abjuration
abjure
ablation
able-bodied
ablegati
ablocatio
abnegation
abnepos
abneptis
abode
abolish
abolition
à bon droit
abordage
abortive
  a. trial
aboutissement
abridge
abridgment
abrogate
abrogation
abscond
absconding
absence

absent
absente
absentee
absoile
absolute
absolutely
absolution
absolutism
absolve
absque
  a. hoc
  a. impetitione vasti
abstain
abstention
abstract
  a. of title
  a. reasoning
abstraction
absurdity
abuse
  a. of distress
  a. of process
abusive
abut
abutment
abuttal
abutter
abutting
  a. owner
academic
academy
a cancellando
a cancellis
a causa de cy
accedas
  a. ad curiam
accede
acceleration
accentuation
accept
acceptance
  a. au besoin
  a. supra protest
acceptare
acceptor
access
accessio
accession

accessory
  a. after the fact
  a. before the fact
  a. during the fact
accident
  inevitable a.
accidere
accion
accomenda
accommodated
  a. party
accommodation
  a. paper
accommodatum
accompany
accomplice
accord
  a. and satisfaction
accordance
accordant
accouchement
account
accountable
  a. receipt
accountant
  certified public a.
account-book
accounting
accouple
accredit
accretion
accroach
accrocher
accrual
  a. basis
accrue
accruer
accruing
accumulated
  a. profits
accumulation
accumulative
  a. sentence
accusation
accusatorial
accusatory
  a. part
accuse
accustom
a ce

a cel jour
acequia
achat
achieve
acknowledge
acknowledgment
  certificate of a.
acolyte
a confectione
a consiliis
acquainted
acquereur
acquest
acquêts
acquiesce
acquiescence
acquiescent
acquire
acquired
  a. rights
acquirer
acquisition
acquit
  autrefois a.
acquitment
acquittal
acquittance
acquitted
act
  a. in pais
  intervening a.
  moiety a.
  a. of bankruptcy
  a. of God
  a. on petition
acte
actio
  a. calumniae
  a. damni injuria
  a. de dolo malo
  a. directa
  a. furti
  a. in factum
  a. mixta
  a. vulgaris
action
  amicable a.
  civil a.
  class a.
  collusive a.

action (*continued*)
  common-law a.
  concerted a.
  matrimonial a.
  noxal a.
actionable
actionary
activity
actual
  a. cash value
  a. practice
  a. residence
actuarial
actuary
aculosure
a cueillette
acuity
acuminate
adapt
adaptation
adapted
a dato
a datu
ad damnum
addendum
addicere
addict
addictio
addiction
addictive
addition
additional
  a. servitude
additionales
additur
addled
address
adduce
adeem
ademptio
ademption
adequate
  a. remedy
adhere
adherence
adherent
adhering
adhesive
adhesiveness
adhibere

ad hoc
ad hominem
adiation
adieu
ad infinitum
adipocere
adiratus
adit
aditus
adjacent
adjective
  a. law
adjoin
adjoining
adjourn
adjournatur
adjourned
  a. summons
  a. term
adjournment
adjudge
adjudicataire
adjudicate
adjudicatee
adjudicatio
adjudication
adjudicative
adjudicatory
adjunct
adjunctio
adjunction
adjunctive
adjuration
adjure
adjust
adjuster
  independent a.
adjustment
adjutant
  a. general
adjuvant
adlegiare
ad litem
admanuensis
admeasurement
  writ of a.
admezatores
adminicle
adminicular
  a. evidence

adminiculate
adminiculator
adminiculum
administer
administration
administrative
  a. law
administrator
administratrix
admiral
admiralitas
admiralty
admissible
admission
admit
admittance
admixture
admonish
admonishment
admonition
admonitory
admortization
adnepos
adneptis
adnihilare
adnotatio
adobe
adolescence
adolescent
adopt
adoption
adoptive
adoptivus
adpromissor
adquieto
adrectare
adrift
adrogation
adscendentes
adscriptus
ad sectam
adsessores
adstipulator
adult
adulter
adultera
adulterant
adulteration
adulterator
adulterer

adulteress
adulterine
adulterous
adultery
  incestuous a.
advance
advancement
advantage
advena
advent
adventitia
adventitial
adventitious
adventitius
adventura
adventure
adventurer
adversaria
adversary
adverse
  a. enjoyment
  a. interest
  a. possession
  a. witness
adversus
advertise
advertisement
advice
advisare
advise
advisedly
advisement
advisory
  a. opinion
advocacy
advocare
advocate
  judge a.
advocator
advocatus
  a. diaboli
advoutrer
advoutry
advowee
advowson
advowtry
aedes
aedificare
aedile
aequitas

aequus
aerodrome
aeronaut
aeronautic
aerostatics
aerostation
aes
aesthetic
affair
affect
affection
affectus
affeer
affeerors
affermer
affiance
affiant
affidare
affidari
affidatus
affidavit
affilare
affile
affiliate
affiliation
affinage
affines
affinitas
affinity
affirm
affirmance
affirmant
affirmantis
  a. est probare
affirmation
affirmative
  a. defense
  a. pregnant
  a. proof
affix
affixing
affixus
affliction
afforare
afforatus
afforce
afforest
afforestation
affouage
affranchir

affranchise
affray
affrectamentum
affreightment
affretement
affront
aforesaid
aforethought
a fortiori
after-acquired
aftermath
afterthought
afterward
against
agalma
agard
agarder
age
   a. of consent
agency
agenda
agenesia
agent
ager
aggravated
   a. assault
aggravating
aggravation
aggregate
aggregation
aggression
aggressive
aggressor
aggrieved
agio
agist
agistor
agitate
agitator
agnates
agnati
agnatic
agnatio
agnation
agnomen
agnomination
agony
agraphia
agrarian
agrarium

a gratia
agree
agreed
   a. order
agreement
agreer
agrez
agri
agricultural
agriculture
aid
   a. and abet
aider
   a. by verdict
air
   a. pollution
aircraft
aisne
a issue
ajournment
ajuar
ajutage
akin
alcabala
alcaide
alcalde
alcove
   a. room
alderman
aleator
aleatory
   a. contract
alia
   a. enormia
aliamenta
alias
   a. dictus
alibi
alien
   a. amy
   a. enemy
alienable
alienage
alienate
alienation
alienee
alieni
   a. juris
alienigena
alienism

alienist
alienor
alienus
alignment
aliment
alimenta
alimentos
alimony
  a. in gross
alio
  a. intuitu
aliquot
aliter
aliunde
alius
allegation
  disjunctive a.
  irrelevant a.
allege
allegiance
alleging
  a. diminution
all fours
alliance
allison
allocable
allocate
allocation
allocatur
allocution
allocutus
allodial
allograph
allonge
allot
allotment
allottee
allow
allowable
allowance
allowed
  a. claim
alloy
allude
allusion
alluvion
ally
almanac
almoin
almoner

almshouse
altenheim
alter
  a. ego
alteration
altercation
alternat
alternate
  a. legacy
alternatim
alternative
  a. writ
alumnus
alveus
amalgamation
amanuensis
ambactus
ambassador
amber
ambiguity
  patent a.
ambiguous
ambit
ambivalence
ambivalent
ambulance
ambush
ameliorating
  a. waste
amelioration
amenable
amend
amendment
amenity
amentia
amerce
amercement
ameublissement
ami
amicable
  a. action
amicus
  a. curiae
amiral
amita
amitinus
amnesty
amok
amorphous
amortissement

amortization
amortize
amotion
amove
amparo
ampliation
analogous
analogy
analytical
   a. jurisprudence
anaphrodisia
anaphrodisiac
anarchist
anarchy
anathema
anathematize
a nativitate
anatocism
ancestor
ancestral
anchor
anchorage
ancient
   a. documents
   a. lights
ancillary
androgynous
androgynus
androlepsy
andromania
androphonomania
angary, right of
anglice
angling
anguish
aniens
anient
animal
animation
animo
   a. et corpore
animus
   a. ad se omne jus ducit
   a. hominis est anima scripti
anker
annals
annex
annexation
anni
   a. nubiles

anniculus
anniented
anniversary
anno
   a. Domini
annotation
announced
annoyance
annual
annually
annuitant
annuity
annul
annular
annulment
annulus
annus
anomalous
anomaly
anonymity
anonymous
answer
ante
   a. litem motam
antecedent
antecessor
antedate
antenatal
antenna
antenuptial
   a. contract
anthracite
anthracosis
anthrax
anthropometric
anthropometry
antichresis
anticipation
anticipatory
   a. breach of contract
antigraphy
antitrust
   a. acts
à outrance
a pais
apartment
apatisatio
apertura
aperture

apex
  a. juris
apices
  a. juris non sunt jura
apocrisarius
apogee
apographia
apologetic
apologia
apologize
apology
apoplexy
apostacy
a posteriori
apostille
apostles
apostoli
apostolus
apotheca
apothecary
appall
apparator
apparatus
apparel
apparent
  a. authority
  a. easement
appeal
  a. bond
  devolutive a.
appealed
appear
appearance
appellant
appellate
  a. court
  a. jurisdiction
appellatio
appellation
appellator
appellee
appello
appellor
append
appendage
appendant
appendices
appenditia
apperception
appertain

appertaining
appliance
applicable
applicant
applicatio
  a. est vita regulae
application
apply
appoint
appointee
appointment
appointor
apportion
apportionment
apposal
apposer
apposition
appostille
appraisal
appraise
appraisement
appraiser
appreciable
appreciate
appreciation
  a. in value
apprehend
apprehensio
apprehension
apprendre
apprentice
apprenticeship
apprise
approach
approbate
approbation
appropriate
appropriation
appropriator
approval
approve
approved
  a. indorsed notes
approvement
approver
approximal
approximate
approximation
appruare
appurtenance

appurtenant
apraxia
à prendre
a priori
aprovechamiento
aqua
   a. cedit solo
aquagium
aquatic
aqueduct
aqueductus
a quo
arable
arbiter
arbitrage
arbitrament
arbitrarily
arbitrariness
arbitrary
   a. punishment
arbitrate
arbitration
   a. and award
   binding a.
arbitrator
arbitrios
arbitrium
archbishop
archdeacon
archdeaconry
archetype
architect
archives
archivist
arcifinious
areal
   a. geology
areaway
arenales
arendator
à rendre
arentare
arere
aretro
a retro
argent
argentum
argot
arguendo
argument

argumentative
arise
arising
aristocracy
aristo-democracy
arma
armistice
armorial
   a. bearings
armory
arpen
arpentator
arra
arraign
arraignment
arrangement
arras
array
arrayer
arrearage
arrears
arrect
arrest
   false a.
   a. of judgment
arrestee
arret
arretted
arrival
arrogate
arrogation
arrondissement
arsenal
arson
artesian
   a. well
article
articled
   a. clerk
articulate
articulately
articuli
articulo
   a. mortis
artifact
artifice
artificer
artificial
   a. persons
artificially

artisan
à savoir
ascend
ascendants
ascendientes
ascending
ascent
ascertain
ascertained
   a. as aforesaid
ascun
asesinato
aspect
aspersions
asphalt
asportation
assart
assassin
assassinate
assassination
assault
  aggravated a.
  felonious a.
assay
assayer
assecurare
assecuration
assecurator
assemblage
assemble
assembly
assent
assert
assertion
assertory
  a. covenant
assess
assessed
assessment
assessor
asset
  intangible a.
asseveration
assewiare
assign
assignability
assignable
assignation
assignee

assignment
  a. for benefit of creditors
  a. of dower
assignor
assigns
assimilate
assimilation
assisa
assise
assiser
assist
assistance
  writ of a.
assistant
assisus
assize
assizes
associate
association
assume
assumed
assumpsit
assumption
  a. of risk
assurance
  common a.
assure
assured
  a. clear distance ahead
assurer
astipulation
astitution
astrum
asylum
asymmetrical
asymmetry
at arm's length
à terme
atheism
atheist
atheistic
atia
atilium
at large
atomize
à tort
à tort et à travers
à tort ou à droit
atravesados
atrocious

atrocity
attach
attaché
attached
attaching
attachment
  a. of privilege
attain
attainder
  bill of a.
attaint
  autrefois a.
attempt
attendant
attentat
attention
attenuant
attenuate
attenuation
attest
attestation
  a. clause
attested
  a. copy
attesting
  a. witness
attestor
attorn
attorney
  a. in fact
  a. general
attornment
attractive
  a. nuisance doctrine
atypical
au besoin
auction
auctioneer
audi
  a. alteram partem
audience
  a. court
audit
audita
  a. querela
auditor
augment
augmentation
aula

Australian
  A. ballot
auter
authentic
  a. act
authenticate
authentication
authentics
authenticum
author
authorities
authority
  apparent a.
authorize
autocracy
autograph
autographic
automatic
autonomous
autonomy
auto-optic
  a. evidence
autopsy
autre
  a. action pendant
  a. droit
  a. vie
autrefois
  a. acquit
  a. attaint
  a. convict
auxilliary
auxiliator
auxilium
availability
available
avails
aval
aventure
avenue
aver
average
averment
  immaterial a.
aversio
  a. periculi
aviation
a vinculo matrimonii
avocat
avocation

avoid
avoidable
avoidance
avoirdupois
avoucher
avoué
avow
avowal
avowry
avulsion
avunculus
award
awareness
axiom
ayuntamiento

B

babbitt
baby
  b. act
bachelor
backadation
backbear
backbite
backbond
backing
  b. a warrant
backside
backward
backwardation
backwater
bad
  b. debt
  b. faith
  b. title
badge
  b. of fraud
badger
baggage
  b. car
bahadum
bail
  b. bond
  justifying b.
bailable
  b. offense
bailee

bailiff
bailiwick
bailment
bailor
bailpiece
baiting
  b. animals
balance
  b. of power
balconies
baldio
bale
balise
balius
ballast
ballastage
ballium
ballot
  b. box
ballottement
ban
banal
banality
banc
banco
Bancus
  B. Reginae
  B. Regis
  B. Superior
bandit
banditry
bane
baneret
banish
banishment
banister
  b. and railing
bankable
  b. paper
banking
bankrupt
  cessionary b.
bankruptcy
  composition in b.
banlieu
banner
bannimus
bannitio

banns
   b. of matrimony
bannum
banque
banyan
bar
   b. association
baragaria
barbarous
bare
   b. patent license
   b. trustee
barebones
   b. parliament
bargain
   b. and sale
bargainee
bargaining
   collective b.
bargainor
barge
barleycorn
baron
   b. et feme
baronage
baronet
barony
   b. of land
barrator
barratrous
barratry
barred
barrel
barren
   b. money
barrenness
barretor
barretry
barricade
barrier
barrister
barter
bas
base
   b. estate
   b. fee
   b. line
basilica
basis
basset

basso
bastard
bastarda
bastardization
bastardize
bastardy
   b. process
batiment
batonnier
battery
   simple b.
battonier
batture
bawd
bawdyhouse
baygall
bayou
beacon
beaconage
beadle
bearer
bearing
   b. date
beaupleader
bedehouse
bedel
bedelary
bedlam
beget
beggar
begotten
begum
behalf
behetria
behoof
belief
belligerency
belligerent
bellum
belongings
bench
   b. warrant
benchers
bene
bénéfice
bénéficiaire
beneficial
   b. interest
   b. power
beneficiary

beneficium
   b. abstinendi
   b. competeniae
   b. separationis
benefit
   b. of clergy
benevolence
benevolent
bequeath
bequest
berbiage
berg
berghmayster
beria
berm bank
Bertillon system
berton
besaile
beseech
besoin
besot
bessemerizing
best
   b. evidence
bestia
bestial
bestiality
bestow
bestowal
betray
betrayal
betrothal
betrothed
betrothment
betterment
betting book
beverage
beyond
   b. a reasonable doubt
bias
biases
bicameral
   b. system
bielbrief
bienes
   b. comunes
biennial
biennially
biens
bigamist
bigamous

bigamus
bigamy
bigot
bigotry
bilagines
bilan
bilateral
   b. contract
bilboes
bilged
biline
bilinguis
bilk
bill
   b. of attainder
   b. of certiorari
   b. of interpleader
   b. of lading
   b. of sale
   b. of sufferance
billa
   b. cassetur
billboard
billet
billy
bimetallic
bimetallism
bind
   b. out
binder
binding
   b. arbitration
   b. instruction
bipartite
bipolar
birretum
bis
bisaile
bishop
bishopric
bissextile
biting rule
bitulithic
bitumen
bituminous
bizarre
black
   B. Book of Admiralty
   b. liquor
   B. Maria
   B. Muslim

blackjack
blackleg
blacklist
blackmail
blacksmith
blank
   b. acceptance
   b. indorsement
blanket
   b. insurance
blasarius
blasphemy
blasting
bleachers
blended
   b. fund
blindcraft
block
blockade
blockage
blockbooking
blockholer
bloodhounds
bludgeon
blue laws
blue sky law
bluff
blumba
blunder
blunderbuss
board
   b. of directors
boarder
boarding
   b. house
boatable
boatswain
bobtail
   b. driver
bobtailed
   b. caboose
boddemerey
bodemerie
bodmerie
body
   b. image
   b. politic
bogus
boilary

boiler
bois
bon
bona fide
   b. f. purchase
bonanza
bond
   appeal b.
   dissolving b.
   fidelity b.
   forthcoming b.
   performance b.
bondage
bonded
   b. indebtedness
   b. warehouse
bondsman
bonification
bonus
boodle
boodling
booked
booking
   b. contract
bookmaker
bookmaking
boom
boomage
boosted
   b. fire
booting
bootlegger
bootstrap
   b. doctrine
booty
bordaria
bordereau
borgbriche
borough
   b. court
borrasca
borrow
borrowed
   b. capital
borrower
borrowing
   b. power
boscage
boscus

bote
bottellaria
bottom
  b. hole contract
  b. land
bottomry
bouche
bought
  b. and sold notes
boulevard
bouncer
bound
boundary
bounded
bounders
bounding
bounty
bourgeois
bourse
  b. de commerce
boussole
bout
bovarius
bovine
boycott
  secondary b.
Boyd rule
bozero
brabanter
bracery
bracinum
branding
brasiator
brasium
brawl
brawling
breach
  b. of contract
  b. of promise
  b. of trust
  b. of warranty
breadth
breakage
breakdown
  b. service
breaking
  b. bulk
breech
breed
brethren

breve
  b. de recto
  b. originale
brevet
brevia
breviate
brewer
brewery
bribe
bribery
bribour
bridge
brief
briefly
brigandine
brine
bris
brisement
Bristol bargain
brocage
broken stowage
broker
brokerage
  b. contract
brothel
brother
brother-in-law
brotherhood
brought
Brown decree
brushing
brutum fulmen
bubble
bucketing
bucket shop
buckstall
buck swamper
budget
budgetary
buffer
buffet
builder
building
  b. and loan association
bulk
  b. sales acts
  b. windows
bulldozer
bullet
bulletin

bullheaded
bullion
bum-bailiff
bunco game
buoy
burden
   b. of proof
bureau
bureaucracy
bureaucratic
burg
burgage-tenure
burgator
burgess
burgh
burglar
burglariously
burglarize
burglary
burgomaster
burial
burking
burkism
burlesque
burned
   b. out of sight
burning fluid
burnt
burrochium
bursar
bursaria
burying-ground
bushel
bushido
business
butane
butcher
butlerage
butt
buttals
butte
butts
   b. and bounds
buyer
by-bidder
bylaw
bypassing
byroad
bystander

C

cabal
cabalist
caballero
cabana
cabaret
cabinet
   c. council
cable
cablish
caboose
cabotage
cacicazgos
cadastre
cadastu
cadaver
cadaverous
cadere
cadet
cadi
caduca
caducary
Caesar
caeterorum
caeterus
cafe
cahier
cahoots
calaboose
calamitous
calamity
calculate
calculated
calculus
calendar
calends
caliche rock
callable
   c. bonds
callers
calling
calumnia
calumniae
   c. jusjurandum
calumniate
calumniator
calumny
Calvo doctrine

camara
camber
cambio
cambist
cambium
camera
  c. stellata
cameralistics
camerarius
camino
camouflage
campaign
campana
campanarium
campanile
campartum
campers
campus
cana
canalization
cancel
cancellaria
cancellarius
cancellation
candidate
candor
canon
  c. law
canonical
  c. disability
  c. obedience
canonist
cantel
cantle
canvass
canvasser
capability
capable
capacity
capax
  c. doli
  c. negotii
capella
caper
capias
  c. ad audiendum judicium
  c. ad respondendum
  c. ad satisfaciendum
  c. pro fine
capita

capital
  floating c.
  c. punishment
  c. stock
capitale
capitalist
capitalization
  c. method
capitalism
capitalize
capitatim
capitation
  c. tax
capite
capitula
capitulary
capitulate
capitulation
capitulum
capper
capricious
  c. disbelief
captain
captation
captator
caption
captive
captor
capture
caput
carat
carcan
carcanum
carcatus
carcer
cardinal
careless
carelessly
carence
carga
cargaison
cargo
caristia
Carlisle tables
carnal
  c. abuse
  c. knowledge
carnaliter
carnally
carrera

carriage
carricle
carrier
  certified c.
carrying away
carta
carte blanche
cartel
carucata
carucate
case
  c. law
  c. system
casement
cash
  c. market value
  c. surrender value
cashier
cashiered
cashier's check
cashlite
casing-head gas
casket
cassare
cassation
  court of c.
cassetur
  c. billa
  c. breve
cassock
cassula
castigate
castigation
casting vote
castle
castrensis
castrum
casual
  c. deficit
  c. ejector
  c. pauper
casualty
casus
  c. belli
  c. fortuitus
catastrophic
catastrophe
catching bargain
catchings
catchland

catchment area
catchpoll
categorical
categorize
category
cathedral
catholic
catoniana regula
cattle
  c. rustling
cattleguard
Caucasian
caucus
causa
  c. mortis
  c. proxima
  c. remota
causation
causator
cause
  c. of action
causeway
caustic
causus
  c. major
cautio
caution
cautionary
  c. judgment
cautioner
cautionnement
cautious
caveat
  c. emptor
  c. venditor
  c. viator
caveator
cavere
cavum
ceap
cease
cede
cedo
cedula
cedule
celibacy
celibate
cemetery
cenninga
cens

censere
censitaire
censive
censo
censor
censorious
censorship
censucre
censurable
censure
census
   c. regalis
cental
centenarii
centeni
centime
centralization
centralize
centumviri
century
certain
certainty
certificate
   c. into chancery
   c. of acknowledgment
   c. of deposit
   c. of stock
certification
   c. proceeding
certified
   c. carrier
   c. check
   c. public accountant
certify
certiorari
cerura
cesionario
cess
cessare
cessation
cesser
cesset
   c. executio
   c. processus
cessio
   c. bonorum
cession
cessionary
   c. bankrupt
cessment

cessor
cessure
cestui
   c. que trust
chaceable
chacer
chaffery
chain of title
chairman
chairmanship
challenge
chamber
   c. surveys
chamberlain
chamberlaria
chamfer
chamotte
champart
champert
champertor
champertous
champerty
champion
chancel
chancellor
chance-medley
chancer
chancery
   certificate into c.
changer
channel
chanter
chantry
chapel
chapelry
chaplain
chapman
chapter
character
   c. evidence
charbon
charge
chargé
   c. d'affaires
chargeable
chargeant
charge-off
charge-sheet
charging
   c. lien

charitable
  c. corporation
  c. trust
charity
charlatan
charta
charte
chartel
charte-partie
charter
chartered
  c. ship
charterer
charter-house
charter-land
charter-party
chassis
chaste
chastity
chattel
  incorporeal c.
  c. mortgage
  c. real
chaud-medley
chauffeur
chaussée
cheat
cheaters
check
checker
checkerboard system
check-off system
check-roll
chemin
cheque
chevisance
cheze
chicane
chicaner
chicanery
chief
  c. baron
  c. justice
  c. magistrate
chilling
  c. a sale
chirograph
chirographa
chirographer
  c. of fines

chirographum
choate lien
choke damp
chose
  c. in action
  c. in possession
chosen
  c. freeholders
churl
Cinque Ports
cipher
circa
circinate
circuit
  c. court
  c. justice
circuity
  c. of action
circulate
circulation
circulatory
circumferential
circumflex
circumscribe
circumstances
circumstantial
  c. evidence
circumvent
circumvention
circus
cista
citacion
citation
cite
citizen
citizenry
citizenship
ciudades
civic
civil
  c. action
  c. inquest
  c. law
  c. liability
  c. rights
  c. wrong
civilian
civilis
civiliter
civilization

civis
civitas
claim
  allowed c.
  c. and delivery
  dormant c.
  c. of ownership, right and title
  placer c.
  c. for relief
claimant
clam
clamor
clandestine
class
  c. action
  c. representation
classiarius
classification
classified
classify
clause
  attestation c.
  commodities c.
  derogatory c.
  enacting c.
  escalator c.
  iron-safe c.
clausula
  c. derogativa
clausum
clean hands
clear
  c. and convincing proof
clearance
clearing
clearing-house
clergy
clergyable
clergyman
clerical
  c. error
clerigos
clerk
  articled c.
clerkship
cliens
client
cloere
close
  c. corporation
  c. season

closed shop
close-hauled
cloture
cloud on title
clough
clubbing
club-law
coach
coadjutor
coadministrator
coadunatio
coadventurer
coalition
coassignee
coaster
coasting
coastwise
cockbill
cocket
cockpit
cocksetus
code
  C. Napoléon
codex
codicil
codicillus
codification
codify
coemptio
coemption
coequal
coerce
coercion
coercive
coexecutor
coffee-house
cognates
cognati
cognatio
cognation
cognatus
cognitio
cognitive
cognitor
cognizable
cognizance
cognizee
cognizor
cognomen
cognovit
  c. actionem

cohabit
cohabitation
　lascivious c.
cohabiting
coheir
coheiress
coherent
coherer
coinage
coinsurance
coinsure
coke
cold blood
collapsible
　c. corporation
collate
collateral
　c. attack
　c. facts
　c. inheritance tax
　c. promise
　c. security
　c. warranty
collation
colleague
collectible
collection
collective
　c. bargaining
collector
collega
collegatarius
collegatary
college
collegia
collegialiter
collegiate
　c. church
collegium
collide
colliery
collision
collobium
collocation
colloid
colloidal gold
colloquial
colloquium
collum
collusion

collusive
　c. action
colony
color
　c. of authority
　c. of office
　c. of title
colorable
colored
colpices
comaker
combe
combination
　c. in restraint of trade
combine
combustible
combustion
comes
　c. and defends
comfortable
　c. speed
cominus
comitas
comitatus
comitia
comity
　judicial c.
　c. of nations
　c. of states
command
commandement
commander-in-chief
commandery
commanditaires
commandité
commandment
commarchio
commence
commencement
　c. of a declaration
commend
commenda
commendam
commendatio
commendation
commendators
commendatory
comment
　c. upon the evidence

commerce
  interstate c.
  intrastate c.
commercia
  c. belli
commercial
  c. agency
  c. court
  c. law
  c. paper
  c. partnership
commercium
comminalty
commingle
commissaire
commissaires-priseurs
commissariat
commissary
commission
  c. merchant
commissioned
commissioner
commissive
commit
commitment
committed
committee
committing
  c. magistrate
committitur
commixtio
commodate
commodato
commodatum
commodities
  c. clause
commodity
commodore
common
  c. assurances
  c. humanity doctrine
  c. knowledge
  c. law
  c. nuisance
  c. pleas
commonable
commonalty
commonance
commoner

common-law
  c. action
  c. court
  c. marriage
  c. wife
commons
commonwealth
commorancy
commorant
commorientes
commotio
commotion
communal
commune
communicable
communicate
communication
communicative
communing
communion
communis
  c. error facit jus
communism
communist
community
  c. of interest
  c. property
commutation
commutative
  c. contract
commute
compact
companage
companion
companulate
company
comparable
  c. accommodation
comparative
  c. interpretation
  c. jurisprudence
  c. negligence
  c. rectitude
comparison
compascuum
compass
compassing
compatibility
compatible
compel

compellativus
compendium
compensable
  c. death
  c. injury
compensacion
compensate
compensatio
  c. criminis
compensation
  facultative c.
compensator
compensatory
  c. damages
comperendinatio
compertorium
compete
competence
competency
competent
  c. evidence
competition
competitive
  c. bidding
  c. traffic
competitor
compilation
compile
compiled
  c. statutes
complainant
complaint
complete
  c. in itself
completion
complex
complexity
compliance
compliant
complicated
complice
comply
composite
  c. work
composition
  c. in bankruptcy
compound
  c. interest
compounder

compounding
  c. a felony
comprehend
comprehension
compremesso
compress
compression
comprint
comprise
compromise
  c. verdict
compromissarius
compromissum
comptroller
compulsa
compulsion
compulsory
compurgator
computation
compute
computing scale
computo
comte
conative
concavity
conceal
concealed
concealment
concede
conceder
concentric
conception
conceptualize
conceptum
concern
concerted
  c. action
concert-room
concessi
concessimus
concession
concessor
concessum
concessus
conciliate
conciliation
conciliatory
concilium
conclude
conclusion

conclusive
   c. presumption
concomitant
concord
concordat
concordia
concubinage
concubinatus
concubine
concur
concurator
concurrence
   c. deloyale
concurrent
   c. jurisdiction
   c. power
concurso
concursus
concuss
concussio
condemn
condemnation
condensation
condense
condescendence
condictio
conditio
condition
   c. precedent
   c. subsequent
conditional
   c. endorsement
   c. sale
   c. stipulation
conditionally
   c. privileged communication
conditioning
conditions of sale
condominia
condominium
condonacion
condonation
condone
conduce
conduct
conductio
conduction
conductor
conductus
confabulation

confectio
confederacy
confederate
confederation
conference
confess
confessing
   c. error
confessio
confession
   c. and avoidance
   c. of defense
confessor
confidant
confidante
confide
confidence
   c. game
confidential
   c. communication
   c. relation
confidentiality
configuration
confine
confinement
confirm
confirmatio
confirmation
confirmavi
confirmee
confirmor
confiscable
confiscate
confiscatee
confiscation
confiscator
confiscatory
   c. rates
confitens reus
conflict
   c. of interest
   c. of laws
   c. of presumptions
conflicting
   c. evidence
confluent
conformity
confreres
confront
confrontation

confusio
confusion
confutation
confute
congé
   c. d'accorder
   c. d'emparler
congeable
congenital
congested
conglomerate
congregate
congregation
congress
congressman
congresswoman
conjectio
conjectural
conjecture
conjoint
   c. robbery
conjugal
   c. rights
conjugium
conjunct
conjuncta
conjunctio
conjunctive
   c. denial
conjuration
conjurator
connect
connection
connexité
connivance
connive
connoissement
connubial
connubium
conociamento
conocimiento
conpossessio
conqueror
conquest
conquestor
conquêts
consanguineous
consanguineus
   c. frater
consanguinity

conscience
conscientious
   c. objector
conscious
consciously
consciousness
conscript
conscription
consecrate
consecutive
consedo
consensual
   c. contract
   c. marriage
consensus
   c. facit legem
consent
   c. decree
   c. rule
consentible
   c. lines
consequence
consequential
   c. damages
conservation
conservative
conservator
conserve
consider
considerable
consideration
consideratum
   c. est per curiam
consideratur
considered
consign
consignation
consignee
consignment
consignor
consilium
consillarius
consist
consistent
consisting
consistor
consistory
   c. courts
consobrini
consociatio

consolation
console
consolidate
consolidated
  c. laws
  c. statutes
consolidation
  c. of corporations
consols
consonant
  c. statement
consort
consortium
consortship
conspicuous
conspiracy
conspirator
conspire
constable
constablewick
constabularius
constabulary
constant
constantly
constat
constate
constituent
constituimus
constituted
  c. authorities
constitutio
constitution
constitutional
  c. convention
  c. right
constitutor
constitutum
constrain
constraint
constrict
constriction
construct
constructio
  c. legis non facit injuriam
construction
constructive
  c. eviction
  c. force
  c. mortgage
  c. notice
  c. willfulness

construe
constuprate
consuetudinary
  c. law
consuetudo
consul
consular
  c. courts
consult
consultant
consultary
  c. response
consultation
consulto
consumer
consumerism
consummate
consummation
consumption
contaminant
contaminate
contamination
contango
contemner
contemplate
contemplation
contempt
  c. of court
contemptuous
contend
contenement
contenementum
contentious
  c. jurisdiction
  c. possession
contents
  c. and not contents
conterminous
contest
contestatio litis
contestation
  c. of suit
contested
  c. election
context
contiguity
contiguous
  c. and compact
continence
continencia

continens
continent
continental
contingency
   c. with double aspect
contingent
   c. claim
   c. estate
   c. fund
continual
continuance
continuando
continuing
continuity
continuous
continuously
contour
contra
   c. bonos mores
   c. pacem
   c. proferentem
contraband
contracausator
contraception
contraceptive
contracoup
contract
   aleatory c.
   antenuptial c.
   bilateral c.
   booking c.
   breach of c.
   brokerage c.
   commutative c.
   consensual c.
   cost-plus c.
   divisible c.
   innominate c.
   marine c.
   requirement c.
   c. of suretyship
   synallagmatic c.
contraction
contractor
contractual
   c. obligation
contractus
contradict
contradiction
   c. in terms

contraescritura
contrafactio
contralateral
contramandatum
contrary
contrat
contratenere
contravene
contravening
   c. equity
contravention
contrefacon
contre-maitre
contribute
contribution
contributory
control
controller
controlment
controversial
controversy
controvert
contumacy
contumax
contumely
contutor
conusance
conusant
conusee
conusor
convenable
convene
convenience
   c. and necessity
convenient
convent
conventio
   c. in unum
   c. vincit legem
convention
conventional
conventione
conventual
   c. church
conventus
converge
convergence
convergent
conversant
conversation

converse
conversion
convex
convey
conveyance
  fraudulent c.
conveyancer
conveyancing
convicium
convict
  autrefois c.
convicted
conviction
  summary c.
convincing
  c. proof
convivium
convocation
convoke
convoy
coobligor
cooperate
cooperation
cooperative
  c. association
  c. negligence
coopertus
cooptation
coordinate
coparcenary
coparceners
copartner
copartnership
copeman
copesman
copesmate
copia
coping
  c. mechanism
coppa
coppice
copse
copula
copulation
copulative
  c. term
copulatory
copyhold
copyright

coram
  c. nobis
  c. non judice
  c. vobis
cordon
corespondency
corespondent
corn
  c. laws
  c. whisky
cornage
corollary
coronation
coronator
coroner
coroner's inquest
corporal
  c. imbecility
  c. oath
  c. punishment
corporate
corporation
  charitable c.
  close c.
  collapsible c.
  eleemosynary c.
corporator
corporeal
  c. hereditaments
corps diplomatique
corpse
corpus
  c. delicti
  c. juris
correct
  c. attest
corrected
  c. policy
correction
corregidor
correlative
correspondence
correspondent
corroborate
corroborating
  c. evidence
corroboration
corrupt
  c. intent
corruption

corruptly
cortes
cortis
corvée
cosmopathic
cosmos
cosmus
coss
costal
costbook
costipulator
cost-plus
  c. contract
costumbre
cosureties
cotenancy
coterie
cottage
cottier tenancy
couchant
coucher
coulisse
council
councillor
counsel
counsellor
countenance
counter
counterclaim
counterextension
counterfeit
counterfeiter
counterfesance
countermand
counterpart
counter-rolls
countersign
countervail
  c. livery
countervailing
  c. equity
countors
count-out
country
county
coupled
  c. with an interest
coupon
cour de cassation

course
  c. of business
  c. of employment
courses
  c. and distances
court
  appellate c.
  audience c.
  borough c.
  c. of cassation
  circuit c.
  civil c.
  commercial c.
  common-law c.
  consistory c.
  consular c.
  criminal c.
  district c.
  divisional c.
  equity c.
  fiscal c.
  inferior c.
  instance c.
  juvenile c.
  magistrate's c.
  moot c.
  orphans' c.
  Palatine c.
  parish c.
  probate c.
  c. of record
  small claims c.
  superior c.
courtbaron
courtesy
courthand
courthouse
courtlands
courtleet
courtmartial
courtyard
cousin
cousinage
cousin-german
coustom
couthutlaugh
couverture
covenable
covenant
  assertory c.

covenantee
covenantor
covenants
  c. performed
covering deed
cover into
covert
coverture
covin
covinous
cowardice
cozen
cracking
cranage
crassa
  c. negligentia
crassus
craven
crazy
creamer
creamus
creance
creancer
creansor
create
creation
credentials
credibility
credible
credibly
  c. informed
credit
crédit
  c. foncier
  c. mobilier
credited
creditor
  judgment c.
creditrix
cremate
cremation
crepusculum
crescent
cretio
crier
crime
crimen
  c. falsi
  c. laesae majestatis

criminal
  c. abortion
criminalist
criminaliter
criminally
  c. insane
criminaloid
criminate
criminological
criminologist
criminology
crimp
cripple
crippling
criteria
criterion
critical
criticism
crook
crooked
crop
cropper
cross-action
cross-claim
cross-demand
cross-errors
cross-examination
cross-examine
cross-examiner
cross-lay
crossmatching
cross-question
cross-sale
cruel
  c. and unusual punishment
cruelty
cryer
crypt
crypta
cuckold
cueillette
cui
  c. bono
  c. in vita
cul de sac
culpa
culpable
  c. act
culprit
cultivate

cultivation
cultivator
cultura
culturally
culture
cum
   c. grano salis
   c. onere
   c. testamento annexo
cumulative
   c. evidence
cuneator
cuneiform
cura
curate
curateur
curatio
curator
curatorship
curatrix
cure
   c. by verdict
curfew
curia
   c. advisari vult
   c. regis
curing
   c. title
currency
current
curricula
curriculum
cursing
cursitor
cursor
cursory
   c. examination
curtail
curtailment
curtesy
curtilage
curtillium
curtis
cussedness
custodes
custodial
custodia legis
custodiam lease
custodian
custody

custom
customarily
customary
   c. freehold
customer
customhouse
customs
custos
   c. rotulorum
cutler
cut-over land
cutpurse
cycle
cyclone
cyphonism
cy-pres
cyrographum
czar
czarevitch
czarevna
czarina

D

dacion
dagger
dais
dalus
damages
   compensatory d.
   discretionary d.
   exemplary d.
   lay d.
   liquidated d.
   punitive d.
damna
damnification
damnify
damnum
   d. absque injuria
   d. fatale
danger
   d. zone
dangerous
   d. per se
danism
dano
dans et retinens nihil dat
dapifer

dare
darraign
darrein
data
date
  d. certaine
  d. of issue
datio
dation
dative
datum
daughter
daughter-in-law
dauphin
day
  d. certain
daybook
daylight
days
  d. of grace
daysman
daytime
deacon
dead
  d. freight
deadborn
deadhead
deadly
  d. weapon
deadman
deadpledge
dealer
dealings
dean
death
  civil d.
  presumptive d.
deathsman
debase
debasement
debasing
debauch
debauchery
debenture
  d. indenture
  d. stock
debet
  d. et solet
  d. sine breve
debilitate

debilitation
debility
debit
debitor
debitrix
debitum
de bonis non
debris
debt
  floating d.
  judgment d.
  liquid d.
debtee
debtor
  common d.
decania
decapitate
decapitation
decease
deceased
decedent
deceit
deceive
deceleration
decency
decennarius
decennary
decent
deception
deceptione
deceptive
decide
decimation
decime
decision
  Durham d.
  d. on merits
decisive
decisory
declarant
declaration
  d. of intention
  d. of trust
declarator
  d. of trust
declaratory
  d. decree
  d. judgment
  d. statute
declare

declination
déclinatoires
declinatory
   d. exceptions
   d. plea
declinature
decline
decoction
decomposed
decomposition
déconfes
decontamination
decorate
decorator
decoy
decree
   Brown d.
   consent d.
   declaratory d.
   foreclosure d.
   d. nisi
decrement
decrepit
decreta
decretal
   d. order
decretals
decreto
decretum
decrowning
decry
dedi
   d. et concessi
dedicate
dedication
dedimus
   d. postestatem
dedition
deduce
deduct
deductible
deduction
deductive
deed
   covering d.
   disentailing d.
   d. indented
   d. in fee
   d. of inspectorship
   d. poll

deem
deemsters
deface
defacement
de facto
defalcation
defalk
defamacast
defamation
defamatory
   d. per quod
   d. per se
defame
default
   d. judgment
defeasance
defeasible
defeasive
defeat
defect
   d. of parties
   d. of substance
defection
defective
defector
defectus
   d. sanguinis
defend
defendant
defendare
defendemus
defender
defendour
defeneration
defense
   affirmative d.
   character d.
   issuable d.
defensive
defenso
defensum
defer
deferred
   d. life annuities
defiance
defiant
deficiency
deficient
deficit
defile

defilement
define
definite
definitio
definition
definitive
deflect
deflection
defloration
deflower
deforce
deforcement
deforceor
deforciant
deforciare
deformed
deformity
defraud
defraudacion
defraudation
defunct
defunctus
defundation
degaster
degenerate
degeneration
degradation
degrade
degrading
degree
dejacion
dejeration
de jure
délaissement
delatio
delator
del credere
   d. c. agent
delegate
delegation
délestage
delete
deleterious
deletion
delf
deliberate
deliberately
deliberation
delict

delictual
   d. fault
delictum
delimit
delimitation
delineate
delineation
delinquency
delinquent
delito
deliverance
delivery
delusion
   d. of persecution
demain
demand
   compulsory d.
   d. deposit
   d. note
demanda
demandant
demandress
demarcate
demarcation
demean
demeanor
demens
demented
demesne
de minimis non curat lex
deminutio
demise
   d. and redemise
demisi
demissio
demobilization
demobilize
democracy
democratic
demographic
demography
demolish
demonetization
demonetize
demonstrate
demonstratio
demonstration
demonstrative
   d. evidence
   d. legacy

demoralize
demote
demotion
demur
demurrable
demurrage
demurrant
demurrer
   d. ore tenus
denarii
denarius
denial
denier
   d. à Dieu
denigrate
denigration
denization
denize
denizen
denomination
denominational
denounce
denouncement
de novo
dense
denshiring
   d. of land
density
denudation
denumeration
denunciation
deny
deodand
depart
department
departmental
departure
depeculation
depend
dependable
dependence
dependency
   d. needs
dependent
   d. relative revocation
depletable
   d. economic interest
deplete
depletion
depolymerization

depone
deponent
deponer
depopulation
deport
deportation
deportee
deportment
depose
deposit
   certificate of d.
depositary
depositation
deposition
   d. de bene esse
deposito
depositor
depository
depositum
depot
depreciate
depreciation
   d. reserve
depredation
depression
deprivation
deprive
deputize
deputy
deraign
derail
derailer
derailment
deranged
derangement
derecho
derelict
dereliction
derivation
derivative
derive
derogate
derogation
derogatory
   d. clause
desafuero
desamortizacion
descend
descendant
descender

descendible
descending
descent
describe
descriptio
   d. personae
description
descriptive
desecrate
desecration
desert
deserter
desertion
deserve
deserving
deshonora
desiccate
design
designate
designating
   d. petition
designatio
   d. personae
designation
designed
designedly
desire
desirous
desist
desistement
deslinde
despacheurs
despatch
desperado
desperate
desperation
despicable
despite
despitus
despoil
despoilment
despojar
despoliation
desponsation
desposorio
despot
despotic
despotism
dessaisissement
destination

destitute
destitution
destroy
destruction
desubito
desuetude
desultory
detach
detachiare
detachment
detail
detain
detainer
    forcible d.
detainment
detect
detectable
detection
detective
detector
detentio
detention
deter
deteriorate
deterioration
determinable
determinant
determinate
determination
determinative
determine
determinism
deterrence
deterrent
detestatio
detinet
detinue
detinuit
detour
detournement
detract
detraction
detractive
detractor
detriment
detrimental
deuterogamy
devadiatus
devastate
devastation

devastavit
develop
developed
   d. water
developer
development
developmental
devest
deviate
deviation
device
devilling
devisable
devisavit vel non
devise
devisee
devisor
devoir
devolution
devolutive
   d. appeal
devolve
devulcanize
devy
dextrarius
diagonal
dialect
dialectic
diallage
dichotomy
di colonna
dicta
dictate
dictation
dictator
dictatorial
dictatorship
dictores
dictum
  judicial d.
diem clausit extremum
dies
   d. a quo
   d. dominicus
   d. gratiae
   d. juridicus
   d. non juridicus
dieta
die without issue
diffacere
differ

difference
different
differentiate
differentiation
difficult
difficulty
diffuse
diffusion
digama
digamy
dignify
dignitary
dignity
dijudication
dike
diking
dilacion
dilapidated
dilapidation
dilatory
   d. exceptions
   d. pleas
diligence
diligent
diligiatus
dilute
dilution
dimidia
dimidietas
dimidium
dimidius
diminished
   d. responsibility doctrine
diminutio
diminution
   alleging d.
dimisi
dimissory
   d. letters
dinarchy
diocesan
diocese
diploma
diplomate
diplomatic
   d. agent
direct
   d. attack
   d. contempt
   d. evidence
   d. examination

directed
  d. verdict
direction
directive
directly
director
directory
  d. statute
disability
disable
disabling
  d. statutes
disadvocare
disaffirm
disaffirmance
disaffirmation
disafforest
disagree
disagreeable
disagreement
disallow
disallowance
disalt
disapproval
disapprove
disaster
disastrous
disavow
disavowal
disbar
disbarment
disbarred
disbursement
discharge
  d. in bankruptcy
disciplinary
discipline
disclaim
disclaimer
disclamation
disclose
disclosure
discommon
discontinuance
disconvenable
discount
discover
discovert
discovery
discredit
discreet

discreetly
discrepancy
discrete
discretely
discretion
discretionary
  d. damages
  d. power
  d. trusts
discriminate
discrimination
discussion
disentail
disentailing
  d. deed
disentailment
disfigure
disfigurement
disfranchise
disfranchisement
disgavel
disgrace
disgrading
disguise
disherison
disheritor
dishonest
dishonesty
dishonor
dishonorable
disincarcerate
disincarceration
disinherison
disinherit
disinheritance
disintegrate
disintegration
disinter
disinterested
disinterment
disjunctim
disjunctive
  d. allegation
dislocation
disloyal
dismes
dismiss
dismissal
  d. agreed
  d. without prejudice
dismortgage

disorder
disorderly
   d. conduct
disorganization
disorientation
disparagation
disparage
disparagement
disparate
dispark
dispatch
dispatcher
dispauper
dispel
dispensable
dispensation
dispense
dispersonare
displace
displacement
display
dispono
disposable
   d. portion
disposal
dispose
disposition
dispositive
   d. facts
dispossess
dispossession
disproval
disprove
dispunishable
disputable
   d. presumption
disputatio
   d. fori
disputation
disputatious
dispute
disqualification
disqualify
disrate
disrationare
disregard
disrepair
disreputable
disrepute
disrespect

disrespectful
disseise
disseisee
disseisin
disseisitrix
disseisitus
disseisor
disseisoress
dissemble
disseminate
dissension
dissensus
dissent
dissenter
dissentiente
dissenting
   d. opinion
dissertation
dissociate
dissociation
dissolute
dissolution
dissolve
dissolving
   d. bond
dissuade
dissuasion
distance
distill
distillation
distiller
distillery
distinct
distinctive
distinguish
distort
distortion
distract
distractibility
distractio
distraction
   d. rule
distrahere
distrain
distrainer
distrainor
distraint
distress
   abuse of d.
   d. and danger
   d. warrant

distribute
distributee
distribution
distributive
  d. justice
distributor
district
  d. attorney
  d. court
districtio
distringas
disturb
disturbance
disturber
ditching
diurnal
diverge
divergence
divergent
divers
diverse
diversion
diversity
  d. of citizenship
divert
dives
divest
divestitive
  d. fact
divide
dividend
divinare
divisa
divisible
  d. contract
  d. offense
division
  d. of opinion
divisional
  d. court
divorce
  d. a mensa et thoro
  d. a vinculo matrimonii
divulge
divulgence
divulsion
docimasia pulmonum
dock
  d. warrant
dockage

docket
dockmaster
doctrinal
  d. interpretation
doctrine
  Calvo d.
  common humanity d.
  Drago d.
  globe d.
  humanitarian d.
  McNabb d.
  rescue d.
  sole actor d.
  switchyard d.
  turntable d.
document
documentary
  d. evidence
documentation
do, dico, addico
dogger
dogma
dogmatic
dole
doleance
do, lego
doles
doli
  d. capax
  d. incapax
dollar
dolly
dolo
dolus
domain
  eminent d.
Domesday Book
domestic
  d. corporations
domesticate
domicile
domiciled
domiciliary
  d. administration
domiciliate
domiciliation
domicilium
domina
dominance
dominant
  d. estate or tenement

dominate
domination
dominical
dominicide
dominicum
dominio
dominion
dominium
    d. directum
    d. directum et utile
    d. eminens
    d. plenum
domitae
dommages
    d. intérêts
donatarius
donatio
    d. mortis causa
    d. non praesumitur
donation
donative
    d. trust
donator
donatorius
donatory
donec
donee
donor
donum
doom
dormancy
dormant
    d. claim
    d. judgment
dormitory
dos rationabilis
dossier
dotal
    d. property
dotation
dote
    d. unde nihil habet
dotissa
double
    d. bond
    d. entry
    d. jeopardy
    d. taxation
    d. use
doubles

doubt
doubtful
    d. paper
    d. title
doun
do ut des
do ut facias
dovetail
dowable
dowager
dowager-queen
dower
dowment
downward
dowress
dowry
dozein
drachma
draconian
draff
draft
draftsman
drag
Drago doctrine
dragoman
drain
drainage
    d. district
dram
dram-shop
draught
draw
drawback
drawee
drawer
drawing
drawlatches
drayage
dredge
dreit-dreit
drift
    d. net
drifting
driftstuff
driftway
drilled
drinkable
drinking-shop
droit
    d. naturel

droit-droit
droits civils
droitural
drop-letter
drove
drummer
drunkard
drunkenness
dry
  d. dock
  d. mortgage
dual
  d. business
  d. nationality
duarchy
dubious
dubitans
dubitante
dubitatur
dubitavit
ducat
duces tecum
duchy
ducroire
due-bill
duel
duelling
due process of law
duke
dulocracy
duly
  d. qualified
dum
dumb-bidding
dummodo
dummy
dump
dumping
dun
dungeon
dunio
dunnage
dunsets
dupla
duplex
  d. house
duplicate
duplicatio
duplication
duplicitous

duplicity
durable
  d. lease
durante
  d. absentia
duration
duress
duressor
Durham decision
Durham rule
duties
  d. of detraction
  d. on imports
duty
dwell
dwelling-place
dying
  d. declaration
  d. without issue
dynamic
dynamics
dynasty

E

eadem est ratio, eadem est lex
earles-penny
earmark
earned income
earner
earnest
earnings
earwitness
easement
  apparent e.
  intermittent e.
easterling
easterly
eastinus
eat inde sine die
eavesdrip
eavesdropping
ebb and flow
ebriety
eccentric
eccentricity
ecclesia
ecclesiarch
ecclesiastic

ecclesiastical
ecdicus
economic
   e. functioning
economist
economizer
economy
e contra
e converso
ecumenical
edict
edictum
edition
efface
effect
effecting
   e. loan
effective
   e. procuring cause
effectiveness
effects
effectus
   e. sequitur causam
effendi
efferent
effet
efficiency
efficient
effigy
efflux
effluxion
   e. of time
efforcialiter
effort
effraction
effractor
egress
eigne
eignesse
einecia
einetia
einetius
eire
eisne
eisnetia
eject
ejection
ejectment
ejector
ejectum

ejercitoria
ejuration
elaborate
elaboration
elaboratus
elastic
elation
elder
eldest
elected
election
   e. dower
   e. returns
elective
   e. franchise
   e. office
elector
electoral
   E. College
electricity
electrocute
electrocution
electronic
eleemosynae
eleemosynaria
eleemosynarius
eleemosynary
   e. corporation
eleganter
elegit
element
elevator
eligibility
eligible
eliminate
elimination
elinguation
elisors
ell
ellipsis
elliptical
elogium
eloigne
eloignment
elongata
elongatus
elongavit
elope
elopement
elsewhere
emaciated

emaciation
emancipate
emancipation
embargo
embassage
embassy
embezzle
embezzlement
emblements
embraceor
embracery
emend
emenda
emendals
e mera gratia
emerge
emergency
emergent
  e. year
emigrant
emigration
émigré
eminence
eminent
  e. domain
emissary
emission
emmenagogue
emolument
emotion
empalement
empanel
emparnours
empathy
emperor
emphasizing
  e. facts
emphyteusis
emphyteuta
emphyteuticus
empire
empiric
empirical
emplazamiento
emplead
emploi
employ
employee
employer
employers' liability acts
employment

emporium
empower
empresario
emprestido
emptio
emptor
emtio
emtor
emtrix
enable
enabling
  e. power
enact
enacting
  e. clause
enajenacion
en banc
enbrever
encaustum
encheson
enclosure
encomienda
encourage
encouragement
encroach
encroachment
encumber
encumbrance
endeavor
endenizen
endenzie
endorse
endorsee
endorsement
  conditional e.
endorser
endow
endowment
endure
endurance
enfeoff
enfeoffment
enfiteusis
enforce
enforceable
enforcement
enfranchise
enfranchisement
  e. of copyholds
engage
engaged
  e. in commerce

engagement
engender
engineer
engrave
engraving
engross
engrosser
engrossing
enhance
enjoin
enjoyment
  adverse e.
enlarge
enlarger l'estate
enlarging
enlist
enlistment
en masse
enormia
enormity
enormous
enquest
enquête
enrégistrement
enroll
enrolled
  e. bill
enrollment
en route
enschedule
enseal
enserver
ensue
entad
entail
entailed
  e. money
entailment
ental
entendment
enterprise
enthusiast
entice
entire
  e. contract
entirely
entireties
entirety
entitle
entity

entrails
entrance
entrap
entrapment
entreat
entreaty
entrebat
entrega
entrepôt
entry
  forcible e.
entryman
enumerated
enumerator
enure
envelope
en ventre sa mere
environment
environmental
  e. law
environmentalist
envoy
eo die
eo instanti
epicycloidal
  e. curve
episcopacy
episcopalia
episcopate
episcopus
epistola
epistolae
e pluribus unum
epoch
equal
  e. degree
  e. protection of the laws
equality
equalization
equalize
equally
equate
equation
equerry
equilibrium
equilocus
equinox
equip
equipment

equitable
  e. conversion
  e. estate
  e. estoppel
  e. lien
equity
  contravening e.
  countervailing e.
  e. of a statute
  e. of redemption
  e. term
  e. to a settlement
equivalent
equivocal
equivocate
equivocation
erabilis
Erastian
erasure
erciscundus
erection
ergo
ergolabi
erigimus
ermine
erode
erosion
erosive
errant
errata
erratum
erroneous
erronice
error
  clerical e.
  invited e.
erupt
eruption
eruptive
escalator
  e. clause
escaldare
escapade
escape
escapee
escapium
esceppa
escheat
escheator
eschipare

escritura
escroquerie
escrow
escurare
escutcheon
esketores
eskippamentum
eskippare
eskipper
eskippeson
esnecy
espedient
espera
espionage
espousal
espurio
esquire
essarter
essartum
essence
essential
essentially
essoin
establish
establishment
estache
estadal
estadia
estandard
estanques
estate
  e. ad remanentiam
  e. at sufferance
  base e.
  e. by the curtesy
  e. by the entirety
  equitable e.
  e. in coparency
  e. in fee conditional
  e. in fee simple
  e. in remainder
  e. in reversion
  landed e.
  life e.
  e. tail
estendard
estendart
estimate
estimated
  e. cost

estimation
estop
estoppel
  e. by verdict
  equitable e.
  judicial e.
  promissory e.
estovers
estranged
estrangement
estray
estreat
estreciatus
estrepe
estrepement
estuary
établissement
et cetera
etching
eternal
  e. security
ethical
ethics
  legal e.
ethnic
etiquette
  e. of the profession
et vir
eunomy
euthanasia
evacuate
evacuation
evanescent
evasion
evasive
event
  e. of any suit
eversion
evert
every
  e. other thing
  e. such provision
evict
eviction
  constructive e.
evidence
  adminicular e.
  auto-optic e.
  character e.
  circumstantial e.

evidence (*continued*)
  competent e.
  conflicting e.
  corroborating e.
  cumulative e.
  demonstrative e.
  direct e.
  documentary e.
  extraneous e.
  fabricated e.
  incompetent e.
  indicative e.
  indirect e.
  mathematical e.
  opinion e.
  preappointed e.
  prima facie e.
  rebutting e.
  satisfactory e.
  state's e.
  substantive e.
  substitutionary e.
  traditionary e.
evident
evidentia
evidentiary
evidently
evil
evocation
evoke
evolution
evolutive
evolve
ewbrice
ewry
exacerbate
exacerbation
exaction
exactor
ex aequo et bono
examen
examination
  direct e.
examine
examined
  e. copy
examiner
excambium
ex cathedra
excavate

excavation
excellency
except
excepting
exceptio
exception
  declinatory e.
  dilatory e.
exceptionable
exceptor
excerpt
excerpta
excess
excessive
  e. drunkenness
  e. verdict
exchange
exchangeable
exchequer
excise
excision
exclude
exclusion
exclusive
exclusively
excommengement
excommunicate
excommunication
ex contractu
excoriation
excrescence
exculpate
exculpation
exculpatory
excusable
  e. homicide
excusatio
excusator
excuse
excuss
excussio
ex delicto
exeat
executant
  e. ego function
execute
executed
  e. consideration
  e. remainder
  e. trust

executio
execution
  e. of instrument
  e. thereof
exécution
  e. parée
executioner
executive
executor
  e. creditor
  e. de son tort
  instituted e.
executorial
executor-trustee
executory
executress
executrix
exemplar
exemplary
  e. damages
exemplification
exemplificatione
exemplify
exempli gratia
exemplum
exempt
exemption
exequatur
exercise
exercitalis
exercitorial
  e. power
exfestucare
exfrediare
ex gratia
exhaeredatio
exhaeres
exhaustion
  e. of administrative remedies
exhibere
exhibit
exhibitant
exhibition
exhibitor
exhumation
exhume
exigence
exigency
exigendary
exigent

exigenter
exigible
exigi facias
exile
exist
existence
existent
exitus
exlegalitus
ex maleficio
ex officio
exoine
exonerate
exoneration
exoneretur
exorbitant
exordium
ex parte
expatriate
expatriation
expectable
expectancy
expectant
   e. heir
expectation
expediency
expedient
expediente
expediment
expeditation
expedite
expediter
expeditio
expedition
expeditious
expel
expend
expendere
expenditor
expenditure
expense
experience
experientia docet
experiment
experimental
   e. testimony
expert
   e. witness
expilare
expilatio
expilator

expiration
expire
explicatio
explicit
explode
exploit
exploitation
exploration
explorator
explore
explosion
explosive
export
exportation
exporter
expose
exposé
expositio
exposition
expository
   e. statute
ex post facto
exposure
express
expressly
expromissio
expromissor
expromittere
expropriate
expropriation
expulsion
expunge
expurgate
expurgation
expurgator
ex tempore
extend
extendi facias
extension
extensive
extent
extenuate
extenuating
   e. circumstances
extenuation
exterior
external
externally
exterritorial
exterritoriality
exterus

extinct
extinction
extinguish
extinguishment
extirpate
extirpation
extirpatione
extorsively
extort
extorter
extortion
extortionary
extract
extraction
extradite
extradition
   interstate e.
extra-dotal
  e. property
extrahazardous
extrajudicial
extrajudicially
extralateral
  e. right
extramural
extraneous
  e. evidence
extraordinary
  e. remedy
extraparochial
extraterritorial
extraterritoriality
extra viam
extreme
  e. and repeated cruelty
extremis
extremism
extremist
extremity
extrinsic
extrude
extrusion
exuperare
ey
eyde
eyewitness
eygne
eyott
eyre
eyrer

F

fabricare
fabricate
fabricated
  f. evidence
fabricating
fabrication
facere
face value
facias
faciendo
facies
facilitate
facilitation
facilities
facility
facing
facio
  f. ut des
  f. ut facias
facsimile
  f. probate
fact
  dispositive f.
  divestitive f.
  investitive f.
facto et animo
factor
factorage
factoring
factorizing
  f. process
factory
factum
facultative
  f. compensation
faculties
faculty
faggot vote
failing
  f. circumstances
faillite
failure
  f. of consideration
  f. of issue
  f. of title
faint pleader

fair
  f. comment
  f. hearing
  f. market value
  f. preponderance
  f. usage
fairly
fairway
fait
  f. accompli
faithful
faithfully
faithless
faitours
faker
falcarious
falcidia
falda
faldage
fallout
fallow
fallowland
falsarius
false
  f. and fraudulent
  f. and misleading statement
  f. arrest
  f. pretenses
falsehood
falsely
falsification
falsify
falsifying
  f. a judgment
falsity
falsonarius
falsum
falsus
fama
famacide
familia
familial
familiar
familiarity
familiarization
familiarize
family
  f. car doctrine
famosus
  f. libellus

fanal
fanatic
fanatical
fanaticism
fanciful
fanega
farding-deal
fare
farinagium
farlingarii
farm
  f. labor
faro
farrier
farthing
farvand
fas
fatal
  f. injury
  f. variance
fatality
father
father-in-law
fathom
fatigability
fatigue
fat spot
fatum
fatuous
fatuus
faubourg
fault
  delictual f.
fautor
faux
favor
favorable
favoritism
feal
fealty
fear
feasance
feasant
feasibility
feasible
feasor
federal
federated
  f. state
federation

fee
  base f.
  finder's f.
  initiation f.
  f. simple
  f. tail
feign
feigned
  f. issue
feld
fele
fellow
  f. heir
  f. servant
felo de se
felon
felonia
felonice
felonious
  f. assault
  f. homicide
feloniously
felony
  substantive f.
felting
female
feme
  f. covert
  f. sole
femicide
feminine
femininity
femme
fenatio
fence
fencing
  f. patent
feneration
fenestra
fenestrated
fenestration
Fenian
feoffamentum
feoffare
feoffee
feoffment
  f. to uses
feoffor
feonatio

ferae
  f. bestiae
  f. naturae
fercosta
ferlingum
ferlingus
ferm
ferment
fermentation
fermented
  f. liquors
fermer
fermier
fermor
ferrator
ferri
ferriage
ferruere
ferrum
ferrura
ferry
festum
fetters
feud
feuda
feudal
  f. tenure
feudalism
feudalize
feudist
feudo
feudum
fiancé
fiancée
fiancer
fianza
fiat
  f. justitia
fiaunt
fictio
fiction
fictitious
  f. payee
  f. plaintiff
fide-commissary
fidei-commissarius
fidei-commissum
fide-jubere
fide-jussio
fide-jussor

fidelitas
fidelity
  f. bond
fides
fiducia
fiducial
fiduciary
  f. capacity
  f. relation
fief
fiel
fieldad
fieri
  f. facias
filch
filed
  f. for record
filiate
filiation
filius
  f. nullius
filly
filum
  f. aquae
final
  f. decision
  f. submission
finance
financial
financially
  f. able
financier
finder
finder's fee
finding
fine
  chirographer of f's
fine-force
finis
finitio
firearm
firebare
firebote
firebug
fire district
fireman
fireproof
fireworks
firkin
firm

firmarius
firmatio
first
  f. blush
  f. impression
fiscal
  f. agent
  f. court
  f. year
fiscus
fishery
fishgarth
fishing
  f. banks
fixed belief
fixture
flaco
flagrans
flagrant
  f. necessity
flagrante
  f. delicto
flagrantly
  f. against evidence
flammable
flank
flattery
flecta
flee
  f. from justice
flemeswite
flexibility
flexible
flim-flam
floatable
floaters
floating
  f. capital
  f. debt
  f. policy
flodemark
flogging
flood
  f. waters
floor
  f. plan rule
floored
flotages
flotsam
  f. and jetsam

flourish
flowage
flowing
fluctuant
fluctuate
fluctuation
fluctus
flume
flumen
fluvius
flying
  f. switch
flypower
foal
focage
fodder
fodina
foedus
foeneration
foenus
  f. nauticum
foetura
foldcourse
folgoth
folio
folk
follow
fonds
  f. et biens
  f. perdus
fonsadera
fontana
foot
  f. acre
  f. drop
footage
footgeld
footprint
forage
foragium
foraneus
forathe
forbannitus
forbarrer
forbear
forbearance
force
  f. majesture
  f. majeure

forced
  f. heir
  f. sale
forcheapum
forcible
  f. detainer
  f. entry
  f. trespass
fordal
foreclose
foreclosure
  f. decree
foregift
forehand
  f. rent
foreign
  f. dominion
  f. exchange
foreigner
forejudge
forejudger
foreman
forematron
forensic
forensis
foresaid
foreschoke
foreseeability
foreseeable
foreshore
foresight
forest
forestall
forestaller
forestalling
forestarius
forester
forethought
forewoman
forfeit
forfeitable
forfeiter
forfeiture
forgabulum
forgavel
forge
forger
forgery
forinsecus
foris

forisfacere
forisfactum
forisfactura
forisfactus
forisfamiliare
forisjudicatus
forisjurare
forma
  f. pauperis
formal
formalities
formality
formata
  f. brevia
formedon
former
  f. acquittal
formication
formulary
forno
foro
foros
forprise
forschel
forses
forspeaker
forswear
forswore
forsworn
fortaxed
forthcoming
  f. bond
forthwith
fortior
  f. est custodia legis quam hominis
fortis
fortlett
fortuit
fortuitous
  f. collision
  f. event
fortuna
forum
forward
forwarder
forwarding
  f. merchant
fossatum
fossellum

foster
  f. child
  f. home
  f. parent
fosterage
fosterlean
fosterling
foundation
founded
founder
founderosa
foundling
  f. hospitals
fourcher
four corners
fourierism
foy
fractio
fraction
fractional
fractionate
fractionation
fractious
fractitium
fragile
fragility
fragment
fragmenta
fragmentary
frais
  f. de justice
  f. jusqu'à bord
frame
frameup
franchise
  f. tax
francus
frank-almoigne
frank-fee
franking
  f. privilege
frank-tenant
frank-tenement
frater
fraternal
fraternia
fraternity
fratriage
fratricidal
fratricide

fraud
fraudare
fraudulence
fraudulent
  f. concealment
  f. conveyance
  f. representation
fraunchise
fraus
fray
free
  f. and clear
  f. entry
  f. on board
free-bench
freedman
freedom
freehold
freeholder
freeman
freeway
freight
freighter
freomortel
frequency
frequent
frequenter
frère
fresh
  f. pursuit
freshet
fret
fréter
fréteur
fretum
fribusculum
friend
  f. of the court
friendly
  f. suit
frigid
frigidity
friscus
frisk
frith
frithbote
frithbreach
frithgar
frithgilda
frithman

frithsocne
frithsplot
frithstool
frivolity
frivolous
frodmortel
frolic
frontage
frontager
front-foot
  f. rule
frontier
fronting
  f. and abutting
frozen
  f. snake
fructuarius
fructus
  f. civiles
  f. fundi
  f. industriales
  f. naturales
fruges
frumentum
frussura
frustra
frustration
frutos
fuero
fugacia
fugitation
fugitive
  f. from justice
fugitivus
full
  f. faith and credit
fully
  f. administered
fulminate
function
functionary
functus
  f. officio
fund
  blended f.
fundamental
  f. error
fundamus
fundatio
fundator

funeral
fungibiles res
fungible things
fur
   f. manifestus
furiosus
furlingus
furlong
furlough
furnish
furniture
further
   f. assurance
furtherance
furtive
furtum
   f. manifestum
future
   f. acquired property
   f. estate
   f. interest
futures
futuri
fyhtwite
fyke

G

gabel
gabella
gablum
gadget
gadgetry
gaffoldgild
gaffoldland
gafol
gage
gager
  g. del ley
gain
gainage
gainery
gainful
gajum
galea
gallivolatium
gallon
gallows
galvanize

gamalis
gambit
gamble
gambler
gambling
  g. device
game
  g. laws
  g. of chance
gamekeeper
gaming
ganancial
  g. property
gananciales
ganancias
gangster
gaol
  g. delivery
gaoler
garage
garandia
garantia
garantie
garble
garbler
garciones
gard
garde
gardein
gardia
garene
garnish
garnishee
garnishment
garrison
garrote
garroting
garter
garth
gasoline
gast
gastaldus
gastel
gastine
gaugeator
gauger
gaugetum
gavel
gavelbred
gavelcester

gavelgeld
gavelherte
gavelkind
gaveller
gavelman
gavelmed
gavelrep
gavelwerk
gazette
gebrauchsmuster
geld
geldable
gelding
gelt
gemma
gemot
gender
genearch
gener
genera
general
   g. assembly
   g. assumpsit
   g. council
   g. verdict
generale
   g. nihil certum implicat
generalization
generalize
generatio
generation
generic
generosa
generosus
geniculum
gens
gentes
gentleman
gentlewoman
genuine
genus
gerens
germane
germanus
gerontocomi
gerontocomium
gerrymander
gest
gestio
gestor

gestum
getaway
ghetto
gibberish
gibbet
gift
   g. causa mortis
   g. inter vivos
giftoman
gild
gill
gilour
gilt edge
gin men
ginning advances
girante
girdle
girth
gisement
giser
gisetaker
gist
give
   g. and bequeath
giver
gladius
glaive
glavea
gleaning
gleba
glebariae
glebe
glider
globe
   g. doctrine
glomerell
glos
gloss
glossa
glossator
glyn
goaf
gob
go-between
going
   g. concern
   g. witness
golda
goldsmiths' notes
goldwit

goliardus
good
  g. and valid
  g. behavior
  g. consideration
  g. faith
  g. title
  g. will
goods
  g. and chattels
gopher holing
gorce
gore
gorge
gors
govern
governance
governess
government
governmental
  g. function
  g. instrumentality
  g. subdivision
governor
grabbots
grace
  days of g.
  g. period
grade
graded
  g. offense
gradient
graduate
gradus
graffer
graffium
grafio
graft
grain
grainage
grammar
  g. school
grammatica
  g. falsa non vitiat chartam
grammatophylacium
gramme
grand
  g. jury
  g. larceny
grandchild

grandfather
  g. clause
grandiose
grandmother
grange
grangearius
granger
  g. cases
grangia
grant
  g. and demise
grantee
grantor
grantor's lien
grasson
grassum
grass widow
gratification
gratify
gratis
  g. dictum
gratuitous
  g. licensee
gratuity
grava
gravamen
grave
gravel
graven dock
graveyard
gravis
gravius
gree
greenback
greenhew
greffiers
Gregorian code
gremio
gremium
gressume
greve
grief
grievance
grievous
griff
grithbrech
grithbreche
grithstole
groat
grocer

grog-shop
gross
  g. inadequacy
  g. negligence
  g. profit
grossement
ground
  g. rent
groundage
group
  g. process
growing crop
gruarii
grub stake
guarantee
guarantied
  g. stock
guarantor
guaranty
guardage
guardian
  testamentary g.
guardianship
guardianus
guarentigio
guastald
gubernator
gubernatorial
guerilla
  g. party
guerpi
guerpy
guerra
guerre
guia
guidage
guideline
guideplate
guild
guildhall
guillotine
guilt
guilty
guinea
guise
gula-thing
gules
gutter
gwalstow
gwayf

gynarchy
gynecocracy
gyration
gyratory
  g. stone crusher
gyves

H

habe
habeas corpus
habendum
habentia
habere
  h. facias
haberjects
habilis
habit
habitable
  h. repair
habitancy
habitant
habitatio
habitation
habitual
habitually
habituate
habituation
hacienda
hackney
haeredes
  h. proximi
haereditas
  h. jacens
  h. testamentaria
haeres
  h. factus
  h. natus
  h. necessarius
  h. suus
hafne
hag
haga
hagia
hagne
hagnebut
hakh
hakhdar
halakar

half
  h. blood
  h. brother
  h. sister
half-life
halfproof
halfseal
halftimer
halfway
  h. house
hali
halimas
hallazco
hallmark
hallucination
hambling
hamel
hameleta
hameling
hamlet
hamleta
hamma
hanaper
  h. office
handbill
handcuff
handgun
handle
handsale
handsel
handwriting
handwritten
hangman
hanig
hanse
hanseatic
hansgrave
haole
hap
happiness
haque
harass
harassment
harbinger
harbor
hard
  h. cases
  h. labor
hardpan
hardship

hariot
harmful
harmless
harmonic plane
harmonize
harmony
harness
hart
harvest
hasp
hasta
hatch
hatchway
hat money
hauber
hauberk
haugh
haula
haulage
  h. royalty
haulm
haustus
haven
hawker
hawking
hazard
hazardous
hazarzamin
header
head money
headnote
headright
hearing
  h. de novo
hearsay
hearth
heave to
hebberman
hebbing-wears
hebdomad
hebdomadius
hebote
heck
heda
hedagium
hedge
hedging
heedless
heeler
hegemony

hegira
hegumenos
heifer
heinous
heir
   h. apparent
   forced h.
   legal h.
   lineal h.
   h. presumptive
   h. testamentary
   h. unconditional
heirdom
heiress
heirloom
heirs
   h. and assigns
heirship
helm
helplessness
henceforth
henchman
henedpenny
heptarchy
herald
heraldic
heraldry
heraud
herbage
herbenger
herbergagium
herbergare
herbergatus
herbery
herbury
hercia
herciare
herciscunda
herd
herder
hereafter
herebote
hereby
heredad
heredero
heredes
hereditagium
hereditament
hereditary

hereditas
   h. jacens
   h. testamentaria
heredity
hereinafter
hereinbefore
heremitorium
heremones
herenach
heres
hereslita
heressa
heressiz
heresy
hereto
heretoch
heretofore
herewith
heriot
heriscindium
herislit
heristal
heritability
heritable
heritage
heritor
hermandad
hermeneutics
hermer
hermetic
hermetically
hernasium
hernescus
hernesium
herst
herus
hesia
hesta
hestha
hetaerarcha
hetaeria
heymectus
hibernagium
hidalgo
hidalguia
hierarchical
hierarchy
highbinder
highgrading
highness

highwayman
highway robbery
higler
higuela
hijack
hijacker
Hilary rules
hinder
   h. and delay
hinegeld
hipoteca
hirciscunda
hireman
hirer
hiring
hirst
hissa
histrionic
hitherto
hobbit
hoc
hodge-podge
   h. act
hoggus
hogietus
hogshead
holder
   h. in due course
holding company
holiday
holm
holografo
holograph
holographic will
homage
homager
homagium
homestall
homestead
homicidal
homicide
   excusable h.
   felonious h.
   justifiable h.
   h. per infortunium
   h. se defendendo
homicidium
   h. ex casu
   h. ex necessitate
   h. ex voluntate

hominatio
homme
homo
homologacion
homologare
homologate
homologation
homonymiae
honestus
honi
honor
honorable
honoraria
honorarium
honorary
hookland
hootch
hoppo
hora
horca
horizontal
   h. price fixing contracts
hornbook
horner
hornswoggle
horreum
hortus
hospes
hospital
hospitalaria
hospitalization
hospitalize
hospitaller
hospitator
hospitia
hospiticide
hospitium
hospodar
hostage
hosteler
hostes
hosticide
hostilaria
hostile
   h. witness
hostility
hostler
hotchpot
hough

house
   H. of Commons
   H. of Delegates
   H. of Representatives
houseage
housebreaking
household
householder
housekeeper
hovel
hove to
howgh
hoy
hoyman
huckster
hue and cry
huebras
hui
huis
huisserium
huissier
hull
humagium
humanitarian
   h. doctrine
hundredweight
hunger
hung jury
hurdereferst
hurdle
hurricane
hurst
hurtadus
hurto
hurtus
husband
husbandman
husbandry
husfastne
hush money
hustings
hutilan
hydage
hypothecaria
   h. actio
hypothecarii
   h. creditores
hypothecary
   h. action
hypothecate

hypothecation
hypothesis
   infirmative h.
hypothesize
hypothetical
   h. question
hysteropotmoi
hythe

I

ibid.
ibidem
icona
idealization
idealize
idem
   i. sonans
identical
identification
identify
identity
ideo
Ides
id est
idiochira
idiota
idoneus
ignominious
ignominy
ignoramus
ignorance
ignorant
ignorantia
   i. legis neminem excusat
ignore
ikbal
ikrah
ikrar
illegal
   i. conditions
illegality
illegitimacy
illegitimate
illeviable
illicit
   i. cohabitation
   i. distillery
illicite

illiteracy
illiterate
illocable
illud
illusion
illusional
illusory
illustrious
imagine
imago
imbasing
  i. of money
imbracery
imbrocus
imitate
imitation
immaterial
  i. averment
  i. issue
immature
immaturity
immediacy
immediate
immediately
immemorial
immeubles
immigrant
immigrate
immigration
imminent
imminently
  i. dangerous
immiscere
immittere
immobilis
immoderate
immoral
immorality
immovables
impair
impairing
  i. the obligation of contracts
impairment
impalare
impanel
impanelment
impargamentum
imparl
imparlance

impartial
  i. jury
impartiality
impartible
impatronization
impeach
impeachable
impeachment
  i. of waste
impechiare
impede
impediatus
impediment
impedimento
impensae
imperative
imperfect
imperitia
imperium
impersonal
impersonalitas
impertinence
impertinent
impier
impierment
impignorata
impignoration
implacitare
implead
impleaded
implement
implementation
implicata
implicate
implication
implicative
implied
  i. contract
imply
import
importation
imports
importune
importunity
impose
imposition
impossibility
impossible
impost
impostor

impotentia
   i. excusat legem
impound
impoundment
impoverish
imprescriptibility
imprescriptible
   i. rights
impress
impressio
impression
impressment
imprest
   i. money
impretiabilis
imprimatur
imprimere
imprimery
imprimis
imprinting
imprison
imprisonment
impristi
improbability
improbable
improbation
improper
impropriate
impropriation
improve
improvement
improvidence
improvident
improvidently
impubes
impugn
impulse
impulsive
impunity
imputatio
imputation
   i. of payment
impute
imputed
   i. negligence
inability
inaccessibility
inaccessible
inadequacy

inadequate
   i. consideration
   i. remedy at law
inadmissible
in adversum
inadvertence
inadvertent
inaedificatio
in aequali jure
inalienable
inappropriate
in articulo mortis
inattentiveness
inaugurate
inauguration
in autre droit
in banco
inboard
inbound
   i. common
in camera
incapacitate
incapacity
incarcerate
incarceration
incastellare
incaustum
incendiary
inception
inchartare
inchoate
   i. right
incidence
incident
incidental
incidere
incile
incinerate
incineration
incipience
incipient
incipitur
incite
incitement
incivile
incivism
inclausa
inclose
inclosure
include

inclusion
inclusive
incoherent
incola
income
   i. tax
in commendam
incommunication
incommutable
incompatibility
incompatible
incompetence
incompetency
incompetent
   i. evidence
inconclusive
inconsistent
inconsulto
incontestability
   i. clause
incontestable
inconvenience
inconvenient
incopolitus
incorporamus
incorporate
incorporation
incorporeal
   i. chattels
   i. hereditaments
incorrigible
incorruptibility
incorruptible
increase
increment
incremental
incrementum
incriminate
incriminating
   i. admission
incrimination
incriminatory
   i. statement
inculpate
inculpation
inculpatory
incumbency
incumbent
incumber
incumbrance

incumbrancer
incur
incurramentum
incursion
in custodia legis
inde
indebitatus
   i. assumpsit
indebitum
indebted
indebtedness
   bonded i.
indecimable
indefeasible
indefensible
indefensus
indefinite
   i. legacy
in delicto
indemnification
indemnificatus
indemnify
indemnis
indemnitee
indemnitor
indemnity
   i. against liability
indenization
indent
indenture
   debenture i.
independence
independent
   i. adjuster
   i. contractor
indeterminate
   i. sentence
index
   i. animi sermo
indicare
indicate
indication
indicative
   i. evidence
indicavit
indices
indicia
indicium
indict
indictable

indicted
indictee
indictio
indictment
indictor
indifference
indifferent
indigenous
indigent
indignity
indirect
  i. evidence
  i. tax
indispensable
  i. parties
indistanter
inditee
individual
individually
individuum
indivisibility
indivisible
indivisum
indolence
indolent
indubitable
  i. proof
induce
inducement
induciae
induct
inductio
induction
inductive
indulgence
indulgent
indument
industrial
  i. and provident societies
industry
inebriate
inebriation
inebriety
inefficiency
inefficient
ineligibility
ineligible

inert
inertia
inescapable
  i. peril
in esse
in est de jure
inevitability
inevitable
  i. accident
in extremis
infamia
infamis
infamous
infamy
infancy
infans
infant
infantia
infanzon
infeoffment
inference
inferential
inferior
  i. court
infeudation
inficiari
inficiatio
infidel
infidelis
infidelity
infiltrate
infiltration
infirm
infirmative
  i. hypothesis
infirmity
inflation
inflexibility
inflexible
influence
  undue i.
influential
informal
informality
in forma pauperis
information
informative
informer

infortunium
infra
   i. aetatem
   i. annos nubiles
   i. annum
   i. corpus comitatus
   i. jurisdictionem
   i. praesida
infraction
infringe
infringement
infringer
infugare
infula
in futuro
inge
ingenium
ingenuitas
ingenuity
ingenuous
ingenuus
ingrate
ingratitude
ingress
   i., egress, and regress
ingressu
ingrossator
inhabit
inhabitant
inhabited
   i. house duty
in haec verba
inhere
inherent
   i. power
inherently
   i. dangerous
inherit
inheritable
   i. blood
inheritance
   i. tax
inhibit
inhibition
inhoc
inhuman
   i. treatment
in infinitum
iniquitous
iniquity

initial
initiate
initiation
   i. fee
initiative
iniurcolleguia
injunction
   mandatory i.
   preliminary i.
   temporary i.
injunctive
in jure
injure
injures graves
injuria
   i. absque damno
   i. non excusat injuriam
   i. non praesumitur
injuries
injurious
   i. words
injury
   compensable i.
injustice
inlagation
inlagh
inland
inlantal
inlantale
inlaw
inleased
in lieu of
in litem
in loco parentis
inmate
in medias res
innavigability
innavigable
innings
innkeeper
innocence
innocent
   i. agent
   i. purchaser
   i. trespass
innocuous
innominate
   i. contract
innotescimus
innovate

innovation
innuendo
inofficiosum
inofficious
   i. testament
inoficiocidad
inops consilii
inordinate
inordinatus
in pais
in pari delicto
in pari materia
in perpetuity
in personam
in posse
in principio
in propria persona
inquest
   civil i.
   coroner's i.
   i. of office
inquilinus
inquirendo
inquiry
   writ of i.
inquisition
inquisitor
in re
in rem
in restraint of trade
insalubrious
insane
inscribere
inscriptio
inscription
inscriptiones
insecure
insecurity
insensibility
insensible
insidiator
insignia
insiliarius
insilium
insimul
insinuacion
insinuare
insinuate
insinuatio
insinuation

insolation
insolvency
insolvent
inspect
inspectator
inspection
   i. laws
   i. of documents
inspector
inspectorship
   deed of i.
inspeximus
install
installation
installment
instance
   i. court
instancia
instant
instantaneous
instanter
instantly
instar
in statu quo
instigate
instigation
instigator
instill
instillation
instirpare
in stirpes
institor
institorial
   i. power
institute
instituted
   i. executor
institution
institutional
institutiones
instruct
instruction
instructive
instructor
instrument
   i. of appeal
   i. of evidence
instrumenta
instrumental

instrumentality
  i. rule
instrumentation
insubordinate
insubordination
insufficient
insula
insulate
insulation
insuper
insurable
  i. interest
insurance
insure
insurer
insurgent
insurrection
intake
intangible
  i. asset
  i. property
integer
integrate
integration
integrity
intelligibility
intelligible
intend
intendant
intended
  i. to be recorded
intendente
intendment
  i. of law
intent
  larcenous i.
intentio
intention
intentional
intentione
inter
  i. alia
  i. alios
intercalare
intercede
intercedere
intercept
interception
intercession
interchangeably

intercommon
intercommuning
intercourse
interdict
interdiction
interesse
interest
  adverse i.
  beneficial i.
interfere
interference
interim
  i. order
interinsurance
interlineation
interlocutor
interlocutory
interloper
intermarriage
intermeddle
intermediary
intermediate
intermittent
  i. easement
intermixture
  i. of goods
internal
  i. revenue
internally
international
  I. Court of Justice
  i. law
internuncio
internuncius
inter partes
interpellate
interpellation
interplea
interpleader
  bill of i.
interpolate
interpolation
interpose
interposition
interpret
interpretation
interpreter
interpretive
interregnum
interrelationship

interrogate
interrogation
interrogatoire
interrogatories
interrogatory
in terrorem
interrupt
interruptio
interruption
inter se
intersect
intersection
inter sese
interspace
interstate
   i. commerce
   i. extradition
intervene
intervening
   i. act
   i. agency
   i. cause
   i. force
intervenor
intervention
inter vivos
intestabilis
intestable
intestacy
intestate
intestato
intestatus
intimacy
intimate
intimation
intimidate
intimidation
intolerable
   i. cruelty
in toto
intoxicant
intoxicated
intoxicating
intoxication
Intoximeter
intra
intractable
intraliminal
intramural
in transitu

intrastate
   i. commerce
intra vires
intra vitam
intrinsic
   i. evidence
introduce
introduction
introject
introjection
intromission
intronisation
intruder
intrusion
intrust
intuitus
inundate
inundation
inure
inurement
invadiare
invadiatio
invadiatus
invasion
invent
inventio
invention
inventiones
inventor
inventory
inventus
inveritare
inverse
   i. order of alienation doctrine
inversion
invest
investigate
investigation
investigative
investitive
   i. fact
investiture
investment
inviolability
inviolable
inviolate
invitation
invited
   i. error
invitee

invito
   i. beneficium non datur
   i. debitore
   i. domino
invoice
involuntary
   i. manslaughter
iota
ipse
   i. dixit
ipsissimis verbis
ipso
   i. facto
   i. jure
irade
irascibility
irascible
ire ad largum
irenarcha
iron-safe
   i. clause
irrational
irrationality
irrecusable
irreducible
irregular
irregularity
irrelevancy
irrelevant
   i. allegation
irremovability
irremovable
irreparable
   i. damages
irrepleviable
irresistible
   i. force
   i. impulse
irreversible
irrevocable
irrigate
irrigation
irrogare
irrotulatio
island
isolate
isolated transaction
isolation
issei
issint

issuable
   i. defense
   i. plea
issue
   feigned i.
   i. in fact
   i. roll
issues and profits
istimrar
istimrardar
ita est
ita lex scripta est
item
itemize
iter
iteratio
itinera
itinerant
   i. peddling
   i. vendor
itinerary

J

jacens
Jacob's ladder
jactitation
jactivus
jactura
jactus
jail
jailer
jake
jamb
Jane Doe
janitor
janitorial
Janus-faced
jargon
jaywalk
jealous
jealousy
jenny
jeofaile
jeopardize
jeopardy
jerguer
jerk
jesse

jetsam
jettison
jetty
jewel
jewelry
jimmy
jitney
jobber
jobbery
jobmaster
jocelet
John Doe
joinder
    j. in demurrer
    j. of parties
joint
    j. action
    j. and several
    j. enterprise
    j. venture
jointist
jointly
jointress
jointure
jointuress
joker
jolt
josh
jostle
jouir
jour
journal
journey
journey-hoppers
journeyman
joust
jubere
jubilacion
jubilation
Judaeus
Judaismus
Judeus
judex
judge
    j. advocate
    J. Advocate General
    j. de facto
    j. pro tem
judger

judgment
    arrest of j.
    j. creditor
    j. debtor
    declaratory j.
    dormant j.
    j. lien
    j. in rem
    self-executing j.
    villenous j.
judicable
judicare
judicatio
judicative
judicator
judicatory
judicature
judices
judicial
    j. comity
    j. dictum
    j. estoppel
    j. writ
judiciary
judicious
judiciously
judicium
juge
jugerum
jugum
juicio
jumenta
juncta
    j. juvant
junior
junkie
junkshop
junta
jura
jural
juramentum
jurare
jurat
juration
jurator
juratores
    j. sunt judices facti
jurats
jure
juridical

juridicus
juris
  j. et de jure
  j. positivi
jurisconsult
jurisconsultus
jurisdiction
  appellate j.
  concurrent j.
  contentious j.
  military j.
  original j.
  pendent j.
  probate j.
  summary j.
jurisdictional
jurisinceptor
jurisperitus
jurisprudence
  analytical j.
  comparative j.
  medical j.
  sociological j.
jurisprudent
jurisprudentia
jurisprudential
jurist
juristic
juro
juror
jury
  j. box
  hung j.
  j. list
  j. room
  struck j.
juryman
jury-packing
jurywoman
jus
  j. belli
  j. cannonicum
  j. civile
  j. gentium
  j. loci
  j. naturale
  j. publicum
  j. sanguinis
jusjurandum

justa
  j. causa
justice
  j. of the peace
justiceship
justiciable
justiciar
justiciary
justiciatus
justicier
justicies
justifiable
  j. homicide
justification
justificator
justified
justify
justifying
  j. bail
justinianist
justitia
justitium
justiza
justness
juvenile
  j. court
juxta
juxtapose
juxtaposition

K

kabani
kaia
kaiage
kaiagium
kalendarium
kalends
kangaroo court
kast
kast-geld
kay
kayage
kazy
keel
keelage
keeper
keeping

kelp-shore
kentlage
kerf
kerhere
kernellatus
kernes
kerosene
keyage
keyus
kickback
kidder
kidnap
kidnapping
kilderkin
kin
kindred
kingdom
king-geld
King's Bench
King's Counsel
kinsfolk
kinship
kinsman
kinswoman
kintlidge
kith
kleptomania
kleptomaniac
kleptophobia
knacker
knave
knaveship
kneading
knight
knighthood
knight-marshal
knowingly
knowledge
knowledgeable
Koshuba

L

label
la belle indifférence
labor
  l. dispute
  l. union

laboratory
laborer
laborious
laches
lacta
lade
laden
  l. in bulk
lading
  bill of l.
lady-court
laenland
laesiwerp
lagan
lageman
laghday
lahdy
lahlslit
laia
laicus
laity
laiz
lamaneur
lame duck
lana
land
  l. grant
  l. office
  l. patent
landa
landed
  l. estate
landefricus
landing
landlocked
landlord
  l. and tenant
landmark
landpoor
lands, tenements, and hereditaments
landslagh
langeman
langemanni
language
languidus
lapidicina
lapilli
lappage
lapse

lapsed
  l. devise
  l. legacy
  l. policy
lapsus linguae
larboard
larcenous
  l. intent
larceny
  l. by bailee
  grand l.
lascar
lascivious
  l. cohabitation
lassitude
last
  l. antecedent rule
  l. clear chance
  l. resort
  l. will and testament
lastage
lata culpa
latching
latens
latent
  l. content
  l. defect
lateral
  l. railroad
  l. support
laterare
lathe
latifundus
latitatio
lator
latrocination
latrocinium
latrociny
lattermath
latitude
laudare
laudatio
laudator
laudemeo
laudemium
laudum
launch
laureate
laurels
lavatorium

lavor nueva
law
  adjective l.
  administrative l.
  canon l.
  case l.
  commercial l.
  common l.
  consuetudinary l.
  environmental l.
  inspection l.
  international l.
  maritime l.
  martial l.
  mercantile l.
  moral l.
  l. of the land
  l. reports
  session l's
  substantive l.
  sumptuary l's
lawful
  l. age
  l. discharge
  l. entry
  l. representative
lawing
  l. of dogs
lawless
lawsuit
lawyer
laxity
lay
  l. damages
  l. judge
laye
laying the venue
layman
layoff
layperson
laystall
laywoman
lazaret
lazaretto
lead
leading
  l. a use
  l. question
league
leakage

leal
lealte
leap year
lease
  l. and release
  custodiam l.
  durable l.
  reversionary l.
leasehold
leasing
leaute
leave
  l. and license
leccator
lecture
lecturer
ledge
ledger
ledo
leet
lega
legabilis
legacy
  alternate l.
  demonstrative l.
  indefinite l.
  lapsed l.
legal
  l. acumen
  l. age
  l. ethics
  l. malice
  l. privity
  l. right
  l. subrogation
  l. tender
  l. wrong
legalis homo
legality
legalization
legalize
legalized
  l. nuisance
legally
  l. competent
legalness
legare
legatarius
legatary
legate

legatee
legation
legator
legatory
legem
legenita
leges
legislate
legislation
legislative
legislator
legislature
legisperitus
legist
legitimacy
legitimate
legitimation
legitime
legitimus
lego
leguleius
lender
lending
leod
leporarius
leporium
leschewes
lese majesty
lesion
lessa
lessee
lesser
  l. offense
lessor
lest
lestage
lestagium
lethal
  l. weapon
letrado
letter
  l. book
  l. carrier
  l. of credence
  l. of credit
letters
  l. rogatory
  l. testamentary
lettres
  l. de cachet

leuca
levee
   l. district
   l. rate
level
leviable
levis
levitical
   l. degrees
levy
lex
   l. domicilii
   l. fori
   l. loci contractus
   l. manifesta
   l. mercatoria
   l. naturale
   l. non curat de minimis
   l. ordinandi
   l. terrae
lexicon
ley
   l. gager
liability
  civil l.
  secondary l.
  vicarious l.
liable
liaison
libel
  seditious l.
libelant
libelee
libellus
libelous
   l. per quod
   l. per se
liber
   l. homo
libera
liberal
   l. construction
liberare
liberate
liberation
libertas
liberticide
liberties
liberty
librarian

librarius
library
licenciado
license
licensee
   l. by invitation
  gratuitous l.
licensing
   l. acts
licensor
licensure
licentia
licentiate
licere
licet
licitacion
licitare
licitation
licitator
Lidford law
liege
liegeman
lieger
lien
   charging l.
   choate l.
   equitable l.
   grantor's l.
   maritime l.
   mechanic's l.
lienee
lienor
lieu
   l. lands
lieutenancy
lieutenant
life
   l. annuity
   l. estate
   l. tenant
lifehold
lifeland
lifeless
lifetime
   l. prevalence
ligan
ligare
ligeance
ligeantia
lighter

lighterage
lighterman
lighthouse
ligius
lignagium
lignamina
ligula
likelihood
likewise
limit
limitation
   l. of actions
limited
   l. administration
   l. divorce
   l. liability
   l. partnership
limitless
limogia
line
   l. of credit
lineage
linea
   l. recta
   l. transversalis
lineal
   l. consanguinity
   l. heir
linear
link
liquere
liquet
liquid
   l. debt
liquidate
liquidated
   l. damages
   l. debt
liquidation
liquidator
liquor
lis
   l. mota
   l. pendens
listing
lite
   l. pendente
litem
   l. denunciare
litera

literal
literary
   l. property
literate
litigant
litigare
litigate
litigation
litigioso
litigious
litis
   l. contestatio
   l. maris
litispendencia
littoral
litura
litus
   l. maris
livelihood
livelode
livery
   l. of seisin
liveryman
livestock
Lloyd's
loadmanage
loadsman
loan
loaned
   l. employee
lobby
lobbying
lobbyist
local
   l. affairs
   l. option
   l. prejudice
   l. statute
locality
locare
locataire
locatarius
locate
locatio
   l. custodiae
   l. operis
   l. operis faciendi
   l. rei
locatio-conductio
location

locative
l. calls
locator
locatum
lockout
lockup
locman
lococession
locomotion
locomotive
loco parentis
locum tenens
locuples
locus
l. contractus
l. publicus
l. regit actum
l. sigilli
lode
lodeman
lodemanage
lodger
lodging
logbook
logging
logia
logic
logical
l. relevancy
logographus
loiter
longitude
longitudinal
longshoreman
lookout
loophole
lopwood
loquela
lordship
loss
l. leader
l. of consortium
lot
l. and scot
l. book
lottery
louage
lowbote
lowers
loyalty

lucrative
lucre
lucri
l. causa
lucrum
luctus
luggage
lumina
luminare
lumping sale
lump-sum
l. settlement
lunacy
lunatic
lupanatrix
lurgulary
luxury
luxus

M

mace
macebearer
maceproof
macer
machination
machine
machinery
macing
McNabb doctrine
M'Naghten rule
mad point
maere
maeremium
magic
magis
magister
m. navis
magisterial
magistracy
magistrate
committing m.
magistrate's court
magistratus
Magna Charta (*or* Carta)
magna culpa
mahlbrief
maignagium
maihematus

mailable
maim
main-à-main
mainoeuvre
mainour
mainovre
mainpernable
mainprise
mainsworn
maintain
maintainor
maintenance
maire
mairie
maisura
maître
majestas
majesty
major
   m. continent in se minus
majority
maker
mal gree
mala
   m. fides
   m. in se
   m. praxis
   m. prohibita
maladministration
malconduct
malcontent
malediction
malefaction
malefactor
maleficium
maleson
malesworn
malevolence
malevolent
malfeasance
malfetria
malice
   m. aforethought
   m. in fact
   m. in law
malicious
   m. mischief
   m. prosecution
   m. trespass
maliciously

maliciousness
malignare
malinger
malingerer
malingering
malitia
   m. praecogitata
malo
   m. animo
   m. grato
malsworn
malt mulna
maltreatment
malt-scot
malt-shot
malt-tax
malum
   m. in se
   m. prohibitum
malveisa
malversation
manacle
manage
management
manager
managerial
managium
manceps
manche-present
mancipare
mancipate
mancipatio
mancipium
manciple
mancomunal
mandamiento
mandamus
mandans
mandant
mandataire
mandatary
mandate
mandato
mandator
mandatory
   m. injunction
mandatum
manera
manhood

manifest
  m. content
manifestation
manifesto
manning
mannire
mannus
manor
manorial
  m. extent
manser
mansion
mansion-house
manslaughter
manstealing
mansuetus
manticulate
manu
  m. brevi
  m. longa
manual
manufactory
manufacture
manufacturer
manumission
manupretium
manurable
manus
  m. mortua
manuscript
marathon
marauder
march
marchandises avariées
marchioness
mare
  m. clausum
  m. liberum
marettum
margin
marginal
  m. street
marihuana (*or* marijuana)
marine
  m. contract
  m. league
mariner
mariscus
maritagium
  m. habere

marital
  m. portion
  m. rights
maritime
  m. belt
  m. law
  m. lien
  m. tort
maritus
market
  m. overt
  m. value
marketable
  m. title
marksman
marque
  m. and reprisal
marquess
marquis
marquisate
marriage
  m. articles
  common-law m.
  consensual m.
  morganatic m.
  m. settlement
marriageable
married
marrow
marshal
marshaling
  m. assets
Marshalsea
mart
martial
  m. law
masagium
mash
mashgiach
Mason-Dixon line
massa
massacre
masseur
masseuse
mass picketing
mass strike
mast
master
  m. in chancery
  m. of the rolls

mate
matelotage
mater familias
materia
material
  m. allegation
  m. fact
materialman
maternal
materna maternis
maternity
matertera
  m. magna
  m. major
  m. maxima
mathematical
  m. evidence
matima
matriarch
matriarchate
matriarchy
matricidal
matricide
matricula
matriculate
matriculation
matrimonial
  m. action
matrimonium
matrimony
matrix
matron
matter
  m. in controversy
  m. in pais
  m. of course
  m. of substance
maturity
maugré
maxim
maximal
maximize
maximum
  m. security
mayhem
mayhemavit
mayn
maynover
mayor
mayoral

mayoralty
mayorazgo
mayoress
mayor's court
McNabb doctrine
mead
meadow
mean
  m. low tide
meander
  m. lines
means
measure
  m. of damages
measurement
measurer
mechanic
mechanical
mechanic's lien
mechanism
media
  m. annata
  m. concludendi
medianus
  m. homo
mediate
  m. datum
mediation
mediator
medical
  m. examiner
  m. jurisprudence
medicine
  forensic m.
medicolegal
medley
medsypp
Meilicke system
meindre age
mejorado
melior
melioration
melius
  m. inquirendum
membership
membrum
mémoire
memorandum
memorial
memories

memoriter
memorization
memorize
memory
menace
menacing
menial
mens
  m. legis
  m. legislatoris
  m. rea
mensa
  m. et thoro
mensalia
mensis
mensor
mensularius
mente
  m. captus
mentiri
mentition
mera noctis
mercable
mercantant
mercantile
  m. law
mercative
mercatum
mercature
mercedary
mercenarius
mercenary
merces
merchandise
merchant
  m. seaman
merchantability
merchantable
merchantman
merciament
merciful
merciless
mercy
mere motion
meretricious
merger
meridian
merino
meritorious
  m. consideration

merit system
merscum
mertlage
merx
mescreauntes
mese
mesne
  m. assignment
  m. incumbrance
  m. process
message
messenger
messuage
mestizo
meta
metachronism
metallic
metallum
meter
metes
  m. and bounds
metewand
meteyard
method
metric
  m. system
metropolis
metropolitan
metus
meubles
  m. meublans
midchannel
middleman
middle thread
midshipman
mieses
mileage
milestone
militant
militare
military
  m. jurisdiction
  m. service
  m. testament
militia
militiaman
mill
  m. privilege
milleate
milled money

mill-holms
milliequivalent
milligram
milliliter
milling
   m. in transit
mill-leat
minable coal
minage
mineral
   m. lode
minimal
minimize
minimum
   m. charge
   m. wage
minimus
mining
minister
   m. plenipotentiary
ministerial
   m. act
ministrant
ministry
minor
minority
mintage
mintmark
mintmaster
minus
minute
   m. book
minutes
minutia
minutio
Miranda rule
mirror
misadventure
misallege
misapplication
misappropriate
misappropriation
misbrand
misbranding
miscarriage
   m. of justice
miscarry
miscasting
mischarge
mischief

mischievous
misconduct
miscontinuance
miscreant
misdate
misdelivery
misdemeanant
misdemeanor
misdescription
misdirection
mise
mise-money
miserable
   m. depositum
misericordia
misfeasance
misfeasor
misfortune
misjoinder
mislay
misleading
misnomer
mispleading
misprision
   m. of felony
   m. of treason
misreading
misrecital
misrepresent
misrepresentation
missa
missal
misshapen
mission
missionary
missive
missura
mistake
mister
mistery
mistress
mistrial
misuse
misuser
mitigate
mitigating
   m. circumstances
mitigation
   m. of damages
mitior sensus

mitoyenneté
mitter
mittimus
mixed question of law and fact
mixtion
M'Naghten rule
mobbing
mobilia
mobilization
mobilize
mock
modality
mode
model
moderate
   m. castigavit
   m. speed
moderation
moderator
modification
modify
modo et forma
modus
   m. habilis
   m. operandi
moeble
moerda
mohatra
moiety
   m. act
molendum
molest
molestation
molitura
molliter
   m. manus imposuit
momentum
monachism
monarchy
monasterium
monasticon
moneta
monetagium
monetary
money
   barren m.
   m. bill
   imprest m.
moneyed
   m. capital
   m. corporation

moneyer
monger
monier
moniment
monition
monitor
monitory
   m. letters
monocracy
monocrat
monogamy
monogram
monograph
monopolium
monopolize
monopoly
monster
monstrans
   m. de droit
monstrous
monstrum
montes
   m. pietatis
monument
monumental
moonshine
moor
moorage
mooring
moot
   m. court
mooter
mooting
mora
   m. reprobatur in lege
moral
   m. certainty
   m. law
   m. turpitude
moratorium
moratory
moratur in lege
morbus sonticus
moreover
morganatic
   m. marriage
morgangina
morgangiva
morgue
mors omnia solvit

mortality
  m. tables
mortgage
  chattel m.
  constructive m.
  dry m.
  purchase-money m.
mortgagee
  m. in possession
mortgagor
morthlaga
morthlage
mortification
mortify
mortis causa
mortmain
mortuary
  m. tables
mortuum vadium
mortuus
  m. civiliter
  m. sine prole
most favored nation clause
mostrencos
mote
mother
mother-in-law
motile
motility
motion
motivation
motive
motorcycle
mounting
mourning
movable
  m. estate
movables
movant
movement
movent
muebles
muffler
mulatto
mulct
mulier
mulieratus
multifactorial
multifarious
multifariousness

multipartite
multiplicity
  m. of actions
multitude
mundbyrd
mundeburde
municeps
municipal
  m. charter
  m. corporation
municipality
municipium
muniments
munitions
  m. of war
murder
murderous
museum
muster
  m. master
  m. out
  m. roll
mustizo
mutation
  m. of libel
mutatio nominis
mutatis mutandis
mutilate
mutilation
mutineer
mutinous
mutiny
mutual
mutuality
mutuant
mutuari
mutuary
mutuatus
mutuum
mysterious disappearance
mystery
mystic testament

N

namare
namely
nantissement
narratio

narration
narrative
narrator
nasciturus
natale
nation
national
nationality
nationalization
nationalize
native
nativitas
nativus
natura appetit perfectum; ita
  et lex
natural
natural-born citizen
naturaleza
naturalization
naturalize
naturalized citizen
natus
nauclerus
naufrage
naufragium
naught
naulage
naulum
nauta
nautical
naval
navarchus
navicularius
navigable
navigate
navigation
navigational
navire
navis
nazeranna
ne admittas
neatland
necation
necessaries
necessarius
necessary
necessitas vincit legem
necessitous
necessitudo
necessity

needful
needless
ne exeat
ne exeat republica
nefas
nefastus
negate
negation
negative
negativism
negativity
neggildare
neglect
neglected minor
negligence
  comparative n.
  cooperative n.
  gross n.
  imputed n.
  n. per se
negligent
negligentia
negligently
negligible
negoce
negotiability
negotiable
  n. instrument
negotiate
negotiation
negotiorum gestor
neighbor
neighborhood
nemo
  n. est haeres viventis
  n. est supra leges
  n. tenetur ad impossibile
nephew
nepos
nepotism
neptis
ne unques accouple
neutral
neutrality
  armed n.
newspaper
nexi
next of kin
nexum
nichills

nickname
nidering
niderling
nient
   n. comprise
   n. culpable
   n. dedire
   n. le fait
nighttime
nihil
nil
nimmer
nisel
nisi
   n. prius
nithing
nobility
nocent
nochell
noctanter
nocturnal
nolens volens
nolis
nolissement
nolle prosequi
nolo contendere
nol-pros
nomen
nomenclature
nominal
   n. damages
   n. plaintiff
nominate
   n. contract
nominatim
nominating
nomination
nomine
nominee
nomographer
nomography
nomotheta
nonacceptance
nonaccess
nonadmission
nonage
nonagium
non assumpsit
noncancellable
non cepit

nonclaim
noncombatant
noncommissioned
noncompetitive
   n. traffic
non compos mentis
nonconforming
   n. uses
nonconformist
non constat
non culpabilis
nondelivery
nondescript
non detinet
nones
nonfeasance
nonfunctional
nonissuable
   n. plea
nonjoinder
non juridicus
nonlacerating
non obstante veredicto
nonpayment
nonprofit
nonpros
nonresidence
nonresident
non sanae mentis
nonsense
non sequitur
nonspecific
nonsuit
nonuser
non vult contendere
nonwaiver
   n. agreement
normal
normality
normally
normative
norroy
nosocomi
nosocomial
nostrum
nota
nota bene
notae
notarial
notarius

notary public
notation
notchell
note of hand
nothus
notice
   n. of dishonor
   n. of lis pendens
   n. to quit
notifiable
notification
notify
noting
notio
notitia
notorial
notoriety
notorious
   n. possession
novale
novalis
novation
novel assignment
novellae
novelty
noverca
novitas
noxa
noxal action
noxia
noxious
nubilis
nuda possessio
nudum pactum
nugatory
nuisance
   n. in fact
   n. per se
nul
   n. tort
null
nulla bona
nullification
nullify
nullity
   n. of marriage
nullius filius
numerical lottery
nummata
nunciatio

nuncio
nuncius
nunc pro tunc
nuncupare
nuncupate
nuncupative
   n. will
nundination
nunquam
   n. indebitatus
nuptial
nurture
nurus
nutrition
nutritive
nycthemeron
nymphomania

O

oath
   corporal o.
   o. of office
   suppletory o.
oathrite
obedience
obedient
obedientia
obediential
   o. obligation
obedientiarius
obedientiary
obfuscation
obit
obiter
   o. dictum
object
   o. relations
objection
oblata
oblatio
oblation
obligate
obligatio
obligation
   contractual o.
   obediential o.
obligatory
   o. pact

oblige
obligee
obligor
obliterate
obliteration
obliterative
oblivion
oblivious
obloquy
obnoxious
obra
obreptio
obreption
obrogare
obrogate
obrogation
obscene
obscenity
obscure
obscurity
observance
observation
observe
obsignare
obsignatory
obsolescence
obsolescent
obsolete
obstante
obstinacy
obstinate
   o. desertion
obstruct
obstructing
   o. justice
obstruction
   o. of justice
obtain
obtemperare
obtest
obtuse
obventio
obvention
obvious
occasio
occasion
occasionari
occupancy
occupant
occupare

occupatile
occupatio
occupation
occupational
occupative
occupier
occupy
occupying
   o. claimant
occur
occurrence
ochlocracy
octave
octroi
odd lot
odious
odium
offender
offense
   bailable o.
   divisible o.
   graded o.
offensive
offering
office
officer
   o. de facto
   o. de jure
official
officially
officialty
officious
   o. will
offset
offspring
oligarchical
oligarchy
oligopolistic
oligopoly
olograph
olographic
   o. testament
ombudsman
omission
omittance
omnibus
omnium
oncunne
oneratio
onerous

onomastic
onus
  o. probandi
open
  o. account
  o. shop
open-end mortgage
opening statement
opentide
operarii
operate
operatio
operation
operative
opetide
opinion
  advisory o.
  dissenting o.
  o. evidence
oppignerare
opposer
opposite
opposition
oppression
oppressor
opprobrium
optimacy
optimal
optimization
optimize
optimum
option
optional
opus
oraculum
oral
  o. contract
  o. evidence
orator
oratory
oratrix
orbation
ordain
ordainer
ordeal
ordeffe
ordelfe
ordenamiento
order
  agreed o.
  decretal o.

order (*continued*)
  interim o.
  o. nisi
  o. of filiation
  o. of revivor
orderly
ordinance
ordinary
ordination
ordines
ordo
ordonnance
ore-leave
ore tenus
organic
  o. act
  o. law
organically
organism
organization
organize
organized
  o. county
  o. labor
orientation
oriented
original
  o. jurisdiction
  o. plat
  o. writ
originalia
orphan
orphanage
orphanotrophi
orphans' court
ortolagium
ostensible
  o. partner
ostensio
ostentum
oust
ouster
outage
outbuilding
outcast
outcrop
outer bar
outhouse
outland
outlaw
outlawry

outlot
outparter
outrage
outrider
outright
outroper
outstanding
outstroke
ovell
overactivity
overawe
overbraided
overbreak
overcharge
overcome
overcyhsed
overcyted
overdraft
overdraw
overdue
overflowed lands
overhaul
overhead
overissue
overlay
overlive
overload
overlying right
overplus
overrate
overreaching
override
overriding royalty
overrule
overseer
oversight
overt
overtake
overtime
overtone
overture
owelty
owing
owner
  abutting o.
ownership
owner's risk
oyer
  o. and terminer
oyez

P

pacare
pacatio
paceatur
pacification
pacifism
pacifist
pacify
pact
  obligatory p.
pactio
paction
pactional
pactitious
pactum
  p. de non alienando
padder
paddock
paga
pagarchus
pairing off
pais
palam
palatine
Palatine court
palatium
palmarium
palmistry
palm off
palpable
pamphlet
pamphleteer
Pandects
pander
panderer
panel
panic
panier
pannage
pannellation
pantomime
papal supremacy
par
  p. delictum
parachronism
paracium
paradox
paradoxical

parage
paragium
paragraph
parallel
paramount
　p. title
parapherna
paraphernalia
paraphernaux
parasceve
parasynexis
paratitla
paravail
parcel
parcels
　bill of p.
parcenary
parcener
parchment
pardon
parens
　p. patriae
parent
parentage
parentela
parenthesis
parenthetical
parenticide
parergon
pares
pari
　p. delicto
　p. materia
　p. passu
pariah
parientes
paries
　p. communis
pari-mutuel
parish
　p. court
parishioner
paritor
parity
park-bote
parkway
parliament
parliamentary
　p. law
parliamentum

parochial
parol
　p. evidence rule
parole
parols de ley
parquet
parricide
parricidium
pars
　p. rationabilis
parson
parsonage
partage
partial
　p. account
　p. average
　p. dependency
partiality
partiarius
particeps
　p. criminis
participant
participate
participation
particula
particular
particularity
partida
parties in interest
partitio
partition
partner
partnership
　p. in commendam
partus
party
parum
parvise
pas
pasch
pascua
pascuage
passage
passbook
passenger
passiagiarius
passim
passing-ticket
passio
passport

pasto
pastor
pastoral
  p. counseling
pasture
patent
  p. ambiguity
  p. defect
  fencing p.
  land p.
  pioneer p.
patentable
patentee
pater
paterfamilias
paternal
paternalism
paternalistic
paternity
patiens
patria
patriarch
patriarchal
patriarchy
patricidal
patricide
patricius
patrimonial
patrimonium
patrimony
patrocinium
patrolman
patron
patronage
patronatus
patronize
patronus
patruelis
patruus
pauper
pauperies
pauperize
pavage
pawn
pawnbroker
pawnee
pawnor
payable
  p. on demand
payee
  fictitious p.

payer
paymaster
payment
payroll
peaceable
pecia
pecora
peculation
peculatus
peculiar
peculiarity
peculium
pecunia
pecuniary
pedagium
pedaneus
pedaulus
peddler
pedigree
pedis
  p. possessio
pedones
peeping Tom
peer
peerage
peeress
pela
peles
pelfe
pelfre
pellage
pellex
pellicia
pelliparius
pellota
pelt-wool
penal
  p. servitude
penalize
penalty
penance
pendency
pendens
pendent
  p. jurisdiction
pendente lite
pendentes
pending
penetration
penitent
penitentiary

pennon
pennyweight
pensam
pensio
pension
pensioner
pent road
peon
peonage
peonia
perambulation
per annum
per autre vie
perca
per capita
perceivablc
   p. risk
perception
perch
percolate
percolating waters
per curiam
perdida
per diem
perduellio
perdurable
peregrini
perempt
peremption
peremptorius
peremptory
   p. challenge
perfect
   p. instrument
perfected
perfidy
performance
   p. bond
periculosus
periculum
péril
perilous
period
   p. prevalence
periodical
periodicity
perish
perishable
perjure
perjurer

perjurious
perjury
permanence
permanent
   p. abode
permission
permissive
   p. waste
permit
permutatio
permutation
permutatione
pernancy
pernicious
pernour
perpars
perpetrate
perpetration
perpetrator
perpetual
   p. succession
perpetuating testimony
perpetuity
perquisites
perquisitio
per se
persecutio
persecution
persequi
perseveration
person
persona
   p. non grata
personable
personal
   p. injury
   p. property
personality
personalty
personate
personation
personero
personne
per stirpes
persuade
persuasion
persuasive
pertain
pertenencia
pertinence

pertinent
perturbation
perturbatrix
perverse
  p. verdict
pesa
pesquisidor
pessurable
  p. wares
petit
  p. larceny
petitio
petition
  designating p.
  p. in bankruptcy
petitioner
petitory action
peto
petra
pettifogger
pettifogging shyster
petty
  p. bag office
picaroon
picket
pickle
picklock
pickpocket
pier
pierage
piety
pignoratio
pignus
pilfer
pilferage
pilferer
pillage
pillar
pillar-and-stall system
pillory
pilot
pilotage
pimp
pin money
pinnage
pinner
pioneer patent
pious
piracy
pirate

piratical
piscary
pistol
pittance
pix
placard
placeman
placer
  p. claim
placet
placit
placita communia
placitare
placitory
placitum
plagiarism
plagiarist
plagiarius
plagiary
plagium
plaint
plaintiff
  fictitious p.
  p. in error
  nominal p.
plantation
plaque
plat
play-debt
plaza
plea
  declinatory p.
  dilatory p.
  p. in abatement
  p. in bar
  issuable p.
  nonissuable p.
  p. of never indebted
plead
pleadable
pleader
pleadings
plebeian
plebeity
plebeyos
plebiscite
plebiscitum
plebity
plebs
pledable

pledge
pledgee
pledgery
pledges
pledgor
plenarty
plenary
plene
   p. administravit praeter
plenipotentiary
plevin
pleyto
plight
plok-pennin
plottage
plow-bote
plowland
plumbatura
plumber
plumbum
plunder
plunderage
plural
pluralist
pluraliter
plurality
pluries
poach
poblador
pocket
poena
poenalis
poenitentia
poinding
point prevalence
poison
poisoning
poisonous
police
   p. de chargement
policies
policy
   floating p.
political
politics
polity
poll
pollengers
pollicitation
polling the jury

poll tax
pollute
pollution
polyandrous
polyandry
polygamous
polygamy
polygarchy
pone
ponere
pooling contracts
poolroom
populace
populacy
popular
populiscitum
populous
populus
porcion
pornographic
pornography
porrect
porrection
porter
porterage
portion
   p. disponible
portionist
portoria
portsoka
portsoken
positive
posse
   p. comitatus
possess
possessed
possessio
possession
   adverse p.
   p. vaut titre
possessor
   p. bona fide
possessory
possibilitas
possibility
   p. of reverter
possible
post act
postage
postal

postdate
post diem
postea
posteriority
posterity
post facto
postfactum
posthumous
postliminium
postman
postmark
postmaster
  p. general
post-mortem
postnatus
post notes
postnuptial
postobit
postpartal
postpone
postponement
potable
potency
potent
potentate
potentia
potential
potestas
poundage
pound breach
poundkeeper
pour acquit
pourparler
pourparty
pourpresture
poverty affidavit
power
  beneficial p.
  p. coupled with an interest
  exercitorial p.
  inherent p.
  p. of appointment
  p. of attorney
  p. of revocation
powerlessness
practicable
practicably
practical
practice
  actual p.

practitioner
praecipe
  p. in capite
praecipitium
praeco
praecognita
praecognitum
praedia
praedial
praedictus
praedium
  p. dominans
  p. rusticum
  p. serviens
praedo
praefatus
praefecturae
praefine
praelegatum
praemunire
praenomen
praescriptio
praescriptiones
praeses
praestare
praesumptio
praeteritio
praetexta
praetextus
praetor
pragmatic
pragmatica
pragmatism
prairie
pratique
praxis
prayer
preamble
preappointed evidence
preaudience
prebend
prebendary
precarious
  p. possession
  p. right
precarium
precatory
  p. words
precaution
precautionary

precedence
precedency
precedent
   p. condition
preceding
precensor
precepartium
precept
preces
precinct
precipe
precipitate
precipitation
préciput
précis
precise
preclude
precognition
preconization
precontract
precursor
predecessor
predial
   p. servitude
predicate
predication
predispose
predisposition
predominance
predominant
preempt
preemption
preemptioner
preemptive
preemptor
preemptory
prefect
prefer
preference
preferential
preferred
   p. dividend
   p. stock
préfet
prejudice
prejudicial
   p. error
prelate
prélèvement

préliminary
   p. examination
   p. hearing
   p. injunction
   p. proof
premeditate
premeditated
   p. design
premeditatedly
premeditation
premier
premise
premium
premonitory
prenda
prenomen
preparation
preparatory
prepare
prepense
preponderance
   p. of evidence
preponderant
prerogative
   p. writ
presbyter
prescribable
prescribe
prescription
prescriptive
presence
presentation
presentative
presentee
presenter
presently
presentment
preservation
preserve
preside
president
presidential
presiding
prestation
presumable
presumably
presume
presumptio

presumption
  conclusive p.
  disputable p.
  p. of survivorship
presumptive
  heir p.
prêt
pretend
prête-nom
pretense
pretensed
pretension
prétention
preterition
pretermission
pretermit
pretermitted
  p. heir
pretext
pretium
  p. affectionis
pretorial
  p. court
pretrial
  p. hearing
preuve
prevail
prevailing
prevalence
prevalent
prevaricate
prevarication
prevaricator
prevent
prevention
preventive
previous
previously
price
  p. discrimination
pricking note
priest
prima facie
primage
primal
primary
  p. purpose
primate
prime

prime minister
primer
  p. election
primitiae
primogeniture
prince
princeps
princess
  p. royal
principal
principalis
principle
prior
priority
prise
prison
prisoner
prist
privacy
private
  p. international law
privateer
privation
privatum
privies
privigna
privignus
privilege
  attachment of p.
privileged
  p. communication
privileges
  p. and immunities
privilegium
privity
privy
  p. council
prize
  p. court
prizefight
proamita
pro and con
proavia
proavunculus
proavus
probability
probable
  p. cause
probably

probate
  p. court
  facsimile p.
  p. jurisdiction
probatio
probation
probationer
probative
probator
probatory
pro bono publico
procedendo
procedural
procedure
proceeding
proceeds
proceres
process
  abuse of p.
  bastardy p.
  judicial p.
procession
processioning
procès-verbal
prochein
  p. ami
prochronism
procinctus
proclaim
proclamation
proclamator
proconsul
procreation
proctor
procuracy
procurare
procuratio
procuration
procurator
procure
procurement
procurer
procureur
prodigal
prodigus
prodition
proditor
proditorie
produce
producent

producer
product
  p. liability
production
profane
profanity
profectitius
pofert
profess
profession
professional
professor
proffer
profile
profit
  p. à prendre
profiteer
pro forma
progener
progression
progressive
pro hac vice
prohibit
prohibition
prohibitive
prohibitory
projection
projective
projet
proles
proletariat
proletarius
prolixity
prolocutor
prolongation
prolytae
promise
promisee
promisor
promissory
  p. estoppel
  p. note
promote
promoter
promotion
promovent
promulgare
promulgate
promulgation
promutuum

pronepos
proneptis
pronounce
pronunciation
pronurus
proof
  affirmative p.
  convincing p.
  indubitable p.
prop
propagate
propagation
proper
property
  community p.
  dotal p.
  extra-dotal p.
  ganancial p.
  intangible p.
  literary p.
propinquity
propios
proponent
proportionate
proposal
proposition
propositus
propound
propres
propriedad
proprietary
  p. rights
proprietas
propriété
proprietor
propriety
proprios
propter
pro rata
prorate
prorogation
prorogue
proscribe
proscription
pro se
prosecute
prosecuting
  p. attorney
prosecution
  malicious p.

prosecutor
  p. of the pleas
prosecutrix
prosequi
prosequitur
prospective
prospectus
pro tanto
protection
protective
protector
protectorate
pro tem
pro tempore
protest
protestando
prothonotarial
prothonotary
protocol
protocolize
protocolo
protutor
provable
proven
provide
provider
province
provincial
provincialis
provision
provisional
  p. government
  p. remedy
provisiones
proviso
provisor
provocation
provocative
provoke
provost
  p. marshal
proxeneta
proximal
proximate
  p. cause
proximately
proximity
proxy
prudence
prudent

prudential
pseudo
pseudograph
public
publican
publicanus
publication
publiciana
publici juris
publicist
publicity
publish
publisher
pueblo
puer
puffer
pugilism
pugilist
puis
puisne
pulsare
pulsator
pundit
punishable
punishment
  arbitrary p.
  cruel and unusual p.
punitive
  p. damages
pur autre vie
purchase
purchase-money mortgage
purchaser
purgation
purge
  p. des hypothèques
purging
purlieu
purloin
purpart
purparty
purport
purpose
purposeful
purposely
purposive
purpresture
purprise
purser
pursuant

pursue
pursuer
pursuit
purvey
purveyance
purveyor
purview
putative
  p. father

Q

qua
quack
quackery
quacunque via data
quadragesima
quadrans
quadrant
quadriennium
quadripartite
quadroon
quadruplatores
quadruplicatio
quadruplication
quae nihil frustra
quaere
quaerens
quaesta
quaestio
quaestionarii
quaestor
quaestus
qualification
qualified
  q. indorsement
  q. nuisance
qualify
qualitative
quality
quamdiu
quando acciderint
quantitative
quantify
quantity
quantum
  q. meruit
  q. valebant
quarantine

quare
quarrel
quarrelsome
quarry
quart
quartan
quarter
  q. day
  q. sessions
quarterization
quarterly
quartermaster
quarterone
quash
quasi
  q. contract
quasi-traditio
quay
quayage
Queen's Counsel
que estate
querela
querens
querulous
questionable
questioner
questionnaire
quia timet
quibble
quidam
quid pro quo
quiescence
quiescent
quietare
quietus
qui facit per alium facit per se
quille
quinquepartite
quintal
quinterone
quiritarian ownership
quit
qui tam
quitclaim
  q. deed
quitrent
quittance
quo ad
quoad hoc
quo animo

quod computet
quo ligatur, eo dissolvitur
quorum
quota
quotation
quotidian
quotient
  q. verdict
quotuplex
quousque
quo warranto

R

raceway
rachat
rachater
racket
racketeer
rack-rent
radical
radour
raffle
railroad
railway
rainwater
rake-off
ramification
ramify
rancho
rancid
rand
range
ranger
ranking of creditors
ransom
rape
  statutory r.
rapine
rapport
rasure
ratable
rate
  r. of exchange
ratification
ratify
ratihabitio
ratio
  r. decidendi

rationes
ravage
ravine
ravish
ravisher
ravishment
raze
razon
ready and willing
reafforest
reafforestation
real
  r. action
  r. covenant
  r. estate
  r. party in interest
  r. property
reality
realization
realize
realm
realtor
realty
reappraise
reappraiser
reargument
reasonable
  r. certainty
  r. doubt
reassurance
reattach
reattachment
rebate
rebel
rebellion
rebellious
  r. assembly
rebound
rebut
rebuttable
  r. presumption
rebuttal
rebutter
rebutting
  r. evidence
recalcitrant
recall
recant
recapitalization
recapitalize

recapitulate
recapitulation
recaption
recapture
receipt
  accountable r.
receiptor
receiver
  r. in bankruptcy
  r. pendente lite
receivership
reception
receptus
recess
recession
recht
recidivation
recidive
recidivism
recidivist
recipient
reciprocal
  r. contract
reciprocate
reciprocation
reciprocity
recital
recite
reck
reckless
recklessness
reclaim
reclamation
  r. district
recluse
reclusion
recognition
recognitor
recognizance
recognizant
recognize
recognizee
recognizor
récolement
recommend
recommendation
recommendatory
recommit
recompensate
recompensation

recompense
reconcile
reconciliation
reconduction
reconsider
reconsideration
reconstruct
reconstruction
recontinuance
reconvenire
reconventio
reconvention
reconventional
   r. demand
reconversion
reconveyance
record
recordare
recordatur
recordum
recoup
recoupment
recourse
recousse
recover
recoveree
recoverer
recovery
recreant
recriminate
recrimination
recruit
rectification
rectifier
rectify
rectitude
   comparative r.
rectitudo
rector
rectorial
rectory
rectum
   r. esse
   r. rogare
rectus
recuperatio
recuperative
recuperatores
recurrence
recurrent

recusant
recusation
reddendum
reddition
redeem
redeemable
   r. bonds
redelivery
redemise
redemption
redeundo
redevance
redhibere
redhibition
redhibitory
   r. action
redimere
redistribute
redistribution
reditus
redraft
redress
redubber
reduce
reducible
reductio ad absurdum
reduction
   r. into possession
redundancy
redundant
reenact
reentry
reestablish
reestablishment
reeve
reexamination
reexamine
reexchange
reextent
refalo
refare
refection
refer
referable
referee
   r. in bankruptcy
reference
referendarius
referendum
referent

refinance
refinement
reform
reformation
reformatory
refresher
refund
refunding bond
refusal
refuse
regalia
regality
regardant
regency
regent
regicide
regidor
regime
regimiento
regina
regional
register
registered bond
registrant
registrar
registrarius
registration
registrum brevium
registry
reglamento
regnant
regrant
regress
regula
regular
  r. on its face
regularity
regularly
regulate
regulation
regulus
rehabilitate
rehabilitation
rehearing
reif
reimburse
reimbursement
reinforce
reinforcement
reinstate

reinstatement
reinsurance
reissuable
  r. notes
rejoin
rejoinder
rejoining
  r. gratis
relate
relation
relationship
relative
relator
relatrix
relaxare
relaxatio
relaxation
release
releasee
releaser
relegatio
relegation
relevance
relevancy
  logical r.
relevant
reliability
reliable
relict
reliction
relief
relieve
religion
religious
relinquish
relinquishment
reliqua
reliquary
relocate
relocatio
relocation
remainder
remainderman
remand
remanent
  r. pro defectu emptorum
remanet
remedial
remedies
remedy
  adequate r.

remembrancer
réméré
remise
remission
remissness
remit
remitment
remittance
remittee
remittent
remitter
remitting bank
remittitur
   r. of record
remittor
remnant
   r. rule
remodel
remonstrance
remonstrate
remonstration
remorse
remote
remoteness
removal
   r. of causes
remover
remunerate
remuneration
rencounter
render
rendezvous
renegade
renew
renewal
renounce
renouncing
   r. probate
rent
  forehand r.
  ground r.
  r. strike
rentage
rental
rente
rentes
rentier
renunciation
renvoi
reo absente

reopening
reorganization
repair
reparable
reparation
repartiamento
repatriate
repatriation
repave
repay
repayment
repeal
repeater
repertory
repetition
repetitive
replace
replacement
replead
repleader
replegiare
repletion
repleviable
replevin
replevisable
replevisor
replevy
repliant
replicant
replicare
replicatio
replication
reposition
repositorium
reprehensible
represent
representation
  class r.
representative
reprieve
reprimand
reprisal
reprise
reprobation
reprobator
republic
republican
republication
repudiate
repudiation

repudium

repugnancy

repugnant

reputable

reputation

repute

reputed

request

require

requirement

   r. contract

requisition

res

resale

rescind

rescissio

rescission

   r. of contract

rescissory

   r. action

rescous

rescript

rescription

rescriptum

rescue

   r. doctrine

resealing

   r. writ

reservando

reservation

reserve

   depreciation r.

reservoir

resettlement

res gestae

resiance

resiant

reside

residence

   actual r.

resident

residential

residual

residuary

   r. clause

   r. devisee

   r. legatee

residue

residuum

resignation

resignee

resilience

resiliency

res ipsa loquitur

resist

resistance

resistant

resisting an officer

res judicata

res nullius

resolucion

resolution

resolutory

   r. condition

resort

resource

respective

respite

respond

respondeat

   r. ouster

   r. superior

respondent

respondentia

responsibility

responsible

responsive

restamping

   r. writ

restaur

restaurant

restitutio

   r. in integrum

restitution

restoration

restorative

restore

restrain

restraining order

restraint

   r. of marriage

   r. of trade

restrict

restriction

restrictive

   r. indorsement

result

resultant

resulting

   r. trust

resummons
resumption
resurrender
retainer
retaliate
retaliation
retaliatory
retention
retinentia
retire
retirement
retorsion
retract
retractation
retraction
retracto
   r. o tanteo
retrait
retraxit
retribution
retro
retroactive
   r. inference
   r. statute
retrocession
retrospective
   r. falsification
rette
return
   r. irreplevisable
returnable
returning board
reus
revel
reveland
revelry
revendicate
revendication
revenue
reversal
reverse
reversible
   r. error
reversion
reversionary
   r. interest
   r. lease
reversioner
revert
reverter

revest
review
revile
revise
revised statutes
revising assessors
revision
revival
revive
revivor
revocable
revocation
revocatur
revoke
revolt
revolution
revolutionary
reward
rex
   r. non potest peccare
rezone
Rhodian laws
ribaud
Richard Roe
ricohome
rider
rider-roll
ridgling
rien
rifflare
rifletum
rigging the market
right
   extralateral r.
   inchoate r.
   r. of action
   r. of survivorship
   r. of tanto
   r. of way
rights
   civil r.
   conjugal r.
rigor
   r. juris
   r. mortis
ring dropping
ringing the changes
rioter
riotose
riotous
   r. assembly

riotously
ripa
riparian
  r. owner
  r. rights
riscus
risk
ristourne
rivage
riveare
rixa
roadbed
roadstead
robber
robbery
rogare
rogatio
  r. testium
rogator
rogatory
rogo
rogue
role
  r. d'équipage
rolling stock
root of title
rosland
roster
rota
rotation
roture
roturier
round-robin
rout
route
routously ·
roy
royal
royalties
royalty
  haulage r.
rubric
ruina
rule
  biting r.
  Boyd r.
  consent r.
  r. day
  distraction r.
  Durham r.

rule (*continued*)
  Hilary r's
  instrumentality r.
  last antecedent r.
  Miranda r.
  M'Naghten r.
  r. nisi
  parol evidence r.
  similitude r.
  substantial compliance r.
  sudden peril r.
  two-issue r.
ruminant
running account
ruptum
rusticum
  r. forum
  r. judicium
rustler
ruta
ryottenure

S

sabbulonarium
sable
sabotage
saboteur
saccularii
sacquier
sacra
sacramentales
sacramentum
sacrilege
sacrilegious
sacrilegium
sacrilegus
sadism
saevitia
safe-conduct
safeguard
safe-pledge
safety island
sagaman
saisie
salable
salarium
salary

sale
  s. and return
  judicial s.
  s. note
  s. with all faults
salesman
saleswoman
saline
  s. land
saloon
saloonkeeper
salus
  s. populi suprema lex
  s. ubi multi consiliarii
salutary
salute
salvage
salvageable
salvo
salvor
sample
sanatorium
sanctio
sanction
sanctuary
sandbag
sanguine
sanguineous
sanguis
sanitary
  s. authority
sanity
sans recours
satisdare
satisdatio
satisfaction
  s. piece
satisfactory
  s. evidence
satisfied
  s. term
satisfy
saunkefin
sauvagine
sauvement
saving clause
saw log
scab
scale
  s. tolerance

scaler
scaling laws
scandal
scandalous
scapha
scaremonger
schedule
scheme
schetes
schism
sciendum est
scienter
scilicet
scintilla
scire
  s. facias
  s. feci
scorn
scot and lot
scottare
scoundrel
scrambling
  s. possession
scratching the ticket
scrawl
screwball
scriba
scribere est agere
scrip
script
scriptum
scrivener
scroll
scruple
scrupulous
scurrilous
scutella
seal
seaman
séance
search
  s. and seizure
  s. warrant
searcher
seashore
seasonal employment
seated land
seaward
seaworthiness
seaworthy

seck
second
secondary
  s. boycott
  s. liability
second-hand
  s. evidence
secret
secretary
Secret Service
sect
secta
sectarian
section
sectores
secular
secundum
secured
  s. creditor
  s. note
securitas
securities
security
secus
sedition
seditious
  s. libel
seduce
seducing to leave service
seduction
seductive
seignior
seignioress
seigniory
seisin
seize
seizure
selda
select
selectman
self-dealing
self-defense
self-executing
  s. judgment
seller
sell short
semble
semestria
semi-matrimonium
seminarian
seminarium

seminary
seminaufragium
semper
  p. paratus
senate
senator
senatus
senda
senectus
senescence
senior
seniority
senorio
sensus
sentence
  accumulative s.
  indeterminate s.
sententia
separable
  s. controversy
separaliter
separate
  s. estate
  s. maintenance
separation
  s. a mensa et thoro
sepulchre
sequela
  s. curiae
sequester
sequestrari facias
sequestratio
sequestration
sequestrator
sergeant
sergeant-at-arms
serial
serially
seriately
seriatim
serious
  s. and wilful misconduct
servant
servi
service
  s. by publication
  s. foncier
  s. of process
servidumbre
servient
  s. tenement

servitude
  additional s.
servitus
sess
session
  s. laws
set aside
seti
set of exchange
set-off
settle
settlement
settler
settlor
sever
severable
  s. statute
several
  s. inheritance
severally
severalty
severance
  s. damage
  s. pay
sewage
seward
sewer
sexton
shakedown
sham
shanghai
share
  s. and share alike
shareholder
sharp
shave
sheepskin
sheeting
Shelley's case
shelter
sheriff
sheriffalty
sheriff's court
sheriff's jury
sheriffwick
shewer
shifting
  s. clause
  s. risk
  s. the burden of proof
shift marriage

shilling
shipment
shipper
shipper's order
shipping
ship's husband
ship's papers
shipwreck
shire
shoot
shop
  s. right
shop-book rule
shopkeeper
shoplift
shoplifter
short
  s. lease
  s. notice
  s. sale
show cause
shutdown
shyster
sib
sibling
sic
sich
side-bar rule
sideline
sidewalk
siervo
sight draft
sigla
sign manual
signa
signal
signatory
signature
signet
significant
signification
signify
signum
silence
silence shows consent
silentiarius
silva
silver
similar
  s. description
similiter

similitude
 s. rule
simony
simpla
simple
 s. battery
 s. sentence
simplex
simpliciter
simul cum
simul et semel
simulate
simulated contract
simulatio
 s. latens
simulation
simultaneous
sinderesis
sine
 s. die
 s. prole
 s. qua non
sinecure
single
 s. juror charge
singular
sinister
sinking fund
sister
sister-in-law
site
sitio
 s. de ganado menor
 s. ganado mayor
situate
situation
situational
situs
six-day license
skeleton
 s. bill
skilled witness
slacker
slander
 s. of title
slanderer
slanderous
 s. per se
slavery
slot machine
slough

sluiceway
slumlord
slungshot
slush fund
small claims courts
smeller
smelt
smelter
smuggling
smut
soakage
sober
sobre
sobre-juezes
socer
social
 s. club
 s. contract
 s. settlement
socida
sociedad
 s. anonima
 s. de gananciales
societas
 s. leonina
 s. navalis
société
 s. anonyme
 s. d'acquets
 s. en commandite
 s. en nom collectif
 s. en participation
 s. par actions
society
sociological
 s. jurisprudence
socius
soil
soit
sojourn
solar
 s. day
 s. month
solares
solatium
sold
 s. note
soldier
sole
 s. actor doctrine
 s. and unconditional owner

solemn
solemnes
  s. legum formulae
solemnity
solemnize
solicit
solicitation
solicitor
  s. general
solidarity
solidary
solidum
solitary
  s. confinement
solutio
  s. indebiti
solutus
solvabilité
solvency
solvendo
solvendum
  s. in futuro
solvent
solvere
solvit
  s. ad diem
sommation
son-in-law
sonticus
soror
sororicide
sors
sortitio
sough
sound
  s. and disposing mind and memory
  s. mind
sounding in damages
soundness
source
sources
  s. of the law
sous
sous seing privé
sovereign
  s. immunity
  s. right
  s. states
sovereignty
sparsim
speaker

speaking
  s. demurrer
special
  s. commission
specialist
specialty
specie
species
specific
  s. performance
specifically
specificatio
specification
specificity
specify
specimen
speculate
speculation
speculative
  s. damages
speculum
spendthrift
  s. trust
sperate
spiritual
spirituous
  s. liquors
spital
spite
  s. fence
split
  s. sentence
splitting
  s. a cause of action
spoliator
spolium
spondeo
sponsio
sponsion
sponsor
spontaneous
  s. combustion
  s. exclamation
sporting house
sportula
spouse
springing use
spur
  s. track
spurious
  s. bank-bill

spurius
squatter
stabilia
stability
stabilization
stabilize
stable
stabularius
stage line
stagiarius
stake
stakeholder
stale demand
stamp
  s. acts
  s. duties
stance
standard
  s. established by law
  s. mortgage clause
  s. of weight
standardization
standardize
standing
  s. aside juror
  s. in loco parentis
staple
starboard
stare decisis
star page
stat pro ratione voluntas
state
  s. experience factor
statement
  consonant s.
  incriminatory s.
  s. of affairs
state's evidence
statesman
station
stationers' hall
stationery office
statist
statistical
statistics
status quo
statute
  declaratory s.
  directory s.
  disabling s.

statute (*continued*)
  expository s.
  s. of frauds
  s. of limitations
  severable s.
  validating s.
statute-merchant
statutes at large
statutory
  s. bond
  s. obligation
  s. rape
statutum
stay
  s. of execution
  s. of proceedings
stealing
stealth
steamfitter
steamship
stellionataire
stellionatus
stenographer
stenography
stepchild
stepfather
stepmother
stereotype
sterility
sterling
stet
  s. billa
  s. processus
stevedore
steward
stifling
  s. a prosecution
stint
stipend
stipendiary
  s. estate
  s. magistrate
stipendium
stipital
stipulate
stipulated
  s. damage
stipulatio
stipulation
  conditional s.

stipulator
stirpes
stock
  certificate of s.
  debenture s.
  s. dividend
  s. exchange
  guaranteed s.
stockade
stockbroker
stockholder
stop order
stoppage
  s. in transitu
storage
storehouse
storeroom
stowage
stowaway
straddle
straggler
straight-line depreciation
stranding
stranger
  s. in blood
strangle
strangulation
strata
stratagem
stratocracy
stratum
straw bail
strepitus
  s. judicialis
stria
strict
  s. liability
stricti
  s. juris
strictissimi
  s. juris
strictly
  s. construed
stricto
  s. jure
strictum
  s. jus
stricture
strike
  s. off
  s. suit

strikebreaker
striking
  s. a docket
  s. a jury
strong hand
strongly
  s. corroborated
struck
  s. jury
structural
  s. alteration
structure
strumpet
stuff gown
stultify
stumpage
stuprum
suable
sua sponte
subagent
subaltern
subcontract
subcontractor
subdivide
subdivision
subduct
subflow
subhastare
subhastatio
subirrigate
subjacent
  s. support
subject matter
subjection
sub judice
sublease
sublet
submarine
submergence
submission
submit
submittal
submortgage
sub nomine
subordinate
  s. officer
suborn
subornation
  s. of perjury
suborner

subpoena
  s. ad testificandum
  s. duces tecum
subreption
subrogate
subrogation
subrogee
subscribe
subscriber
subscribing
  s. witness
subscriptio
subscription
subsequent
subsidiary
  s. corporation
subsidy
sub silentio
subsistence
subsoil
substance
substantial
  s. compliance rule
  s. performance
substantially
substantiate
substantiation
substantive
  s. evidence
  s. felony
  s. law
substitute
substituted
  s. executor
  s. service
substitution
substitutional
substitutionary
  s. evidence
substraction
subtenant
subterfuge
subterranean
subtraction
  s. of conjugal rights
subversion
subversive
successio
succession
  s. duty

successive
successor
succinct
sudden
  s. affray
  s. peril rule
sue out
suerte
sufferance
  bill of s.
  s. wharves
suffering
  s. a recovery
sufficient
  s. evidence
suffocate
suffrage
suggest
suggestio
  s. falsi
suggestion
suggestive
  s. interrogation
sui
  s. generis
  s. juris
suicide
suing
  s. and laboring clause
suit
suitable
suitas
suite
suitor
sulcus
sum
  s. in gross
  s. payable
summarily
summary
  s. conviction
  s. court-martial
  s. jurisdiction
  s. proceedings
  s. process
summing up
summon
summoner

summons
   adjourned s.
   s. ad respondendum
   s. and order
   s. and severance
sump
sumptuary
   s. laws
sundries
sundry
super
supercargo
superfetation
superficiarius
superfluous
superinductio
superinstitution
superintend
superintendent
superior
superiority
supersede
supersedeas
superseding
   s. cause
superstitious
supervene
supervening
   s. cause
   s. negligence
supervise
supervision
supervisor
supervisory
   s. control
supplemental
   s. bill
   s. pleading
supplementary
   s. proceedings
suppletory
   s. oath
suppliant
supplicant
supplicatio
supplication
supplicavit
supplicium
supposition
suppress

suppressible
suppressio
   s. veri
suppression
suppressive
supra
   s. protest
supremacy
supreme
   S. Court of Judicature
   S. Court of the United States
supremus
surcharge
   s. and falsify
surdus
surenchère
surety
   s. of the peace
suretyship
   contract of s.
surface
surmise
sur mortgage
surname
surplice fee
surplus
surplusage
surprise
surrebutter
surrejoinder
surrender
   s. by operation of law
   s. of copyhold
   s. of a preference
surrenderee
surrenderor
surreptitious
surrogate
surrogate's court
surround
surrounding
   s. circumstances
surveillance
survey
   chamber s.
surveyor
survival
   s. statutes
survive
surviving

survivor
survivorship
susceptibility
susceptible
suspect
suspend
suspense
suspension
suspensive
   s. condition
suspensory
   s. condition
suspicion
suspicious
   s. character
sustain
sustenance
sutler
swatch
swear
swearing
   s. the peace
sweating
sweat shop
sweeping
sweepstakes
swift
   s. witness
swindle
swindler
switch
switching movement
switchyard doctrine
sworn
syllabus
syllogism
symbolic
   s. delivery
sympathetic
   s. strike
sympathy
synallagmatic
   s. contract
synchronism
synchronization
synchronize
syncopare
syndic
syndicalism
syndicate

syndicating
synod
synodal
synonymous
synopsis
system
   bicameral s.

T

tabard
tabarder
tabella
tabellio
tabernaculum
tabernarius
table
   t. of cases
tableau
   t. of distribution
tabula
tabulae
   t. nuptiales
tabularius
tacit
tacite
taciturnity
tail
   estate in t.
tailage
taille
tail light
tailor
   t. to the trade
taint
takeover
   t. bid
tales
   t. de circumstantibus
talesman
talio
talion
   t. law
tallage
tallager
tallagium
tallatio
tallia
tally

talweg
tamen
tamper
tam quam
tanamoshi
tangible
  t. property
tankage
tanteo
tanto
  right of t.
tare
tariff
tautology
tavern
taverner
tax
  t. certificate
  t. evasion
  t. ferret
  franchise t.
  indirect t.
  inheritance t.
  t. levy
  t. lien
taxa
taxable
taxare
taxatio
taxation
taxer
tax-exempt
taxicab
taxing
  t. power
taxpayer
teacher
teamster
tearing
  t. of will
technical
technicality
tegula
telegram
telegraph
telephone
teletype
television
televise
teller

telltale
tellworc
tementale
temere
temperance
templar
temple
temporalities
temporality
temporarily
temporary
    t. injunction
    t. restraining order
tempore
tempus
    t. continuum
    t. fugit
tenancy
    t. in common
tenant
    t. as sufferance
    t. by the curtesy
    t. in fee
    t. in severalty
    t. in tail
tenantable repair
tenant-right
tencon
tender
tenement
tenendum
tenens
tenere
teneri
tenet
tenor
tenseriae
Tenterden's act
tenths
tenuit
tenure
terce
tercerone
ter in die
term
    adjourned t.
terminable
    t. property
terminal
terminate

terminating
termination
terminer
termini
termino
terminum
terminus
   t. ad quem
   t. a quo
termor
terrages
terre
   t. tenant
terrier
territorial
territoriality
territory
terror
tertiary
testable
testacy
testament
   inofficious t.
   military t.
   mystic t.
   olographic t.
testamentary
   t. capacity
   t. cause
   t. guardian
   heir t.
testamentum
testari
testate
testation
testator
testatrix
testatum
   t. writ
testatus
teste
   t. of a writ
testify
testimonial
testimonio
testimonium
   t. clause
testimony
   experimental t.
   perpetuating t.

theft
theftbote
thelonmannus
theme
themmagium
theocracy
theoretical
theoretician
theory
thereabout
thereafter
thereby
therefore
therin
thcrctofore
thereupon
thesaurer
thesaurium
thesaurus
thesmothete
thethinga
thia
thievery
third
   t. degree
   t. party
thirdborough
thirdings
thoroughfare
threatening
ticket of leave
tidal
tidesmen
tidewater
tiel
tierce
tignum
tillage
timber
timberlode
timocracy
tinbounding
tinel
tinkerman
tinpenny
tippling
   t. house
tipstaff
tithe
tither

tithing
titius
title
  abstract of t.
  chain of t.
  curing t.
  t. deed
  doubtful t.
  marketable t.
  t. retention
titulada
titular
titulus
tobacconist
toft
togati
token
tolerance
tolerant
tolerate
toleration
toll
  t. the statute
tollage
tollbooth
tolldish
toller
tollere
tolt
tomb
tombstone
tonnage
  t. duty
tonsure
tontine
Torrens title system
tort
  maritime t.
  nul t.
tortfeasor
tortious
torts
  abandonment for t.
tortuous
torture
total
  t. dependency
  t. disability
totidem verbis
toties quoties

totted
to wit
towage
township
townsite
toxicate
toxicity
toxin
trabes
trade
  t. agreement
trademark
trade name
trader
tradesman
tradicion
trading
  t. stamps
traditio
tradition
traditional
traditionary
  t. evidence
traffic
trahens
trailer
trainbands
traitor
traitorously
trajectitius
trajectory
trammer
transact
transacting
transactio
transaction
transazione
transcribe
transcultural
transfer
  t. tax
transferable
transferee
transference
transferor
transgressio
transgression
transgressione

transgressive
  t. trust
transient
transire
transit
  t. in rem judicatam
  t. terra cum onere
transition
transitive
  t. covenant
transitory
transitus
translado
translate
translation
translative
  t. fact
transmission
transmit
transport
transportation
transship
transshipment
traslado
trassans
trassatus
trauma
traumatic
traumatism
travail
traveler
traverse
traverser
traversing
  t. note
treacher
treacherous
treachour
treadmill
treadwheel
treason
treasonable
treasure
treasurer
treasure-trove
treasury
treatment
treaty
treble damages
trechetour

tresael
trespass
  forcible t.
  innocent t.
  malicious t.
trespasser
  t. ab initio
tret
treyt
trial
  abortive t.
tribal
tribuere
tribunal
tributary
tribute
triennial
trinepos
trineptis
Trinity House
trinket
trior
tripartite
triple
triplicacion
triplicatio
tritavia
tritavus
triverbial
  t. days
trivial
triviality
tronage
tronator
troops
trophy
trover
truce
true bill
trust
  t. allotments
  charitable t.
  discretionary t.
  donative t.
  t. receipt
  resulting t.
  transgressive t.
trustee
trustor
tubman

tuchas
tuerto
tuition
tumbrel
tumultuous
tungreve
tunnage
turba
turbary
turf
turnkey
turnout
turnpike
turntable
   t. doctrine
turpis
   t. causa
turpitude
turpitudo
tutela
tutelage
tuteur
tutor
tutorship
tutrix
two-issue rule
tyburn ticket
tylwith
tyrranical
tyranny
tyrant

U

uberrima fides
ubiquitous
ubiquity
udal
uffer
ukase
ullage
ulnage
ulterior
ultimate
ultimatum
ultimum
ultimus
   u. haeres

ultra
   u. reprises
   u. vires
umpirage
umpire
unable
unaccrued
unadjusted
unalienable
unambiguous
unanimity
unanimous
unascertained
unavoidable
unbroken
uncertainty
uncia
unconditional
unconscionable
   u. bargain
unconstitutional
uncontrollable
uncore prist
uncovenanted
undefended
undercurrent
underflow
underlease
underlie
underlying
under-sheriff
undersigned
understand
understanding
understood
undertake
undertaker
undertaking
undertenant
undertook
undertutor
underwrite
underwriter
undesirable
undisclosed
   u. principal
undisputed
undivided
undoing

undue
  u. influence
unduly
unearned
uneasiness
uneducated
unemployable
unemployment
unequal
unequivocal
unerring
unethical
unexceptionable
unexpected
unexpired
unfair
  u. competition
unfaithful
unfinished
unfit
unforeseen
unharmed
unifactoral
  u. obligation
unified
uniform
uniformity
unify
unigeniture
unilateral
  u. contract
unimpeachable
unimproved
uninsured
unintelligible
unio
union
unit
  u. rule
unitary
unite
unity
  u. of interest
  u. of possession
  u. of title
universal
  u. agent
  u. legacy
  u. partnership
  u. representation
universitas

university
universus
unjust
  u. enrichment
unlawful
  u. assembly
unlawfully
unlicensed
unlimited
unliquidated
unlivery
unloading
unmarketable
unmarried
unnatural
unnecessary
unoccupied
uno flatu
unprecedented
unpremeditated
unprofessional
unques
unreality
unreasonable
unruly
unsafe
unseated
  u. land
unseaworthy
unsightly
unsolemn
  u. war
  u. will
unsound
unsubstantiated
untenable
unthrift
untoward
unusual
unvalued
unwholesome
unworthy
unwritten law
upkeep
uplands
uplifted
upset
  u. price
urban
  u. renewal
urbs

ure
usage
  u. of trade
usance
use and occupation
usee
useful
usefulness
user
usher
uso
usque
usual
usuarius
usucapio
usucaptio
usufruct
usufructuary
usufruit
usura
usurious
usurp
usurpatio
usurpation
usurped
  u. power
usurper
usury
utensil
uterque
utilidad
utilis
utility
utilization
utilize
uti possidetis
utlage
utlesse
utter
  u. barrister
utterance
uxor
uxoricide
uxorious

V

vacancy
vacantia bona
vacant succession

vacate
vacatio
vacation
vacatur
vacatura
vacillate
vacillation
vacuity
vacuous
vacuum
vacuus
vades
vadimonium
vadium
vagabond
vagrancy
vagrant
vale
valentia
valid
validate
validating
  v. statute
validation
validity
valuable
valuation
value
  v. judgment
  v. received
value-added tax
valued policy
valueless
valuer
vandal
vandalic
vandalism
vandalize
vara
variability
variable
variance
variant
variation
vassal
vassalage
vasseleria
vastum
vaudeville
vavasory
vavasour

vectigalia
vectura
vegetable
vehicle
vehicular
veies
veiling
vejours
vel non
veltraria
veltrarius
venal
venality
venaria
venatio
vend
vendee
vendetta
vendible
venditio
vendition
venditioni exponas
venditor
venditrix
vendor
  itinerant v.
vendor's lien
vendue
vengeance
vengeful
venia
venire
  v. facias
  v. facias ad respondendum
  v. facias de novo
venireman
vente
venter
venture
venue
veranda
veray
verba
verbal
verbalize
verbatim
verderer
verdict
  aider by v.
  compromise v.

verdict (*continued*)
  directed v.
  excessive v.
  perverse v.
  quotient v.
veredictum
verge
vergence
verger
verification
verified
verify
verily
verity
verna
vernacular
versari
versus
vert
vertex
vertical
  v. price fixing
verus
vesta
vested
  v. remainder
vestige
vestigial
vestigium
vesting order
vestry
  v. clerk
vestryman
vestura
vesture
veteran
veto
vex
vexari
vexata quaestio
vexation
vexatious
  v. suit
vexed question
via
viability
viable
viands
vicar
vicarage

vicarial
vicario
vicarious
   v. liability
vice
vice-chancellor
vice-president
viceroy
vice versa
vicinage
vicinetum
vicinity
vicious
vicontiel
victimize
victualler
victuals
victus
vidame
vide
   v. infra
   v. supra
videlicet
viduity
vie
vi et armis
view
viewer
vigil
vigilance
vigilant
vigilante
vigor
vill
village
villain
villein
villenage
villenous
   v. judgment
vinagium
vinculacion
vinculo
   v. matrimonii
vinculum
   v. juris
vindex
vindicare
vindicate
vindicatio

vindication
vindicatory
vindicta
vindictive
   v. damages
vinous
vintner
viol
violate
violation
violence
violent
violently
vir
vires
vires majores
virgata
virgate
virge
virtual
virtuous
vis
visa
vis á vis
viscount
visé
visible
via impressa
visitation
visitor
vis major
visne
vital
   v. statistics
vitality
vitiate
vitiation
vitiligate
vitricus
vivarium
vivary
viva voce
vocabula
   v. artis
vocation
vocational
   v. counseling
vociferatio
vociferous
voco

void
voidable
voidance
voir dire
voiture
volatile
volens
volitional
Volstead Act
volume
volumen
volumus
voluntarily
voluntary
voluntas
volunteer
voter
voting trust
votum
vouch
vouchee
voucher
vouching to warranty
vox emissa volat; litera
   scripta manet
voyage
voyeurism
vraic
vulgar

W

wabble
wacreour
wadia
wadset
waftor
wage earner
wager
wagering contract
wages
Wagner Act
wagonage
wagonway
waif
wainagium
waive
waiver
wakening

waleschery
Walsh-Healey Act
wampum
wantage
wanton
wapentake
war
   w. crime
   w. criminal
warabi
ward
   w. of the court
warda
warden
wardship
warcctarc
warehouse
warehouseman
warning
warp
warrant
   bench w.
   distress w.
   dock w.
   w. of attorney
warrantee
warrantor
warranty
   w. of fitness
   w. of land
   w. of merchantability
warren
wash sale
waste
   ameliorating w.
wastel
wasting property
wastrel
watchman
water
   w. bailiff
   w. course
   w. pollution
watered
   w. stock
watermark
watershed
waterway
waybill
way-going crop

wayleave

waynagium

waywarden

weald

wealth

weapon

weaponry

weathering

wed

wedlock

weighage

weight

weir

welfare

wellborn

wellhead

welsh

welsher

wend

werelada

wergild

werp-geld

whack

whale

whaler

wharf

wharfage

wharfing out

wharfinger

wheelage

wheeler

whelk

whelp

whereas

whereby

whereupon

wherever

while

whipping

whipping-post

whiskey

white

   w. acre

   w. rents

   w. slavery

wholesale

wholesaler

wholesome

wholly

wic

wica

widow

widower

widowhood

wife

Wild's case

will

   w. contest

   holographic w.

   nuncupative w.

   officious w.

willful

willingly

winding-up acts

windshake

windstorm

winze

witchcraft

withdraw

withdrawal

withdrawing a juror

withernam

withersake

withhold

without

   w. prejudice

   w. recourse

witness

   adverse w.

   attesting w.

   expert w.

   going w.

   hostile w.

   skilled w.

   subscribing w.

   swift w.

   zealous w.

witnessing part

wittingly

witword

wold

woodsrider

woodward

woodwork

woodworker

woolsack

words

   w. of limitation

workaway

workhorse

workhouse
working
  w. capital
workman
workmen's compensation
workshop
worldly
worship
worsted
wort
worth
worthier title
worthiest
worthless
worthy
wrath
wreck
wrecker
wreckfree
wrench
writ
  w. of admeasurement
  alternative w.
  w. of assistance
  w. of election
  w. of entry
  w. of error
  w. of inquiry
  judicial w.
  prerogative w.
  w. of prohibition
  resealing w.
  restamping w.
  w. of summons
  testatum w.
written contract
wrong
wrongdoer
wrongful
wrongfully
wye

X

xenodochy
xerographic
xerography
xylon

Y

yardland
yardman
yea
yearling
yen hock
yen pock
yen shee
yeoman
yeomanry
yeoven
yeven
yield
yielding
  y. and paying
yokelet

Z

zanja
zanjero
zealot
zealous
  z. witness
zeolite process
zetetick
zone
zoning
zonula
zygocephalum
zygostates
zythum

Legal Abbreviations

A

A — about
accepted
adversus
aged
amateur
anonymous
answer
ante
area
A. — Atlantic Reporter
A.2d — Atlantic Reporter, Second Series
AAA — Agricultural Adjustment Act
AAC — anno ante Christum (the year before Christ)
AACN — anno ante Christum natum (the year before the birth of Christ)
AB — able-bodied seaman
ABA — American Bar Association
A.B.A.J. — American Bar Association Journal
A.B.A.Rep. — American Bar Association Reports
Abb.App.Dec. — Abbott's Appeal Decisions (N.Y.)
Abb.N.Cas. — Abbott's New Cases (N.Y.)
Abb.Pr. — Abbott's Practice Reports (N.Y.)
Abb.Pr.(n.s.) — Abbott's Practice Reports, New Series (N.Y.)
Abp — archbishop
Abr — abridged
abridgment
AC — anno Christi (the year of Christ); Appeal Court, Chancery
A/C — account
Acad. Pol. Sci. Proc. — Academy of Political Science Proceedings
ACC — Agricultural Credit Corporation
Acct — account
A.D. — anno Domini (in the year of Our Lord)
Ad — administrative
Adams — Adams' Reports

Ad.&.E. — Adolphus & Ellis' Reports
Ad fin. — ad finem (at or near the end)
Adj — adjourned
adjudged
Adm — Admiralty
Adm'r — administrator
Admx — administratrix
ads — ad sectam (at the suit of)
AEC — Atomic Energy Commission
Afr. — Africa
AG — Attorney General
Agri.Dec. — Agriculture Decisions
Ag't — agent
AID — Agency for International Development
AJ — Associate Judge
Ala. — Alabama
Ala.App. — Alabama Appellate Court Reports
Alas. — Alaska
All E.R. — All England Law Reports
All India Crim. Dec. — All India Criminal Decisions
All India Rptr. — All India Reporter
All Pak. Leg. Dec. — All Pakistan Legal Decisions
Allen — Allen's Massachusetts Reports
A.L.R. — American Law Reports Annotated
A.L.R.2d — American Law Reports Annotated, Second Series
A.L.R.3d — American Law Reports Annotated, Third Series
Alt — Alter
Alta. — Alberta Law Reports
A.M. — ante meridiem (before noon)
Am. — amended
American
AMA — Agricultural Marketing Act
Am.Ann.Cas. — American Annotated Cases
Am.Bankr.R. — American Bankruptcy Reports
Am.Bankr.R.(n.s.) — American Bankruptcy Reports, New Series
Am.Bankr.Rev. — American Bankruptcy Review

A.M.C. — American Maritime Cases
Am.Dec. — American Decisons
Am.&Eng.Ann.Cas. — American and
English Annotated Cases
Ames — Ames' Reports (R.I.)
Am.Fed.Tax.R. — American Federal Tax
Reports
Am.Fed.Tax.R.2d — American Federal Tax
Reports, Second Series
Am.Hist.Rev. — American Historical
Review
Am.J.Comp.L. — American Journal of
Comparative Law
Am.J.Int'l.L. — American Journal of
International Law
Am.J.Legal Hist. — American Journal of
Legal History
Am.J.Pol. — American Journal of Politics
Am.J.Soc. — American Journal of Sociology
Am.L.Rev. — American Law Review
Am.Lab.Leg.Rev. — American Labor
Legislation Review
Am.R. — American Reports
Am.St.R. — American State Reports
And. — Andrew's Reports (Conn.).
Ann. — annotated
Ann.Tax Cas. — Annotated Tax Cases
(Eng., Scot.)
Annals — Annals of the American Academy
of Political and Social Science
Annot. — annotation
Anon — anonymous
Ans — answer
AOC — anno orbis conditi (the year of the
creation of the world)
APC — Alien Property Custodian
Ap.C. — Appeal Cases, Law Reports
APCN — anno post Christum natum (the
year after the birth of Christ)
App.Ct. — Appellate Court
App.D.C. — Appeals Cases, District of
Columbia
App.Div. — Appellate Division Reports,
N.Y. Supreme Court
App.Div.2d — Appellate Division Reports,
N.Y. Supreme Court, Second Series
APRC — anno post Romam conditam (the
year after the foundation of Rome)
AR — anno Regni (in the year of the reign)

Arb.J.(n.s.) — Arbitration Journal, New
Series
ARC — American Red Cross
arg. — arguendo
Argen. — Argentina
Ariz. — Arizona
Ark. — Arkansas
AS, A/S, *or* **A/s** — account sales
after sight
at sight
ASCS — Agricultural Stabilization and
Conservation Service
Ashm. — Ashmead's Pennsylvania Reports
Ass'n — association
Atty — Attorney
Atty Gen — Attorney General
ATU — Alcohol Tax Unit
Aus. — Austria
Austl. — Australia
Austl.Argus L.R. — Australian Argus Law
Reports
Auto.Cas. — Automobile Cases (CCH)
Auto.Cas.2d — Automobile Cases, Second
Series (CCH)
Av.Cas. — Aviation Cases (CCH)

B

B — bancus
bar
Baron
bench
Barb. — Barbour's Supreme Court Reports
(N.Y.)
Barb.Ch. — Barbour's Chancery Reports
(N.Y.)
BC — bail court
bankruptcy cases
B.C. — before Chirst
British Columbia
British Columbia Law Reports
B.C.Ind.&Com.L.Rev. — Boston College
Industrial and Commercial Law Review
BDSA — Business and Defense Services
Administration
BE — Baron of the Court of Exchequer
Belg. — Belgium

BF — bonum factum (a good or proper act, deed, or decree)

Binn. — Binney's Pennsylvania Reports

B.J. — Bar Journal

bkcy — bankruptcy

BL — Bachelor of Laws

Black — Black's United States Supreme Court Reports

BLS — Bureau of Labor Statistics

B.Mon. — B. Monroe's Kentucky Reports

Bol. — Bolivia

Boyce — Boyce Reports (Del.)

BR — Bancus Reginae (Queen's Bench) Bancus Regis (King's Bench)

B.R. — Bankruptcy Reports

Braz. — Brazil

BS — Bancus Superior (upper bench)

BTA — Board of Tax Appeals

B.T.A. — Board of Tax Appeals Reports

BTU — British thermal units

bus. — business

Bush — Bush (Ky.) Bush's Reports (Ky.)

Buxton — Buxton (N.C.) Buxton's Reports (N.C.)

C

C — cases
chancery
chapter
codex
common
court

CA — Court of Appeals

ca.sa. — capias ad satisfaciendum

CAA — Civil Aviation Administration

C.A.A. — Civil Aeronautics Authority Reports

CAB — Civil Aeronautics Board

C.A.B. — Civil Aeronautics Board Reports

Cai.Cas. — Caines' Cases (N.Y.)

Cai.R. — Caines' Reports (N.Y.)

Cal. — California

Cal.App. — California Appellate Reports

Cal.App.2d — California Appellate Reports, Second Series

Cal.Rptr. — California Reporter

Calcutta W.N. — Calcutta Weekly Notes

Calif.L.Rev. — California Law Review

Call — Call's Virginia Reports

Can. — Canada

Can.Crim. — Criminal Reports (Canada)

Can.Crim.Cas.Ann. — Canadian Criminal Cases Annotated

Can.Crim.Cas.(n.s.) — Canadian Criminal Cases, New Series

Can.Exch. — Canada Law Report Exchequer

Can.S.Ct. — Canada Law Reports Supreme Court

Can.Tax App.Bd. — Canada Tax Appeal Board Cases

Can.Tax Cas.Ann. — Canada Tax Cases Annotated

cas — cases
casualty

CaseW.Res.L.Rev. — Case Western Reserve Law Review

CAV — curia advisari vult (the court will be advised, will consider, will deliberate)

CB — Chief Baron of the Exchequer Common Bench

CC — cepi corpus (I have taken his body)
chancery cases
Chief Commissioner
Circuit Court
City Court
civil cases
civil code
County Court
criminal cases
Crown cases

CCA — Circuit Court of Appeals
County Court of Appeals

CCC — Civilian Conservation Corps
Commodity Credit Corporation

CCH — Commerce Clearing House

CCH Lab.Cas. — Labor Cases

CCH Tax Ct.Mem. — Tax Court Memorandum Decisions

CCP — Code of Civil Procedure
Court of Common Pleas

CCPA — Court of Customs and Patent Appeals

CCR — Crown Cases Reserved

cent. — central

Cent.L.J. — Central Law journal

cf — compare
    confer
C & F — cost and freight
CFI — cost, freight, and insurance
CFR — code of federal regulations
CH — Chancellor
    chancery
    chapter
    chief
chap. — chapter
chem. — chemical
Chi.-Kent L.Rev. — Chicago-Kent Law
    Review
CIA — Central Intelligence Agency
Cir Ct — Circuit Court
civ app — civil appeals
CJ — Chief Justice
    Circuit Judge
    corpus juris
CJB — Chief Judge in Bankruptcy
CJS — corpus juris secundum
CL — civil law
Clev.-Mar.L.Rev. — Cleveland-Marshall
    Law Review
CLP — Common Law Procedure
CMA — Court of Military Appeals
C.M.R. — Court-Martial Reports
c/o — care of
COD — collect on delivery
Cold. — Coldwell's Reports (Tenn.)
Cole.Cas. — Coleman's Cases (N.Y.)
Cole.&Cai.Cas. — Coleman & Caines'
    Cases (N.Y.)
Colo. — Colorado
Colo.App. — Colorado Court of Appeals
    Reports
Colom. — Colombia
Colum.J.Transnat'l.L. — Columbia Journal
    of Transnational Law
Colum.L.Rev. — Columbia Law Review
com — commentaries
    Commissioner
    common
    company
Com.Cas. — Commercial Cases (Eng.)
Com.L.J. — Commercial Law Journal
comm — committee
comm'n — commission
Comm'r — Commissioner
Commw.L.R. — Commonwealth Law
    Reports (Austl.)

Comst. — Comstock's Reports (N.Y.)
Cong. — Congress
Cong.Dig. — Congressional Digest
Conn. — Connecticut
Conn.Supp. — Connecticut Supplement
consol — consolidated
const — constitution
constr — construction
Cornell L.Rev. — Cornell Law Review
corp — corporation
Cow. — Cowen's New York Reports
Cox Crim.Cas. — Cox's Criminal Cases
    (Eng.)
CP — Common Pleas
CPA — Certified Public Accountant
CPSC — Consumer Product Safety
    Commission
CR — Curia Regis
C.R. — Chancery Reports
Cranch — Cranch (U.S. and D.C.)
CRC — Civil Rights Commission
crim — criminal
Crim.App. — Criminal Appeal Reports
    (Eng.)
crimcon — criminal conversation
Crim.L.Rev. — Criminal Law Review
CSC — Civil Service Commission
Ct. Cl. — Court of Claims
Ct.Cust.App. — Court of Customs Appeals
    Reports
Ct. Mil. App. — Court of Military Appeals
CTA — cum testamento annexo (with the
    will annexed)
cur — curia
Current Medicine — Current Medicine for
    Attorneys
Cush. — Cushing's Massachusetts Reports
Cust.Ct. — Customs Court Reports
cwt — a hundred-weight; one hundred and
    twelve pounds
C.Z. — Canal Zone
Czech. — Czechoslovakia

D

D — day
    dialogue
    dictum
    digest

D—(*continued*)
  digesta
  digestum
  district
  division
  Doctor
Dak. — Dakota Territorial Reports
Dall. — Dallas (U.S. and Pa.) Reports
Daly — Daly (N.Y.) Common Pleas Reports
DB — day book
  Doomsday Book
  double biased
DBA — doing business as
DBE — de bene esse (conditonally; provisionally)
DBN — de bonis non (of the goods not [administered])
DC — District Court
  District of Columbia
DEA — Drug Enforcement Administration
Dec.Com.Pat. — Commissioner of Patents Decisions
Del. — Delaware
Del.Ch. — Delaware Chancery
Dem. — Demerest's Surrogates Reports (N.Y.)
dem — demise
Den. — Denmark
Denio — Denio's New York Reports
dep — department
  deputy
dep't — department
Dep't.State Bull. — Department of State Bulletin
Dick.L.Rev. — Dickinson Law Review
di et fi — dilecto et fideli (to his beloved and faithful)
dist — district
distrib — distributing
  distributor
div — division
DJ — District Judge
D.L.R. — Dominion Law Reports (Can.)
D.L.R.2d — Dominion Law Reports, Second Series (Can.)
DMC — Defense Manpower Commission
do — ditto (the same)
DOD — Department of Defense
Dom. Proc. — Domus Procerum (the House of Lords)
Dom. Rep. — Dominican Republic

DOT — Department of Transportation
DP — Domus Procerum (the House of Lords)
D.P.R. — Decisiones de Puerto Rico
Dr. — doctor
dr. — debit
  debtor
DS — Deputy Sheriff
DSB — debitum sine brevi (debt without writ)
DSM-II — Diagnostic and Statistical Manual of Mental Disorders, Second Edition
Duv. — Duvall's Kentucky Reports
DWI — died without issue

E

E — east
  Easter
  ecclesiastical
  equity
  exchequer
E. — Edward
  East's Reports
  English
E.Afr.L.R. — East Africa Law Reports
ecc — ecclesiastical
econ — economic
  economics
  economy
ed — edition
  editor
educ — education
  educational
EEOC — Equal Employment Opportunity Commission
e.g. — exempli gratia (for the sake of example)
El.Sal. — El Salvador
elec — electric
  electrical
  electricity
Em Ct App — Emergency Court of Appeals
Eng. — England
  English
Eng.Rep. — English Reports, Full Reprint
eng'r — engineer
  eingineering
EOE — errors and omissions excepted
EPA — Environmental Protection Administration

equip. — equipment
er — error
ERDA — Energy Research Development
Administration
Esq — Esquire
et al. —et alii (and others)
etc. — et cetera (and others; and other things;
and so forth)
et seq. — et sequens (and the following one)
et sequentes (and those that follow)
et ux — and wife
et uxor — and wife
et vir — and husband
ex rel. — ex relatione (at the instance of; on
behalf of)
exch — exchange
exr — executor
exrx — executrix
ex'x — executrix

F

F. — Federal Reporter
F.2d — Federal Reporter, Second Series
F.Cas. — Federal Cases
F.Supp. — Federal Supplement
FAA — Federal Aviation Administration
free of all average
FAS — free alongside ship
FBI — Federal Bureau of Investigation
FCA — Farm Credit Administration
F.C.A. — Federal Code Annotated
FCC — Federal Communications
Commission
F.C.C. — Federal Communications
Commission Reports
FCSC — Foreign Claims Settlement
Commission
FDA — Food and Drug Administration
FDIC — Federal Deposit Insurance
Corporation
FEA — Federal Energy Administration
Fed. — Federal Reporter
Fed.Cas. — Federal Cases
Fed.Com.B.J. — Federal Communication
Bar Journal
Fed'n — federation
FGA — foreign general average
free from general average

FHA — Federal Highway Administration
Federal Housing Administration
FHLBB — Federal Home Loan Bank Board
fi. fa. — fieri facias (order to be done)
FIC — Federal Information Center
Fin. — Finland
fin. — finance
FJ — First Judge
Fla. — Florida
Fla.Supp. — Florida Supplement
FMC — Federal Maritime Commission
FMCS — Federal Meditation and
Conciliation Service
FNMA — Federal National Mortgage
Association
FOB — free on board
Food Drug Cosm.L.J. — Food Drug
Cosmetic Law Journal
FPA — free from particular average
FPC — Federal Power Commission
F.P.C. — Federal Power Commission
Reports
Fr. — France
fr. — fragmentum (a fragment)
F.R.D. — Federal Rules Decisions
FRS — Federal Reserve System
FSS — Federal Supply Service
FTC — Federal Trade Commission
F.T.C. — Federal Trade Commission
Decisions
FTS — Federal Telecommunication System

G

Ga. — Georgia
Ga.App. — Georgia Appeals Reports
GAO — General Accounting Office
Gaz.L.R. — Gazette Law Reports (N.Z.)
gen — general
Geo.L.J. — Georgetown Law Journal
Geo.Wash.L.Rev. — George Washington
Law Review
Ger. — Germany
Gilm — Gilman's Reports (Ill.)
Gilmer's Reports (Va.)
Gov — Governor
gov't — government
GPO — Government Printing Office
Gr.Brit. — Great Britain

Gratt. — Grattan's Virginia Reports
Gray — Gray's Massachusetts Reports
Greene — Greene's Iowa Reports
GSA — General Services Administration
guar — guaranty
Guat. — Guatemala

H

H — House
H. — Henry
  Hilary
  Howard's U.S. Supreme Court Reports
HA — hoc anno (this year; in this year)
Harr. — Harrington's Reports (Del.)
Harv.Bus.Rev. — Harvard Business Review
Harv.Civ.Rights-Civ.Lib.L.Rev. — Harvard Civil Rights-Civil Liberties Law Review
Harv.Int'l.L.J. — Harvard International Law Journal
Harv.J.Legis. — Harvard Journal on Legislation
Harv.L.Rev. — Harvard Law Review
Hay. — Haywood's Tennessee Reports
HB — house bill
HC — habeas corpus
  House of Commons
Heisk. — Heiskell's Tennessee Reports
Hemp. — Hempstead's Circuit Court Reports (Ark. Terr.)
Hen.&M. — Hening and Munford (Va.) Reports
HEW — Health, Education and Welfare, Dept. of
HHFA — Housing and Home Finance Agency
Hill — Hill's New York Reports
HL — House of Lords
HOLC — Home Owners Loan Corporation
Hond. — Honduras
hosp — hospital
Houst. — Houston's Delaware Reports
How. — Howard's U.S. Supreme Court Reports
How.L.J. — Howard Law Journal
How.Pr. — Howard's Practice (N.Y.)
How.St.Tr. — Howell's English State Trials
HR — House of Representatives
HT — hoc titulo (this title; under this title)

HUD — Housing and Urban Development, Dept. of
Humph. — Humphrey's Tennessee Reports
Hun — Hun's New York Reports
Hung. — Hungary
HV — hac voce (by this voice)
  hoc verbo (by this word)

I

i-ctus — jurisconsultus (one learned in the law)
I.&N.Dec. — Immigration and Nationality Decisions
ib — ibidem (in the same place, volume, or case)
ibid — ibidem (in the same place, volume, or case)
ICC — Indian Claims Commission
  Interstate Commerce Commission
I.C.C. — Interstate Commerce Commission Reports
ICC Prac.J. — ICC Practitioners' Journal
id. — idem (the same)
i.e. — id est (that is; that is to say)
Ill. — Illinois
Ill.App. — Illinois Appellate Court Reports
Ill.App.2d — Illinois Appellate Court Reports, Second Series
Ill.Cir.Ct. — Illinois Circuit Court Reports
Ill.Ct.Cl. — Illinois Court of Claims Reports
Inc. — incorporated
Ind. — Indiana
Ind.App. — Indiana Appellate Court Reports
Ind.&Lab.Rel.Rev. — Industrial and Labor Relations Review
indem — indemnity
India Crim.L.J.R. — Criminal Law Journal Reports (India)
India S.Ct. — India Supreme Court Reports
Indian Cas. — Indian Cases
Indian L.R. Allahabad Series — Indian Law Reports, Allahabad Series
Indian R. — Indian Rulings
Indian Terr. — Indian Territory Reports
indus — industrial
  industries
  industry
ins — insurance

INS — Immigration and Naturalization
Service
Interior Dec. — Interior Department
Decisions
Int'l — International
Int'l.Aff. — International Affairs
inv — investment
Ir. — Ireland
Irish
Ir.Jur. — Irish Jurist Reports
Ir.L.T.R. — Irish Law Times Reports
IRS — Internal Revenue Service
ITC — International Trade Commission

J

J — journal
Judge
Justice
J.Air L.&Com. — Journal of Air Law and
Commerce
J.Am.Jud.Soc'y. — Journal of American
Judicature Society
J.Comp.Leg.&Int'l.L. — Journal of
Comparative Legislation and International
Law
J.Crim.L.C.&P.S. — Journal of Criminal
Law, Criminology and Police Science
J.For.Sci. — Journal of Forensic Sciences
J.Land&P.U.Econ. — Journal of Land &
Public Utility Economics
J.Law&Econ. — Journal of Law &
Economics
J.Legal Ed. — Journal of Legal Education
J.Pat.Off.Soc'y. — Journal of Patent Office
Society
JA — Judge Advocate
Jac — Jacobus
JAG — Judge Advocate General
JAGJ. — JAG Journal
JCP — Justice of the Common Pleas
JCS — Joint Chiefs of Staff
JJ — judges or justices
Junior Judge
JKB — Justice of the King's Bench
Johns. — Johnson's Reports (N.Y.)
Johns.Cas. — Johnson's Cases (N.Y.)
Johns.Ch. — Johnson's Chancery Reports
(N.Y.)

JP — Justice of the Peace
JQB — Justice of the Queen's Bench
Jr. — junior
JUB — Justice of the Upper Bench
Just.Cas. — Justiciary Cases (Scot.)
Juv.Ct. — Juvenile Court

K

K — King
Kan. — Kansas
KB — King's Bench
KC — King's Counsel
Kenya L.R. — Kenya Law Reports
Kern. — Kernan's Reports (N.Y.)
KRC — Kentucky Revised Statutes
Ky. — Kentucky
Ky.L.Rptr. — Kentucky Law Reporter

L

L. — law
liber (a book)
Lord
L ct — law court
L div — law division
L.Ed. — Lawyers' Edition, U.S. Supreme
Court Reports
L.Ed.2d — Lawyers' Edition, U.S. Supreme
Court Reports, Second Series
La. — Louisiana
La.Ann. — Louisiana Annual Reports
La.App. — Louisiana Courts of Appeals
Reports
Lab. — Labrador
Lab.L.J. — Labor Law Journal
Lans. — Lansing's New York Supreme Court
Reports
Law & Contemp.Prob. — Law and
Contemporary Problems
Lawyer & Banker — Lawyer and Banker
and Central Law Journal
LC — leading cases
Lord Chancellor
lower Canada
Ld — Lord
LEAA — Law Enforcement Assistance
Administration

Leigh — Leigh's Virginia Reports
LJ — law journal
law judge
L.J.K.B.(n.s.) — Law Journal Reports, King's Bench, New Series
LL — law Latin
LL.B. — Bachelor of Laws
LL.D. — Doctor of Laws
LL.M. — Master of Laws
Lloyd's List L.R. — Lloyd's List Law Reports (Eng.)
Local Gov't. — Local Government and Magisterial Reports
L.R. — law reports
L.R.A. — Lawyers Reports Annotated
L.R.A.(n.s.) — Lawyers Reports Annotated, New Series
L.R.Adm.&Eccl. — Admiralty and Ecclesiastical Cases
L.R. Indian App. — Law Reports, Indian Appeals
L.R.Ir. — Law Reports, Ireland
L.R.R.M. — Labor Relations Reference Manual
LS — locus sigilli (the place of the seal)
Ltd. — limited
L.T.R.(n.s.) — Law Times Reports, New Series

M

MacArth. — MacArthur's District of Columbia Reports
MacArth.&M. — MacArthur and Mackey Reports (D.C.)
mach — machine
machinery
Mackey — Mackey's Reports (D.C.)
Mag.Cas. — Magisterial Cases (Eng.)
Man. — Manitoba
Manitoba Law Reports
Mann.Unrep.Cas. — Manning's Unreported Cases (La.)
mar. — marine
maritime
Mar.L.Cas.(n.s.) — Maritime Cases, New Series (Eng., Scot., Ire.)
Mar.Prov. — Maritime Provinces Reports (Can.)

Marq.L.Rev. — Marquette Law Review
Marv. — Marvel's Reports (Del.)
Mass. — Massachusetts
Mass.App.Dec. — Massachusetts Appellate Decisions
Mass.App.Div. — Massachusetts Appellate Division Reports
MC — magistrates' cases
Master Commissioner
member of Congress
Municipal Court
M.C.C. — Motor Carrier Cases
McCahon — McCahon's Reports (Kan.)
MD — middle district
Md. — Maryland
M.D. — Doctor of Medicine
Me. — Maine
Med.Trial.Tech.Q. — Medical Trial Technique Quarterly
mem — memoranda
memorandum
Met. — Metcalf's Kentucky Reports
Metcalf's Massachusetts Reports
Mex. — Mexico
mfg — manufacturing
mfr — manufacturer
Mich. — Michigan
Mills — Mills Surrogate (N.Y.)
Minn. — Minnesota
Misc. — New York Miscellaneous Reports
Misc.2d — New York Miscellaneous Reports, Second Series
Miss. — Mississippi
mkt — market
Mo. — Missouri
Mo.App. — Missouri Appeal Reports
Mont. — Montana
MP — member of Parliament
MR — Master of the Rolls
Munf. — Munford's Virginia Reports

N

N.A. — North America
n.a. — non allocatur (it is not allowed)
NACCA L.J. — NACCA Law Journal
narr — narratio (narrative)
NARTU — Naval Air Reserve Training Unit
NASA — National Aeronautics and Space Administration

N.B. — New Brunswick
New Brunswick Reports
n.b. — nota bene (mark well; observe)
nulla bona (no goods)
NBS — National Bureau of Standards
N.C. — North Carolina
n.c.d. — nemine contra dicente (no one
dissenting)
NCPC — National Capital Planning
Commission
ND — northern district
N.D. — North Dakota
N.E. — North Eastern Reporter
N.E.2d — North Eastern Reporter, Second
Series
Neb. — Nebraska
Negl.Cas. — Negligence Cases
Negl.Cas.2d — Negligence Cases, Second
Series
n.e.i. — non est inventus (he is not found)
Neth. — Netherlands
Nev. — Nevada
Newf. — Newfoundland
Newf.S.Ct. — Newfoundland Supreme Court
Decisions
N.H. — New Hampshire
NHTSA — National Highway Traffic Safety
Administration
Nicar. — Nicaragua
Nigeria L.R. — Nigeria Law Reports
NIH — National Institutes of Health
N.Ir.L.R. — Northern Ireland Law Report
N.J. — New Jersey
New Jersey Reports
N.J.Eq. — New Jersey Equity
N.J.L. — New Jersey Law Reports
N.J.Misc. — New Jersey Miscellaneous
N.J.Super. — New Jersey Superior Court
Reports
n.l. — non liquet (it is not clear)
NLRB — National Laobr Relations Board
N.L.R.B. — National Labor Relations Board
Decisions
N.M. — New Mexico
NMB — National Mediation Board
NOAA — National Oceanic and Atmospheric
Administration
NODC — National Oceanographic Data
Center

NOL — Naval Ordnance Laboratory
nol pros — nolle prosequi (to be unwilling to
proceed further with the matter)
non pros — non prosequitur (he will not
prosecute)
non seq — non sequitur (it does not follow)
Nor. — Norway
n.o.v. — non obstante veredicto (not
withstanding the verdict)
NP — Notary Public
n.p. — nisi prius (unless before)
N.R. — new reports
nonresident
not reported
NRC — Nuclear Regulatory Commission
NRL — Naval Research Laboratory
N.S. — new style
Nova Scotia
n.s. — new series
NSA — National Security Agency
NSF — National Science Foundation
NSVP — National Student Volunteer
Program
N.S.W. — New South Wales State Reports
NTSB — National Transportation Safety
Board
N.W. — North Western Reporter
N.W.2d — North Western Reporter, Second
Series
Nw.Terr. — Northwest Territory
Nw.U.L.Rev. — Northwestern University
Law Review
N.Y. — New York
N.Y.Civ. Proc. — New York Civil
Procedure
N.Y.Civ.Proc.(n.s.) — New York Civil
Procedure, New Series
N.Y.Crim. — New York Criminal Reports
N.Y.Dep't.R. — New York Department
Reports
N.Y.S. — New York Supplement
N.Y.S.2d — New York Supplement, Second
Series
N.Y.U.7th Inst. on Fed. Tax. — New York
University Institute on Federal Taxation
N.Y.U.Intra.L.Rev. — New York
University Intramural Law Review
N.Z. — New Zealand
N.Z.L.R. — New Zealand Law Reports

O

OAG — Opinions of the Attorney General
OC — Orphans' Court
OEO — Office of Economic Opportunity
Ohio — Ohio Reports
Ohio App. — Ohio Appellate Reports
Ohio C.C.R. — Ohio Circuit Court Reports
Ohio C.C.R.(n.s.) — Ohio Circuit Court Reports, New Series
Ohio C.Dec. — Ohio Circuit Decisions
Ohio Ct.App. — Ohio Court of Appeals Reports
Ohio Dec. — Ohio Decisions
Ohio Dec.Reprint — Ohio Decisions Reprint
Ohio L.Abs. — Ohio Law Abstract
Ohio N.P. — Ohio Nisi Prius Reports
Ohio N.P.(n.s.) — Ohio Nisi Prius Reports, New Series
Ohio Op. — Ohio Opinions
Ohio Op.2d — Ohio Opinions, Second Series
Ohio St. — Ohio State Reports
Ohio St.2d — Ohio State Reports, Second Series
Okla. — Oklahoma
Okla.Crim. — Oklahoma Criminal Reports
OMB — Office of Management and Budget
ONB — Old Natura Brevium
Ont. — Ontario
Ontario Reports
Ont.L.R. — Ontario Law Reports
Ont.W.N. — Ontario Weekly Notes
Ore. — Oregon
O.S. — old style
o.s. — old series
OSHRC — Occupational Safety & Health Review Commission

P

P. — Pacific Reporter
P.2d — Pacific Reporter, Second Series
Pa. — Pennsylvania
Pennsylvania State Reports
Pa.County Ct. — Pennsylvania County Court Reports

Pa.D.&C. — Pennsylvania District and County Reports
Pa.D.&C.2nd — Pennsylvania District and County Reports, Second Series
Pa.Dist. — Pennsylvania District Reports
Pa.Super. — Pennsylvania Superior Court Reports
Pan. — Panama
Para. — Paraguay
Pat.&T.M.Rev. — Patent and Trade Mark Review
P.C. — Parliamentary Cases
Patent Cases
Penal Code
Pleas of the Crown
Political Code
Practice Cases
Privy Council
Penn.&W. — Penrose and Watts (Pa.) Reports
Penne. — Pennewill's Delaware Reports
per proc. — per procurationem (by proxy; by letter of attorney)
Pet. — Peters' U.S. Supreme Court Reports
P-H Am.Lab.Arb.Awards — American Labor Arbitration Awards
P-H Am.Lab.Cas. — American Labor Cases
P-H Tax Ct.Mem. — Tax Court Memorandum Decisions
PHA — Public Housing Administration
Phil. — Philippines
PHS — Public Health Service
PHV — pro hac vice (for this turn; for this purpose)
Pick. — Pickering's Massachusetts Reports
Pin. — Pinney's Wisconsin Reports
P.J. — Presiding Judge
Presiding Justice
P.L. — pamphlet laws
public laws
Pl. — placita (pleas)
P.M. — Postmaster
post meridiem (afternoon)
PO — post office
public officer
Pol. — Poland
Port. — Portugal
Portia L.J. — Portia Law Journal
Pp — pages

pp — per procurationem (by letter of attorney; by proxy)
propria persona (in his proper person; in his own person)
PPI — policy proof of interest
P.R. — Puerto Rico
Prac.Law. — Practical Lawyer
P.R.F. — Puerto Rico Federal Reports
pro tem — pro tempore (for the time being)
prod. — product
production
prox. — proximo (the coming month)
P.R.R. — Puerto Rico Reports
PS — postscript
Public Statutes
PSIA — pounds per square inch absolute
Pub. — public
pub.doc. —* public documents
Publ.Util.Fort. — Public Utilities Fortnightly
P.U.R. — Public Utilities Reports Annotated
P.U.R.(n.s.) — Public Utilities Reports, New Series
P.U.R.3d — Public Utilities Reports, Third Series

Q

Q. — quaere (question; query)
quarterly
Quebec
Queen
question
QB — Queen's Bench
QBD — Queen's Bench Division
QC — Queen's Counsel
q.c.f. — quare clausum fregit (unlawful entry on land)
q.d. — quasi dicat (as if he should say)
q.e.n. — quare executionem non (wherefore execution [should] not [be issued])
QS — Quarter Sessions
q.t. — qui tam (who as well)
Que. — Quebec
Que.L.R. — Quebec Law Reports
Queensl. — Queensland Reports
q.v. — quod vide (which see)

R

R — range
regina (queen)
rex (king)
R&D — research and development
Race Rel.L.Rep. — Race Relations Law Reporter
Rand. — Randolph's Virginia Reports
Rawle — Rawle's Pennsylvania Reports
Rd. — road
re.fa.lo. — recordari facias loquelam (cause the plaint to be recorded)
REA — Rural Electrification Administration
Record of N.Y.C.B.A. — Record of the Association of the Bar of the City of New York
Ref — referee
refining
Ref.J. — Referees' Journal; Journal of National Association of Referees in Bankruptcy
reg. gen. — regula generalis (a general rule)
reg. jud. — registrum judiciale (the register of judicial writs)
reg. lib. — registrarii liber (the register's book in chancery)
reg. orig. — registrum originale (the register of original writs)
reg. pl. — regula placitandi (rule of pleading)
Rep. — reporter
reports
Rev — review
revised
Rev.R. — Revised Reports (Eng.)
RG — regula generalis (a general rule)
R.I. — Rhode Island
R.L. — revised laws
Roman law
RLA — Redevelopment Land Agency
Rob. — Robinson's Virginia Reports
Rocky Mt.L.Rev. — Rocky Mountain Law Review (*now* University of Colorado Law Review)
Rom. — Roman
Romania
Rome

R.S. — Revised Statutes
RSVP — Retired Senior Volunteer Program
Ry — railway

S

S — section
  series
  south
  southern
  statute
S.&M. — Smedes and Marshall (Miss.)
  Reports
S.&R. — Sergeant and Rawle (Pa.) Reports
S.Afr.L.R. — South African Law Reports
S.Austl. — South Australia State Reports
S.Austl.L.R. — South Australia Law Reports
S.Cal.L.Rev. — Southern California Law
  Review
S.Tex.L.J. — South Texas Law Journal
Sask. — Saskatchewan
  Saskatchewan Law Reports
SB — senate bill
SBA — Small Business Administration
SC — same case
  scilicet (that is to say)
  Scotch
  select cases
  South Carolina
  Supreme Court
sci. — science
sci.fa. — scire facias (cause to know)
SCORE — Service Corps of Retired
  Executives
Scot. — Scotland
Scots L.T.R. — Scots Law Times Reports
SCS — Soil Conservation Service
S.Ct. — Supreme Court Reporter
SD — Southern district
S.D. — South Dakota
S/D B/L — sight draft, bill of lading attached
S.E. — South Eastern Reporter
S.E.2d — South Eastern Reporter, Second
  Series
SEC — Securities and Exchange Commission
S.E.C. — Securities and Exchange
  Commission Decisions and Reports

Seld. — Selden's Reports (N.Y.)
sem. — semble (it seems)
Sen — senate
  Senator
seq. — sequitur (it follows)
serv. — service
Sess.Cas. — Scottish Court of Session Cases
SFS — sine fraude sua (without fraud on his
  part)
SL — session laws
  statute laws
Sneed — Sneed's Tennessee Reports
So. — Southern Reporter
So.2d — Southern Reporter, Second Series
soc'y. — society
sol. — solicitor
SP — same point
  same principle
  sine prole (without issue)
SSA — Social Security Administration
SSS — Selective Service System
St. — state
  street
Stan.L.Rev. — Stanford Law Review
State Gov't. — State Government
Storey — Storey (Del.) Reports
Sup. Ct. — Supreme Court
Sup.Jud.Ct. — Supreme Judicial Court
Super.Ct. — Superior Court
Sur. — surety
Sur. Ct. — Surrogates' Court
S.W. — South Western Reporter
S.W.2d — South Western Reporter, Second
  Series
Swed. — Sweden
Switz. — Switzerland
Sw.L.J. — Southwestern Law Journal
sys. — system

T

T — tempore (in the time of)
  term
  territory
  title
  trinity
Tasm. — Tasmanian State Reports

Tasm.L.R. — Tasmanian Law Reports
TaxCas. — Tax Cases (Eng.)
Tax.R. — Taxation Reports (Eng.)
T.B.Mon. — T.B. Monroe's Kentucky
Reports
TC — Tax Court
T.C. — Tax Court of the United States
Reports
T.D. — Treasury Decisions
Tel — telegraph
telephone
Temp.L.Q. — Temple Law Quarterly
Ten.App. — Tennessee Appeals Reports
Tenn. — Tennessee
Tenn.Ch. — Tennessee Chancery Reports
Tex. — Texas
Tex.Civ.App. — Texas Civil Appeals
Reports
Tex.Crim. — Texas Criminal Reports
Tex.Ct.App.Dec.Civ. — Texas Court of
Appeals Decisions, Civil Cases
Tex.Ct.App.R. — Texas Court of Appeals
Reports
Texas L.Rev. — Texas Law Review
T.L.R. — Times Law Reports (Eng.)
Trade Cas. — Trade Cases
Trademark Bull. — Trademark Bulletin
Trademark Bull.(n.s.) — Bulletin of U.S.
Trademark Association, New Series
Tul.L.Rev. — Tulane Law Review
Tur. — Turkey
TVA — Tennessee Valley Authority

U

U. — university
U.Chi.L.Rev. — University of Chicago Law
Review
U.Cin.L.Rev. — University of Cincinnati
Law Review
U.Det.L.J. — University of Detroit Law
Journal
U.K. — United Kingdom
U.Mo.Bull.L.Ser. — University of Missouri
Bulletin Law Series
U.Pitt.L.Rev. — University of Pittsburgh
Law Review
UB — Upper Bench

UC — Upper Canada
UCC — Uniform Commercial Code
UCCC — Uniform Consumer Credit Code
U.C.L.A.Intra.L.Rev. — U.C.L.A.
Intramural Law Review
UCMJ — Uniform Code of Military Justice
ult. — ultimo (last month)
UN — United Nations
Univ — University
u.r. — uti rogas (be it as you desire)
Uru. — Uruguay
U.S. — United States
United States Supreme Court Reports
U.S.&Can.Av. — United States and
Canadian Aviation Reports
USAF — United States Air Force
U.S.Av. — United States Aviation Reports
USC — United States Code
USCA — United States Code Annotated
United States Court of Appeals
USCC — United States Circuit Court
USCCA — United States Circuit Court of
Appeals
USCG — United States Coast Guard
U.S.C.M.A. — United States Court of
Military Appeals Reports
USDA — United States Department of
Agriculture
USDC — United States District Court
USDJ — United States Department of Justice
USES — United States Employment Service
USFS — United States Forest Service
USGS — United States Geological Survey
USIA — United States Information Agency
USMC — United States Marine Corps
USNA — United States Naval Academy
USPHS — United States Public Health
Service
USPS — United States Postal Service
U.S.P.Q. — United States Patent Quarterly
U.S.R.S. — United States Revised Statutes
U.S.S.R. — Union of Soviet Socialist
Republics
U.S.Tax Cas. — United States Tax Cases
Utah — Utah Supreme Court Reports
Utah L.Rev. — Utah Law Review
util. — utilities
utility
ux. — wife

V

V. — verb
versus
Victoria
vide (see)
volume
VA — Veterans Administration
Va. — Virginia
Va.Cas. — Virginia Cases (Criminal)
Va.L.Reg.(n.s.) — Virginia Law Register, New Series
Vand.L.Rev. — Vanderbilt Law Review
VC — Vice-Chancellor
VCC — Vice-Chancellor's Court
v.e. — venditioni exponas (you expose to sale)
Venez. — Venezuela
v.g. — verbi gratia (for the sake of example)
V.I. — Virgin Islands
Vict. — Victorian Reports
Vict.L.R. — Victorian Law Reports
vid. — videlicet (to wit; namely)
Vill.L.Rev. — Villanova Law Review
VISTA — Volunteers in Service to America
viz. — videlicet (to wit; namely; you may see)
VOA — Voice of America
VP — Vice President
vs. — versus
Vt. — Vermont

W

W — west
western
W.&S. — Watts and Sargeant (Pa.) Reports
W.Austl.L.R. — Western Australian Law Reports
W.Va. — West Virginia
Wage & Hour Cas. — Wage and Hour Cases
Wall. — Wallace's U.S. Supreme Court Reports
Wash. — Washington
Wash. & Lee L.Rev. — Washington and Lee Law Review

Wash.Terr. — Washington Territory Reports
Watts — Watts' Pennsylvania Reports
W.D. — western district
Wend. — Wendell's New York Reports
West.Austl. — Western Australian Reports
Whart. — Wharton's Pennsylvania Reports
Wheat. — Wheaton's U.S. Supreme Court Reports
Wis. — Wisconsin
W.L.R. — Weekly Law Reports (Eng.)
Wm. & Mary L.Rev. — William and Mary Law Review
W.N. — Weekly Notes (Eng.)
WRC — Water Resources Council
W.W.R. — Western Weekly Reports (Can.)
W.W.R.(n.s.) — Western Weekly Reports, New Series (Can.)
Wyo. — Wyoming

Y

Yale L.J. — Yale Law Journal
Yeates — Yeates' Pennsylvania Reports
Yugo. — Yugoslavia

Z

Zab. — Zabriskie's New Jersey Reports
Zane — Zane's Reports (Utah)

Part 2

Business Vocabulary

Advertising

A

AA — author's alterations
aa — average audience
AAA — American Academy of Advertising
AAAA — American Association of
Advertising Agencies
AAF — American Advertising Federation
AAIE — American Association of Industrial
Editors
AANR — American Association of
Newspaper Representatives
AAW — Advertising Association of the West
ABC — American Broadcasting Company
ABC — Audit Bureau of Circulations
above-the-line cost
ABP — American Business Press
ABP — Associated Business Publications
a-b split
abstraction
Academy leader
ACB — Advertising Checking Bureau
account executive
accumulated —
a. audience
a. households
accuracy
acetate
acetate sleeve
acid bath
Acme punched
across-the-board
ad — advertisement
AD —
art director
assistant director
associate director
Ad Council — Advertising Council
addressograph plate
ADI — Area of Dominant Influence
ADI Rating — Area of Dominant Influence
Rating
adjacency — a broadcast following or
preceding another on the same station

ad-lib
adnorms
ADP — automatic data processing
advance proof
advertisement
advertiser's copies
advertising —
a. agency
a. allowance
classified a.
a. content
corporate image a.
corrective a.
a. costs
a. linage
a. network
a. pages
a. readership
a. specialty
a. spiral
a. weight
Advertising Association of the West
Advertising Checking Bureau
Advertising Council
Advertising Federation of America
Advertising Hall of Fame
Advertising Register
Advertising Research Foundation
AFA — Advertising Federation of America
affidavit
affiliate
AFM — American Federation of Musicians
AFTRA — American Federation of
Television and Radio Artists
agate
agate line
agency —
a. charges
a. commission
modular a.
a. network
a. of record
a. recognition
Agency List
agent

Agricultural Publishers Association
AIA — Association of Industrial Advertisers
aided recall interview
air —
  a. check
  a. time
airbrushing
à la carte agency
algorithm
all caps — all capital letters
allocation
allotment
alphameric
alphanumeric — alphabetic-numeric
alternate sponsorship
AM — amplitude modulation
AMA — American Marketing Association
American Advertising Federation
American Association of Advertising
  Agencies
American Association of Industrial Editors
American Association of Newspaper
  Representatives
American Broadcasting Company
American Business Press, Inc.
American Federation of Musicians
American Federation of Television and
  Radio Artists
American Marketing Association
American Newspaper Publishers
  Association
American Research Bureau
American Society of Composers, Authors,
  and Publishers
American Transit Association
amplitude modulation
ANA — Association of National Advertisers
analog — representation of numerical
  quantities by means of physical variables.
  Contrasted with digital.
analyst
analyst/programmer
angle shot
angled poster panel
animation
announcement
announcer
ANPA — American Newspaper Publishers
  Association
Ansco color
answer print

antique finish paper
APA — Agricultural Publishers Association
aperture
appeal
apperception
application
approach —
  copy a.
  outdoor a.
appropriation
apron — lattice or other decoration at the
  bottom of a poster panel
apx — average page exposure
ARB — American Research Bureau
arbitrary mark
Arbitron
arc
Area of Dominant Influence Rating
area sampling
ARF — Advertising Research Foundation
arithmetic unit
arrears
art —
  artwork
  a. buyer
  a. gum
  a. order
  a. representative
artist
art-type mechanical
artwork
ASCAP — American Society of Composers,
  Authors, and Publishers
ascender
ascending letters
ASI Market Research
aspect ratio
as produced script
Associated Business Publications
Association of Industrial Advertisers
Association of National Advertisers
association test
ATA — American Transit Association
audience —
  a. accumulation
  a. breakdown
  a. characteristics
  a. composition
  a. duplication
  a. flow
  a. measurement

audience (*continued*)
  a. participation
  pass along a.
  primary a.
  a. profile
  secondary a.
  share of a.
  a. survey
  a. turnover
audimeter
audio
Audit Bureau of Circulations
audit report
audition
audition record
authentication
author's alterations
automatic data processing
automation
autopositive
avail — availability
availability
average —
  a. audience
  a. audience rating
  a. exposure
  a. net paid circulation
  a. page exposure
  a. paid
Ayer Directory of Publications

B

back —
  b. copies
  b. lighting
background —
  b. music
  b. plate
backlighted transparency
back-to-back
back up — to print the second side of a sheet
bad break — an incorrect or awkward word division
bait advertising
balance — the relationship between the elements of any work of art
balloon — encircled words or thoughts in a cartoon
balop — balopticon

balopticon
b and w — black and white
banner
barn doors — flaps controlling the beam of a spotlight
barter plan
baseboard — the solid base below a painted bulletin or poster panel
basic —
  b. bus
  b. network
  b. price
  b. rate
  b. stations
  b. weight
bastard —
  b. face
  b. size
batch processing
BBB — Better Business Bureau
BBC — British Broadcasting Corporation
bearers — the metal rule around type to be electrotyped
beep
below-the-line cost
benchmark
Ben Day process
Better Business Bureau
bf — boldface
bias of nonresponse
Billboard — a trade publication in show business
billboard
billing
bin
binary
birdability
bit —
  b. part
  b. player
black and white
black plate
blanket contract
blanking area
bleed — an illustration printed to the very edges of a page
bleed face
blend
blind emboss
blinking — short periods of alternating advertisement

blister pack
block
block paragraph
blowup
blue plate
blueprint
blurb
BMI — Broadcast Music, Inc.
board
body —
  b. copy
  b. size
  b. type
bold — boldface
boldface type
Boldger — a research service
bond — an adhesive
bond paper
bonus circulation
booked
book paper
boom — a mount that raises or lowers a
  motion picture or TV camera
booth
bounce back
Bourges
boutique
box
boxholder
box set
box-top offers
BPA — Business Publications Audit of
  Circulation, Inc.
brand —
  b. consciousness
  b. image
  b. loyalty
  b. name
  b. rating
  b. selection
  b. switching
Brand Names Foundation
break — the time within a program used for
  announcements
breakdown
bridge — a visual or musical interlude
  between scenes in a broadcast or
  commercial
bristol board
British Broadcasting Corporation
broadcasting

Broadcast Music, Inc.
broadcast spectrum
broadside
brochure
bronze
Bruning
bubble card
budget
bug — a standardized piece of art or a union
  insignia appearing in motion pictures or
  publications
bulk —
  b. mailing
  b. sales
bulkhead card
bulldog edition
bullet — a boldface mark calling attention to
  part of a text
bumper — transition between story action
  and commercial in a TV program
Bureau of Advertising of the American
  Newspaper Publishers Association
buried —
  b. advertisement
  b. offer
Burke Television Day-After Recall
burnish
business —
  b. paper
  b. publication
Business Publications Audit of Circulation,
  Inc.
butterfly — a cloth used to diffuse light in
  photography
buying —
  b. services
  b. space
by-line
byte

C

cablecasting
cable TV
calendered paper
call —
  c. letters
  c. sheet
  c. sign
call-back

calligraphy
camera —
  c. angle
  c. chain
  c. light
  c. lucida
  c. mixing
  c. rehearsal
  c. shot
campaign
Campbell's Soup position
Canadian Broadcasting Corporation
Canadian Circulation Audit Bureau
candid — candid photograph
caps — capital letters
captain agency
caption
captive rotary
carbon arc
carbro
car card
card —
  c. deck
  c. punch
  c. rate
  c. reader
cardboard engineer
cartouche
casein
cash discount
cast —
  c. commercial
  c. off
  c. up
catalog saver
cathode-ray tube
CATV — Community Antenna Television
CBC — Canadian Broadcasting Corporation
CBS — Columbia Broadcasting System
CCAB — Canadian Circulation Audit Bureau
cel (cell)
cell — a celluloid sheet on which drawings
  are painted for animation
census
center spread
central processing unit
certification mark
chain
chain break
channel
character — a single unit of type

character printer
charcoal
chase — a metal frame in which type is
  locked up for printing or for plating
cheat — positioning of performers to achieve
  a better TV picture
checkerboard — layout in advertising
  allowing an advertisement to dominate the
  whole page
checking
checking copy
Chinese white
chisel point
choreographer
Chroma-key
Chromolite
circle-in
circle-out
circular
circulation —
  c. per $
  c. certification
  city zone c.
  controlled c.
  effective c.
  franchise c.
  nonpaid c.
  paid c.
  qualified c.
  request c.
  c. waste
clap stick
Class A time
classification
classified advertising
class magazine
clean proof
clear —
  c. a number
  c. -channel station
  c. time
client rough
clip — a portion of film used within another
  film
clipping
clipsheet
closed —
  c. circuit
  c. -end question
  c. set
close shot

close-up
closing —
  c. date
  c. hour
cluster sample
clutter
CMX — computer editing
coarse-screen halftone
coated paper
coaxial cable
COBOL — common business-oriented
  language
code —
  alphabetic c.
  error detecting c.
  numeric c.
coding
coincidental survey
coined word
cold type
collage
collate
collateral services
collective mark
collotype
colophon
color —
  c. corrected print
  c. form
  c. overlay
  c. plate
  c. print
  c. proof
  c. separation
  c. stat
  c. tape
  c. toning
  c. transparency
Columbia Broadcasting System
column
column inch
combination —
  c. buy
  c. cut
  c. plate
  c. rate
comic strip
command — an electronic pulse or signal

commercial —
  c. audience
  c. impressions
  integrated c.
  c. lead-in
  c. program
  c. protection
commission
Community Antenna Television
comp —
  comprehensive
  complimentary
comparability
comparative advertising
comparison advertising
competitive stage
compilation — the process of translating
  from one language into another or into
  machine language
composing stick
composite print
composition —
  cold c.
  computerized c.
  hand c.
  hot c.
  photo c.
compositor
comprehensive — an advertising layout in
  near-final form
computer —
  analog c.
  digital c.
computer-graphics
computerized composition
conditioning bias
confirmation
connect-time
console
console message
consumer —
  c. advertising
  c. diary
  c. goods
  c. magazine
  c. panel
  c. products
  c. promotion

contact print
contemporary
contest
contiguity discount
continuity —
c. acceptance
c. clearance
c. department
c. discount
continuous —
c. roll insert
c. tone
contract year
contrast
controlled circulation business and
professional publications
controlled experiment
control room
convenience —
c. goods
c. sample
conversion table
co-op —
cooperative
cooperative program
cooperative —
c. advertising
c. mailing
c. program
coordinated advertising
copper halftone
copperplate engraving
copy —
c. approach
c. cast
c. negative
c. order
c. platform
c. print
c. research
c. testing
copyright
copywriter
core — the magnetic core of a computer
corner bullets
corporate image advertising
corrective advertising
correlation

cosponsor
cost —
c. efficiency trends
c. forecasts
c. per commercial minute
c. per thousand
Council of Sales Promotion Agencies
countdown
counter card
counting station
county size group
coupon
couponing
cover —
c. paper
c. position
c. stock
coverage
cowcatcher — a commercial preceeding a
broadcast but part of it
cpi — characters per inch
CPM — cost per thousand
C print
CPS — characters per second
CPU — central processing unit
Craftint
crash finish
crawl — an optical effect in which artwork
moves upward across a TV screen
credits
crew
Cronar film and Cronar plates
Cronopaque
crop — to mask or cut off part of a
photograph
crop marks
cropping
cross —
c. dissolve
c. fade
c. plug
crosshatch
CRT — cathode-ray tube
CSPA — Council of Sales Promotion
Agencies
CU — closeup
cue —
c. card
c. sheet

cukaloris
cume — cumulative audience
cumulative audience
cushion — the portion of a broadcast that can be either lengthened or shortened
customer profile
cut
cut-in
cut-in cost
cutline
cutoff rule
cutout
cut-out extension
cutter
cyclorama

D

dailies
daily
daily effective circulation
data —
    d. bank
    d. base
    d. processing
dateline
Day-glo colors
day parts
daytime station
DB — delayed broadcast
deadline
dead metal
dealer —
    d. imprint
    d. mat
    d. tie-in
deals
debug
decal
decalcomania
decibel
deckle edge
deck panels
decorative
define — to name in user language a problem and how to solve it through a computer system
definition — clean-cut broadcast transmission and reception

delayed broadcast
delete
demo — demonstration; demonstration recording
demo —
    d. record
    d. reel
demographic characteristics
demographics
depth —
    d. interview
    d. of columns
    d. of focus
descender
design
Designated Market Area Rating
Designer colors
DGA — Directors Guild of America
diary method
die-cut
die-stamping
differential
diffuser
digit
dimmer
diorama
direct —
    d. advertising
    d. mail advertising
    d. marketing
    d. process
    d. recording
    d. response advertising
    d. response marketing
Direct Mail Advertising Association
Direct Mail Marketing Association
director
Directors Guild of America
disc
disc jockey
discount
disk — a flat circular plate on which computer data may be stored
disk pack
display —
    d. advertising
    d. tube
    d. type
dissolve — a technique through which a picture fades out and into another

distribution —
mail order d.
nonqualified d.
distributor
ditto
DMA Rating — Designated Market Area
Rating
DMAA — Direct Mail Advertising
Association
DMMA — Direct Mail Marketing
Association
documentation
dodger — a single-sheet circular carrying
advertising
dolly shot
double —
d. decker
d. exposure
d. image
d. leaded
d. page spread
d. print
d. spotting
d. spread
d. system
d. truck
d. weight
down-and-under
DP — data processing
dress — dress rehearsal
dress rehearsal
drive time
drop-in
drop-out halftone
dry —
d. mount
d. offset
d. run
drybrush drawing
dub
dubbing in
due bill
dummy
dumpbin
duograph
duotone
dupe — duplicate
dupe negative
duplicate —
d. coverage
d. plates

duplicated audience
duplication
Dutch door
Dycril plate
dye transfer print

E

early fringe
earned rate
ears of newspaper
earth station
echo chamber
ECU — extreme close-up
edge number
edit
editing charge
edition —
demographic e.
editorial —
e. classifications
e. content
e. pages
EDP — electronic data processing
8mm — 8 millimeter film
Ektachrome
Ektacolor
electrical transcription
electric spectaculars
electronic —
e. data processing
e. editing
e. flash
e. insertion
e. matting
electrotype
elite — a size of typewriter type with twelve
spaces to the inch
em — a unit of type measurement
embellishment
embossed sign
emcee — master of ceremonies
en — a unit of type measurement, half the
width of an em
enamel-coated stock
enameled paper
end-aisle display
end-product advertising
end rate

English finish
engraver's spread
engraving
enlargement
envelope stuffer
equivalent weight of paper
erase
error list
establishment
estimate
estimating
estimator
ET — electrical transcription
etch
ethical advertising
Eurovision
execute — to interpret a machine instruction and perform the indicated operation
exposure
extended covers
extension
exterior
extra
extrapolation
extreme close-up
eye-movement camera

F

face — printing surface of type
facing
facing-text matter
facsimile
facsimile signature
factor analysis
fact sheet
fade — a gradual change in loudness or visibility or a transition from one picture to the next
fade-in
fade-out
fading
fair trade
family of type
fanfare
farm publication
fast motion
fax — complete studio facilities for TV rehearsal

FCC — Federal Communications Commission
FDA — Food and Drug Administration
Federal Communications Commission
Federal Trade Commission
fee
feedback
field —
 f. intensity map
 f. intensity measurement
 f. served
 f. work
50 showing — standard purchase options in outdoor advertising
file — a collection of computer records considered as a unit
file maintenance
fill-in letter
film —
 f. chain
 f. clip
 f. loop
 f. negative
 f. positive
 f. transfer
filmsetting
filmslide
filmstrip
filter mike
final proof
fine grain
finished —
 f. art
 f. art-type mechanical
firm order
first —
 f. proof
 f. proof print
fixative
fixed —
 f. location
 f. position
flag
flap — protective cover for artwork
flasher
flat —
 f. colors
 f. rate
Flexichrome
flier

flight — part of a campaign divided into segments of advertising and lapses of time without advertising
flighting
flip —
 f. cards
 f. chart
float — an advertisement used on a space larger than that for which it was designed
floor —
 f. manager
 f. pyramid
flowchart
fluff — a mistake made during a broadcast
Fluorographic
flush —
 f. left
 f. right
FM — frequency modulation
focus in
focus out
folio
follow —
 f. shot
 f. style
 f. -up ad
font — a complete assortment of type
Food and Drug Administration
for approval script
forced combination
form — type locked up for printing
format
forms close
FORTRAN — formula translating system
Fototype
foundry —
 f. proof
 f. type
4A's — American Association of Advertising Agencies
four-color process
frame
free —
 f. lance
 f. publication
freehand signature
freestanding insert
freeze frame
French fold

frequency —
 f. discount
 f. distribution
 f. modulation
fringe —
 f. publication
 f. time
frisket
from the top
frontispiece
FTC — Federal Trade Commission
fulfillment
full —
 f. position
 f. run
 f. service agency
 f. showing
 f. time station
function
furnish
furniture — pieces of wood inserted in a type form to keep it rigid

G

gaffer — head electrician of a motion-picture crew
gain — adjustment in the strength of current for picture or sound contrast
galley
galley proof
Gallup & Robinson
gatefold
gauge
general —
 g. magazine
 g. rate
generate
generation — a master film or tape considered to be the first generation
geostationary
gestalt — perceiving the whole of an advertisement to have greater impact than the sum of its parts
ghost — an unwanted image appearing on a television picture
ghosted view
giveaway

glassine
glossy —
   g. photograph
   g. photostat
   g. velox
gobo
gondola — island shelving in self-service
   stores
good music
gouache — (pronounced gwash)
grain
graphic
graphic arts
gravure
Greek — to treat a photograph so that details
   are recognizable but not identifiable
grid
grip — a helper in a motion-picture or TV
   crew
gripper
gripper margin
gross —
   g. audience
   g. national product
   g. rating points
ground —
   g. bulletin
   g. waves
group —
   g. discount
   g. subscription
guaranteed —
   g. circulation
   g. position
guards
guest shot
gutter — the space between two facing pages
gutter bleed

H

hairline — a fine or unwanted line in printing
halation
half —
   h. run
   h. service
   h. showing
   h. title

halflap
halftone engraving
Hall, The Lloyd H., Company, Inc.
hand —
   h. composition
   h. lettering
   h. proof
   h. tooling
   h. type
handbill
hanging sign
hard —
   h. copy
   h. edge
   h. goods
hardware — physical elements used in data
   processing
head — headline
headlight display
headline
head-on location
head-on position
heaviside layer
heavy-half users
Hertz
hiatus
hickey — a speck or mark that must be
   routed from an engraving
hidden offer
hi-fi — high fidelity
hi-fi —
   h.f. color
   h.f. insert
high —
   h. band
   h. key
highlight
hitchhike — a commercial attached to the
   end of a TV or radio program
hold frame
holding power
holdover audience
Homosote board
Hooven letter
horizontal —
   h. buy
   h. publications
   h. saturation
hot-metal typesetting

house —
  h. agency
  h. line
  h. mark
  h. order
  h. organ
  h. rough
household —
  h. characteristics
  h. combinations of magazines
  h's reached
  h's using television
  h's using televison rating
housewife times
100 showing — the saturation coverage in outdoor advertising
HUR — homes using radio
HUT — households using television
HUT rating — households using televison rating
hypothesis

I

IAA — International Advertising Association
IARS — Industrial Advertising Research Institute
IATSE — International Association of Theater and Stage Employees
ICIE — International Council of Industrial Editors
iconoscope
ID — identification spot
idea development interview
identification spot
IDI — idea development interview
idiot cards
IDP — integrated data processing
illuminated
illumination
illustration board
image — the total perception of an advertised product
impact — the extent of consumer awareness of advertising
implementation
impression — the pressure of type in printing
impressions — the total audience for all commercials in an advertiser's schedule

imprint
imprinting
impulse buying
in-ad coupon
inch — column inch
inches per second
income
income of household
incremental analysis
independent —
  i. contractor
  i. station
India ink
indicia
individual location
industrial —
  i. advertising
  i. goods
  i. product
Industrial Advertising Research Institute
inherited audience
in-house agency
input data
inquiry — a request to retrieve computer data
inquiry test
insert
insertion order
inserts
inside —
  i. panel
  i. transit advertising
Institute of Outdoor Advertising
institutional advertising
institutions advertising
instruction
in sync — in synchronization
intaglio printing
integrated —
  i. commercial
  i. data processing
intensity
interactive processing
intercut
interlock
International Advertising Association
International Association of Theater and Stage Employees
International Council of Industrial Editors
International Radio and Televison Society
interview

interviewer bias
involuntary attention
IOA — Institute of Outdoor Advertising
ionosphere
IP — immediately preemptible
IPS — inches per second
iris in
iris out
IRTS — International Radio and Television
  Society
island —
  i. display
  i. position
isolated 30 — a 30-second commercial
  surrounded by program matter
issue —
  i. audience
  i. life
italic type
iteration

keying an advertisement
keyline
keypunch
kill — to cancel or delete
kill a widow — to run back or delete a short
  line at the top of a succeeding column or
  page.
kilocycle
kilohertz
kine — kinescope
kinescope
king-size poster
klieg light
kneaded eraser
known-probability sample
Kodachrome
Kodamontage
kraft
Kromekote
Krylon

J

JCL — job control language
jingle — a commercial set to music
job —
  j. control language
  j. ticket
jobber
journal
judgment sampling
jumble display
jumbo stat
junior —
  j. page unit
  j. panel
justification of type
justify — to distribute type so that left and
  right margins are even

K

Kemart
key —
  k. light
  k. plate
  k. station
keyboard

L

laid paper
L and M — layout and manuscript
language — a system of symbols and words
  that a computer can understand and
  interpret
Lanham Act
lap dissolve
late fringe
lateral reasoning
layout
layout and manuscript
layout order
lc — lowercase
lead — (pronounced 'led') a metal strip
  inserted between lines of type
leader — a blank segment of film or tape
leaders — dots or dashes to guide the eye
  from one word or figure to another
lead-in
leading
Leading National Advertisers
lead-out
lead time
leave behind
ledger — a high-grade writing paper
leftover matter

legend
length of commercial
Leroy letter
letter
letterpress printing
letterset
lettershop
letterspace
lf — lightface
librarian
library — a collection of related computer files
life — the time during which response from an advertisement may be measured
life-style
ligature — a single piece of type on which two or three letters have been cast together
light box
lightface
limbo — apparent absence of background in a scene
limited animation
limited-hours station
limited-time station
linage
line — agate line
line —
　l. and Ben Day
　l. and wash drawing
　l. comprehensive
　l. copy
　l. drawing
　l. plate
　l. printer
linear programming
linecut
Linotype composition
lip sync — lip synchronization
list
list broker
listener —
　l. characteristics
　l. diary
listening
listening area
lithograph
lithography
live —
　l. action
　l. matter

local —
　l. advertising
　l. channel station
　l. program
　l. rate
location
lock up — to fix type into a form for printing or plating
log — listing of a station's programs in the order of the day's broadcast
logegram
logo — logotype
logotype
long shot
loop — a piece of film spliced end-to-end for continuous projection
loose — sketchiness of details in a drawing
lottery
lowercase
low-key
LS — long shot
lucy — camera lucida
Ludlow
luminous

MAB — Magazine Advertising Bureau
Macbeth viewer
machine —
　m. composition
　m. language
machine-finish paper
mag —
　magazine
　magnetic
　magtrack
magazine
　m. inserts
　m. supplement
Magazine Advertising Bureau
Magazine Publishers Association
Magic Markers
magnetic —
　m. core
　m. disk
　m. recording
　m. tape
　m. track

mailing list
mail order —
  m.o. advertising
  m.o. campaign
  m.o. selling
make good
makeready
makeup —
  m. of a page
  m. restrictions
mandatory copy
manuscript
map — a screen layout
market —
  m. analysis
  m. index
  m. profile
  m. research
  m. segmentation
  m. share
marketing —
  m. concept
  m. research
Marketing Communications Executives
  International
mask — to cover areas of a picture for
  desired effects
masking tape
mass —
  m. media
  m. medium
master —
  m. agency
  m. contract
  m. file
  m. of ceremonies
  m. print
  m. size
masthead
mat — matrix
mat —
  m. print
  m. surface
match dissolve
matched samples
mathematical model
matrix
matrix film
matt — mat
matte — mat

matter — composed type
matting amplifier
maximal line rate
maximum depth
MC — master of ceremonies
MCEI — Marketing Communications
  Executives International
McKittrick's Dictionary
MCU — medium close-up
mean — the arithemetic average
measure — width of a line of type
mechanical — a finished layout ready for
  offset photography
media —
  m. buyer
  m. coverage
  m. survey
  m. vehicle
Media Records, Inc.
median
medium —
  m. close-up
  m. shot
megacycle
memory — a device in data processing by
  which information can be stored and
  retrieved
men —
  m. readers
  m. viewers
merchandising
merchandising materials
merge/purge
Metro Area Rating
MF — machine-finish paper
middle-of-the-road
middletone
mike — microphone
milline rate
mimeograph
minimum depth
mix — to rerecord sound tracks into a single
  track
mm — millimeter
mobile unit
mock-up
mode — the value that occurs most often in a
  set of data
model release
Modern Roman

modular agency
mold
monitor
monopack
Monotype
montage
monthly
month preceding
mortise
Motion Picture Association of America
motivational research
mount
moviola
MPA — Magazine Publishers Association
MPAA — Motion Picture Association of
  America
mr — motivational research
MS — medium shot
mss — manuscript
multigraph
multilith
multi-network area
multiple —
  m. color press
  m. correlation
multiprogramming
multi-vision
multo ring
musical clock
Mutual — Mutual Broadcasting System

N

NAB — National Association of Broadcasters
NAD — National Advertising Division
NAEA — Newspaper Advertising Executives
  Association
NARB — National Advertising Review Board
NATA — National Association of
  Transportation Advertising
national —
  n. advertising
  n. brand
  n. plan
  n. rates
  n. spot
National Advertising Division
National Advertising Review Board
National Association of Broadcasters

National Association of Transportation
  Advertising
National Broadcasting Company
National Business Publications
National Industrial Advertisers Association
National Newspaper Promotion Association
National Outdoor Advertising Bureau
National Retail Merchants Association
NBC — National Broadcasting Company
NBP — National Business Publications
negative — a still or motion film whose
  image is the reverse of reality
negative photostat or stat
nemo
net —
  n. audience
  n. paid circulation
  n. unduplicated audience
network —
  n. affiliate
  n. participation
  n. promo
  n. rating
  n. spot buy
  n. time
Newspaper Advertising Executives
  Association
newspaper supplement
newsprint
news release
newsstand circulation
next-to-reading matter
NG — no good
NIAA — National Industrial Advertisers
  Association
Nielsen Station Index
Nielsen Television Index
NNPA — National Newspaper Promotion
  Association
NOAB — National Outdoor Advertising
  Bureau
non-bleed
nonilluminated
nonpaid —
  n. circulation
  n. distribution
  n. request
nonprobability sample
non-program material
nonresponse
nonstructured interview

noodled — highly detailed for photographic realism

no-stretch paper

notch — an area cut out of a printing plate for insertion of type

noted — describing a reader of a publication who recognizes a particular page or advertisement from it

NRMA — National Retail Merchants Association

NSI — Nielsen Station Index

NTI — Nielsen Television Index

number 50 showing — one of several standard purchase options in outdoor advertising; ½ the number of boards of the industry's basic number 100 showing

number 100 showing — the purchase of saturation coverage in outdoor advertising

number 10 — standard size of a business envelope

numeric

O

OAAA — Outdoor Advertising Association of America, Inc.

OAI — Outdoor Advertising, Inc.

O and O station — owned and operated station

object program

occupation

occupational classification

off —
  o. camera
  o. -line
  o. screen announcer

offset —
  o. lithography
  o. printing

ogive curve

oil — a painting made with an oil-based pigment

Old English

Old Style Roman

on camera

one-shot

100 showing (See number 100 showing)

one-time-only

one-time rate

on-line

on-page coupon

opacity

opaque

opaque projector

open —
  o. end
  o. rate

open-end —
  o. diary
  o. question
  o. transcription

operand

operations research

operator

optical —
  o. center
  o. effect

opticals

option time

original

OTC — over-the-counter

OTO — one-time-only

outdoor —
  o. advertising
  o. plant

Outdoor Advertising Association of America, Inc.

Outdoor Advertising, Inc.

out-of-home media

out of register

output — information provided by a computer in permanent form

output data

outsert

outtake

overall

overlapping circulation

overlay

overprint

overrun

overset

over-the-counter

overtime

owned and operated station

Oxberry

Ozalid

P

P — page
package —
 p. insert
 p. plan
 p. show
packaged goods
page proof
pagination
painted —
 p. bulletin
 p. display
 p. wall
paired comparison rating
pamphlet
pan — to rotate a camera to keep an object in view or to get a panoramic effect
panchromatic
P and W — Pension and Welfare
panel
pantry inventory
participating sponsorship
participation
participation program
pass-along reader
pasted proof
pastel
paste-up
patch — a correction or revision incorporated within an original
pattern plate
PD — public domain
pencil test
penetration
Pension and Welfare
performance index
per-inquiry advertising
periodical
Periodical Publishers Association
peripheral — data processing devices distinct from a central processing unit
permastat
personal interview
photocomposition
photoengraving
photogelatin process
photogram

photographic justification
photography
photogravure
photolettering
photomicrograph
photomontage
photo-offset printing
photoplatemaking
photoprint
photoscript
photostat
phototypesetting
phototypography
photounit
pi — per inquiry
PIB — Publishers Information Bureau
pic — picture
pica — a size of typewriter type with ten spaces to the inch
pica em
pickup — dry rubber cement used to remove excess cement from a paste-up
pick up — slang for "to insert"
pictograph
picture resolution
pied type
piggyback
pilot film
pioneering stage
pix — pictures
plan
planography
plans board
plant —
 p. capacity
 p. operator
plate —
 Dycril p.
 printing p.
plated stock
platter — a record on which sound is recorded
playback
playback machine
Pliofilm
PM — evening newspaper
point — the unit of measurement of type
point-of-purchase advertising
Point-of-Purchase Advertising Institute

point-of-sale advertising
Politz, Alfred, Media Studies & Research
poll
pop — contemporary music
POP — point of purchase
POPAI — Point of Purchase Advertising
  Institute
population — the total number of units
  studied in sampling
positioning — the technique of fitting a
  product into a broad market in order to set
  it apart from competition
position request
positive — a photographic print in which
  light and dark values correspond to reality
postage saver
poster —
  p. panel
  p. plant
  p. showing
posting —
  p. date
  p. leeway
postsync — postsynchronize
postsynchronize
posttesting
potential audience
pp — pages
PPA — Periodical Publishers Association
PR —
  public relations
  public relations and publicity
predate
preemptible —
  p. time
  p. rate
preemption
preferred position
premium
premium price
preprint
preprint insert
prescore
press —
  p. kit
  p. proof
  p. run
pressing — manufacturing a disc in large
  quantities
prestige advertising

pretesting
preview
primary —
  p. audience
  p. circulation
  p. household
  p. readers
  p. service area
prime —
  p. rate
  p. time
Prime Time Access Rule
principal register
print — a positive copy on paper or film
Printer's Ink Model Statute
printon
printout
private —
  p. brand
  p. label
probability sample
process —
  p. plates
  p. printing
  p. shot
processing
Pro-color slide
producer
production —
  p. department
  p. director
product protection
professional advertising
profile — an analysis of audience in terms of
  its characteristics
program —
  p. analyzer
  p. compatability
  counter p.
  p. effectiveness
  p. following
  p. opposite
  p. package
  p. profile
  p. preceding
  p. rating
programmer
programmer/analyst
programming
progressive proofs

progressives
projective technique
promo — promotional announcement
promotion
promotional —
 p. allowance
 p. announcement
proof — a trial reproduction from type, plate, or film
prop — property
proportion
protection shell
PRSA — Public Relations Society of America
psychographic characteristics
psychographics
pt — point
PUAA — Public Utilities Advertising Association
public —
 p. domain
 p. relations
 p. relations and publicity
 p. service advertising
 p. service announcements
publicity
Public Relations Society of America
Public Utilities Advertising Association
Publishers Information Bureau
publisher's statement
pull a proof
pulsation — a short burst of advertising
Pulse — The Pulse, Inc.
pulsing
punched card
purchasing power
pyramid makeup

Q

quad — a blank piece of type
qualified circulation
quantity discount
quarter —
 q. run
 q. showing
queen-size poster
questionnaire
quintile
quota sample

R

® — registered trademark
RAB — Radio Advertising Bureau
rack —
 r. folder
 r. jobber
Radio Advertising Bureau
Radio and Television Directors Guild
railroad showing
randomization
random sampling
rate —
 r. base
 r. card
 r. differential
 r. holder
 r. protection
rates
rating —
 r. point
 r. service
raw —
 r. data
 r. stock
reach — cumulative audience
reader —
 r. characteristics
 r. response
 r. traffic
 r's per copy
readership
reading —
 r. days
 r. notice
 r. time
read most
real time
ream
rear —
 r. projection
 r. projection slide
rebate
rebroadcast
recall interview
recipient
recognition
recognized agency
record
recording studio

red plate
reduction print
reflector buttons
regional —
   r. channel station
   r. facilities
   r. rate
register
registering trademark
register marks
relay station
release —
   r. date
   r. print
   r. sticker
reliability
relief — release of a sponsor
relief printing
reminder advertising
remote —
   r. broadcast
   r. pickup
renewal
repetition
reportage
reportorial
reprint
repro — reproduction proof
reproduction proof
repro proof — reproduction proof
request circulation
rerecord
rerun
rescale
research service
residual
Resisto print
resize
resizing
respondent
retail —
   r. advertising
   r. trading area
   r. trading zone
retentive stage
retouch
retoucher
reversal film
reverse plate
revise
revised proof

ride the gain
riding the showing
ripple dissolve
river — spaces between words accidentally
   forming continuous vertical white space
Robinson-Patman Act
rock — rock music
rollei
roll-in
roll-in charge
roll-out
Roman type
ROP color — run-of-paper color
ROP position — run-of-paper position
ROS —
   run of schedule
   run-of-station
rotary —
   r. plan
   r. press
rotating plan
roto — rotogravure
roto comp — rotogravure comprehensive
rotogravure
rough — preliminary layout
rough cut
round robin
rout
route
routine
routing out
RP — rear projection
RPM — revolutions per minute
RTDG — Radio and Television Directors
   Guild
rule — border or divider
run —
   r. -of-paper color
   r. -of-paper position
   r. of schedule
   r. -of-station
   r. through
running head
rush — unedited film print

SAA — Specialty Advertising Association
saddleback stitch
saddle stitching

saddle-wire stitch
safety shell
SAG — Screen Actors Guild
sales —
   s. aids
   s. -area test
   s. forecast
   s. manager
   s. potential
   s. promotion
sample —
   s. adequate
   s. error
sampling error
sans serif
satellite —
   s. earth station
   s. station
saturation — heavy use of commercials in a
   short period
save — to turn off or to stop
SC — single column
sc — small caps
scale
scale rates
scaling down
scatter plan
schedule
score
Scotchlite
scotchprint
Scotch spread
scrap — products, photographs, etc. used to
   help artists
scratchboard
screamer — exclamation point
screen —
   s. layout
   s. printing
   s. velox
Screen Actors Guild
Screen Directors Guild
Screen Extras Guild
screening
Screen Writers Guild
scrim
script
SDG — Screen Directors Guild
secondary —
   s. audience
   s. coverage

secondary (*continued*)
   s. meaning
   s. service area
sectional announcements
seen-associated
SEG — Screen Extras Guild
segmentation
segue (pronounced 'segway')
self —
   s. -cover
   s. -liquidating point-of-purchase unit
   s. -liquidating premium
   s. -mailer
semi-spectacular
separation
separation negative
sepia print
serif
service mark
set — studio location
sets in use
sets-in-use rating
set size
set solid
setup
SFX — sound effects
SGA — Screen Actors Guild
shadows
share — share of audience
share
   s. of audience
   s. of market
shared ID
sheet — unit of paper or unit for billboard
   poster
sheet-fed press
sheetwise
shelter —
   s. book
   s. publication
Shiva colors
shoot — to take still photographs or motion
   film
shooting schedule
shopper
short rate
shot — still photograph
shoulder — that part of type on which the
   raised image is set
shout — exclamation mark

showing — coverage buy in outdoor advertising
show-through
SIC — Standard Industrial Classifications
side stitching
side-thread stitch
side-wire stitch
signal area
signature —
  1. In advertising the name of a sponsoring company.
  2. In broadcasting a fixed musical theme.
  3. In printing a large sheet on which a number of pages are printed.
signature plate
sign-off
sign-on
silhouette
silhouette halftone
silk screen
silver print
Simmons, W.R. & Associates Research, Inc.
simulation
simulcast
Sindlinger & Co., Inc.
single-rate card
single system
SIU — sets in use
SIU rating — sets-in-use rating
60 — 60-second commercial
16 mm — 16 millimeter film
60-second commercial
sized —
  s. and supercalendered paper
  s. paper
sketch
skin pack
skip frame
sky waves
slate — identification board in motion picture production
sleeve — protective casing for photographs or artwork
slide
slide motion picture
slip sheeting
slogan
slow motion
slug — a blank line in machine composition or a release date or credit in a news release.

small capitals
small caps — small capitals
SMSA — Standard Metropolitan Statistical Area
snapper — an extra incentive used to stimulate purchases
snipe — an additional piece of copy affixed to outdoor advertising.
SOF — sound-on-film
soft —
  s. copy
  s. goods
software
solid matter
SOP — standard operating procedure
sort
sound —
  s. effects
  s. -effects man
  s. film
  s. man
  s. -on-film
  s. track
  s. truck
source program
space —
  s. buyer
  s. charge
  s. discount
  s. position value
  s. rep
  s. representative
  s. schedule
  s. spots
space rep — space representative
Sparkle Disc
spec — speculation
special —
  s. effects
  s. event
  s. interest publication
  s. representative
Specialty Advertising Association
SpectaColor
spectacular
spec type — to specify faces and sizes of type
speculation
speed
Speedball
spill light

spiral
splice
splicing charge
split —
  s. run
  s. screen
sponsor
sponsor identification
spot —
  s. buy
  s. color
  s. drawing
  s. program
  s. radio
  s. television
spotlight
spread — an advertisement on two facing pages
spread posting dates
square finish
SRA — Station Representatives Association
SR & DS — Standard Rate & Data Service, Inc.
SS — same size
stability of sample
stagehand
staggered schedule
standard —
  s. deviation
  s. error
  s. operating procedure
Standard Advertising Register
Standard Industrial Classifications
Standard Metropolitan Statistical Area
Standard Rate & Data Service, Inc.
stand by
standby space
Starch, Daniel, & Staff, Inc.
Starch rating
star-route boxholder
stat — photostat
station —
  s. break
  s. clearance
  s. identification
  s. promo
  s. rep
  s. representative
  s. satellite
station rep — station representative

Station Representatives Association
stat-type paste-up
steel-die —
  s. embossing
  s. engraving
stereo —
  stereotype
  stereophonic
stereophonic
stereotype
stet — leave as originally was; disregard the attempted changes or revisions
still — a still photograph from a motion picture
still picture
stipple
stock —
  s. footage
  s. music
  s. sets
  s. shot
stop —
  s. action
  s. motion
storage
storecasting
storyboard
straight 60 — 60-second commercial
Strathmore
stratification
stretch — any part of a broadcast that can be lengthened or shortened
strike — to dismantle anything on a set
string and button
strip —
  1. To arrange negatives in correct position.
  2. To mount together separate pieces of art.
  3. To remove film images.
  4. A broadcast program that appears same time every weekday.
stripfilm
strip in
stripping film
strobe — stroboscope
stroboscope
stroboscopic
studio
stump — an implement for touching up charcoal drawings.
stylus

subcaption
subhead
subscription circulation
substance number
super —
  s. in sync
  s. slide
superimposition
supplements
supplier
surprint
sustaining program
swatch
sweepstakes
SWG — Screen Writers Guild
sworn statement
sync — synchronize
synchronize
syndicate
syndicated —
  s. mailings
  s. program
  s. research services
  s. TV program
syndication
system — the hardware or software
  application in data processing
systems analyst

T

t — time
TA — total audience
TAA — Transit Advertising Association
TAB — Traffic Audit Bureau
tabloid
tag — short announcement at the end of a
  program
tailpiece
take — a single shot of a scene or action
take one
talent
talent cost
talk
tape —
  t. librarian
  t. library
Target Group Index

TBA — to be announced; Television Bureau
  of Advertising, Inc.
TCRB — Television Code Review Board
tear sheet
teaser
teaser campaign
technique
telecast
telegenic
telephone —
  t. coincidental
  t. interview
  t. survey
telephoto
teletypewriter exchange
televiewer
Television Bureau of Advertising, Inc.
Television Code
Television Code Review Board
television —
  t. recording
  t. satellite
telop
tempera
ten — a ten-second commercial
tent card
terminal
test —
  t. campaign
  t. market
  t. marketing
text
TF — till forbidden; to fill; to follow
TGI — Target Group Index
Thermofax
thermography
35 mm — 35-millimeter film
30 — a 30-second commercial or the symbol
  after a news story to mark its completion,
  often written ''30''
30 mark — ''30''
30-sheet poster
Three Sigma Research, Inc.
throw a cue
thumbnail sketch
tie-in
tight — highly detailed descriptions or
  artwork
till forbidden

time —
t. buyer
t. charge
t. classification
t. clearance
t. discount
t. -sharing
t. sheet
t. signal
t. slot
t. spent reading
t. spent viewing
t. standards for advertising copy
tint
tint block
tip on
tissue — a rough layout on semitransparent paper
titles
to fill
tombstone advertising
tone
total —
t. advertising
t. audience
t. circulation
t. net paid
tr. — transpose type as indicated
traceoline
track — film on which sound has been recorded
trade —
t. advertising
t. area
t. character
t. journal
t. name
t. paper
t. promotion
t. publication
trademark
trade-out syndication
trading area
traffic —
t. count
t. department
t. flow map
Traffic Audit Bureau
trailer — a spot announcement
Transadhesive tape

transcribed program
transcription program library
transfer
transfer negative
transient rate
transit
transit advertising
Transit Advertising Association
transition time
translation
translucency
transparency
transportation advertising
traveler — traverse rod
traveling —
t. display
t. matte
Trendex, Inc.
trimmed flush
trims — any film shot not used in a completed commercial
trim size
triple spotting
tri-vision
trompe l'oeil(pronounced trom ploy) "fool the eye"
trucking shot
truck shot
tune-in —
t. advertising
t. audience
turnover
TV — television
TvQ score — the percentage of people who consider a specific TV program a favorite
TVR — television recording
TV week
20 — 20-second commercial
24-sheet poster
20-second commercial
two —
t. -color
t. -fold
t. -shot
TWX — teletypewriter exchange
type —
t. comprehensive
t. C print
t. family

type (*continued*)
   t. -high
   t. page
   t. spec
typeface
types —
   t. of advertising
   t. of magazines
   t. of programs
typo — typographical error
typographical error

uc — uppercase
UHF — ultrahigh frequency
ultrahigh frequency
unaided recall interview
unduplicated audience
unit count
universe — a census or enumeration of characteristics being studied, or total units or individuals under consideration
up-and-over
update
uppercase
Upson board
user
utility program

V

VAC — Verified Audit Circulation Corporation
validate
validation
value goal
Vandyke
Variac
Varityper
vehicle — an advertising medium
velox
Verifax
Verified Audit Circulation Corporation
verify

vertical —
   v. buy
   v. publications
   v. saturation
very high frequency
VHF — very high frequency
video
videotape
videotape recording
viewer
viewer characteristics
vignette
visual
visual display
VOC — voice-over-credits
voice-over
voice-over-credits
voice track
VTR — videotape recording
Vu-Graph
Vu-Lyte

wait order
wall banner
warm-up
wash — a drawing made with water-soluble paint
wash drawing
waste — the part of a publication's distribution without value to an advertiser
watermark
watts
wave posting
weather contingency
web —
   w. -fed press
   w. press
   w. printing
weekly
weight
wet printing
wf — wrong font
Whatman paper
whip pan
white space

wide-angle lens
widow — the last line of a paragraph
  appearing at the head of the succeeding
  column or page
wild —
  w. recording
  w. spot
  w. track
window —
  w. display
  w. envelope
  w. streamer
wipe — an optical effect in which a scene is
  erased to reveal the succeeding scene
withholding — the right of a network, with
  notice, to take over a broadcast time period
women —
  w. readers
  w's service publications
  w. viewers
woodcut
word space
work —
  w. -and-tumble
  w. -and-turn
  w. print
wove paper
wrong font

X

xerography
Xerox

Y

Yankelovich, Daniel
yardstick
yellow plate

Z

Ziff-Davis
zinc —
  z. etching
  z. halftone
Zip-a-tone
zone plan
Zoomar lens
zoom shot

Computer Language

A

aberration

abnormal termination

abort

absolute —
a. address
a. addressing
a. code
a. coding
a. error
a. value computer

acceleration time

access —
a. arm
a. control register
a. level
a. method
parallel a.
a. permission
random a.
a. right
serial a.
simultaneous a.
a. time

accountable time

accounting —
a. journal
a. machine

accumulator register

accuracy

AC dump — removal of all alternating current from a system

acknowledgement — the reply given to signals within a computer system where an immediate response is not required

acoustic —
a. delay line
a. memory
a. store

acronym

action period

active element

activity

activity ratio

actual —
a. address
a. code
a. decimal point
a. instruction

adaptive control system

addend

adder —
binary half a.
a.-subtractor

addition —
a. record
a. table
a. without carry

additional characters

address —
a. computation
direct a.
a. format
a. generation
indirect a.
instruction a.
machine a.
a. mapping
a. modification
multi-a.
one a.
one-plus-one a.
a. part
real a.
a. register
specific a.
three a.
a. track
a. translation slave store
variable a.
virtual a.
zero level a.

addressing

addressless instruction format

add-subtract time

add time

ADP — automatic data processing

advance feed tape

after-look journalizing
agenda — a set of operations forming a procedure for solving a problem
agendum call card
ALGOL — ALGOrithmic Language
algorithm
algorithmic
algorithm translation
allocate
allocation —
  dynamic a.
all-purpose computer
alphabetic —
  a. code
  a. string
alphameric code
alphanumeric code
alteration — a logical operation which will produce a result depending on its patterns
alteration switch
alternative denial
ALU — arithmetic and logic unit
ambiguity error
amendment —
  a. file
  a. record
  a. tape
amplifier —
  directly coupled a.
  inverting a.
  sign-changing a.
amplitude
analog —
  a. adder
  a. channel
  a. computers
  a. digital converter
  a. network
  a. representation
analogue
analysis —
  systems a.
analyst —
  systems a.
analyst/programmer
analytical function generator
analyzer —
  digital differential a.
  electronic differential a.
  mechanical differential a.

and —
  a. circuit
  a. element
  a. gate
  a. operation
anticoincidence —
  a. circuit
  a. element
  a. operation
aperture plate
application —
  a. package
  a. program
  a. system
  a. virtual machine
arbitrarily sectioned file
arbitrary function generator
architectural protection
architecture — design of a computer in which hardware and software interact to provide basic facilities
archived file
archiving
area —
  common storage a.
  a. search
  working a.
argument — the key that specifies the location of a particular item within a system
arithmetic —
  a. address
  a. and logic unit
  a. check
  floating-decimal a.
  a. instruction
  multi-length a.
  a. operation
  a. organ
  a. overflow
  a. register
  a. shift
  a. unit
arithmetical —
  a. instruction
  a. operation
  a. shift
array — an arrangement of data identified by a key
artificial intelligence
ASCII — American Standard Code for Information Interchange

ASR — automatic send-receive set
assemble
assembler
assembly —
   a. language
   a. list
   a. program
   a. routine
   a. system
   a. unit
assign
associative —
   a. memory
   a. store
assumed decimal point
asynchronous —
   a. computer
   a. working
asyndétic
attended time
attentuate — to cause reduction in amplitude
   of a signal
attenuation
atto — prefix denoting one million-million-
   millionth or 10^{-18}
audio
audio response unit
audit —
   a. of computer systems
   a. trail
augend
augment
augmenter
auto-abstract
autocode
automatic —
   a. abstract
   a. carriage
   a. check
   a. coding
   a. data processing
   a. dictionary
   a. error correction
   a. exchange
   a. feed punch
   a. hardware dump
   a. interrupt
   a. message switching center
   a. paper tape punch

automatic (*continued*)
   a. program interrupt
   a. programming
   a. punch
   a. restart
   a. send-receive set
   a. stop
   a. switching center
   a. tape punch
   a. verifier
automatically —
   a. cleared failure
   a. corrected error
automatics
automation
automonitor
autopolling
auxiliary —
   a. equipment
   a. store
availability ratio

B

background —
   b. job
   b. processing
   b. program
   b. reflectance
backgrounding
backing store
backspace
backup
backup storage
backward recovery
badge reader
balanced error
balance error
band — a group of magnetic tracks or a
   range of frequencies
bar-code scanner
barrel printer
base —
   b. address
   b. notation
   b. number
BASIC — Beginner's All-Purpose Symbolic
   Instruction Code

basic —
  b. coding
  b. instruction
  b. language
  b. linkage
  b. mode
batch —
  b. job
  b. mode
  b. processing
  b. processing mode
  b. total
batching
baud
BCD — binary coded decimal
bead — a small module performing a specific function
beam store
beat — a time unit related to the execution of an instruction
before-look journalizing
beginning —
  b. of file label
  b. of file section label
  b. of volume label
  b. of information marker
benchmark
benchmark problem
bias — an error range having a value of more than zero
bias testing
bi-conditional operation
billi — a prefix denoting one thousand million or 10^9, synonymous with giga
bimag core
binary —
  b. arithmetic operation
  b. Boolean operation
  b. cell
  b. chop
  b. code
  b. -coded character
  b. -coded decimal notation
  b. -coded decimal representation
  b. -coded digit
  b. counter
  b. digit
  b. dump
  b. half adder
  b. image

binary (*continued*)
  b. incremental representation
  b. notation
  b. number
  b. numeral
  b. operation
  b. pair
  b. point
  b. representation
  b. search
  b. -to-decimal conversion
  b. variable
bionics
bipolar
biquinary code
bistable —
  b. circuit
  b. magnetic core
  b. trigger circuit
bit —
  check b.
  b. density
  b. location
  b. pattern
  b. position
  b. rate
  sign b.
  b. string
  b. track
bite — byte
blank —
  b. form
  b. medium
  b. tape
blast — to release external or internal memory areas
bleed — the printing of characters for optical recognition
block —
  b. copy
  b. diagram
  b. header
  b. ignore character
  input b.
  b. length
  b. list
  b. mark
  output b.
  b. sort
  b. transfer

blocking — grouping of individual records into blocks
blocking factor
bobbin core
Boolean —
  B. algebra
  B. calculus
  B. complementation
  B. connective
  B. logic
  B. operation
  B. operation, dyadic
  B. operation table
bootstrap —
  b. input program
  tape b. routine
border-punched card
borrow — the carry signal in subtraction when the difference between digits is less than zero
box —
  connection b.
branch — departure from the normal sequence of program steps
branch instruction
branchpoint
breadboard — a mock-up or model of any device
breakdown
breakpoint —
  b. instruction
  b. symbol
bridge limiter
bridgeware
bridging — the conversion of systems written for one kind of computer for use in another kind
broadband
brush —
  b. compare check
  b. station
brute-force approach
bucket — a unit of storage distinct from the data contained in the unit
budgetary control
budgeting
buffer —
  b. amplifier
  double b.
  b. store

buffered —
  b. computer
  b. input/output
bug — a mistake or malfunction in a computer program
built-in check
bulk —
  b. storage
  b. store
burst
burster
burst mode
bus (highway) — the route along which signals travel
bus driver —
  output b.d.
byte —
  b. mode
  b. track

C

calculating punch
calculator
calendar time
call —
  c. direction code
  c. instruction
calling sequence
capacitor store
capacity
capstan
card —
  c. back
  c. bed
  c. code
  c. column
  c. deck
  edge-punched c.
  eighty-column c.
  c. face
  c. feed
  c. field
  c. fluff
  c. format
  c. hopper
  c. image
  c. jam

card (*continued*)
c. leading edge
c. loader
margin-notched c.
ninety-column c.
c. punch
c. punch buffer
c. punch, duplicating
c. punching
c. reader
c. reproducer
c. row
c. stacker
c. systems
c. -to-card
c. -to-magnetic-tape converter
c. -to-tape
c. -to-tape converter
c. track
c. trailing edge
verge-perforated c.
c. verifier
c. verifying
c. wreck
carriage —
c. return
c. tape
carrier system
carry —
addition without c.
c. -complete signal
ripple-through c.
standing-on-nines c.
c. time
cascade control
cascaded carry
casting-out-nines
catalogue
category — a group of disks or volumes
containing a given set of information
category storage
catena
catenate
cathode —
c. follower
c. ray tube
c. ray tube visual display unit
cell — the smallest unit capable of storing a
single bit

cell —
static magnetic c.
cellar — storage that works on the principle
of a push-down list, so that when new
items of data are added, previous items
move back
center —
automatic switching c.
c. -feed tape
semi-automatic switching c.
torn-tape switching c.
central —
c. control unit
c. processing unit
c. processors
c. terminal
centralized data processing
chad
chadded tape
chadless tape
chain —
c. code
c. printer
chained —
c. list
c. record
chaining search
change —
c. dump
c. file
intermediate control c.
major control c.
minor control c.
c. of control
c. record
step c.
c. tape
channel —
paper tape c.
peripheral interface c.
c. status table
c. -to-channel connection
chapter — a self-contained section of a
computer program
character —
c. -at-a-time printer
c. code
c. code, forbidden
c. crowding
c. density

character (*continued*)
c. emitter
erase c.
c. fill
functional c.
c. modifier
c. oriented
c. printer
c. reader
c. reader, magnetic ink
c. reader, optical
c. recognition
redundant c.
c. repertoire
c. set
c. string
c. subset
characteristic —
c. overflow
c. underflow
chart —
systems c.
check —
c. bit
c. character
c. digits
c. indicator
marginal c.
c. number
c. problem
redundant c.
c. register
c. row
c. sum
c. symbol
c. total
c. word
checking —
c. program
c. routine
checkout routine
checkpoint
checkpoint dump
checkpointing
chip tray
chopper — a device interrupting a beam of
light to produce a pulsating signal
chopper-stabilized amplifier

circuit —
and c.
duplex c.
half-duplex c.
c. noise level
simplex c.
circular shift
circulating register
clear — to replace data in a storage device
with a standard character, often a zero or
blank
clear band
clock —
c. pulses
c. rate
c. signal
c. signal generator
c. track
closed —
c. loop
c. shop
c. subroutine
cluster —
tape c.
clutch point
coalesce
COBOL — Common Business Oriented
Language
code —
alphabetic c.
alphameric c.
c. area
binary c.
column-binary c.
computer c.
cyclic c.
direct c.
c. -directing characters
c. elements
error checking c.
error correcting c.
error detecting c.
c. holes
c. line
macro c.
micro c.
minimum latency c.
mnemonic operation c.

code (*continued*)
  numeric c.
  one-level c.
  optimum c.
  c. position
  c. segment
  self-checking c.
  single-address c.
  specific c.
  symbolic c.
coded —
  c. decimal
  c. stop
coder
coding —
  c. check
  c. sheet
  specific c.
coefficient
coincidence —
  c. element
  c. gate
collate
collator
collector
column —
  c. binary
  c. binary code
  c. 1 leading
  c. split
COM — computer output on microfilm
combined —
  c. head
  c. read/write head
command
command chain
comment — written notes that can be included in coding of computer instructions
commercial —
  c. data processing
  c. language
commission — installation of a computer so that it is capable of effective operation
common —
  c. area
  c. business oriented language
  c. language
  c. storage area
  c. target machine

communication —
  c. channel
  c. devices
  c. link
  c's line control procedure
  c's link controller
commutator pulse
comparator
compare
comparing control change
compatibility —
  equipment c.
compilation
compilation time
compile — to create an object program
compiled module format
compiler —
  c. diagnostics
  c. manager
  c. target machine
compiling system
complement
complementary operation
complementing
complete —
  c. carry
  c. operation
  c. routine
compute mode
computer —
  analogue c.
  all-purpose c.
  c. applications
  c. code
  digital c.
  c. efficiency
  c. instruction
  c. operation
  parallel c.
  c. personnel
  c. program
  stored program c.
  c. system
  c. word
computer-graphics
computing amplifier
conceptual modeling
concurrent —
  c. conversion
  c. processing

condensing routine
conditional —
  c. branch instruction
  c. breakpoint
  c. breakpoint instruction
  c. implication operation
  c. jump
  c. stop instruction
  c. transfer
  c. transfer of control
configuration —
  c. block
  c. state
  c. table
configured-in
configured-off
configured-out
conjunction
connection —
  c. box
  c. of a node
connective
connector
connect-time
consistency check
console —
  data station c.
  c. display register
  c. message
  c. switch
  c. typewriter
constant area
constants
construct — a statement in a source program
  that will produce a predetermined effect
container file
content
content-addressed storage
contention — the condition that arises in time
  sharing when more than one unit attempts
  to transmit simultaneously
continuous stationery
contrast
control —
  c. break
  c. card
  c. change
  c. change, intermediate
  c. change, major
  c. change, minor
  c. character

control (*continued*)
  c. circuits
  c. computer
  c. counter
  c. data
  c. field
  flow c.
  c. holes
  input/output traffic c.
  c. language
  c. language interpreter
  c. loop
  c. mark
  c. -message display
  numerical c.
  panel c.
  c. punchings
  c. register
  c. sequence
  c. stack
  c. statement
  c. tape
  c. total
  c. totals
  c. transfer
  c. transfer instruction
  c. unit
  c. unit, peripheral
  c. word
controlling file
conventional — describing punched card
  equipment
conversational —
  c. compiler
  c. mode
conversion —
  c. equipment
  c. program
converter
coordinate store
copy
CORAL — a high-level language for real-
  time applications
cordless plug
core —
  core store c.
  c. dump
  c. memory
  c. memory resident
  c. storage
corner cut

correction —
   automatic error c.
corrective maintenance
corruption — mutilation of data caused by
   the failure of hardware or software
cost analysis
count
counter —
   control c.
   program address c.
cpi — characters per inch
CPM — critical path method; cards per
   minute
CPS — characters-per-second; cycles-per-
   second
CPU — central processing unit
creation — organization of raw data into a
   file
crippled leap-frog test
crippled mode
criteria
criterion
critical path method
cross —
   c. -check
   c. compiler
   c. talk
crowd — a collection of punched cards
   having something in common
CRT — cathode ray tube
cryogenics
current instruction register
customer acceptance test
customizing
cybernetics
cycle —
   c. count
   c. index counter
   c. reset
   c. shift
   store c.
   c. time
cyclic —
   c. code
   c. redundancy check
   c. shift
   c. store
cylinder — an area of storage holding
   specified records and permitting rapid
   access to them

D

dagger operation
damping — decreasing unwanted oscillation
   or wave motion
data —
   d. acquisition control system
   d. adapter unit
   d. administrator
   d. analysis display unit
   d. area
   d. bank
   d. base
   d. base management systems
   d. capture
   d. carrier
   d. carrier store
   d. cell drive
   d. channel multiplexor
   d. collection
   d. collection and analysis
   d. communications
   d. communications exchange
   d. communication terminal
   d. control
   d. conversion
   d. conversion language
   d. delimiter
   d. description
   d. description language
   d. description library
   d. display unit
   d. division
   d. element
   d. format
   d. gathering
   d. handling equipment
   d. item
   d. level
   d. link
   d. management
   d. management utility system
   d. manipulation language
   d. matrix
   d. -names
   d. net
   d. phone
   d. plotter
   d. preparation

data (*continued*)
  d. processing
  d. processing, automatic
  d. processing center
  d. processing department organization
  d. processing, electronic
  d. processing standards
  d. processor
  d. purification
  d. record
  d. reduction
  d. reduction, on-line
  d. representation
  d. retrieval
  d. segment
  d. set
  d. statements
  d. station
  d. station console
  d. storage
  d. terminal
  d. transmission
  d. unit
  d. word

DC amplifier — directly coupled amplifier; direct current amplifier

DCF — discounted cash flow

DDA — digital differential analyzer

DDL — data description language

dead —
  d. halt
  d. time
  d. zone unit

deadly embrace — a condition when processes simultaneously active within a computer become suspended

debatable time

deblocking

debug

debugging

debugging aid routine

debug on-line

decade — a group of ten storage locations

decay time

deceleration time

decentralized data processing

decibel

decimal —
  binary coded d.
  d. notation
  d. notation, coded

decimal (*continued*)
  d. numeral
  d. point
  d. representation, binary coded

decision —
  d. box
  d. instruction
  d. plan
  d. table
  d. tables

deck —
  tape d.

declaration — an instruction written as part of a source program

declarative —
  d. macro instruction
  d. statement

decode

decoder

decollator

decrement

defect

defective

deferred addressing

define — to name in user/human language a problem and how to solve it through a computer

degradation — lowering the level of service in a computer system because of failures in certain equipment areas

delay —
  d. device, digit
  d. element, digit
  d. line
  d. line, acoustic
  d. line, magneto-strictive acoustic
  d. line, mercury
  d. line, quartz
  d. line register
  d. line, sonic
  d. line store
  d. unit

delayed updating

delete

deleted representation

deletion record

delimit

demand —
  d. processing
  d. reading
  d. writing

demodifier
demodulator
denial —
  alternative d.
  joint d.
dependent — in data structure, an item or set
  of items dependent upon a nominal point
deposit — to preserve the contents of a
  memory area by writing
description —
  problem d.
design —
  logical d.
designating device, independent sector
designation — coded information forming
  part of a computer record, or special
  punching in a card column
designation holes
desk checking
destination —
  d. file
  d. warning marker
destruction (of a node)
destructive —
  d. addition
  d. reading
DETAB (DETAB X, DETAB 65)
detachable plugboard
detail —
  d. file
  d. flowchart
detected error
de-updating
device control character
devices —
  input/output d.
DFG — diode function generator
diagnosis
diagnostic —
  d. check
  d. program
  d. routine
  d. test
diagram —
  logical d.
dichotomizing search
dictionary —
  automatic d.
difference —
  symmetric d.

differential —
  d. amplifier
  d. analyzer
  d. analyzer, digital
  d. gear
differentiating amplifier
differentiator
digit —
  d. compression
  d. delay device
  d. delay element
  d. emitter
  d. emitter, selective
  equivalent binary d's
  d. filter
  d. period
  d. place
  d. plane
  d. position
  d. pulse
  d. selector
  d. time
digital —
  d. adder
  d. /analog converter
  d. clock
  d. computers
  d. differential analyzer
  d. divider
  d. incremental plotter
  d. integrator
  d. multiplier
  d. representation
  d. subtractor
digitize
digitizer
diminished radix complement
diode
direct —
  d. access storage
  d. address
  d. allocation
  d. code
  d. coding
  d. control
  d. current amplifier
  d. display
  d. insert subroutine
  d. instruction
  d. serial file organization

directive
directly coupled amplifier
director — an integral part of a computer operating system that controls its internal resources
directory — a device in standard file-processing programs to specify the size and structure of the file to be processed
dirigible linkage
disable
disc (magnetic disk)
discounted cash flow
discrimination instruction
disjunction
disk —
  d. file
  d. file controller
  d. pack
  d. store, magnetic
disperse
dispersed intelligence
dispersion
display —
  d. console
  d. console, message
  d. control
  data analysis d.
  inquiry and subscriber d.
  d. tube
distance —
  hamming d.
diversity — a logical operation intended to produce a result depending on its bit patterns
dividend
divider
division
division subroutine
divisor
document —
  original d.
documentation —
  d. book
  d. programming
  d. systems
docuterm
do-nothing instruction
dope vector
dot printer

double —
  d. buffering
  d. -ended amplifier
  d. -length number
  d. -precision arithmetic
  d. -precision hardware
  d. -precision number
  d. -pulse reading
  d. punching
  d. tape mark
down time
DP — data processing
drift —
  d. -corrected amplifier
  d. error
drive —
  data cell d.
  magnetic tape d.
  d. pulse
  d. winding
  d. wire
drop —
  false d.
drop dead halt
drop-in
drop-out
drum (magnetic drum)
drum mark
dry running
dual —
  d. operation
  d. recording
ducol punched card system
dummy — a feature of a computer routine to satisfy a specific logical or structural requirement, but which in a particular circumstance is not used
dummy instruction
dump —
  d. and restart
  d. check
  d. cracking
  d. point
  storage d.
dumping
duodecimal number system
duplex —
  d. channel
  d. computer system
  d. console

duplexing
duplicate
duplicate record
duplicated records
duplicating card punch
duplication
duplication check
dyadic —
   d. Boolean operation
   d. operation
dynamic —
   d. allocation
   d. allocation (of memory)
   d. buffering
   d. check
   d. dump
   d. error
   d. memory
   d. memory relocation
   d. stop
   d. storage allocation
   d. store
   d. subroutine
   d. test
dynamicizer

E

E 13 B — a type font used for character recognition machines
EAM — electrical accounting machines
EBR — electron beam recording
eccles jordan circuit
echo check
econometrics
edge —
   card leading e.
   card trailing e.
   e. -notched card
   e. -punched card
edit — to arrange data in a format required for subsequent processing
EDP — electronic data processing
EDPM — electronic data processing machine
EDS — exchangeable disk store
effective —
   e. address
   e. instruction
   e. time

efficiency
eighty-column card
either-or operation
elapsed time
electrical accounting machine
electron beam recording
electronic —
   e. calculating punch
   e. data processing
   e. data processing machine
   e. differential analyzer
   e. switch
electrostatic —
   e. printer
   e. storage
element —
   combinational logic e.
   digit delay e.
   equivalent-to e.
   logical e.
   nand e.
   non-equivalence e.
   non-equivalent-(to) e.
   not e.
elementary item
eleven —
   e. position
   e. punch
else rule
emitter —
   e. pulse
   selective digit e.
empty medium
emulated executive
emulation — the process of using a computer to operate on data originally produced for a different type of computer
emulator
enable pulse
enabling signal
encode
encoder
end —
   e. mark
   e. of data marker
   e. of field marker
   e. of file indicator
   e. of file marker
   e. of file routine
   e. of file spot

end (*continued*)
  e. of first file section label
  e. -of-job card
  e. -of-message
  e. of record word
  e. of run
  e. of run routine
  e. of tape marker
  e. of tape routine
  e. printing
end-around —
  e. carry
  e. shift
endwise feed
engineering time —
  scheduled e.t.
engineer's journal
enquiry (inquiry)
entry —
  e. block
  e. condition
  e. instruction
  keyboard e.
  e. point
enveloped file
EOF — end of file
EOR — end of run
equality —
  e. circuit
  e. unit
equal zero indicator
equipment —
  e. compatibility
  data transmission e.
  electronic data processing e.
  e. failure
  input e.
  on-line e.
  output e.
  peripheral e.
equivalence —
  e. element
  operation e.
equivalent —
  e. binary digits
  e. -to element
erasable storage
erase —
  e. character
  e. head

error —
  e. character
  e. checking code
  e. code
  e. correcting code
  e. correction routine
  e. detecting code
  e. detection routine
  e. diagnostics
  e. interrupts
  e. list
  e. message
  e. range
  e. rate
  e. report
  e. routine
  e. tape
escape character
evaluation
even parity check
event — any occurrence that affects an item
  on a file of data
except gate
exception principle system
exception reporting
excess fifty
excess-three code
exchange —
  remote computing system e.
exchangeable disk store
exclusive-or element
exclusive-or operation
execute —
  e. cycle
  e. phase
execution —
  e. cycle
  e. time
executive —
  e. program
  e. system
exit — the last instruction in a routine or
  program
exjunction
exponent
expression — the symbolic representation of
  a mathematical or logical statement
extended —
  e. basic mode
  e. time scale

exterior label
external —
  e. delays time
  e. memory
  e. store
extract
extract instruction
extractor
extrapolation

face —
  f. down feed
  f. up feed
facsimile —
  f. posting
  f. telegraph
factor
fail —
  f. safe
  f. soft
failure —
  f. logging
  f. rate
  f. recovery
false —
  f. drop
  f. error
  f. retrieval
fast-access storage
fast time scale
fault
fault time
feasibility studies
feed —
  f. holes
  f. pitch
  f. tract
feedback
femto — prefix denoting one thousand
million-millionth or 10^{-15}
ferrite core
field — subdivision of a record containing a
unit of information
field length
file —
  f. conversion
  f. extent

file (*continued*)
  f. identification
  f. label
  f. layout
  f. maintenance
  f. name
  on-line central f.
  f. organization
  f. print
  f. processing
  f. protection
  f. protection ring
  f. recovery
  f. reconstitution
  f. section
  f. set
  shared f's
  f. tidying
filestore
film —
  f. optical sensing device
  f. reader
  f. recorder
filter — a pattern of characters designed to
alter or isolate specific bit positions in
another bit pattern
final result
fine index
first —
  f. generation computer
  f. item list
  f. -level address
  f. remove subroutine
fixed —
  f. block length
  f. field
  f. form coding
  f. length record
  f. placement file
  f. point arithmetic
  f. point part
  f. point representation
  f. radix notation
  f. word length
flag — a piece of information added to a data
item; an error flag indicating that the data
item has given rise to error
flag event
flip-flop — a device or circuit assuming one
of two possible states

float — to add origins to data in a program, thus determining its area of memory
float factor
floating —
  f. address
  f. point arithmetic
  f. point number
  f. point package
  f. point radix
  f. point representation
flow —
  f. diagram
  f. direction
  f. -process diagram
flowchart
flowcharting
flowchart symbols
flowline
font-change character
forbidden character code
force — to intervene in the operation of a computer program by executing a branch instruction
forced checkpoint
forecasting
foreground —
  f. processing
  f. program
foregrounding
format
format effectors
form —
  f. feed
  f. feed character
FORTRAN — FORmula TRANslation
forward compatibility standards
foundation virtual machine
four address instruction
four-wire channel
fractional part
fragmentation
frame — a transverse section of magnetic tape
free field
free-standing display
frequency
frequency band
full —
  f. adder
  f. duplex

function —
  f. code
  f. generator
  f. holes
  f. polling
  f. table
functional —
  f. character
  f. design
  f. diagram
  f. unit
future labels

G

gain — the ratio of output signal to the original signal
gang punch
gap —
  g. digit
  g. scatter
garbage — meaningless data in a storage device
gate —
  and g.
  coincidence g.
  nor g.
  one g.
  or g.
gather write
gathering —
  data g.
general —
  g. peripheral controller
  g. purpose computer
  g. purpose function generator
  g. purpose program
generate
generated address
generating —
  g. program
  g. routine
generation number
generator —
  analytical function g.
  arbitrary function g.
  diode function g.
  general purpose function g.
  manual word g.

generator (*continued*)
  natural function g.
  natural law function g.
  number g.
  output routine g.
  program g.
  random number g.
  report program g.
  sorting routine g.
  tapped potentiometer-function g.
gibberish total
giga — a prefix denoting one thousand million or 10⁹, synonymous with billi.
gigo — garbage in, garbage out
graceful degradation
grandfather tape
graphic —
  g. panel
  g. solution
graphical display
graph plotter
graunch
gray code
grid
gross index
group —
  g. code
  g. indication
  g. mark
  g. marker
  g. polling
  g. printing
grouped records
guard —
  g. band
  g. signal
guide —
  g. edge
  g. margin
gulp — a group of binary digits

H

half —
  h. adder
  binary h. adder
  h. -duplex
  h. -duplex channel
  h. subtracter

halt —
  dead h.
  drop dead h.
  h. instruction
hamming —
  h. code
  h. distance
hand —
  h. feed punch
  h. punch
hang-up
hard —
  h. copy
  h. dump
hardware —
  h. availability ratio
  h. check
  h. dump
  h. dump area
  h. recovery
  h. serviceability ratio
hash — meaningless information put into storage to comply with length requirements
hashed random file organization
hash total
head —
  combined h.
  combined read/write h.
  h. gap
  playback h.
  read h.
  reading h.
  record h.
  writing h.
header
header label
hesitation
heuristic —
  h. approach
  h. program
heuristics
hexadecimal notation
high —
  h. level filestore
  h. level language
  h. level recovery
  h. order
  h. performance equipment
  h. -speed carry
highway — the route along which signals travel

highway width
hit —
  h. -on-the-fly printer
  h. on the line
hold —
  h. facility
  h. mode
holding —
  h. beam
  h. gun
holes —
  designation h.
  function h.
  sprocket h.
hole sight
Hollerith card
Hollerith code
homeostasis — the state of a system in which input and output are exactly balanced
home record
hoot stop
hopper
horizontal —
  h. feed
  h. flowcharting
housekeeping —
  h. operation
  h. run
hub — a hole in the middle of magnetic tape that fits over the capstan when the reel is mounted
hunting — an unstable condition that results from the attempt by an automatically controlled loop to find equilibrium
hybrid —
  h. computers
  h. interface

I

IAL — International Algebraic Language
identification
identification division
identifier
identity —
  i. element
  i. unit
idle time
IDP — integrated data processing

if and only if operation
if-then operation
ignore character
illegal character
image
IMIS — integrated management information system
immediate —
  i. access
  i. access store
  i. address
  i. processing
imperative —
  i. macro instructions
  i. statements
implementation
implication —
  material i.
  i. operation, conditional
impulse
incident — a failure requiring activity to correct or remove the matter concerned
incidentals time
inclusion
inclusive-or operation
incomplete —
  i. program
  i. routine
inconsistency
increment
incremental —
  i. computer
  i. display
  i. dump
  i. plotter
  i. representation
  i. representation, binary
  i. representation, ternary
independent sector designating device
index —
  i. point
  i. positions
  i. register
  i. sequential access method
  i. sequential file
  i. sequential file organization
  i. word
indexed address
indexing

indicator —
i. chart
end of file i.
sign check i.
indirect —
i. addressing
i. control
inductive potential divider
industrial data processing
ineffective time
infix notation
information —
i. bits
i. channel
i. -feedback system
i. flow analysis
loss of i.
i. processing
i. requirements
i. retrieval
i. retrieval techniques
i. separator
i. system
i. theory
i. word
inherent store
inherited error
inhibit
inhibiting signal
inhibit pulse
initial —
i. condition
i. condition mode
i. instructions
i. orders
initialization
initialize
initiate
ink —
i. bleed
i. ribbon
i. smudge
i. squeezeout
in-line —
i. coding
i. processing
i. subroutine
in-plant
in-plant system

input —
i. area
i. block
i. buffer
i. devices
i. instruction code
i. limited
i. loading
i. log
i. magazine
i. /output buffers
i. /output channel
i. /output control
i. /output control systems
i. /output devices
i. /output interrupt
i. /output interrupt identification
i. /output interrupt indicators
i. /output library
i. /output limited
i. /output referencing
i. /output routines
i. /output switching
i. /output traffic control
i. /output trunks
i. /output unit
i. program
i. record
i. register
i. routine
i. section
i. stacker
i. station
i. storage
i. unit
i. unit, manual
inquiry —
i. and communications system
i. and subscriber display
i. display terminal
remote i.
i. station
i. unit
inscribe — to rewrite data in a form that can
be read by a character recognition device
inside-plant
installation —
i. processing control
i. tape number
i. time

instruction —
actual i.
i. address
i. address register
i. area
arithmetic i.
i. code
conditional branch i.
conditional stop i.
control transfer i.
i. counter
discrimination i.
dummy i.
i. format
i. format, one-plus-one
i. format, zero address
machine code i.
i. modification
multiple address i.
no-op i.
null i.
i. register
i. repertoire
i. set
table look-up i.
i. time
unconditional branch i.
unconditional control transfer i.
unconditional jump i.
waste i.
i. word
zero address i.
integer
integral
integrated —
i. circuit
i. data processing
i. management information system
integrator —
digital i.
integrator (computing unit)
integrity — self-consistency in a set of data
intelligence — the ability of a device to
improve its effectiveness by repeated
performance of the same task
intelligent terminal
interactive —
i. batch job
i. display
i. mode
i. processing

interblock —
i. gap
i. space
interchangeable type bar
intercycle
interface —
i. channel
i. routines
interference
interfix
interior label
interlace
interleaved carbon set
interleaving
interlude
intermediate —
i. control
i. control change
i. control data
i. result
i. storage
i. total
internal —
i. memory
i. store
i. timer
internally stored program
international algebraic language
interpolator
interpret — to print information on a
punched card from the code punched in the
card
interpreter —
punched card i.
transfer i.
interpretive —
i. code
i. programming
i. routine
i. trace program
interrecord gap
interrogating typewriter
interrupt —
i. event
i. mask
i. mode
i. signal
i. trap
interruption
intersection
interstage punching

intersystem communications
inventory control
inversion
inverted file
inverter
inverting amplifier
invigilator
invisible failure
I/O — input/output
IPOT — inductive potential divider
irrecoverable error
irreversible —
  i. magnetic process
  i. process
ISAM — index sequential access method
isolated locations
item —
  i. advance
  i. design
  i. of data
  i. size
iteration
iterative —
  i. process
  i. routine

J

jack
jack panel
jam
JCL — job control language
jitter
job —
  j. control language
  j. control program
  j. flow control
  j. oriented terminal
  j. restart
  j. stream
joggle
join
joint denial
journal
jump —
  conditional j.
  j. instruction
  unconditional j.
jumper

justification
justify

K

k — kilo
KCS — a thousand characters per second
kernel — a set of procedures controlling real
  resources
key —
  k. change
  k. -driven
  load k.
  k. punch
  k. -to-disk unit
  k. verify
keyboard —
  k. computer
  k. entry and inquiry
  k. inquiry
  k. lockout
  k. punch
keying-error rate
keyword
kill — to prematurely terminate a computer
  run
kilo
kilobaud
kilocycle
kilomega
kilomegacycle

L

label —
  l. group
  l. identifier
  magnetic tape l.
  l. record
  l. set
  tape l.
laced card
language —
  ALGOrithmic L.
  programming l.
languages
latency
lattice file

layout character
leader — a length of unpunched paper
    preceding the recorded data
leading —
    l. edge
    l. end
leapfrog test
leased line
least significant character
left —
    l. justified
    l. shift
leg — a path in a routine or subroutine
length —
    fixed l.
    variable l.
letter
librarian
librarian program
library —
    l. facilities
    l. program
    l. routine
    l. software
    l. subroutine
    l. tape
    tape l.
light pen
limited integrator
limiter
line —
    acoustic delay l.
    l. -feed code
    magneto-strictive delay l.
    mercury delay l.
    nickel delay l.
    l. noise
    l. printer
    quartz delay l.
    sonic delay l.
linear —
    l. equation
    l. optimization
    l. program
    l. programming
    l. unit
line-at-a-time printer
link — a branch instruction given in order to
    return to some desired point in a program
linkage

linked subroutine
list —
    first item l.
literal operands
liveware
load —
    l. -and-go
    l. key
    l. point
    l. program
loader
loading —
    l. program
    l. routine
local system library
location
location counter
lock — a method by which a process is given
    exclusive use of a resource within an
    operating system
locked down
locking of files
lock-out
log
logger
logic —
    l. chart
    l. symbol
logical —
    l. comparison
    l. connectives
    l. decision
    l. design
    l. diagram
    l. element
    l. flowchart
    l. instruction
    l. multiply
    l. operation
    l. operator
    l. product
    l. record
    l. shift
    l. sum
    l. symbol
    l. track
    l. unit
longitudinal —
    l. check
    l. -mode delay line

look-up
look-up table
loop —
  l. checking
  l. stop
loosely coupled twin
loss — the difference in amplitude between the transmission and reception of a signal
loss of information
low —
  l. level filestore
  l. level language
  l. order
  l. -order position
lower curtate
LP — linear programming
LPM — lines per minute

MAC — multi-access computing
MAC background job
MAC mode
MAC sub-system
machine —
  electrical accounting m's
  m. address
  m. code
  m. cycle
  electrical accounting m's
  m. error
  m. instruction
  m. instruction code
  m. interruption
  m. language
  m. language code
  m. learning
  m. logic
  m. operation
  m. operator
  m. processible form
  m. run
  m. script
  m. sensible
  m. -spoilt work time
  m. word
macro —
  m. assembly program
  m. code

macro (*continued*)
  m. -coding
  m. flow chart
  m. instruction
  m. -programming
magazine — an input hopper that holds punched cards
magnetic —
  m. card
  m. card file
  m. cell
  m. cell, static
  m. character
  m. core
  m. core storage
  m. disk
  m. disk file
  m. drum
  m. film store
  m. head
  m. ink
  m. ink character reader
  m. ink character recognition
  m. ink document reader
  m. ink document sorter/reader
  m. memory
  m. store
  m. tape
  m. tape deck
  m. tape drive
  m. tape file
  m. tape group
  m. tape head
  m. tape librarian
  m. tape library
  m. tape parity
  m. tape plotting system
  m. tape reader
  m. tape unit
  m. thin film
  m. wire store
magnetized ink character
magneto-strictive acoustic delay line
magneto-strictive effect
magnitude
main —
  m. frame
  m. memory
  m. path
  m. program

main (*continued*)
  m. routine
  m. storage
  m. store
  m. store quota
maintenance —
  m. contract
  file m.
  m. of programs
  m. routine
  schedule m.
major —
  m. control change
  m. control cycles
  m. control data
  m. cycle
majority element
malfunction routine
management information system
manipulated variable
mantissa
manual —
  m. control
  m. input
  m. input unit
  m. operation
  m. (operations)
  m. word generator
  m. word unit
marginal —
  m. checking
  m. cost
  m. testing
margin-notched card
margin-punched card
mark —
  control m.
  m. hold
  m. reading
  m. scanning
  m. scanning document
  m. sense cards
  m. sensing
  m. -space multiplier
  m. -to-space ratio
mask — a pattern of characters devised to alter or isolate specific bit positions
masking
mask register

mass —
  m. data
  m. storage
master —
  m. card
  m. clock
  m. control routine
  m. console
  m. data
  m. file
  m. instruction tape
  m. library tape
  m. operating station
  m. program file
  m. record
  m. /slave system
  m. tape
match
matching
material implication
mathematical —
  m. analysis
  m. check
  m. logic
  m. model
  m. subroutine
matrix —
  m. printer
  m. store
mean —
  m. repair time
  m. time between failures
  m. time to repair
medium
meet operation
mega — a million; as in 10 megacycles per second, meaning 10 million cycles per second
megabit
memory —
  acoustic m.
  address register m.
  associative m.
  m. buffer register
  m. capacity
  m. core
  m. cycle
  m. dump
  dynamic m.
  external m.

memory (*continued*)
   m. fill
   m. guard
   internal m.
   mercury m.
   m. overlays
   permanent m.
   m. power
   m. print
   m. protect
   random access m.
   rapid-access m.
   thin-film m.
   m. unit
menu selection — a method of displaying a list of optional facilities in the different functions of a system
mercury —
   m. delay line
   m. memory
merge
message —
   m. display console
   m. exchange
   m. queuing
   m. routing
   m. switching system
method study
MICR — magnetic ink character recognition
micro — a prefix denoting one millionth (10^{-6}), as in microsecond
micro —
   m. code
   m. -coding
   m. instruction
microprogram
microsecond
microwave — pertaining to data communications systems using ultra high-frequency wave forms to transmit messages
middleware
milli — a prefix meaning one thousandth (10^{-3}), as in millivolt, millisecond, etc.
millisecond
millivolt
minimum —
   m. access code
   m. access coding
   m. delay code
   m. delay coding
   m. latency code

minor —
   m. control change
   m. control data
   m. cycle
minuend
minus zone
misfeed
MIT — master instruction tape
mixed —
   m. base notation
   m. number
   m. radix notation
mnemonic —
   m. operation codes
mode
model —
   m. building
modem — modulator/demodulator
modification
modifier —
   m. register
modify
modular —
   m. programming
modularity
modulation —
   m. code
modulator
modulator/demodulator
module —
   m. key
modulo —
   m. *n* check
   m. 2 sum
monadic operation
monitor —
   m. display
   m. routine
   m. system
monostable device
most significant character
MTBF — mean time between failures
MTTR — mean time to repair
multi-access
multi-address instruction
multi-aspect search
multi-cycle feeding
multi-length arithmetic
multi-level addressing

multiple —
  m. address
  m. -address code
  m. connector
  m. -length arithmetic
  m. -length number
  m. -length working
  m. punching
  m. recording
multiplex
multiplex data terminal
multiplexer (multiplexor)
multiplexing
multiplexor —
  m. channel
  m. -channel time sharing
  data channel m.
multiplicand
multiplication —
  m. table
  m. time
multiplier —
  m. register
multi-precision arithmetic
multiprocessor —
  m. interleaving
  m. system
multiprogramming
multi-read feeding
multi-reel file
multistation
multivibrator
mylar

nand —
  n. element
  n. operation
nano — prefix denoting one thousand-millionth or 10^{-9}
narrative
natural —
  n. function generator
  n. law function generator
negation
negative indication
negator
neither-nor operation

nesting —
  n. loops
  n. store
  n. subroutines
network —
  n. analog
  n. analyser
  n. analysis
nexus
nickel delay line
nine-edge leading
nines complement
ninety-column card
no-address instruction
node — an expression used to define the location of information about a specific object
noise
noise digit
noisy mode
non-accountable time
non-arithmetic shift
non-destructive read
non-equivalence operation
non-erasable store
non-numeric character
non-print code
non-reproducing codes
non-resident routine
non-volatile memory
no-operation instruction
no-op instruction
nor —
  n. circuit
  n. element
  n. gate
  n. operation
normal —
  n. range
  n. stage punching
normalize
not —
  n. -and
  n. -and element
  n. -and operation
  n. -both operation
  n. circuit
  n. -element
  n. operation

notation —
  binary n.
  binary coded decimal n.
  coded decimal n.
  mixed radix n.
nought —
  n. output signal
  n. state
noughts complement
n-plus-one address instruction
null instruction
number —
  n. cruncher
  n. generator
  n. representation
  n. system
numeral
numeric —
  n. character
  n. coding
  n. control
  n. data
  n. punching
numerical —
  n. analysis
  n. control
  n. tape

O

O and M — organization and methods
object —
  o. computer
  o. configuration
  o. language
  o. machine
  o. program
observation matrix
OCR — optical character recognition
octal —
  o. digit
  o. notation
odd —
  o. -even check
  o. parity check
off-line —
  o. equipment
  o. processing
  o. storage

off-line (*continued*)
  o. unit
  o. working
off punch
OLRT — on-line real time
one —
  o. address instruction
  o. condition
  o. digit adder
  o. digit subtracter
  o. element
  o. -for-one
  o. gate
  o. level address
  o. level code
  o. level store
  o. level subroutine
  o. output signal
  o. -over-one address format
  o. -plus-one address
  o. shot circuit
  o. shot multivibrator
  o. shot operation
  o. state
  o. to one assembler
  o. to one translator
  o. to zero ratio
ones complement
on-line —
  o. central file
  o. data reduction
  o. equipment
  o. processing
  o. programming
  o. real time operation
  o. storage
  o. typewriter
  o. unit
  o. working
on-the-fly printer
op code — operation code
open —
  o. loop
  o. routine
  o. shop
  o. subroutine
open ended
opening a file
operand

operating —
o. delays
o. display
o. instructions
o. ratio
o. station
o. systems
operation —
biconditional o.
binary (Boolean) o.
o. code
o. cycle
dagger o.
decoder o.
dyadic Boolean o.
either-or o.
meet o.
nand o.
neither-nor o.
non-equivalence o.
not-both o.
one shot o.
or o.
o. part
o. register
single shot o.
o's research
step by step o.
o. time
unary o.
operational —
o. amplifier
o. research
operator —
o. command
o. name
o. part
operators — characters designating different
computer operations
operator's —
o. console
o. control language
o. control panel
optical —
o. bar-code reader
o. character reader
o. character recognition
o. scanner
o. type font
optimization

optimum —
o. code
o. coding
o. programming
optional stop instruction
OR — operational research
or —
o. circuit
o. element
o. gate
o. operation
order —
o. code
o. code processor
o. structure
ordered serial file
orders —
initial o.
organization and methods
origin — the location of specific items in
computer storage
original document
out —
o. device
o. of line coding
o. of service time
o. -plant system
outline flowchart
output —
o. area
o. block
o. buffer
o. bus driver
o. data
o. devices
o. program
o. punch
o. record
o. routine
o. routine generator
o. section
o. table
o. unit
overall —
o. availability ratio
o. serviceability ratio
overflow —
o. bucket
o. records

overlay — a technique by which the same area of computer storage is used to contain successively different parts of a program

overpunch

overwrite

own coding

owner — a process or user that exercises control over resources or data

ownership

P

pack — a collection of punch cards having something in common

package — a general program written so that a user's particular problem will not make the program any less useful in general

packing density

padding

page —
  p. -at-a-time printer
  p. printer
  p. turning

paged segment

paging

pair —
  binary p.
  trigger p.

panel —
  patch p.

paper —
  p. advance mechanism
  p. low condition
  p. tape
  p. tape channel
  p. tape code
  p. tape loop
  p. tape punch
  p. tape punching
  p. tape reader
  p. tape reproducer
  p. tape verifier
  p. throw

parallel —
  p. access
  p. allocation
  p. computer
  p. feed
  p. running
  p. search storage

parallel (*continued*)
  p. storage
  p. transfer

parameter —
  p. card
  p. word

parity —
  p. bit
  p. check
  p. check, even
  p. check, odd
  p. error

partial —
  p. carry
  p. system failure

pass — passage of magnetic tape across the read heads; or a single execution of a loop

password

patch — a group of instructions added to a program to correct error

patchboard

patchcord

patch panel

patchplug

path — a logical sequence of instructions in a computer program

pattern-sensitive fault

PCM — punched card machine; pulse code modulation

pecker — a sensing device in a mechanical paper tape reader

perforated tape

perforation rate

perforator —
  keyboard p.

performance monitoring journal

period —
  scan p.

peripheral —
  p. buffers
  p. controller
  p. control unit
  p. device
  p. equipment
  p. interface channel
  p. limited
  p. manager interface
  p. processor
  p. prompt
  p. transfer
  p. units

permanent memory
personnel records
PERT — Project Evaluation and Review
Technique
physical —
p. address
p. data independence
p. file
p. file copy
p. file report
p. track
pico — prefix denoting one million-millionth
or 10^{-12}
picture
pilot system
pinboard
ping-pong — a technique for processing
multi-reel files
pipelining
PL/1 — Programming Language 1
place — a digit position within an ordered set
of digits
plant — to place the result of an operation
where it will be used later in a program
platen
playback head
plot
plotter —
digital incremental p.
x-y p.
plotting —
p. board
p. table
plug
plugboard
plugging chart
plug-in unit
plugwire
pneumatic computer
pocket — a receptacle for holding processed
punched cards
point —
fixed p.
floating p.
p. mode display
Polish notation
poll — a technique of data transmission
through which several terminals share
communication channels

portability — a characteristic of code or data
that can be used in more than one system
positional —
p. notation
p. representation
post — to update a record with information
posting interpreter
post-mortem —
p. dump
p. program
p. routine
p. time
P-pulse
precision —
double p.
pre-edit
prefix notation
pre-read head
preset parameter
presort
pre-store
presumptive —
p. address
p. instruction
preventive maintenance
PRF — pulse repetition frequency
primary storage
primitive file
print —
p. bar
p. barrel
p. format
p. hammer
p. member
p. position
p. totals only
p. wheel
printer —
hit-on-the-fly p.
line-at-a-time p.
matrix p.
wire p.
xerographic p.
printout —
memory p.
priority —
p. indicator
p. processing
privacy

private volume
privilege
probability
problem —
  p. board
  p. definition
  p. description
  p. oriented language
procedure —
  p. analysis
  p. oriented language
process —
  p. chart
  p. control
  p. image
  irreversible p.
  p. limited
  reversible p.
  p. state
processing —
  automatic data p.
  centralized data p.
  conversational p.
  electronic data p.
  in-line p.
  integrated data p.
processor —
  p. error interrupt
  p. limited
product —
  logical p.
production —
  p. control
  p. run
productive time
program —
  p. address counter
  p. cards
  p. compatibility
  p. compilation
  p. control
  p. controller
  p. control unit
  p. counter
  p. development time
  diagnostic p.
  p. documentation
  p. file
  p. flowchart

program (*continued*)
  general p.
  p. generator
  p. generator, report
  p. instruction
  internally stored p.
  p. language
  p. library
  p. maintenance
  master control p.
  p. modification
  p. overlay
  p. parameter
  p. register
  p. segment
  p. -sensitive fault
  p. specification
  p. step
  p. storage
  supervisory p.
  p. tape
  p. test
  p. testing
  p. testing time
  utility p.
programmed —
  p. check
  p. dump
  p. halt
  p. instruction
  p. switch
programmer
programmer/analyst
programmer defined macro
programming —
  automatic p.
  heuristic p.
  p. language
  micro p.
prompt — a message given to an operator by an operating system
prompt identifier
proof total
propagated error
propagation time
protected —
  p. location
  p. record (or field)

protection — techniques of preventing interference between units of software or areas of data
protection mechanism
proving
proving time
PRR — pulse repetition rate
pseudocode
pseudo —
  p. instruction
  p. off-lining
  p. operation
  p. -random sequence
pulse —
  p. code
  p. code modulation
  P-p.
  p. recording, double
  p. repetition frequency
  p. repetition rate
  p. train
punch —
  automatic feed p.
  automatic tape p.
  p. card
  duplicating card p.
  eleven p.
  hand p. (card)
  hand-feed p.
  hand p. (paper tape)
  keyboard p.
  p. knife
  p. position
  p. tape
  p. tape code
  twelve p.
  zone p.
punched —
  p. card
  p. card duplicating
  p. card, edge
  p. card field
  p. card interpreter
  p. card machine
  p. card system, ducol
  p. card tabulator
  p. card verifier
  p. paper tape
  p. tape

punching —
  designation p's
  normal stage p.
  p. positions
  p. rate
  p. station
  p. track
punctuation bits
push —
  p. down list
  p. down store
  p. -pull amplifier
  p. up list

Q

quanta
quantity —
  double-precision q.
quantization
quantizer
quantum
quartz delay line
quasi instruction
queuing theory
QUICKTRAN — a subset of FORTRAN
quinary
quotient

R

rack-up
radix —
  r. complement
  r. complement, diminished
  r. -minus-one complement
  r. notation
  r. point
RAMPS — resource allocation in multi-project scheduling
random —
  r. access storage
  r. number generator
  r. numbers
  r. number sequence
range — the difference between upper and lower limits of a function

range independence
rank
rapid-access loop
rate —
  pulse repetition r.
  residual error r.
raw data
read —
  r. -around ratio
  r. head
  r. -only storage
  r. -out
  r. -punch unit
  r. rate
  r. time
  r. while writing
  r. /write channel
  r. /write head
reader —
  magnetic tape r.
  paper tape r.
reading —
  r. head
  r. station
real —
  r. address
  r. file
  r. store
  r. time
  r. time clock
recompile
reconfiguration —
  r. console
reconnection
reconstitution
record —
  r. access management
  r. access mechanism
  r. blocking
  r. count
  r. format
  r. head
  r. header
  r. list
  reference r.
  r. section
recording density
recovery
recovery file

red-tape operations
redundancy
redundancy check
redundant —
  r. character
  r. check
  r. code
reel —
  r. number
  r. sequence number
re-entrant —
  r. code
  r. procedure
reference —
  r. address
  r. listing
  r. picture
  r. supply
  r. time
regeneration period
regenerative —
  r. reading
  r. store
  r. tracks
regional address
register —
  r. capacity
  console display r.
  control r.
  current instruction r.
  delay line r.
  r. dump
  r. length
  memory buffer r.
  program r.
  sequence control r.
rejection
relative —
  r. address
  r. addressing
  r. code
  r. coding
  r. error
relay —
  r. amplifier
  r. center
release
reliability
reload time

relocatable program
relocate
remainder
remedial maintenance
remote —
  r. calculator
  r. computing system
  r. computing system exchange
  r. computing system language
  r. computing system log
  r. console
  r. data stations
  r. data terminal
  r. debugging
  r. inquiry, real time
  r. job entry
  r. processing
  r. processor
  r. testing
removable plugboard
reorganize
repair —
  r. delay time
  r. time
  r. time, mean
reperforator
repertoire — the range of characters or codes
  available in a system of coding
repetition —
  r. frequency, pulse
  r. instruction
  r. rate, pulse
repetitive —
  r. addressing
  r. operation
replication
reply
report —
  r. generation
  r. generator
  r. program
  r. program generator
representation —
  binary-coded decimal r.
  binary incremental r.
  positional r.
  ternary incremental r.
reproducer —
  paper tape r.
reproducing punch

request slip
rerouting
rerun —
  r. point
  r. time
rescue dump
research —
  operations r.
reservation — allocation of memory areas in
  a multiprogrammed computer
reserve
reserved word
reset —
  r. cycle
  r. mode
  r. pulse
reshaping —
  signal r.
resident routine
residual —
  r. error
  r. error rate
residue check
resilience
resolution error
resolver
resolving potentiometer
resource
resource allocation in multi-project
  scheduling
response —
  r. duration
  r. time
restart
restart point
restore — to set a counter or indicator to
  some previous value
result
retained peripheral
retention period
retrieval
return —
  r. address
  r. instruction
  r. -to-bias recording
  r. -to-reference recording
reversible —
  r. counter
  r. magnetic process
  r. process

revolver track
rewind
rewrite
right —
  r. justified
  r. shift
ring —
  r. counter
  r. shift
ripple-through carry
rise time
RJE — remote job entry
RJE mode
role indicator
roll —
  r. in
  r. off
  r. on
  r. out
round — to alter the value of digits at the least significant end of a number
rounding —
  r. error
  r. off
route
routine —
  assembly r.
  checking r.
  closed r.
  compiling r.
  debugging r.
  executive r.
  floating point r.
  heuristic r.
  housekeeping r.
  interpreter r.
  r. maintenance
  r. maintenance time
  master r.
  object r.
  open r.
  test r.
  trace r.
  tracing r.
  translating r.
routing —
  r. indicator
row —
  r. binary
  r. binary code
  r. pitch

run —
  r. book
  r. chart
  r. diagram
  r. duration
  r. locator routine
  machine r.
  r. phase
  r. time
running accumulator

S

sampling —
  s. rate
satellite processor
scale —
  extended time s.
  s. factor
  fast time s.
  s. of two
  slow time s.
scaling factor
scan —
  s. period
  s. rate
scanner
scanning —
  s. rate
scatter read
scheduled —
  s. engineering time
  s. maintenance
scheduling
schema
scientific —
  s. computer
  s. data processing
  s. language
scratch —
  s. pad memory
  s. tape
screen —
  s. layout
  s. mode
search
search time
second —
  s. generation computers

second (*continued*)
  s. level address
  s. remove subroutine
secondary storage
section —
  input s.
  output s.
sector
security
seek
seek area
see-saw circuit
segment
segment mark
segmented program
segregating unit
select
selecting
selection sequential access
selective —
  s. digit emitter
  s. dump
  s. sequential
  s. trace
selector
selector channel
self —
  s. -checking code
  s. -checking number
  s. -resetting loop
  s. -triggering program
semantic error
semantics
semi-automatic switching center
semiconductor
sense — to test the condition of some part of computer hardware
sense switch
sensing station
sentinel
separator
sequence —
  s. check
  s. checking routine
  s. control register
  s. error
  s. register
sequential —
  s. access storage
  s. control
  s. processing
  s. -stacked job control

serial —
  s. access
  s. feeding
  s. processing
  s. transfer
service —
  s. bits
  s. programs
  s. routines
serviceability —
  s. ratio
serviceable time
servo
servo-mechanism
set —
  s. pulse
  s. up
  s. up time
several-for-one
shared files system
shift —
  arithmetic s.
  non-arithmetic s.
  s. register
  ring s.
shifting register
sideways feed
sight check
sign — an arithmetical symbol distinguishing positive from negative quantities
sign —
  s. bit
  s. check indicator
  s. -changing amplifier
  s. check indicator
  s. digit
  s. position
signal —
  s. conditioning
  s. distance
  s. normalization
  nought output s.
  one output s.
  s. regeneration
  s. reshaping
  s. standardization
signalling rate
signed field
significance
significant —
  s. digits
  s. figures

simplex —
  s. channel
simulation — the representation of problems allowing physical situations to be expressed mathematically
simulator
simulator routine
simultaneity
simultaneous —
  s. access
  s. computer
single —
  s. address code
  s. address instruction
  s. column pence coding
  s. -ended amplifier
  s. length
  s. shot circuit
  s. shot operation
  s. step operation
sizing — evaluation of resources and facilities required to perform a data-processing task
skeletal code
skip
skip-sequential access
slave store
slow time scale
smudge
snapshot dump
socket
soft —
  s. copy
  s. dump
software
solid —
  s. state computer
  s. state device
sonic delay line
SOP — standard operating procedure
sort
sorter
sort generator
sorting —
  s. needle
  s. routine
  s. routine generator
source —
  s. code
  s. computer
  s. document

source (*continued*)
  s. language
  s. machine
  s. module
  s. program
space —
  s. character
  s. suppression
span
spanned record
special —
  s. characters
  s. purpose computer
specific —
  s. address
  s. code
  s. coding
  s. program
specification
splicer
split-word operations
spool
spooling
spot —
  s. carbon
  s. punch
sprocket —
  s. holes
  s. pulse
squeezeout
stability
stable trigger circuit
stack — an area for temporary storage of data
stacker —
  card s.
standard —
  s. costing
  s. form
  s. interface
  s. operating procedure
  s. subroutine
standardization
standardize
standards
standing-on-nines carry
start-stop time
state —
  one s.
statement — a source language instruction
statement number

static —
　　s. dump
　　s. magnetic cell
　　s. store
　　s. subroutine
staticizer
stationery
status word
step —
　　s. -by-step operation
　　s. change
　　s. counter
stock control
stop —
　　s. code
　　s. instruction
　　s. instruction, conditional
　　s. instruction, optional
　　s. time
storage —
　　s. allocation
　　s. allocation, dynamic
　　s. block
　　buffer s.
　　s. capacity
　　s. cell
　　s. compacting
　　content-addressed s.
　　s. cycle
　　s. density
　　s. devices
　　direct access s.
　　disk s.
　　drum s.
　　s. dump
　　dynamic s.
　　erasable s.
　　internal s.
　　s. location
　　magnetic s.
　　magnetic core s.
　　magnetic disk s.
　　magnetic drum s.
　　magnetic film s.
　　magnetic tape s.
　　main s.
　　mercury s.
　　non-erasable s.
　　parallel search s.
　　s. register
　　secondary s.
　　Williams tube s.

store —
　　cathode ray tube s.
　　core s.
　　s. cycle time
　　s. dump
　　erasable s.
　　magnetic s.
　　magnetic disk s.
　　magnetic drum s.
　　magnetic film s.
　　magnetic tape s.
　　magnetic wire s.
　　non-volatile s.
　　random access s.
　　secondary s.
　　volatile s.
　　Williams tube s.
stored —
　　s. program
　　s. program computer
　　s. routine
straight line coding
stream — the data route from a resource to a controller
string —
　　s. break
　　s. length
　　s. manipulation
stunt box
style — the distinctive optical proportions of characters remaining constant, whatever the size of the characters
stylus —
　　s. input device
　　light pen s.
　　s. printer
subprogram
subroutine
subroutine library
subroutines
subscriber station
subscript
subset
subtracter
subtracter-adder
subtraction
subtrahend
suite (of programs)
sum —
　　modulo 2 s.
sumcheck
sum-check digit

summary —
  s. card
  s. punch
  s. punching
summation check
supervising system
supervisor
supervisory —
  s. control
  s. program
supplementary —
  s. maintenance
  s. maintenance time
suppression
switch
switched-message network
switching —
  s. center
  message s.
symbol —
  s. table
symbolic —
  s. address
  s. assembly-language listing
  s. assembly system
  s. code
  s. coding
  s. debugging
  s. instruction
  s. language
  s. name
  s. programming
symmetric difference
synchronizer
synchronous —
  s. computer
  s. working
syntax
synthesis
synthetic —
  s. address
  s. language
system —
  s. chart
  s. checks
  s. control language
  ducol punched card s.
  s. failure
  s. generation
  hybrid computer s.
  information s.
  information retrieval s.

system (*continued*)
  management information s.
  real time s.
  s. reliability
  s. structure
  time-sharing monitor s.
systematic error checking code
systems —
  s. analysis
  s. analyst
  s. definition
  s. design
  s. flowchart
  inquiry and communications s.
  s. recovery time
  specification s.

T

table —
  t. look-at
  t. look-up
  t. look-up instruction
tabular language
tabulate
tabulation —
  t. character
tabulator
tag —
  t. converting unit
  t. format
takedown —
  t. time
tally
tally reader
tandem system
tank — colloquialism for an acoustic delay line in which mercury is used to recirculate sonic signals
tape —
  t. alternation
  t. bootstrap routine
  chadded paper t.
  chadless paper t.
  t. cluster
  t. code, paper
  t. comparator
  t. controlled carriage
  t. core
  t. deck

tape (*continued*)
t. drive
t. feed
t. file
t. group
t. labels
t. librarian
t. library
t. mark
master instruction t.
perforated t.
t. plotting system
t. processing simultaneity
t. punch
t. punch, automatic
punched t.
t. reader
t. reader, magnetic   .
t. reproducer
t. serial number
t. sort
t. splicer
t. station
t. thickness
t. transport
t. transport mechanism
t. unit
t. verifier
t. width
t. wound core
tapped potentiometer function generator
target —
t. computer
t. configuration
t. language
t. machine
t. phase
t. program
teaching machines
telecommunication
telegraphic communication
telemeter
telemetering
telephone data set
telephonic communication
teleprinter
teleprocessing
Teletype
teletype —
t. grade
t. input/output unit

teletypewriter
teletypewriter exchange
telex
temporary storage
ten position
tens complement
teracycle
terminal —
data communication t.
job-oriented t.
multiplex-data t.
t. symbol
t. user
termination
ternary
ternary incremental representation
test —
crippled leapfrog t.
t. data
t. pack
t. program
t. routine
t. run
testbed
testing envelope
text — the information element of a message, excluding those characters required to facilitate transmission
text editor
thin-film memory
third generation computers
thread — small modules performing a specific function in a computer program
three address instruction
three-input adder
three-input subtracter
three-level subroutine
threshold
threshold element
throughput
tie-line
tightly coupled twin
time —
t. -derived channel
t. -division multiplexing
t. division multiplier
fault t.
latency t.
machine-spoilt t.
mean repair t.

time (*continued*)
 t. -of-day clock
 t. origin
 program development t.
 program testing t.
 routine maintenance t.
 t. scale (factor)
 scheduled engineering t.
 t. series
 t. shared input/output system
 t. shared system
 t. sharing
 t. sharing dynamic allocator
 t. sharing monitor system
 t. slicing
 start t.
 t. study
 supplementary maintenance t.
timer —
 t. clock
timing —
 t. considerations
 t. error
TLU — table look-up
toggle —
 t. switch
torn-tape
torn-tape switching center
torsional mode delay line
total —
 t. system
 t. time
 t. transfer
totals only
TP — transaction processing
trace —
 t. program
 t. routine
 t. statement
track —
 t. labels
 t. pitch
 reading t.
trailer —
 t. label
 t. record
trailing —
 t. edge
 t. end
transacter

transaction —
 t. data
 t file
 t. processing
 t. record
 t. tape
transactor
transceiver
transcribe
transcriber
transducer
transfer —
 t. card
 t. check
 t. control
 t. function
 t. instruction
 t. instruction, condition control
 t. instruction, control
 t. instruction, unconditional control
 t. interpreter
 t. of control
 t. of control, conditional
 t. operation
 t. rate
 t. time
 unconditional t.
transfluxor
transform
transient
transistor
transition
transition card
translate
translater (translator)
translation
translator
transmission —
 t. control character
 t. interface converter
 t. loss
 parallel t.
 serial t.
 t. speed
transmit
transparency
transport —
 t. delay unit
 t. mechanism, tape
 t. unit

trap — a branch operation initiated automatically by hardware on detection of an unusual condition in the running of a program
trapezoidal integration
trapping
trap setting
tree — graphic representation of input and output lines resembling a tree
triad
tributary circuit
trigger —
    t. circuit, bistable
    t. circuit, monostable
    t. circuit, stable
    t. pair
triple-length working
trouble shooting
true —
    t. complement
    t. -time operation
truncate — to suppress insignificant digits of a number
truncation error
trunk —
    t. circuit
    t. link
truth table
turn —
    t. around document
    t. around time
twelve punch
twenty-nine feature
twin check
two —
    t. address instruction
    t's complement
    t. -core-per-bit store
    t. -dimensional storage
    t. gap head
    t. input adder
    t. input subtracter
    t. -level subroutine
    t. -out-of-five code
    t. -plus-one address
    t. state variable
    t. -valued variable
    t. -wire channel
TWX — teletypewriter exchange

type —
    t. bar
    t. bar, interchangeable
    t. drum
    t. face
    t. font, optical
typewriter

U

ultrasonics
unary operation
unattended time
unconditional —
    u. branch instruction
    u. jump instruction
    u. transfer instruction
underflow
underpunch
undisturbed —
    u. one output signal
    u. output signal
    u. response voltage
    u. zero output signal
unexpected halt
uniformly accessible store
union
union catalogue
unipolar
unipunch
unit —
    anti-coincidence u.
    card punch u.
    card reader u.
    central processing u.
    magnetic tape u.
    manual input u.
    manual word u.
    output u.
    u. record
    u. string
uniterm system
unmodified instruction
unpack
unpaged segment
unset
unused time
unwind

update
updating and file maintenance
upper curtate
up time
user —
  u. group
  u. hook
utility —
  u. programs
  u. routines
utilization ratio

validation
validity check
variable —
  v. address
  v. block
  v. connector
  v. field
  v. length
  two-valued v.
VDU — visual display unit
vector mode display
verge-perforated card
verification
verifier
vertical feed
video
virgin medium
virtual —
  v. address
  v. machine
  v. machine environment
  v. storage
visual display unit
voice-grade channel
volatile memory
volume — a unit of magnetic storage
  connected to a computer system

waiting time
walk down
warm restart

waste instruction
wheel printer
Williams tube
Williams tube storage
wire printer
word —
  w. length
  w. oriented
  w. time
work —
  w. area
  w. assembly
  w. measurement
  w. tape
  w. time
working —
  double-length w.
  off-line w.
  on-line w.
  real time w.
  w. storage
wrap round
wreck — a machine fault that causes a piling
  up of punched cards on the card track
write —
  w. head
  w. inhibit ring
  w. permit ring
  w. pulse
  w. ring
  w. time
writing head

xerographic printer
xerography
X-position
X-punch
X-Y plotter

Y-edge leading
Y-position
Y-punch

Z

zero —
z. access storage
z. address instruction format
z. balance
z. condition
z. elimination
z. fill
z. -level address

zero (*continued*)
z. output
z. output signal
z. output signal, undisturbed
z. state
z. suppression
zeroize
zone —
z. bit
z. digit
z. punch

Economics and Finance

A

AAA — American Arbitration Association
abandonment
abatement
ability-to-pay principle of taxation
abrasion — loss of weight in coins due to wear while in circulation
absolute advantage
abstinence theory of interest
accelerated —
a. amortization
a. depreciation
accelerating premium
acceleration —
a. clause
a. premium
a. principle
acceptance —
anticipated a.
bank a.
a. bill
a. credit
dollar a.
a. liability
qualified a.
a. supra protest
accommodation —
a. bill of lading
a. endorsement
a. paper
account —
a's payable
a's receivable
controlling a.
custodian a.
expense a.
frozen a.
impersonal a.
memorandum a.
nominal a.
open a.
personal a.
property a.
real a.

account (*continued*)
rubricated a.
sequestered a.
subsidiary a.
suspense a.
tax and loan a.
accountabilities
accountant
accrual basis
accrued —
a. income
a. interest
accumulated —
a. dividend
a. profits tax
accumulation
accumulative dividend
acid-test ratio
acknowledgment
across-the-board
active —
a. stock
a. trade balance
actuary
Adamson Act
ADB — Asian Development Bank
added value tax
add-on-loan
adjusted —
a. gross income
a. trial balance
adjuster
adjustment bond
administered price
administrative budget
administrator
admission temporaire (Fr) — free admission of dutiable goods destined for export
ADP — automatic data processing
ad valorem (Lat) — according to the value
a. v. duty
advance bill
advertising —
a. agency
AEC — Atomic Energy Commission
affidavit

afforestation
AFL — American Federation of Labor
agency —
  mercantile a.
  a. shop
  specialized a.
Agency for International Development
agent —
  corporate a.
  a's of production
  trade a.
aggregate corporation
aggregative index number
agio theory of interest
agreement —
  clearing a.
  commodity a.
  del credere a.
  gentlemen's a.
  joint a.
  marketing a.
  multilateral a.
  standstill a.
  trade a.
agricultural —
  a. economics
  a. ladder
  a. parity
  a. price support
  a. revolution
Agricultural Adjustment Act
Agricultural Credit Act
Agricultural Research Service
Agricultural Stabilization and Conservation
  Service
AID — Agency for International
  Development
Air Quality Act
Aldrich-Vreeland Act
Alliance for Progress
allocation
allonge
allotment
allowance —
  a. for bad debts
  a. for depreciation
allowed time
AMA — American Management Association
amalgamation
American Arbitration Association
American depository receipt

American Economic Association
American Farm Bureau Federation
American Federation of Labor
American Management Association
American selling price
American Statistical Association
American Stock Exchange
American system
amortization —
  accelerated a.
amortized value
analog computer
anarchism
annual wage
annuity —
  a. bond
  deferred a.
  life a.
  survivorship a.
  variable a.
antagonistic cooperation
antibank movement
anticipation rate
Anti-Corn-Law League
antidumping duty
Anti-injunction Act
Antiracketeering Act
Antistrikebreaking Act
antitrust —
  a. acts
Antitrust Division
applied economics
apportioned tax
appraisal
appreciation
apprentice
appropriation —
  itemized a.
  lump-sum a.
  segregated a.
arbitrage
arbitration —
  a. of exchange
area —
  a. agreement
  a. sample
arithmetic —
  a. chart
  a. mean
  a. progression
arm's length

arrears
ARS — Agricultural Research Service
articles of Incorporation
artificial capital
artisan
Asian Development Bank
assaying
assay office
assembly-line technique
assented —
   a. bond
   a. stock
assessable stock
assessment —
   special a.
   tax a.
assessor
asset —
   a. and liability statement
   capital a.
   contingent a.
   current a.
   a. enter mains
   fixed a.
   floating a.
   frozen a's
   hidden a's
   intangible a.
   legal a.
   liquid a.
   ordinary a.
   quick a.
   slow a.
   unencumbered a.
   wasting a.
assignat
assignee
assignment
assimilation
association —
   a. agreement
   trade a.
assumed bond
assumption of risk
assurance
astronomical theory of the business cycle
Atomic Energy Act
Atomic Energy Commission
atomistic society
at the market
auction sale

audit
auditor
austerity program
Austrian school
autarchy
authorized —
   a. capital stock
   a. investment
   a. issue
automatic —
   a. balance
   a. checkoff
   a. data processing system
   a. stabilizer
   a. wage adjustment
automation
autonomous —
   a. investment
   a. tariff system
   a. variable
avail
average —
   arithmetic mean a.
   Dow-Jones a's
   geometric mean a.
   harmonic mean a.
   median a.
   mode a.
   moving a.
   quadratic mean a.
   weighted a.

B

backlog
back spread
backtracking
bad faith
bailment
balance —
   adjusted trial b.
   automatic b.
   compensating b.
   b. of payments
   b. of trade
   b. sheet
   passive trade b.
balloon —
   b. loan
   b. note

ballooning
bank —
   b. acceptance
   b. call
   b. clearings
   b. credit
   b. credit proxy
   b. debits
   b. deposit
   b. examiner
   b. for cooperatives
   b. holiday
   industrial b.
   joint stock land b's
   land b.
   member b.
   national b.
   b. note
   b. of issue
   par-list b.
   pet b's
   private b.
   b. post remittance
   b. rate
   b. reserves
   savings b.
   state b.
   b. term loan
   world b.
bankable bill
banker's bill
Bank for International Settlements
Bankhead-Jones Farm Tenant Act
Banking Act
banking system
Bank of North Dakota
Bank of the United States
bankruptcy —
   b. acts
   involuntary b.
   voluntary b.
bantam store
bargaining unit
barometer stock
barter
base —
   b. pay
   b. period
   b. rate

basic —
   b. crops
   b. yield
basing-point system
bazaar
bear — a trader in stocks who believes that
   their value will decline
bearer
bear vs. bull
BEC — Bureau of Employees' Compensation
beneficiary
benefit society
benefits-received principle of taxation
Benelux
bequest —
   charitable b.
betterment tax
Beveridge plan
bidding
big —
   b. board
   b. business
   b. steel
bilateral —
   b. agreement
   b. monopoly
bill —
   acceptance b.
   advance b.
   bankable b.
   banker's b.
   blank b.
   clean b.
   continental b.
   credit b.
   demand b.
   documentary b.
   domestic b.
   finance b.
   foreign b.
   inland b.
   investment b.
   b. of credit
   b. of exchange
   b. of lading
   b. of sale
   b's payable
   payment b.
   prime b.

bill (*continued*)
  b's receivable
  sight b.
  time b.
  treasury b.
bimetallism
binary notation
binder
birth rate
BIS — Bank for International Settlements
black —
  b. Friday
  b. list
  b. market
Bland-Allison Act
blank —
  b. bill
  b. endorsement
blanket bond
blighted area
block diagram
blocked —
  b. currency
  b. exchange
BLS — Bureau of Labor Statistics
blue —
  b. chip
  b. eagle
  b. sky laws
board —
  b. of directors
  b. of trade
Board of Governors of the Federal Reserve System
boiler room
bonanza
bond —
  adjustment b.
  annuity b.
  assented b.
  assumed b.
  blanket b.
  bottomry b.
  callable b.
  collateral trust b.
  colonial b.
  consol b.
  consolidated b.
  continued b.

bond (*continued*)
  convertible b.
  coupon b.
  currency b.
  debenture b.
  deferred b.
  divisional b.
  endorsed b.
  equipment trust b.
  extended b.
  extension b.
  fidelity b.
  first-lien b.
  gold b.
  guaranteed b.
  income b.
  industrial b.
  industrial revenue b.
  installment b.
  insular b.
  interchangeable b.
  interest b.
  interim b.
  irredeemable b.
  joint and several b.
  junior-lien b.
  land-grant b.
  legal-tender b.
  liberty b.
  mortgage b.
  municipal b.
  nonassented b.
  noninterest-bearing discount b.
  optional b.
  overlying b.
  participating b.
  passive b.
  perpetual b.
  plain b.
  prior-lien b.
  profit-sharing b.
  public b.
  railroad b.
  redeemable b.
  refunding b.
  registered b.
  registered coupon b.
  reorganization b.
  revenue b.

bond (*continued*)
  savings b.
  serial b.
  series b.
  sinking-fund b.
  special-assessment b.
  stamped b.
  state b.
  surety b.
  tax-anticipation b.
  ten-forty b.
  terminal b.
  territorial b.
  underlying b.
  unified b.
bondage
bonded —
  b. goods
  b. warehouse
Bonneville Power Administration
bonus —
  b. stock
book —
  b. credit
  b. value
bookkeeping
boom — rapid growth in business activity and in market values
boondoggling
boot — something given in addition to an exchanged thing to equalize the exchange
bootlegging
bordereau
borrowing
bottomry bond
bounty —
  export b.
bourgeoisie
bourse
boycott —
  primary b.
bracero
branch banking
brand — a symbol or name used to identify a product
Brannan plan
brassage
brazen law of wages
break-even chart
breakthrough

broad market
broker —
  bond b.
  insurance b.
  odd-lot b.
  real-estate b.
  ship b.
  stock b.
brokerage
bubble — an unsound business venture in which the price of participation bears no relation to the value of assets
bucket shop
budget —
  administrative b.
  capital b.
  double b.
  national income accounts b.
  unified b.
Budget and Accounting Act
budgetary control
buffer stock plan
builder's lien
building and loan association
building society
built-in — indicating laws, contracts or customs that speed or retard current economic trends
bulk-line costs
bull — a trader in stocks who believes that their value will increase
bullion —
  standard b.
  unparted b.
bull vs. bear
bumping — the policy of retaining employees with longer records of service in preference to those with shorter records
Bureau of Employees' Compensation
Bureau of Engraving and Printing
Bureau of Family Services
Bureau of Federal Credit Unions
Bureau of International Commerce
Bureau of Labor Standards
Bureau of Labor Statistics
Bureau of Land Management
Bureau of Mines
Bureau of Public Roads
Bureau of Reclamation
Bureau of the Budget

Bureau of the Census
Bureau of the Customs
Bureau of the Mint
Bureau of the Public Debt
business —
    b. affected with a public interest
    b. agent
    b. barometer
    b. cycle
    b. interruption insurance
buyers' —
    b. market
    b. monopoly
    b. strike
    b. surplus
buying —
    memorandum b.
    b. on margin
by-product
Byrnes Act

C

CAB — Civil Aeronautics Board
cable —
    c. rate
    c. transfer
cadastre
call —
    c. back pay
    bank c.
    c. compensation
    c. loan
    margin c.
callable —
    c. bond
    c. preferred stock
cambism or **cambistry**
cambist
Cambridge school
Cameralism (also spelled Kameralism)
canons of taxation
capillarity —
    law of c.
capital —
    artificial c.
    c. asset
    c. budget
    consumers' c.

capital (*continued*)
    c. consumption allowance
    equity c.
    floating c.
    c. formation
    frozen c.
    c. gain
    c. gains tax
    c. goods
    impaired c.
    instrumental c.
    c. levy
    c. liability
    liquid c.
    c. loss
    lucrative c.
    c. market
    money c.
    c. movement
    natural c.
    producer's c.
    property c.
    c. rent
    risk c.
    security c.
    c. stock
    c. stock tax
    c. surplus
    venture c.
    working c.
capitalism
capitalist
capitalistic production
capitalization of land taxes
capitalized —
    c. value
    c. value standard
capitation tax
Capper-Volstead Act
capsule cargo
captive mine
car loadings
carrier's lien
carry-back
carryover funds
cartel
cash —
    c. flow
    c. items
    c. market

cash (*continued*)
  c. on delivery
  c. position
  c. reserve
  c. sale
  c. surrender value
cashier's check
caste system
casualty insurance
casual workers
caveat emptor (Lat) — let the buyer beware
caveat venditor (Lat) — let the seller beware
CCC — Commodity Credit Corporation
CEA — Commodity Exchange Authority;
  Council of Economic Advisers
CED — Committee for Economic
  Development
ceiling prices
central —
  c. bank
  c. reserve cities
  c. reserve city banks
Central Certificate Service
certificate —
  c. of beneficial interest
  debenture c.
  c. of deposit
  gold c.
  c. of incorporation
  c. of indebtedness
  c. of origin
  participating c.
  c. of public convenience and necessity
  receiver's c.
  script c.
  silver c.
  stock c.
  street c.
  union c.
  unqualified c.
  validation c.
  voting-trust c.
  warehouse c.
certified —
  c. check
  c. public accountant
chain —
  c. banking
  c. store
  c. store tax

chamber of commerce
chapel — in printing, a division of a local
  union composed of members who are
  employed by one plant
charitable —
  c. bequest
  c. devise
  c. trust
charter
Chartism
chattel —
  c. mortgage
  personal c.
cheap money
check —
  cashier's c.
  certified c.
  counter c.
  c. credit
  c. currency
  traveler's c.
  voucher c.
checkoff —
  automatic c.
  compulsory c.
  voluntary c.
checkweighman
chemurgy
Chicago Board of Trade
child labor
chrematistic
Christian Socialism
churning — continuous buying and selling of
  securities, often to generate commissions
CIO — Congress of Industrial Organizations
circular letter of credit
circulating —
  c. capital good
  c. medium
Civil Aeronautics Board
civil corporation
Civil Service anti-strike law
class —
  c. price
  c. struggle
Classical school
classified —
  c. stock
  c. tax
Clayton Act

clean bill
Clean Waters Act
clearing agreement
clearinghouse —
  c. agent
  c. stock
clearings —
  bank c.
close corporation
closed —
  c. corporation
  c. end investment company
  c. mortgage
  c. shop
  c. union
CMEA — Council for Mutual Economic
  Assistance
CMS — Consumer and Marketing Service
coalition bargaining
coaxial cable
cobweb chart
codes of fair competition
codetermination
coefficient —
  c. of acceleration
  c. of correlation
  c. of cross-elasticity
  c. of elasticity
  c. of variation
cognovit note
coin —
  subsidiary c.
  token c.
coinage
Coinage Act
coinsurance
collateral —
  c. heir
  c. loan
  c. note
  c. security
  c. surety
  c. trust bond
  c. value
collective —
  c. bargaining
  c. ownership
collectivism
collector of the customs

collusion —
  tacit c.
Colombo Plan
colonial —
  c. bond
  c. system
column diagram
comaker
combination —
  c. in restraint of trade
  c. rate
combined entry
Comecon — Council for Mutual Economic
  Assistance
commerce —
  interstate c.
  intrastate c.
commercial —
  c. bank
  c. credit
  c. credit company
  c. paper
  c. policy
  c. revolution
  c. treaty
commission
Commissioner of Customs
commissioner of deeds
Commissioner of Internal Revenue
Committee for Economic Development·
commodity —
  c. agreement
  c. dollar
  c. exchange
  c. paper
  c. standard
  c. theory of money
Commodity Credit Corporation
Commodity Exchange Authority
common —
  c. carrier
  c. law trust
  c. stock
  c. stock index
  c. trust
Common Market
commonwealth
Communications Satellite Corporation
communism

community-property principle
company —
  holding c.
  investment c.
  joint stock c.
  management c.
  mutual c.
  safe-deposit c.
  split investment c.
  c. store
  subsidiary c.
  c. town
  trust c.
  c. union
comparative —
  c. advantage
  c. costs
compensated dollar
compensating balance
compensatory —
  c. duty
  c. fiscal policy
  c. principle of money
  c. principle of taxation
  c. spending
competition —
  cutthroat c.
  destructive c.
  free c.
  imperfect c.
  monopolistic c.
  open c.
  perfect c.
  pure c.
complex trust
compliance director
composite —
  c. commodity standard
  c. demand
  c. supply
composites
composition
compound —
  c. duty
  c. entry
  c. interest
Compromise Tariff
comptroller (sometimes spelled controller)
compulsory —
  c. arbitration
  c. checkoff

computer —
  c. assisted instruction
Comsat — Communications Satellite
  Corporation
concentration
concession
conciliation
condemnation
conditional —
  c. endorsement
  c. gift
  c. sale
  c. sales contract
condominium
confirmed letter of credit
confiscation
conflict of interest
conglomerate
Congress of Industrial Organizations
consent decree
conservation
conservator
consignment
consol bond
consolidated —
  c. balance sheet
  c. bond
  c. mortgage
consolidation
conspicuous consumption
constant —
  c. costs
  c. dollar
consular —
  c. agent
  c. invoice
consul general
consumer —
  c. cooperative
  c. credit
  c. economics
  c. good
  c. price index
  c's capital
  c. sovereignty
Consumer and Marketing Service
Consumers Advisory Council
consumption —
  conspicuous c.
  c. tax
  unproductive c.

containerized freight
continental bill
contingency reserve
contingent —
  c. asset
  c. duty
  c. fund
  c. liability
continued bond
continuous market
contract —
  c. clause
  conditional sales c.
  future-exchange c.
  c. labor
  labor c.
  open c.
  open-end c.
  c. rent
  c. research
  sweetheart c.
  c. system
  tying c.
  voidable c.
  yellow-dog c.
contributory —
  c. negligence
  c. pension
control —
  budgetary c.
  credit c.
  exchange c.
  inventory c.
  manpower c.
  pollution c.
  price c.
  quality c.
  rent c.
  standby c.
  wage and salary c.
controlled economy
controller (see comptroller)
controlling —
  c. account
  c. company
convenience store
conventional tariff system
conversion price
convertible —
  c. bond
  c. money
  c. stock

convict —
  c. labor
  c. lease system
cooling-off period
cooperative —
  c. commonwealth
Cooperative Marketing Act
copyright
corner — buying a stock or commodity in
  sufficient quantity to give the buyer control
  of its price
corn laws
corporate —
  c. agent
  c. depository
  c. fiduciary
  c. resolution
  c. shell
  c. stock
  c. surety
  c. trust
corporation —
  aggregate c.
  civil c.
  close c. (closed)
  ecclesiastical c.
  eleemosynary c.
  foreign c.
  c. income tax
  lay c.
  limited-dividend c.
  municipal c.
  private c.
  public c.
  public-service c.
  quasi c.
  quasi-public c.
  sole c.
correspondent bank
cost —
  c. accounting
  bulk line c.
  comparative c.
  constant c.
  decreasing c.
  depreciable c.
  direct c.
  c. factor
  fixed c.
  imputed c.
  increasing c.

cost (*continued*)
  incremental c.
  indirect c.
  joint c.
  marginal c.
  c. of living adjustment
  c. of production theory of value
  c. of service principle of taxation
  operating c.
  opportunity c.
  overhead c.
  c. plus contract
  prime c.
  running c.
  social c.
  standard c.
  sunk c.
  supplementary c.
  unit c.
  user c.
  variable c.
Council for Mutual Economic Assistance
Council of Economic Advisers
counter check
counterfeit money
counterpart fund
countervailing —
  c. duty
  c. excise duty
county agricultural agent
coupon —
  c. bond
  ex c.
covenant
craft —
  c. guild
  c. union
credit —
  acceptance c.
  bank c.
  c. bill
  book c.
  c. card
  check c.
  commercial c.
  consumer c.
  c. control
  frozen c's
  c. life insurance
  c. money

credit (*continued*)
  c. rating
  reserve bank c.
  social c.
  store c.
  swap c.
  c. theory of the business cycle
  c. union
Crédit Mobilier
creditor —
  judgment c.
  c. nation
Crime of 1873
critical material
crop insurance
cross —
  c. -elasticity
  c. of gold
  c. picketing
  c. purchase
  c. -rate
crude —
  c. birth rate
  c. death rate
culture lag
cum rights
cumulative —
  c. dividend
  c. stock
  c. voting
curb —
  c. exchange
  c. stock
currency —
  blocked c.
  c. bond
  fractional c.
  reserve c.
  Treasury c.
current —
  c. asset
  c. liability
  c. ratio
  c. yield
Current Tax Payment Act
curtail schedule
custodian account
customers' net debit balances
customhouse

customs —
  c. broker
  c. duty
  c. union
cutback
cutthroat competition
cybernetics
cyclical —
  c. fluctuations
  c. unemployment

D

datamation
Dawes plan
day loan
days of grace
dead —
  d. rent
  d. time
deadheading
dear money
death —
  d. rate
  d. sentence
debasement
debenture —
  d. bond
  d. certificate
  d. stock
  subordinated d.
debit —
  bank d's
debt —
  d. ceiling
  floating d.
  funded d.
  gross national d.
  interallied d.
  d. limit
  d. monetization
  national d.
  private d.
  public d.
  secured d.
  d. service
  unfunded d.
  unsecured d.

debtor —
  judgment d.
  d. nation
decentralization
deciles
declining-marginal-efficiency-of-capital theory
decreasing —
  d. costs
  d. returns
dedication
deductible clause
deductive method
deed
defalcation
Defense Production Act
defensive portfolio
deferred —
  d. annuity
  d. bond
  d. demand
  d. income
deficiency supply bill
deficit —
  dollar d.
  d. financing
  trade d.
definitive
deflation
deflationary gap
degressive taxation
del credere (Lat) — of trust
  d.c. agreement
delinquency
delinquent tax
demand —
  d. and supply curves
  d. bill
  d. deposit
  derived d.
  d. draft
  elastic d.
  joint d.
  d. loan
  d. note
  potential d.
  d. rates
  replacement d.
democratic socialism
demonetization

demurrage
denominational value
Department of Agriculture
Department of Commerce
Department of Defense
Department of Health, Education, and
    Welfare
Department of Housing and Urban
    Development
Department of Justice
Department of Labor
Department of State
Department of the Interior
Department of the Treasury
Department of Transportation
depletion allowance
deposit —
    bank d.
    d. bank
    d. currency
    demand d.
    derivative d.
    d. insurance
    primary d.
    d. slip
    time d.
depositary
depository —
    corporate d.
depreciable cost
depreciated money
depreciation —
    accelerated d.
    allowance for d.
depression
derivative deposit
derived demand
descriptive —
    d. economics
    d. labeling
destructive competition
devaluation
development
devise —
    charitable d.
diagonal expansion
differential —
    d. duty
    port d.
    d. wage rate

diffusion theory of taxation
digital computer
Dillon Round
dilution
diminishing —
    d. productivity
    d. returns
    d. utility
Dingley Tariff
direct —
    d. cost
    d. financing
    d. production
    d. reduction mortgage
    d. strike
    d. tax
    d. verification
directed economy
director of internal revenue
disability benefits
disagio
disaster relief program
disbursement —
    d. schedule
discontinuous market
discount —
    d. house
    d. loan
    d. market
    d. rate
    d. store
    trade d.
discounting the news
discretionary trust
discriminating duty
discrimination
discriminatory taxation
disguised unemployment
dishoarding
disinflation
disintermediation
disinvestment
dismal science
dismissal wage
disposable personal income
dissaving
distribution —
    physical d.
    temporal d.
disutility

diversification
dividend —
accumulated d.
accumulative d.
cumulative d.
ex d.
optional d.
d. payment ratio
scrip d.
stock d.
wage d.
divisional bond
division of labor
documentary bill
dole
dollar —
d. acceptance
compensated d.
constant d.
d. -cost averaging
d. deficit
d. exchange
d. gap
d. stabilization
domestic —
d. bill
d. exchange
d. industry
d. system
donated —
d. stock
d. surplus
double —
d. budget
d. entry
d. liability
d. standard
d. taxation
Dow-Jones averages
down period
Dow theory
draft —
demand d.
sight d.
time d.
drawback
drayage
drummer — a salesman who solicits business
by showing samples
dry farming

dual —
d. pay system
d. purpose fund
dummy —
d. directors
d. incorporators
dumping
Dun and Bradstreet
duopoly
duopsony
Dutch auction
duty —
ad valorem d.
antidumping d.
compound d.
contingent d.
countervailing d.
countervailing excise d.
customs d.
differential d.
discriminating d.
import d.
preferential d.
retaliatory d.
specific d.
dynamic economics

E

eagle — a United States $10 gold coin
early vesting
earmarked gold
earned —
e. income
e. surplus
earnest money
earning-capacity standard
easement
ecclesiastical corporation
ECCS — European Community for Coal and
Steel
econometrics
economic —
e. abundance
e. democracy
e. determinism
e. equality
e. friction
e. good

economic (*continued*)
  e. growth rate
  e. harmonies
  e. history
  e. imperialism
  e. independence
  e. interpretation of history
  e. law
  e. liberalism
  e. man
  e. mobilization
  e. nationalism
  e. planning
  e. rent
  e. royalist
  e. sanctions
  e. scarcity
  e. self-sufficiency
  e. system
  e. union
  e. warfare
  e. wealth
economics —
  agricultural e.
  applied e.
  consumer e.
  descriptive e.
  dynamic e.
  econometric e.
  home e.
  institutional e.
  international e.
  Keynesian e.
  macroeconomic e.
  mathematical e.
  microeconomic e.
  static e.
  welfare e.
Economic and Social Council
Economic Commission for Africa
Economic Commission for Asia and the Far East
Economic Commission for Europe
Economic Commission for Latin America
Economic Cooperation Administration
Economic Opportunity Act
economist
economy —
  handicraft e.
  mature e.

economy (*continued*)
  mixed e.
  political e.
Edge Act
Edge banks
educational tariff
EEC — European Economic Community
effective demand
efficiency engineer
EFTA — European Free Trade Association
EIB — Export-Import Bank of the United States
elastic —
  e. demand
  e. money
  e. supply
electronic data processing
eleemosynary corporation
eligible —
  e. paper
  e. security
embargo
embezzlement
eminent domain
emolument
Empire preference
employers' —
  e. associations
  e. liability insurance
  e. liability laws
employment —
  e. agency
Employment Act of 1946
emporium
enclosures
end —
  e. money
  e. product
endogenous change
endorsed bond
endorsement —
  accommodation e.
  blank e.
  conditional e.
  qualified e.
  restrictive e.
  special e.
endowment —
  e. fund
  e. plan of life insurance

Engel's law
entail
enterprise —
  private e.
entrepot
entrepreneur
entrepreneurship
Environmental Science Services
  Administration
equalization —
  e. of assessments
  e. fee
equation of exchange
equimarginal principle
equipment trust bond
equity —
  e. capital
  e. trading
Erdman Act
escalator clause
escape clause
Esch-Cummins Act
escheat
escrow
ESSA — Environmental Science Services
  Administration
essential industry
establishment
estate —
  residuary e.
  e. tax
EURATOM — European Atomic Energy
  Community
Eurobonds
Eurodollars
Euromarket
Euromart
European Atomic Energy Community
European Commission
European Community for Coal and Steel
European depository receipt
European Economic Community
European Free Trade Association
European Monetary Agreement
European Payments Union
European Recovery Program
ever-normal granary
ex —
  e. coupon
  e. dividend

ex (*continued*)
  e. interest
  e. officio
  e. rights
  e. warrants
excess —
  e. condemnation
  e. profits tax
  e. reserves
exchange —
  commodity e.
  e. control
  curb e.
  dollar e.
  foreign e.
  forward e.
  pecuniary e.
  e. rate
  e. stabilization fund
  unregistered e's
exchequer
excise tax
executive
Executive Office of the President
Executive Peace Corps
executor
exhaust price
exogenous change
expediter
expendable
expense —
  e. account
  nonrecurring e.
  prepaid e.
export —
  e. association
  e. bounty
  e. license
  e. tax
Export-Import Bank of the United States
expropriation
extended —
  e. bond
extension bond
Extension Service
extensive cultivation
external public debt
extractive industry
extrapolation

F

FAA — Federal Aviation Agency
Fabian socialism
FAC — Federal Advisory Council
face value
factor —
  f. cost
  f. reversal test
  f's of production
factorage
factory system
faculty principle of taxation
fair —
  f. employment practices legislation
  international trade f.
  f. price
  f. return
  f. trade practices acts
Fair Deal
Fair Labor Standards Act
falling-rate-of-profit theory
family industry
Fannie Mae — Federal National Mortgage
  Association
FAO — Food and Agriculture Organization
  of the United Nations
farm —
  f. bloc
  f. subsidies
  f. surpluses
Farm Bureau
Farm Credit Administration
Farmers Home Administration
Farmers Union
f.a.s. — free alongside ship
fascism
favorable balance of trade
FCA — Farm Credit Administration
FCC — Federal Communications
  Commission
FCIC — Federal Crop Insurance Corporation
FDA — Food and Drug Administration
FDIC — Federal Deposit Insurance
  Corporation
featherbedding
Fed. — Federal Reserve System

federal —
  f. intermediate credit bank
  f. land bank
  f. land bank association
  f. reserve agent
  f. reserve bank
  f. reserve bank float
  f. reserve bank note
  f. reserve city
  f. reserve notes
  f. savings and loan association
  f. trust fund
Federal Advisory Council
Federal-Aid Highway Acts
Federal Aviation Administration
Federal Communications Commission
Federal Crop Insurance Corporation
Federal Deposit Insurance Corporation
Federal Farm Loan Act
Federal Food, Drug, and Cosmetic Act
Federal funds market
Federal Home Loan Bank Act
Federal Home Loan Bank Board
Federal Home Loan Bank System
Federal Housing Administration
Federal Maritime Commission
Federal Mediation and Conciliation Service
Federal National Mortgage Association
Federal Open Market Committee
Federal Power Act
Federal Power Commission
Federal Prison Industries, Inc.
Federal Reserve Act
Federal Reserve Banks
Federal Reserve Board
Federal Reserve System
Federal Savings and Loan Insurance
  Corporation
Federal Tort Claims Act
Federal Trade Commission
Federal Trade Commission Act
Federal Water Pollution Control
  Administration
fee —
  equalization f.
fellow-servant doctrine
feudal system
FHA — Farmers Home Administration;
  Federal Housing Administration

FHLBB — Federal Home Loan Bank Board
fiat money
fidelity —
  f. bond
fiduciary —
  corporate f.
  f. money
  f. standard
fifo — first in, first out
final —
  f. good
  f. utility theory of value
finance —
  f. bill
  public f.
financial —
  f. investment
  f. statement
fine — term designating pure metal
fink
first-lien bond
fiscal —
  f. monopoly
  f. policy
  f. year
Fisher's ideal index
five percenter
five-twenty bond
fixed —
  f. asset
  f. capital good
  f. cost
  f. investment trust
  f. liability
  f. shift
flat —
  f. money
  f. standard
flexible —
  f. schedule
  f. tariff
flight —
  f. of capital
  f. of the dollar
float — uncollected checks and commercial paper in process of transfer from bank to bank
floating —
  f. asset
  f. capital

floating (*continued*)
  f. debt
  f. exchange rate
  f. supply
floor trader
flotsam
flow —
  cash f.
  f. chart
fluid savings
FMC — Federal Maritime Commission
FMCS — Federal Mediation and Conciliation Service
FNMA — Federal National Mortgage Association
Food and Agriculture Organization of the United Nations
Food and Drug Administration
food stamp plan
forced —
  f. loan
  f. sale
Fordney-McCumber Tariff
foreclosure
foreign —
  f. bill
  f. corporation
  f. exchange
  f. trade zone
  f. valuation
Foreign Investors Tax Act
Foreign Securities Act
Foreign Service officer
Forest Service
forfeiture
form utility
Fort Knox
forward exchange
forwarding agent
4-H Club agent
Fourierism
FPC — Federal Power Commission
fractional —
  f. currency
  f. reserve
frame of reference
franchise —
  f. tax
franking
Frazier-Lemke Act

free —
    f. and clear
    f. banking system of New York
    f. capital good
    f. coinage
    f. competition
    f. enterprise
    f. good
    f. list
    f. market
    f. port
    f. silver
    f. trade
freedom of contract
Freedom Shares
frequency —
    f. curve
    f. distribution
    f. polygon
    f. table
frictional unemployment
fringe benefit
frozen —
    f. account
    f. assets
    f. capital
    f. credits
FRS — Federal Reserve System
FTC — Federal Trade Commission
full —
    f. employment
    f. -paid stock
    f. stock
function
functional —
    f. distribution
    f. finance
functions of money
fund —
    carryover f.
    contingent f.
    counterpart f.
    dual purpose f.
    endowment f.
    exchange stabilization f.
    federal trust f.
    general f.
    hedge f.
    imprest f.
    interdistrict settlement f.

fund (*continued*)
    International Monetary F.
    leverage f.
    mutual f.
    no-load f.
    revolving credit f.
    revolving f.
    sinking f.
    stabilization f.
    trust f.
    unsatisfied judgment f's
fundamental disequilibrium
funded debt
future-exchange contract
futures

G

gain sharing
Gantt chart
GAO — General Accounting Office
garnishment
GATT — General Agreement on Tariffs and
    Trade
general —
    g. equilibrium
    g. equilibrium theory of international trade
    g. fund
    g. property tax
    g. strike
    g. tariff
General Accounting Office
General Agreement on Tariffs and Trade
General Assembly of the United Nations
General Services Administration
genetic industry
gentlemen's agreement
geometric —
    g. mean ·
    g. progression
George-Deen Act
George-Ellzey Act
George-Reed Act
ghetto
G.I. Bill of Rights
gift —
    conditional g.
    g. tax

gilt-edge security
give-up
Glass-Steagall Act
GNP — gross national product
going —
  g. business
  g. value
  g. wage
gold —
  g. bond
  g. bullion standard
  g. certificate
  g. clause
  g. cover
  earmarked g.
  g. exchange standard
  g. points
  g. price
  g. standard
  sterilized g.
Gold-cover Repeal Act
Gold Pool
Gold Reserve Act
Gold Standard Act
good —
  g. faith
  fixed capital g.
  g. will
government depository
Government Printing Office
GPD — general purpose data
GPO — Government Printing Office
grace period
graded tax
grade labeling
graduated tax
Grain Futures Act
grain pit
Grain Standards Act
Grange
granger legislation
grant
gratuitous coinage
gratuity
graveyard shift
gray market
greenbacks
Gresham's law
grievance

gross —
  g. income
  g. interest
  g. national debt
  g. national product
  g. national products deflator
  g. profit
ground rent
group —
  g. banking
  g. insurance
  g. medicine
Group of Ten
growth stock
Grundy tariff
GSA — General Services Administration
guaranteed —
  g. annual income
  g. annual wage
  g. bond
  g. stock
  g. wage plan
guaranty savings bank
Guffey Coal Act
guild —
  g. socialism

H

half stock
hallmark
handicraft economy
hard —
  h. money
  h. sell
harmonic —
  h. mean
  h. progression
harmonies — in economic theory, the
  doctrine that economic forces are essentially
  in accord with one another
Hatch Act
Hawes-Cooper Act
Hawley-Smoot Tariff
head —
  h. of family
  h. tax
headright

health insurance
hedge fund
hedging
hedonistic principle
Hepburn Act
HEW — Department of Health, Education,
    and Welfare
hidden —
    h. assets
    h. inflation
    h. tax
highway
higgling
hi-lo index
hire purchase
histogram
Historical school
hoarding
hold-back pay
holder —
    h. in due course
    h. of record
holding —
    h. company
    h. the line
    h. the market
holograph
home —
    h. demonstration agent
    h. economics
    h. industry
homestead —
    h. aid benefit association
Homestead Act
homework — the practice of providing
    materials to workers so that they perform
    some operations in the production of a
    commodity at home
Hoover moratorium
horizontal —
    h. expansion
    h. labor union
hot money
household system
HUD — Department of Housing and Urban
    Development
hypothecate
hypothecation
hypothesis

I

IAEA — International Atomic Energy
    Agency
IBRD — International Bank for
    Reconstruction and Development
ICAO — International Civil Aviation
    Organization
ICC — Interstate Commerce Commission
ICFTU — International Confederation of
    Free Trade Unions
ICJ — International Court of Justice
IDA — International Development
    Association
IDB — Inter-American Development Bank
idle money
IFC — International Finance Corporation
illegal strike
illiquid
illth
ILO — International Labor Organization
IMF — International Monetary Fund
immigrant remittances
immigration
impacted area
impaired capital
impair investment
impartial chairman
imperfect competition
impersonal account
import —
    i. duty
    i. license
    i. quota
impost
imprest fund
improved good
imputed —
    i. cost
    i. interest
    i. rent
inactive stock
incentive —
    i. taxation
    i. wage system
incidence of taxation
in-clearing items

income —
 accrued i.
 adjusted gross i.
 i. and expenditure equation
 i. bond
 deferred i.
 disposable personal i.
 earned i.
 gross i.
 guaranteed annual i.
 maintenance i.
 national i.
 net i.
 personal i.
 psychic i.
 i. statement
 i. tax
 unearned i.
inconvertible money
incorporation
increasing —
 i. costs
 i. misery (theory of)
 i. returns
increment —
 unearned i.
incremental cost
indemnity
indent — a purchase order to an importer to buy specified goods at a stated price
indenture
indentured servant
independent —
 i. treasury system
 i. union
index number
indifference —
 i. curve
 i. map
 i. schedule
indirect —
 i. cost
 i. exporting
 i. foreign-exchange standard
 i. production
 i. tax
individualism
Individualist school
individual proprietorship

induced —
 i. consumption
 i. investment
inductive method
industrial —
 i. bank
 i. bond
 i. democracy
 i. life insurance
 i. relations
 i. relations court
 i. research
 i. revenue bond
 i. type farming
 i. union
Industrial Revolution
Industrial Workers of the World
industry —
 genetic i.
 infant i.
 key i.
 seasonal i.
 i. wide bargaining
inelastic —
 i. demand
 i. supply
infant industry
inflation —
 hidden i.
 runaway i.
inflationary gap
inherent vice
inheritance tax
injunction
in kind
inland bill
input and output analysis
inside director
insolvency
installment —
 i. bond
 i. buying
 i. interest
instant vesting
institutional —
 i. economics
 i. investor
institutionalism
instrument

instrumental capital
insular bond
insurance —
    term plan of life i.
intangible —
    i. asset
    i. property
integration —
    vertical i.
Intelsat — International Telecommunications
    Satellite Consortium
intensive cultivation
Interallied debts
Inter-American Development Bank
interchangeable —
    i. bond
    i. parts
interdistrict settlement fund
interest —
    accrued i.
    i. bond
    compound i.
    i. equalization tax
    ex i.
    gross i.
    imputed i.
    installment i.
    legal i.
    loan i.
    net i.
    pure i.
    i. rate
    short i.
    simple i.
    true i.
Intergovernmental Maritime Consultative
    Organization
interim bond
interlocking directorate
intermediate good
internal —
    i. improvement
    i. public debt
    i. revenue
Internal Revenue Service
international —
    i. commodity agreement
    i. double taxation
    i. economics
    i. gold-bullion standard
    i. stock

international (*continued*)
    i. transit
    i. union
    i. unit
International Atomic Energy Agency
International Bank for Reconstruction and
    Development (World Bank)
International Chamber of Commerce
International Civil Aviation Organization
International Confederation of Free Trade
    Unions
International Cotton Advisory Committee
International Court of Justice
International Development Association
International Executive Service Corps
International Finance Corporation
International Labor Organization
International Monetary Fund
International Patents Bureau
International Rubber Study Group
International Statistical Institute
International Telecommunications Satellite
    Consortium
International Telecommunications Union
International Wheat Agreement
interpolation
interstate —
    i. commerce
    i. trade barriers
Interstate Commerce Act
Interstate Commerce Commission
intrastate commerce
intrinsic value
invention
inventory —
    i. control
    perpetual i.
    physical i.
    i. valuation adjustment
investment —
    authorized i.
    autonomous i.
    i. banking
    i. bill
    i. company
    i. counselor
    financial i.
    impair i.
    induced i.
    negative i.
    i. portfolio

investment (*continued*)
  real i.
  i. trust
Investment Advisors Act
Investment Company Act
invisible —
  i. hand
  i. items of trade
invoice —
  consular i.
involuntary —
  i. bankruptcy
  i. servitude
iron law of wages
irredeemable —
  i. bond
  i. foreign-exchange standard
  i. money
irrevocable letter of credit
IRS — Internal Revenue Service
issue —
  authorized i.
  term i.
itemized appropriation
ITU — International Telecommunications Union
IWW — Industrial Workers of the World

J

jetsam
job —
  j. action
  j. classification
  j. evaluation
jobber
Johnson Act
joint —
  j. agreement
  j. and several bond
  j. cost
  j. council
  j. demand
  j. rate
  j. return
  j. stock company
  j. stock land banks
  j. supply
  j. venture

Joint Economic Committee
journeyman
judgment —
  j. creditor
  j. debtor
  j. lien
  j. note
junior-lien bond
junket
jurisdictional strike
just compensation

K

Kameralism (also spelled Cameralism)
Kansas Industrial Court
Keating-Owen Act
Kennedy Round
key industry
Keynesian economics
Keynes' law of consumption
kickback
kiting
Knights of Labor
kurtosis

L

labor —
  l. agreement
  l. dispute
  l. exchange bank
  l. force
  l. grade
  l. piracy
  l. relations
  l. theory of value
  l. union
Labor-Management Relations Act (Taft-Hartley)
Labor Reform Act
laborsaving machinery
La Follette Seamen's Act
laissez faire (Fr) — Let things proceed without interference
lamb — a novice at speculation and hence likely to be quickly shorn
lame duck — a speculator whose ventures have failed of success

land —
 l. bank
 l. grant
 l. grant bond
 l. grant college
 l. patent
 l. tax
 l. value tax
Landrum-Griffin Act
lapping — the practice of covering theft from one customer by stealing from another
large-scale production
Laser technology
Latin Monetary Union
lawful money
law of capillarity
lay corporation
lead time
leakage
lease
leaseback
leased life insurance
least-squares method
legacy
legal —
 l. asset
 l. interest
 l. person
 l. rate
 l. reserves
 l. security
 l. tender
 l. tender bond
lending authority
Lend-Lease Act
letter —
 l. of credit
 l. of lien
 l. of marque
 l. of trust
letters patent
level of living
liability —
 acceptance l.
 contingent l.
 current l.
 fixed l.
 limited l.
 long-term l.
Liberal school
liberty bond

license —
 export l.
 import l.
lien —
 builder's l.
 carrier's l.
 vendor's l.
life —
 l. annuity
 l. estate
 l. insurance
lifo (last in, first out)
limited —
 l. dividend corporation
 l. liability
 l. partnership
 l. payment plan of life insurance
limping standard
line —
 holding the l.
 l. of regression
liquid —
 l. asset
liquidation
liquidity —
 l. preference
 l. preference theory of interest
listed —
 l. security
 l. stock
list price
little steel
loan —
 add-on l.
 balloon l.
 bank term l.
 call l.
 collateral l.
 day l.
 demand l.
 discount l.
 forced l.
 l. interest
 nonrecourse l.
 l. shark
 soft l.
 term l.
 tied l.
 time l.
 warehouse l's
loanable-funds theory of interest

localization of labor
local rate
lockout
logistics
London Economic Conference
long —
  l. and short haul
  l. position
  l. term liability
Lorenz curve
loss —
  capital l.
  l. leader
lucrative capital
Luddite
lump-sum appropriation
luxury tax

McFadden Act
McKinley Tariff
McNary-Haugen Bill
MA — Maritime Administration
macroeconomics
maintenance —
  m. of membership
make-work fallacy
malfeasance
malpractice
Malthusian theory of population
managed money
management —
  m. company
  m. science
  m. stock
Manchester school
man-hour
manifest
man-land ratio
Mann-Elkins Act
manorial system
Manpower Administration
manpower control
margin —
  m. call
  m. of cultivation
  m. of safety

marginal —
  m. borrower
  m. buyer
  m. cost
  m. desirability
  m. disutility of labor
  m. efficiency of capital
  m. land
  m. lender
  m. producer
  m. product
  m. productivity
  m. productivity theory of wages
  m. propensity to consume
  m. propensity to save
  m. rate of substitution
  m. revenue
  m. seller
  m. trading
  m. utility
  m. utility theory of interest
Maritime Administration
market —
  black m.
  broad m.
  buyers' m.
  capital m.
  cash m.
  continuous m.
  m. demand
  discontinuous m.
  discount m.
  federal funds m.
  free m.
  gray m.
  holding the m.
  law of m's
  money m.
  narrow m.
  open m.
  over-the-counter m.
  m. price
  rigged m.
  sellers' m.
  sensitive m.
  thin m.
  m. value
marketing agreement
markon
markup

Marshall plan
Marxian law of capitalist accumulation
Marxian school
mass —
   m. picketing
   m. production
Massachusetts Trust
matched and lost — refers to the flip of a
   coin to determine what bid secures a stock
   when there is a disparity between buy and
   sell orders
mathematical economics
mature economy
maturity
maximum —
   m. and minimum tariff system
   m. hour legislation
mean deviation
means test
measured day rate
median
mediation
mediator
Medicaid
Medicare
medium of exchange
melon — extraordinary profits awaiting
   distribution
member bank
memorandum —
   m. account
   m. buying
mercantile agency
mercantilist school
merchant —
   m. guild
   m. marine
merchantman
merger
merit rating
microeconomics
middleman
middleway
migrant worker
Miller-Tydings Act
minimum —
   m. rate
   m. wage
minor coin

mint —
   m. par of exchange
   m. price of gold
   m. ratio
mintage
misfeasance
Mississippi bubble
mixed economy
mode
modified union shop
modular housing
monetary —
   m. policy
   m. reserves
   m. sovereignty
   m. system
   m. union
   m. unit
money —
   m. capital
   depreciated m.
   earnest m.
   elastic m.
   fiat m.
   hot m.
   idle m.
   m. in circulation
   inconvertible m.
   irredeemable m.
   lawful m.
   managed m.
   m. market
   near m.
   neutral m.
   occupation m.
   m. order
   paper m.
   primary m.
   real m.
   representative m.
   soft m.
   spearhead m.
   stable m.
   standard m.
   m. wage
monometallism
monopolistic competition
monopoly —
   partial m.

monopoly (*continued*)
  public consumption m.
  special-privilege m.
  trade m.
monopsony
moonlighting
moratorium
more-favorable-terms clause
Morrill Act
Morrill Tariff
Morris Plan bank
mortgage —
  m. bond
  chattel m.
  closed m.
  consolidated m.
  direct reduction m.
  purchase-money m.
mortgagee
mortgagor
most-favored-nation clause
Motor Carrier Act
moving average
multicraft union
multilateral agreement
multilinear tariff
multiple —
  m. commodity reserve dollar
  m. currency system
  m. expansion of credit
  m. tariff system
multiplier principle
municipal —
  m. bond
  m. corporation
  m. socialism
mutual —
  m. company
  m. fund
  m. loan association
  m. savings bank
mutualism

NAM — National Association of
  Manufacturers
narrow market

NASA — National Aeronautics and Space
  Administration
national —
  n. bank
  n. debt
  n. economy
  n. forests
  n. income
  n. income accounts budget
  n. income and product account
  n. insurance
  n. minimum
  n. product
  n. security exchange
  n. union
  n. wealth
National Academy of Sciences
National Advisory Council on International
  Monetary and Financial Policies
National Aeronautics and Space
  Administration
National Association of Manufacturers
National Bank Act
National Bureau of Standards
National Currency Act
National Defense Education Act
National Farmers Union
National Grange Order of the Patrons of
  Husbandry
National Industrial Recovery Act
National Institutes of Health
nationalization
National Labor Relations Act
National Labor Relations Board
National Mediation Board
National Monetary Commission
National Railroad Adjustment Board
National Science Foundation
National Security Council
National Transportation Safety Board
natural —
  n. capital
  n. monopoly
  n. order
  n. resources
  n. rights
Natural Gas Act
navicert
NBS — National Bureau of Standards

near money
negative —
  n. income tax
  n. investment
  n. -pledge clause
negotiability
Neoclassical school
neoclassical theory of value
net —
  n. borrowed reserves
  n. free reserves
  n. income
  n. interest
  n. lease
  n. national product
  n. price
  n. product
  n. profit
  n. worth
neutral money
New Deal
Newlands Act
New York Stock Exchange
NIH — National Institutes of Health
NLRB — National Labor Relations Board
NMB — National Mediation Board
no-load fund
nominal —
  n. account
  n. price
  n. yield
nonassented —
  n. bond
  n. stock
nonassessable stock
nonclearinghouse stock
noncontributory pension
noncumulative stock
nonfeasance
Nonimportation Act
nonimportation agreement
Nonintercourse Act
noninterest-bearing discount bond
nonrecourse loans
nonrecurring expense
no-par-value stock
normal —
  n. curve of distribution
  n. curve of error
  n. price

Norris-LaGuardia Act
nostro overdraft
notary public
note —
  balloon n.
  bank n.
  cognovit n.
  collateral n.
  demand n.
  federal reserve bank n.
  federal reserve n.
  judgment n.
  n's payable
  promissory n.
  n's receivable
  savings n.
  Sherman n.
  treasury n.
  United States n.
NSC — National Security Council
NSF — National Science Foundation
nuisance tax

O

OAS — Organization of American States
obligational authority
obsolescence
occupational level
occupation —
  o. money
  o. tax
odd-lot broker
OECD — Organization for Economic
  Cooperation and Development
OEEC — Organization for European
  Economic Cooperation
OEO — Office of Economic Opportunity
OEP — Office of Emergency Planning
Office of Business Economics
Office of Comptroller of the Currency
Office of Economic Opportunity
Office of Education
Office of Emergency Planning
Office of Science and Technology
Office of Tax Legislative Counsel
Office of the Special Representative for
  Trade Negotiations
Office of the Treasurer of the United States

official exchange rate
offsets to savings
ogive
old-age (retirement), survivors' and disability
  insurance
oligopoly
one-thousand-hour clause
open —
  o. account
  o. commitments
  o. competition
  o. contracts
  o. -door policy
  o. -end contract
  o. -end investment company
  o. interest
  o. letter of credit
  o. market
  o. market operations
  o. market paper
  o. mortgage
  o. price system
  o. shop
  o. union
Open Market Committee
operating —
  o. cost
  o. profit
  o. ratio
operations research
opportunity cost
Optimist school
optimum population
option —
  stock o.
optional —
  o. bond
  o. dividend
order bill of lading
ordinary —
  o. asset
  o. rent
  o. stock
Organic school
Organization for Economic Cooperation
  and Development
Organization for European Economic
  Cooperation
Organization of American States

original —
  o. cost standard
  o. -issue stock
  o. package doctrine
Orthodox school
Ottawa agreements
Outer 7 (European Free Trade Association)
outlaw strike
outside director
overcertification
overdraft
overdraw
overextended
overhead cost
overheating
overinvestment theory of the business cycle
overlying bond
overproduction
oversaving —
  o. theory of the business cycle
over-the-counter market
Owenism
ownership utility

P

pace setter
Packers and Stockyards Act
paid-in surplus
paid-up stock
Pan American Union
panic
paper —
  accommodation p.
  eligible p.
  p. gold
  p. money
par —
  p. exchange rate
  p. -list bank
  p. value
  p. -value stock
parallel standard
Pareto's law
parity
Parkinson's laws
partial monopoly
partial or particular equilibrium

participating —
p. bond
p. certificate
p. preferred stock
partner —
silent p.
partnership —
limited p.
part-paid stock
passbook
passive —
p. bond
p. trade balance
p. trust
patent
Patent Office
paternalism
Patrons of Husbandry
patroon
Paunch Corps
pauper
pawnbroker
pay-as-you-go
payment —
p. bill
transfer p.
Payne-Aldrich Tariff
payola
payroll tax
Peace Corps
peasant movement
pecuniary exchange
pegged price
pegging
peg point
pension —
noncontributory p.
p. pool
portable p.
peonage
peppercorn rent
per —
p. capita
p. -contra item
p. diem
percentiles
perfect competition
peril point
permissive wage-adjustment clause

permit
perpetual —
p. bond
p. inventory
perquisite
personal —
p. account
p. chattel
p. distribution
p. finance company
p. income
p. property
p. property tax
pet banks
petty cash
phalanstery
Phillips curve
PHS — Public Health Service
physical —
p. distribution
p. inventory
physiocrats
picketing
piecework
piggyback
pit —
grain p.
place utility
plain bond
plane of living
planning
plantation system
Plumb plan
plunger
plutocracy
P.O. — post office
P.O.B. — post office box
point —
p. -and-figure charting
p. of ideal proportions
p. of indifference
Point Four Program
policy
political —
p. arithmetic
p. economy
poll tax
pollution control
polymetallism

polypoly
pool — a combination of business
organizations for a specific and often
temporary purpose
population pyramid
port —
p. authority
p. differential
p. of entry
portable pension
Portal-to-Portal Act
portal-to-portal pay
portfolio —
defensive p.
Port of New York Authority
possession utility
postal savings
postaudit
postdate
Post Office Department
potential —
p. demand
p. stock
poverty
power —
p. in trust
p. of alienation
p. of attorney
preaudit
preclusive buying
preemptive rights
prefabricate
preference stock
preferential —
p. duty
p. shop
preferred stock
premium —
acceleration p.
p. for risk
p. pay
p. stock
prepaid expense
prepayment —
p. penalty
p. plan
prescription
price —
p. consumption curve
p. control

price (*continued*)
p. control legislation
p. -earnings ratio
exhaust p.
f.a.s p.
p. fixing
p. leadership
p. level
list p.
p. loco
market p.
net p.
nominal p.
normal p.
pegged p.
reservation p.
p. rigidity
p. specie-flow theory
subscription p.
p. support
p. system
pricing out of the market
primary —
p. boycott
p. deposit
p. money
prime —
p. bill
p. cost
p. rate
primogeniture
prior —
p. lien bond
p. stock
priority system
private —
p. bank
p. corporation
p. debt
p. enterprise
p. property
privateering
privilege tax
probability curve
probable error
proceeds
process effects
processing tax
procurement
producer's capital

production —
p. allocation program
capitalistic p.
p. factors
indirect p.
mass p.
roundabout p.
productivity
profit —
p. and loss statement
gross p.
net p.
operating p.
pure p.
p. sharing
p. -sharing bond
windfall p.
pro forma (Lat) — as a matter of form. In importing, an invoice presented in advance to arrange for payments, with the understanding that this estimate may not correspond precisely to the later actual invoice.
p.f. statement
program
progression
progressive taxation
proletariat
promissory note
promoter
propensity —
p. to consume
p. to hoard
p. to invest
p. to save
property —
p. account
p. capital
intangible p.
personal p.
private p.
real p.
tangible p.
p. tax
unencumbered p.
proportionality —
law of p.
proportional taxation
proprietorship

prospectus
protectionism
protective tariff
protest —
acceptance supra p.
prudent-investment-cost standard
psychic income
Psychological school
psychological theory of the business cycle
public —
p. bond
p. carrier
p. consumption monopoly
p. corporation
p. debt
p. domain
p. finance
p. goods
p. lands
p. opinion survey
p. ownership
p. relations
p. revenue
p. service commission
p. service corporation
p. utility
p. utility bond
p. welfare
p. works
p. works and ways system
Public Health Service
Public Utility Holding Company Act
pump priming
punched-card data processing
purchase-money mortgage
purchasing —
p. power
p. power parity
pure —
p. competition
p. interest
p. profit
Pure Food and Drugs Act
purposive sample
put — in security trading, an option that permits an investor to sell a specific security at an agreed-upon price within a stipulated period of time
pyramiding

Q

quadratic mean
qualified —
  q. acceptance
  q. endorsement
  q. report
quality control
quantity theory of money
quarter stock
quartile deviation
quartiles
quasi —
  q. corporation
  q. public corporation
quick —
  q. asset
  q. ratio
quickie strike
quitrent
quota —
  import q.
  q. sample

R

racism
rack rent
railroad bond
Railroad Retirement Act
Railroad Retirement Board
Railroad Unemployment Insurance Act
Railway Labor Act
rally — a brisk rise in the stock market or in the price of an individual stock
random sample
range
rate —
  anticipation r.
  bank r.
  cable r.
  demand r's
  differential wage r.
  r. discrimination
  floating exchange r.
  joint r.
  legal r.

rate (*continued*)
  minimum r.
  official exchange r.
  prime r.
  rediscount r.
  r. regulation
  tax r.
  r. war
ratio chart
rationalization
rationing —
  r. of foreign exchange
raw material
REA — Rural Electrification Administration
real —
  r. account
  r. chattel
  r. -estate tax
  r. investment
  r. money
  r. property
  r. wage
realistic method
realization — conversion of assets into cash
rebate
recapitalization
recapture of earnings
receipt —
  warehouse r.
receiver
  r.'s certificate
recession
reciprocal trade agreement
reciprocity principle
reclamation
Reconstruction Finance Corporation
reconversion
recourse
redeemable —
  r. bond
  r. preferred stock
redemption agent
rediscount —
  r. rate
re-export
referee
  r. in bankruptcy
refined —
  r. birth rate
  r. death rate

reflation
reforestation
refunding —
  r. bond
regional —
  r. division of labor
  r. economic commissions of the United
    States
  r. pension system
registered —
  r. bond
  r. coupon bond
registration —
  r. statement
registry
regressive —
  r. supply curve
  r. taxation
regulation
rehypothecate
reinsurance
relative-value index number
release
remainderman
remargining
remonetization
renegotiation
rent —
  capital r.
  r. contract
  r. control
  dead r.
  economic r.
  ground r.
  imputed r.
  ordinary r.
  peppercorn r.
  rack r.
rentier
reorganization bond
reparations
repatriation
replacement —
  r. cost standard
  r. demand
replevin
representative —
  r. good
  r. money
repressive tax
reproduction-cost standard

repudiation
resale price agreements
reservation price
reserve —
  bank r's
  r. bank credit
  cash r.
  r. city banks
  contingency r.
  r. currency
  excess r's
  fractional r.
  r. ratio
  secondary r's
  unearned premium r.
residuary estate
resources —
  natural r.
restraint of trade
restrictive —
  r. covenant
  r. endorsement
Resumption Act
retaliatory duty
retroactive restoration
returns to scale of plant
revaluation
revenue —
  r. bond
  r. expenditure
  internal r.
  marginal r.
  public r.
reverse split — the opposite of a stock split;
  reduction in the number of outstanding
  shares of a corporation
reversing entries
reversion
revocable letter of credit
revolving —
  r. credit fund
  r. fund
  r. letter of credit
RFC — Reconstruction Finance Corporation
Ricardian theory of rent
rigged market
rights —
  ex r.
  preemptive r.
  subscription r.
right-to-work laws

risk —
   r. capital
   r. capital pooling
   widow and orphan's r.
rival —
   r. demand
   r. supply
Robinson-Patman Act
Rochdale principles
roll-back
rolling stock
rotating shifts
roundabout production
round-of-wage increases
royalty
RRB — Railroad Retirement Board
rubricated account
rule of reason
runaway —
   r. inflation
   r. shop
running cost
run on a bank
Rural Electrification Administration

S

sabotage
safe-deposit company
safety —
   s.-fund bank system
   margin of s.
Saint-Simonians
salary
sales —
   s. finance company
   s. tax
salvage —
   s. value
sample —
   random s.
   stratified s.
satiety —
   law of s.
savings —
   s. and loan association
   s. bank
   s. bond
   s. notes

Say's law
Say's theory of markets
SBA — Small Business Administration
scab — anyone who works under conditions
   contrary to those enforced by a labor union,
   or anyone who works in a business whose
   employees are on strike
Scandinavian Monetary Union
scarcity value
scatter chart
schedule —
   curtail s.
   s. demand
   disbursement s.
   indifference s.
   s. supply
school lunch program
schools of economic thought
Schuman Treaty
scrip —
   s. dividend
script certificate
SCS — Soil Conservation Service
SDR's — special drawing rights
seasonal —
   s. fluctuations
   s. industry
   s. unemployment
seasoned security
seat on the exchange
SEC — Securities and Exchange Commission
secondary —
   s. boycott
   s. offering
   s. picketing
   s. reserves
   s. strike
Second Industrial Revolution
secular —
   s. stagnation
   s. trend
secured debt
Securities Act
Securities and Exchange Commission
Securities Exchange Act
security —
   s capital
   collateral s.
   eligible s.
   s. exchange
   gilt-edge s.

security (*continued*)
  listed s.
  seasoned s.
  unlisted s.
Security Council
segregated appropriation
segregation
seigniorage
self —
  s.-interest
  s.-interest, law of
  s.-liquidating
  s.-sufficient nation
seller's —
  s. market
  s. seven sale
  s. surplus
selling short
semilogarithmic chart
seniority
sensitive market
sequestered account
serial bond
series bond
Servicemen's Readjustment Act
service utility
servitude
settlor
severance —
  s. tax
  s. wage
share —
  s. the wealth
  s. -the-work-plan
sharecropper
shares
Sheppard-Towner Act
Sherman Antitrust Act
Sherman notes
Sherman Silver Purchase Act
shift —
  fixed s.
shifting of taxation
shinplaster — a term of derision applied to depreciated paper currency
ship broker
shop —
  runaway s.
shopping —
  s. center
  s. mall

short interest
sight —
  s. bill
  s. draft
silent partner
silver certificate
Silver Purchase Act
simple interest
sinecure
single —
  s. entry
  s. -schedule tariff
  s. standard
  s. tax
sinking —
  s. fund
  s. -fund bond
sit-down strike
situs picketing
sixteen to one
skewness
sliding-scale tariff
slow asset
slowdown strike
slum clearance
small —
  s. business
  s. business investment company
  s. loan law
Small Business Administration
Smith-Hughes Act
Smith-Lever Act
smuggling
social —
  s. costs
  s. credit
  s. insurance
  s. security tax
  s. wealth
  s. workshop
Social and Rehabilitation Service
socialism
Social Security Act
Social Security Administration
soft —
  s. loan
  s. money
soil —
  s. bank program
  s. conservation

soil (*continued*)
  s. conservation district
  s. erosion
Soil Conservation Service
sole corporation
solidarism
solvency
Southeastern Power Administration
South Pacific Commission
South Sea Bubble
Southwestern Power Administration
span of control
spearhead money
special —
  s. assessment
  s. assessment bond
  s. endorsement
  s. -privilege monopoly
  s. stock
Special Drawing Rights
specialist
specialization of labor
specialized —
  s. agency
  s. capital good
specie
Specie Circular
specific —
  s. duty
  s. performance
speculation
speed-up
spending unit
spendthrift trust
spill-over
spin-off
split investment company
split-up
spot delivery
spread — in security trading, the difference between two options: a *put* specifying a price below the market and a *call* specifying a price above the market
SSA — Social Security Administration
stabilization —
  dollar s.
  s. fund
stable money
stamped bond
stamp tax

standard —
  s. bullion
  s. cost
  s. cost system
  s. deviation
  s. error of estimate
  s. error of the mean
  s. metropolitan area
  s. money
  s. of living
standardization
standby controls
standstill agreement
state —
  s. bank
  s. bond
  s. capitalism
  s. socialism
  s. use system
  welfare s.
statement —
  registration s.
static economics
statism
statute of limitations
stay law
sterilized gold
sterling —
  s. area
  s. bloc
steward
stipend
stock —
  assented s.
  assessable s.
  authorized capital s.
  barometer s.
  bonus s.
  capital s.
  s. certificate
  classified s.
  s. clearing agency
  clearinghouse s.
  common s.
  convertible s.
  corporate s.
  cumulative s.
  curb s.
  debenture s.
  s. dividend

stock (*continued*)
  donated s.
  s. exchange
  full s.
  growth s.
  guaranteed s.
  half s.
  inactive s.
  international s.
  listed s.
  management s.
  nonassented s.
  nonassessable s.
  nonclearinghouse s.
  noncumulative s.
  no-par-value s.
  s. option
  ordinary s.
  original-issue s.
  paid-up s.
  par-value s.
  participating preferred s.
  part-paid s.
  potential s.
  preference s.
  preferred s.
  premium s.
  prior s.
  quarter s.
  redeemable preferred s.
  s. rights
  rolling s.
  s. savings bank
  special s.
  s. transfer tax
  treasury s.
  unissued s.
  unlisted s.
  unvalued s.
  s. warrant
  watered s.
stockholder
stockpiles
stop-loss order
store credit
straddle — the simultaneous purchase of
  options both to buy and sell the same
  security
straight
  s. bill of lading

straight (*continued*)
  s. letter of credit
  s. -life plan of insurance
strategic materials
stratified sample
street certificate
stretch-out
strike —
  illegal s.
  jurisdictional s.
  outlaw s.
  quickie s.
  secondary s.
  sit-down s.
  slowdown s.
  sympathetic s.
  wildcat s.
strikebreaker
stringency
structural unemployment
subjective value
subordinated debenture
subscription —
  s. price
  s. rights
subsidiary —
  s. account
  s. coin
  s. company
  s. ledger
subsidy
subsistence law of wages
substitution —
  law of s.
subtreasury system
subvention
Suffolk Bank system
sumptuary law
sunk cost
sunspot theory of the business cycle
supermarket
superseniority
supersession
supplementary cost
supply and demand —
  law of s. and d.
surety —
  s. bond
  collateral s.
  corporate s.

suretyship
surplus —
  donated s.
  earned s.
  s. labor and value theory
  paid-in s.
  s. value
surtax
survivorship annuity
survivors' insurance
suspense account
swap credits
sweating
sweetheart contract
symmetallism
sympathetic strike
syndicalism
syndicate
systems research

T

Tableau économique (Fr) — a graphic
  representation of what was believed to be
  the flow of wealth, published in 1758 by
  Francois Quesnay, a French physician
tabular standard of value
tacit collusion
Taft-Hartley Act
take-home pay
talon — the remaining part of a debt
  instrument after its interest coupons have
  been presented
tangible property
tare — a deduction from gross weight to
  allow for the weight of a container
tariff —
  educational t.
  flexible t.
  t. for revenue only
  general t.
  Grundy t.
  multilinear t.
  protective t.
  single-schedule t.
  sliding-scale t.
  unilinear t.
  t. union
  t. war

Tariff Commission
Tariff Information Catalogue
Tariff of Abominations
task — the amount of work that must be done
  within a given length of time to secure an
  assigned minimum wage
tax —
  t. and loan accounts
  t. anticipation bond
  apportioned t.
  t. assessment
  t. avoidance
  t. base
  betterment t.
  capital gains t.
  capitation t.
  classified t.
  t. collector
  t. commission
  consumption t.
  delinquent t.
  direct t.
  t. dodging
  estate t.
  t. evasion
  excess profits t.
  excise t.
  t. exemption
  export t.
  t. farming
  franchise t.
  general property t.
  gift t.
  graded t.
  graduated t.
  head t.
  hidden t.
  income t.
  indirect t.
  inheritance t.
  interest equalization t.
  land t.
  t. lien
  t. limit
  luxury t.
  negative income t.
  nuisance t.
  occupation t.
  payroll t.
  personal property t.

tax *(continued)*
  privilege t.
  processing t.
  property t.
  t. rate
  real estate t.
  repressive t.
  sales t.
  severance t.
  t. sharing
  single t.
  social security t.
  stamp t.
  stock transfer t.
  transactions t.
  turnover t.
  undistributed-profits t.
  use t.
  value-added t.
  war-profits t.
  withholding t.
taxation —
  regressive t.
  shifting of t.
Tax Court of the United States
taxpayer
Taylorism
Taylor Law
teaching machine
technical —
  t. assistance
  t. position
technocracy
technological unemployment
technology
teller
temporal distribution
temporary admission
Temporary National Economic Committee
ten-forty bond
Tennessee Valley Authority
tenure
term —
  t. issue
  t. loan
  t's of trade
  t. plan of life insurance
terminal —
  t. bond
  t. wage
territorial bond

theory
thin market
through bill of lading
tied loan
tie-in sale
till money
time —
  t. and motion study
  t. bill
  t. deposit
  t. draft
  t. loan
  t. reversal test
  t. series
  t. utility
timework
title
token coin
tolerance
toll
tonnage
total utility
Totten trust
Townsend plan
trade —
  t. acceptance
  t. agreement
  t. association
  t. barrier
  t. bloc
Trade Agreements Act
Trade Expansion Act
trademark
trading stamp
transactions tax
transfer —
  t. agent
  cable t.
  t. payment
Transportation Act
traveler's —
  t. check
  t. letter of credit
Treasurer of the United States
treasury —
  t. bill
  t. certificates of indebtedness
  t. note
  t. stock
Treasury currency
trial balance

triangular trade
Tripartite Currency Agreement
true interest
Truman Plan
trust —
charitable t.
common t.
t. company
complex t.
discretionary t.
fixed investment t.
t. fund
investment t.
passive t.
power in t.
t. receipt
spendthrift t.
t. territory
Totten t.
voluntary t.
trustee
Trusteeship Council
Trust Indenture Act
Truth-in-Lending Act
Truth-in-Packaging Act
turnover —
t. tax
TVA — Tennessee Valley Authority
two —
t.-dollar broker
t.-name paper
t.-tier gold price
tycoon
tying contract

U

UN — United Nations
unconfirmed letter of credit
UNCTAD — United Nations Conference on
Trade and Development
underdeveloped area
underemployment equilibrium
underlying bond
under the rule — when a stock-exchange
member fails to deliver a security, the
security is purchased by an exchange
official and delivered under the rule
Underwood Tariff

underwriting
undistributed-profits tax
unearned —
u. income
u. increment
u. premium reserve
uneconomic
unemployment —
u. insurance
seasonal u.
structural u.
technological u.
unencumbered —
u. asset
u. property
UNESCO — United Nations Educational,
Scientific and Cultural Organization
unfair labor practice
unfavorable balance of trade
unfunded debt
unified —
u. bond
u. budget
uniform laws
unilinear tariff
union —
u. certification
craft u.
independent u.
industrial u.
international u.
u. label
labor u.
monetary u.
multicraft u.
national u.
open u.
u. security clause
u. shop
vertical labor u.
unissued stock
unit —
u. banking
u. cost
monetary u.
United Nations
**United Nations Conference on Trade and
Development**
**United Nations Educational, Scientific and
Cultural Organization**

United Nations Relief and Rehabilitation Administration
United States Chamber of Commerce
United States Civil Service Commission
United States Court of Claims
United States Court of Customs and Patent Appeals
United States Customs Court
United States Employment Service
United States Fish and Wildlife Service
United States note
United States Tariff Commission
United States Travel Service
Universal Postal Union
unlisted —
  u. security
  u. stock
  u. trading privileges
unparted bullion
unproductive consumption
unqualified certificate
unregistered exchanges
UNRRA — United Nations Relief and Rehabilitation Administration
unsatisfied —
  u. judgment funds
unsecured debt
unvalued stock
UPU — Universal Postal Union
Urban Mass Transportation Act
urban renewal
usance
use-and-occupancy insurance
user cost
USES — United States Employment Service
use tax
USTC — United States Tariff Commission
usury
utility —
  ownership u.
  place u.
  possession u.
  public u.
  service u.
  u. theory of value
  time u.
  total u.
utopia
utopian socialism

V

VA — Veterans Administration
validation certificate
valorization
valuation
value —
  v. added
  v. -added tax
  amortized v.
  book v.
  capitalized v.
  cash surrender v.
  collateral v.
  denominational v.
  face v.
  going v.
  intrinsic v.
  market v.
  par v.
  salvage v.
  scarcity v.
  subjective v.
  surplus v.
  tabular method of v.
  tabular standard of v.
variable —
  v. annuity
  v. cost
  v. proportions
velocity of circulation
vendee
vendor —
  v.'s lien
venture —
  v. capital
  joint v.
vertical —
  v. expansion
  v. integration
  v. labor union
vested interests
Veterans Administration
veterans' preference
vice-consul
vice propre
visible items of trade
VISTA — Volunteers in Service to America

vital statistics
Vocational Education Act
voidable contract
voluntary —
  v. bankruptcy
  v. checkoff
  v. plan
  v. trust
Volunteers in Service to America
voting-trust certificate
voucher —
  v. check
  v. register
  v. system

W

wage —
  w. and price guidelines
  w. and salary control
  dismissal w.
  w. dividend
  w. fund theory
  guaranteed annual w.
  w. leadership
  minimum w.
  w. -price spiral
  real w.
  severance w.
  terminal w.
Wage and Hour Law
Wage and Hour and Public Contracts
  Divisions
Wagner-Connery Act
waiver
Walker Tariff
walkout
Walsh-Healey Public Contracts Act
war —
  w. economy
  w. -profits tax
warehouse —
  w. certificate
  w. loans
  w. receipt
warrant —
  ex w's
  stock w.

wash sale
wasting asset
watered stock
waybill
wealth —
  economic w.
  social w.
Webb-Pomerene Act
weighted average
welfare —
  w. economics
  w. state
Western Hemisphere trade corporation
wetback
WFTU — World Federation of Trade Unions
Wheeler-Lea Act
when issued — a conditional transaction in
  investment trading for a security authorized
  but not yet issued
WHO — World Health Organization
widow and orphan's risk
wildcat —
  w. banking era
  w. strike
Wilson-Gorman Tariff
windfall profit
withholding tax
Women's Bureau
work —
  w. relief
  w. sharing
working capital
workmen's compensation laws
world bank
World Bank Group
World Federation of Trade Unions
World Health Organization
write —,
  w. -down
  w. -off
  w. -up

Y

yardstick
yellow —
  y. -dog contract
  y. pages

yellow (*continued*)
  y. seal dollar
yield —
  safe y.
  specific y.
  y. to maturity
Young plan
youth employment service

Z

Zollverein (Gr) — customs union; such unions were formed between Prussia and other German states in which it was agreed to impose no tariff duties among themselves
zoning

Engineering and Construction

A

AASHO — American Association of State Highway Officials
abaca
Abney level
Abrams' law
abscissa
absolute humidity
absorbing well
absorption —
 a. loss
 a. pit
abutment —
 a. wall
Abyssinian well
ac — alternating current
accelerated curing
accelerator
accidental error
accuracy
ACI — American Concrete Institute
acid steel
acoustic strain gauge
acre foot
Ac system — an airfield classification of soils based on sieve analysis
activated sludge process
active —
 a. earth pressure
 a. layer
additive —
 a. constant
adhesion —
 specific a.
adhesive water
adit
adjusting screw
adjustment —
 permanent a.
 temporary a.
admixture
adopted street
adsorption

advanced waste water treatment
aeolian
aerated concrete
aeration —
 a. tank
 zone of a.
aerial —
 a. ropeway
 a. surveying
 a. tramway
aerobic treatment
aerodynamic instability
A-frame
aftercooler
agent —
 contractor's a.
 dispersing a.
 parting a.
 peptizing a's
 release a.
 surface-active a.
aggregate —
 coarse a.
 fine a.
 gap-graded a.
 graded a.
 grouted a.
 half-sized a.
 lightweight a.
 single-sized a.
aggregate/cement ratio
aging
agitating —
 a. truck
 a. lorry
Aglite
agonic line
agricultural drain
A–horizon — the uppermost of the three layers of soil
air —
 a. base
 compressed a.
 a. compressor
 a. content of fresh concrete

air (*continued*)
  a. domes
  a. embolism
  a. -entrained concrete
  a. -entraining agent
  a. -flush drilling
  a. houses
  humidity of a.
  a. -lift pump
  a. lock
  a. pump
  saturated a.
  a. survey
  a. valve
  a. vessel
airfield soil classification
airplane mapping
Akashi-Kaikyo Bridge
Alclad
alidade
align
alignment —
  a. chart
  vertical a.
alloy —
  light a.'s
  a. steel
  wrought aluminum a.
altar — a step in the wall of a dry dock, used
  for holding the wooden shores that steady
  the vessel
alternator
altitude —
  a. level
alumina
alumino-thermic reaction
aluminous cement
aluminum —
  a. oxide
**American Association of State Highway
  Officials**
American caisson
American Ephemeris and Nautical Almanac
American Society for Testing and Materials
American Society of Civil Engineers
American wire gauge
amplitude
anallatic —
  a. lens
  a. telescope

analogy —
  membrane a.
analysis —
  dimensional a.
  mechanical a.
  model a.
  particle-size a.
  screen a.
  sieve a.
  size a.
  soil a.
  stress a.
  structural a.
  wet a.
anchor —
  a. and collar
  a. block
  a. bolt
  a. gate
  ground a.
  a. ice
  a. pile
  a. plate
  rock a.
  suspension-cable a.
  a. tower
  a. wall
anchorage —
  a. distance
anchoring spud
aneroid barometer
angle —
  a. bar
  a. cleat
  equal a.
  intersection a.
  a. iron
  a. -iron smith
  a. of friction
  a. of internal friction
  a. of repose
  a. of shearing resistance
  a. section
  shelf a.
  unequal a.
angledozer
anion
anisotropic
annealed wire
annealing

annual variation
anode —
  sacrificial a.'s
anodic oxidation
anodizing
anticlastic
anti-crack reinforcement
antidune
anti-flood and tidal valve
anti-friction metal
anti-sag bar
apparent horizon
apron —
  falling a.
  ice a.
aquaplaning
aqueduct
aquiclude
aquifer
aquifuge
aquitard
arbor
arc welding
arch —
  a. dam
  floor a.
  jack a.
  a. rib
  rigid a.
  a. ring
  three-hinged a.
  three-pinned a.
  trussed a.
  two-hinged a.
  two-pinned a.
  voussoir a.
Archimedean screw
Archimedes —
  principle of A.
are — the metric unit of area, 100 sq. meters
argon-arc welding
arm —
  cantilever a.
  lever a.
armor — permanent protection to any
  structure in water
armored —
  a. cable
  a. pipe
Armstrong scale

arrest point
arrissing tool
arrow — a short piece of galvanized wire for
  temporarily marking ground points
arterial road
artesian well
artificial —
  a. cementing
  a. harbor
  a. horizon
  a. islands
  a. recharge
asbestos
ASCE — American Society of Civil
  Engineers
ASCE MEP — American Society of Civil
  Engineers Manuals of Engineering Practice
asphalt —
  a. cement
  fine cold a.
  mastic a.
  natural a.
  natural rock a.
  rolled a.
asphaltic concrete
ASTM — American Society for Testing and
  Materials
astronomical eyepiece
astronomy
atomic-hydrogen welding
Atterberg limits
auger —
  earth a.
  post-hole a.
  power earth a.
  soil a.
autoclaving
autocollimation
autogenous —
  a. healing
  a. welding
automatic —
  a. compensation
  a. level
  a. siphon spillway
  a. welding
automation
autopatrol
autoplumb
autoset level

avenue
average —
  a. distribution
  weighted a.
axial-flow fan
axman
axonometric projection
azimuth
azimuthal projection

B

back —
  b. cutting
  b. gauge
  b. -inlet gulley
  jig b.
  b. mark
  b. observation
  poling b.
  b. prop
  b. sight
  b. water
backacter
backwater curve
bacteria bed
baffle —
  b. pier
  b. plate
baffler
bagwork
bail — a steel half hoop hanging from a hoisting rope
bailer
Bailey Bridge
Baker bell dolphin
balance —
  b. bar
  b. beam
  b. box
  b. bridge
  b. point
balanced earthworks
balancing
balata
balk — earth between excavations
ballast
ball mill

balloon —
  b. skin
  b. structures
band —
  b. chain
  b. screen
  steel b.
banderolle
bank —
  driving b.
  duct b.
  b. of transformers
  outburst b.
  b. protection
  b. storage
banking
banksman
banquette — a bridge footway
bar —
  angle b.
  anti-sag b.
  balance b.
  b. bender
  deformed b's
  indented b's
  jiggle b's
  kelly b.
  sag b.
  splice b.
  spray b.
  starter b.
  subtense b.
Barber Greene tamping levelling finisher
barge —
  b. bed
  dumb b.
  lay b.
Barnes's formula
barometer —
  aneroid b.
barometric pressure
barrage
barrel —
  core b.
  oriented-core b.
  Sprague and Henwood core b.
  b. vault
  wire-line core b.
bascule bridge

base —
comparator b.
b. course
b. exchange
b. flow
b. line
b. plate
basic —
b. refractory
b. steel
bastard cut
batching plant
batch mixer
bat faggot
bathotonic reagent
batten plate
batter —
b. level
b. pile
battery
battledeck
baulk
bauxite
beach —
expending b.
b. replenishment
shingle b.
beaching
beacon
beaded section
beam —
b. and slab floor
b. bender
b. bridge
castellated b.
b. compasses
continuous b.
b. engine
fixed b.
ground b.
b. loading
main b.
parallel-flanged b.
plated b.
secondary b.
simple b.
simply-supported b.
slender b.
soldier b.
spreader b.

beam (*continued*)
stringer b.
tapered-flange b.
b. test
trussed b.
universal b.
wind b.
Beaman stadia arc
beamless floor
bearing —
bridge b.
b. capacity
grid b.
magnetic b.
b. pile
b. pressure
quadrantal b.
reduced b.
rocker b.
roller b's
b. stratum
b. stress
b. test
thrust b.
true b.
whole-circle b.
Beaufort scale
bed —
barge b.
contact b.
equalizing b.
filter b.
b. load
b. plate
road b.
bedplate
bedrock
beetle head — a drop hammer
Belanger's critical velocity
Belgian truss
bell —
diving b.
b. dolphin
helium diving b.
belling tool
bellmouth overflow
belly rod
belt —
b. conveyor
safety b.

bench —
b. mark
benched foundation
benching —
b. iron
bend —
expansion b.
b. test
bending —
b. formula
b. moment
b. -moment diagram
b. -moment envelope
b. schedule
simple b.
bends — caisson disease
bent
bentonite —
b. mud
berm
Bernoulli's —
B. assumption
B. theorem
berth
berthing impact
bevelled washer
B-horizon — the second of the three layers of soil
bhp — brake horsepower
bi-cable ropeway
billet
bi-metal strip
binder
binding wire
bio-chemical oxygen demand
biological —
b. filter
b. shield
b. treatment
birdseye view
Birmingham wire gauge
bit —
detachable b.
fishtail b.
roller b.
bitumen —
filled b.
b. road emulsion
straight-run b.

bituminous —
b. carpet
b. emulsion
black —
b. bolts
b. diamond
blade —
b. grader
switch b's
blading back
Blake breaker
blank —
b. carburizing
b. flange
b. nitriding
blast —
b. furnace
b. -furnace cement
sand b.
blasting —
bog b.
deep b.
b. fuse
grit b.
b. machine
peat b.
shot b.
steel-grit b.
bleeding — the separation of clear water from the cement paste of mortar or concrete
blind drain
blinding — a layer of lean concrete put down on soil to seal it
bloated clay
block —
anchor b.
chain b.
concrete b.
differential pulley b.
end b.
fall b.
filter b's
foot b.
hoisting b.
b. -in-course
keel b's
lifting b.
lip b.
b. pavement
scotch b.
snatch b.

blockwork —
  coursed b.
  sliced b.
blockyard
Blondin — a cableway
bloom — a half-finished rolled or forged
  piece of steel used as a stanchion base
blow —
  b. down
  b. off
  b. out
blower —
  Rootes b.
  rotary b.
blowing down
blueprint
Board of Trade unit
boart
BOD — bio-chemical oxygen demand
bog blasting
boil — a flow of soil into the bottom of an
  excavation
boiler —
  fire-tube b.
  b. -house foundations
  b. rating
  steam b.
  water-tube b.
bollard
bolster
bolt —
  anchor b.
  black b's
  bright b.
  chair b.
  deck b.
  drift b.
  expansion b.
  eye b.
  fishtail b.
  fitted b.
  foundation b's
  gland b.
  high-strength friction-grip b's
  holding-down b.
  indented b.
  interference-body b.
  Lewis b.
  load-indicating b.
  rag b.
  Raw b.

bolt (*continued*)
  rock b.
  roof b.
  b. sleeve
  tight-fitting b.
  Torshear b.
  turned b.
bond —
  b. breaker
  b. length
  mechanical b.
  b. stress
boning —
  b. in
  b. pegs
  b. rod
boogie box
boojee pump
booking
boom — a beam used in lifting tackle
booster
boot —
  b. man
Bordeaux connection
border stone
bore — a borehole or the internal diameter of
  a pipe
bored —
  b. cast-in-place
  b. cast-in-situ
  b. pile
borehole —
  b. log
  b. logging
  b. pump
  b. samples
  b. surveying
borer —
  well b.
boring — making a hole in rock for blasting
borrow —
  b. pit
bort
Bosporus Bridge
Boston caisson
bottom —
  b. cut
  b. sampler
bottoming
bottom-opening skip
bottom sampler

boulder clay
boulevard
Bourdon pressure gauge
Boussinesq equation
Bowditch's rule
bowk
bowl scraper
bowstring girder
box —
  b. beam
  boogie b.
  b. caisson
  core b.
  b. culvert
  b. dam
  b. drain
  b. frame construction
  b. girder
  grout b.
  b. heading
  joint b.
  b. pile
  b. sextant
  b. shear test
  silt b.
  spreading b.
  stuffing b.
  trench b.
boxing —
  b. up
brace —
  diagonal b.
  knee b.
  sway b.
bracing —
  counter b.
  cross b.
Braithwaite piles
branding iron
brass
braze welding
brazing spelter
breakdown
breaker —
  Blake b.
  bond b.
  circuit b.
  concrete b.
  gyratory b.
  ice b.

breaker (*continued*)
  jaw b.
  primary b.
  road b.
breaking —
  b. ground
  b. of an emulsion
  b. piece
  b. point
  b. strength
  b. stress
break-pressure tank
breakwater —
  floating b.
  mound b.
  rubble-mound b.
breast — the mouldboard of a plough or
  dozer
bridge —
  balance b.
  bascule b.
  beam b.
  b. bearing
  cable-stayed b.
  cantilever b.
  b. cap
  counterpoise b.
  b. deck
  deck b.
  girder b.
  movable b.
  b. pier
  b. pier cap
  pile b.
  pivot b.
  pontoon b.
  retractable b.
  rolling lift b.
  self-anchored suspension b.
  skew b.
  stiffened suspension b.
  suspension b.
  swing b.
  through b.
  b. thrust
  transporter b.
  traversing b.
  trestle b.
  b. truss
  turn b.

Bridge —
  Akashi-Kaikyo B.
  Bailey B.
  Bosporus B.
  Britannia B.
  Forth B.
  Forth Road B.
  Golden Gate B.
  Hooghly B.
  Humber B.
  Irish B.
  Kill Van Kull B.
  Lake Washington B.
  Parramatta B.
  Plougastel B.
  Quebec B.
  Sandö B.
  Severn B.
  St. Nazaire B.
  Sydney Harbor B.
  Tacoma Narrows B.
  Träneberg B.
  Verrazano Narrows B.
bright bolt
Brinell hardness test
briquette
Britannia Bridge
British Standard
British Standards Institution
British Standard Specification
British Thermal Unit
brittle fracture
broach channelling
broaching
broad —
  b. gauge
  b. irrigation
bronze welding
brooming
brothers — a sling of rope or chain; either a
  two-leg or four-leg sling
Brown and Sharp wire gauge
brushwood
BS — British Standard
BSCP — British Standard code of practice
BSI — British Standards Institution
BSS — British Standard Specification
BTU — British Thermal Unit
bubble —
  b. level

bubble (*continued*)
  optical coincidence b.
  prismatic coincidence b.
  split b.
  b. trier
  b. tube
bucket —
  drop-bottom b.
  b. elevator
  grab b.
  b. -ladder dredger
  b. -ladder excavator
  orange-peel b.
  scraper b.
  sinking b.
  b. -wheel excavator
buckle —
  turn b.
buckling load
buffer stop
buggy — a concrete cart
building —
  b. code
  b. inspector
  b. owner
  b. paper
  b. surveyor
built up
bulb —
  b. angle
  b. of pressure
bulk —
  b. density
  b. modulus
  b. spreader
bulking
bulldog grip
bulldozer
bullhead rail
bull wheel
bump —
  b. cutter
bunker
buoyancy
buoyant —
  b. foundation
  b. raft
burden
burn — to cut metal with a gas flame
burnt shale

bush —
  b. hammer
  b. hammering
butane
butt —
  b. strap
  b. weld
  b. -welded tube
butterfly valve
buttress —
  b. drain
  flying b.
  b. screw thread
BWG — Birmingham wire gauge
byatt
bye —
  b. channel
  b. wash
by-pass

C

cabinet projection
cable —
  armored c.
  c. drill
  c. duct
  c. -laid rope
  c. railway
  c. -stayed bridge
  suspension c.
  track c.
  trailing c.
cableway —
  excavating c.
  c. excavator
  inclined c.
  slack-line c.
  c. transporter
cadastral mapping
caisson —
  American c.
  Boston c.
  box c.
  Chicago c.
  cylinder c.
  c. disease
  Gow c.
  open c.

caisson (*continued*)
  c. pile
  pneumatic c.
  ship c.
  sliding c.
  stranded c.
calcine
calcite
calcium —
  c. aluminate
  c. chloride
  c. silicate
calfdozer
caliber
calibrate
California —
  C. bearing ratio method
  C. bearing ratio test
calking
calliper log
callipers
calorific value
camber —
  c. rod
camel — a large hollow steel float
camouflet
camp —
  c. sheathing
  c. shedding
  c. sheeting
canal —
  lateral c.
  c. lift
  main c.
  summit c.
canalization
cant — superelevation
cantilever —
  c. arm
  c. bridge
  c. crane
  c. formwork
  c. foundation
  c. wall
cantledge
cap — a detonator
capacity —
  bearing c.
  c. curve
  infiltration c.
  struck c.

cape chisel
capel
capillarity —
   water of c.
capillary —
   c. fringe
   c. pressure
   c. rise
   c. water
capping —
   c. piece
capstan
carbide —
   cemented c's
   silicon c's
   sintered c's
   tungsten c.
carbon —
   c. -arc welding
   c. -dioxide recorder
   c. -dioxide welding
   c. monoxide
   c. silicide
   c. steel
carbonado
Carborundum
carburizing —
   gas c.
carpet —
   bituminous c.
carriageway
carriers
Cartesian coordinates
cartographer
cartridge paper
cascade
case —
   c. -hardening
cased pile
casing
cast —
   c. -in-place
   c. -in-situ
   c. iron
   c. steel
   c. -welded rail joint
castellated beam
casting yard
catch —
   c. basin
   c. drain

catch (*continued*)
   c. feeder
   c. pit
   c. points
catchment area
catchwater
catenary —
   c. corrections
   hydrostatic c.
   c. suspension
caterpillar gate
caterpillars — a popular name for crawler
   track for tractors
cat-head sheave
cathode
cathodic protection
cation
caulking —
   c. tool
causeway
caving
cavitation
cavity tanking
CBR — California bearing ratio
cc — cubic centimeter
celerity
cellular —
   c. cofferdam
   c. concrete
cellulose nitrate
cement —
   aluminous c.
   asphalt c.
   blast-furnace c.
   expanding c.
   c. grout
   c. gun
   high-alumina c.
   high-early-strength c.
   hydraulic c.
   hydrophobic c.
   c. joggle
   Lossier's c.
   low heat c.
   masonry c.
   metallurgical c.
   c. mortar
   oil-well c.
   ordinary Portland c.
   Portland blast-furnace c.
   Portland c.

cement (*continued*)
 Portland-pozzolana c.
 rapid-hardening c.
 self-stressing c.
 slag c's
 soil-c.
 sulphate-resisting c.
 supersulphated c.
 ultra-high-early-strength c.
 water repellent c.
 white c.
cementation
cemented carbides
cementite
center —
 c. cut
 mass c.
 c. of gravity
 c. of mass
 c. of pressure
 c. of stiffness
 c. punch
 rib c.
 shear c.
 c. to center
centesimal measure
centi — a prefix meaning a hundredth part of
central —
 c. reservation
 c. reserve
centrifugal —
 c. blower
 c. brake
 c. compressor
 c. force
 c. pump
centrifuge —
 c. moisure equivalent
centroid
cess
cesspit
cesspool
chain —
 band c.
 c. block
 c. book
 c. -bucket dredger
 Gunter's c.
 land c.

chain (*continued*)
 measuring c.
 c. of locks
 c. pump
 c. saw
 c. sling
 c. survey
chainage
chainman
chair —
 c. bolt
 rail c.
chalk —
 French c.
 c. line
chamber —
 decompression c.
 detritus c.
 dosing c.
 gate c.
 grit c.
 hyperbaric c.
 inspection c.
 working c.
chambered-level tube
chambering
change —
 c. face
 modulus of volume c.
 c. point
channel —
 bye c.
 ebb c.
 flood c.
 intercepting c.
 c. iron
 open c.
 c. section
 C. Tunnel
channeler
characteristic strength
charging hopper
Charpy test
chartered civil engineer
check —
 contour c.
 c. rail
 c. valve
checker

chemical —
  c. gauging
  c. hydrometry
  c. precipitation
chemi-hydrometry
chemise — a wall that protects the surface of
an earth bank
chequer plate
chequered plate
chert
chevron drain
Chicago —
  C. caisson
  C. well
chief draftsman
chilled cast iron
Chinaman chute
chipping —
  c. chisel
  c. hammer
chippings —
  coated c.
  pre-coated c.
chisel —
  cape c.
  chipping c.
  cold c.
  crosscut c.
chlorination
chord
C-horizon — the third of the three layers of
soil
chuck
churn drill
chute —
  Chinaman c.
  log c.
Ciment Fondu
Cipolletti weir
circle —
  Mohr's c. of stress
  stress c.
  vertical c.
circuit —
  c. breaker
  pilot c.
circular —
  c. -arc method
  c. level
  c. mil

circulating water
circumpolar stars
civil —
  c. engineer
  c. engineering
  c. engineering assistant
  c. engineering draftsman
  c. engineering technician
clack
clad steel
clamp handle
clamping screw
clamshell grab
clapotis
clap sill
claquage grouting
clarification
classification of soils
classifier
classify
clay —
  bloated c.
  boulder c.
  c. cutter
  expanded c.
  firm c.
  fissured c.
  intact c.
  London c.
  organic c.
  over-consolidated c.
  c. puddle
  puddle c.
  refractory c.
  c. sampler
  sensitive c.
  sintered c.
  slickensided c.
  soft c.
  c. spade
  stiff c.
  stiff-fissured c.
cleaning
clear —
  c. span
  c. -water reservoir
clearance —
  c. hole
clearing —
  c. and grubbing
  c. hole

cleat —
  angle c.
cleavage fracture
clevis
client
climbing formwork
clinograph
clinometer
clipping screw
clip screw
close —
  c. boarding
  c. timbering
closed traverse
closer
closing error
clough
clutch
cm — centimeter
CME — centrifuge moisture equivalent
coach screws
coagulation
coarse aggregate
coat —
  sealing c.
  tack c.
coated —
  c. chippings
  c. grit
  c. macadam
cobbles
code of practice
coefficient —
  c. of compressibility
  c. of consolidation
  c. of contraction
  c. of discharge
  c. of expansion
  c. of friction
  hygroscopic c.
  c. of imperviousness
  c. of internal friction
  c. of permeability
  run-off c.
  c. of thermal expansion
  c. of traction
  c. of uniformity
  c. of variation
  c. of velocity
  c. of volume change
  c. of volume decrease
  wilting c.

coffer
cofferdam —
  cellular c.
  double-wall c.
  full-tide c.
  half-tide c.
  Ohio c.
  whole-tide c.
cogging
cohesionless soil
cohesion of soil
cohesive soil
Colcrete
cold —
  c. bend test
  c. chisel
  c. drawing
  c. rolling
  c. sett
  c. shortness
  c. working
Colgrout
collapse design
collecting system
collimation —
  c. error
  c. line
  c. mark
  c. method
colloidal grout
colloids
column —
  c. analogy
  c. head
  laced c.
  Lally c.
  long c.
  short c.
combined —
  c. stresses
  c. system
comminutor
compact material
compacting factor test
compaction —
  deep c.
  explosive c.
  relative c.
  superficial c.
compactor —
  trench c.

comparator —
c. base
compass —
dip c.
magnetic c.
c. needle
prismatic c.
c. traverse
compasses —
beam c.
compensating —
c. diaphragm
c. error
compensation —
automatic c.
optical c.
c. water
composite construction
composites
compound —
c. air lift
curing c.
c. curve
c. dredger
c. engine
c. girder
liquid-membrane curing c.
parting c.
c. pipe
c. pump
sealing c.
compounding
compressed —
c. air
c. -air disease
compression —
c. boom
c. failure
c. flange
four-stage c.
isothermal c.
c. testing
two-stage c.
compressive strength
compressor —
air c.
centrifugal c.
free-piston c.
single-stage c.
concentrated load

conchoidal
concrete —
aerated c.
air-entrained c.
asphaltic c.
c. block
c. breaker
c. cart
cellular c.
c. cutting
dense c.
fiber-reinforced c.
c. -finishing machine
foamed c.
gas c.
glassfiber reinforced c.
grouted c.
light weight c's
mass c.
c. mixer
c. paver
c. pile
c. pipe
c. placer
plain c.
plant-mixed c.
Portland-cement c.
precast c.
prepacked c.
prestressed c.
c. properties
c. pump
ready-mixed c.
reinforced c.
c. roofs
rubble c.
special structural c.
sprayed c.
c. spreader
vacuum c.
vibrated c.
c. -vibrating machine
concreting boom
condensate
conduit
cone penetration test
confined —
c. compression test
c. water
conglomerate

consistence
consistency —
  c. index
  c. limits
consistometer —
  V. -B c.
consolidated quick test
consolidation —
  dynamic c.
  c. press
  c. settlement
  soil c.
consolidometer
construction —
  composite c.
  geodetic c.
  c. joint
  lift-slab c.
  mushroom c.
  sandwich c.
  c. spanner
  stressed-skin c.
  c. way
constructional —
  c. engineer
  c. fitter
consultant
consulting engineer
consumptive use
contact —
  c. aerator
  c. bed
  c. pressure under foundations
  c. print
contactor
continuity
continuous —
  c. beam
  c. filter
  c. gabion
  c. grading
  c. mixer
  c. rate
  c. rating
  c. ropeway
continuously —
  c. moving forms
  c. welded track

contour —
  c. check
  c. gradient
  c. interval
  c. line
  c. ploughing
contracted weir
contraction —
  end c.
  c. in area
  c. joint
contract manager
contractor —
  general c.
  main c.
contractor's agent
contraflexure
control —
  c. flume
  ground c.
  horizontal c.
  level of c.
  c. point
  remote c.
  c. valve
  vertical c.
  water pollution c.
conversion factor
conveyor —
  belt c.
  helical c.
  pneumatic c.
  screw c.
  worm c.
coordinates —
  Cartesian c.
  rectangular c.
copper —
  c. -bearing steel
  electrolytic c.
  c. welding
cordage rope
Cordeau
Cordtex
corduroy road
core —
  c. barrel
  c. box

core (*continued*)
  c. catcher
  c. cutter
  c. drill
  c. lifter
  loose c.
  pile c.
  c. wall
cored —
  c. hole
  c. slab
corers
coring tools
corporate member
correction(s) —
  catenary c.
  gravity c.
  sag c.
  sea-level c.
  slope c.
  standardization c.
  tape c.
  temperature c.
  tension c.
corrosion —
  c. fatigue
  c. resistant
corundum
Coulomb's equation
Council of Engineering Institutions
counter —
  c. -arched revetment
  c. bore
  c. bracing
  c. drain
counterfort
counterpoise bridge
course —
  racking c.
  regulating c.
  snow c.
  wearing c.
coursed —
  c. blockwood
  c. masonry
cover —
  manhole c.
  c. meter
  c. plate
  c. strap

covered electrode
crab — the moving hoist of an overhead
  traveling crane
crack inducer
cracking in concrete
cradle
craftsman
crane —
  cantilever c.
  creeper c's
  c. driver
  derrick c.
  floating c.
  gantry c.
  Goliath c.
  jib c.
  level-luffing c.
  locomotive c.
  luffing jib c.
  mobile c.
  monotower c.
  overhead traveling c.
  portable c.
  portal c.
  portal jib c.
  c. post
  revolver c.
  c. slinger
  swing-jib c.
  Titan c.
  tower c.
  transporter c.
  truck-mounted c.
  Whirley c.
crawler track
creep slide
creosote
creosoting —
  pressure c.
crest gate
crib —
  c. dam
  c. wall
cribwork
Crimp and Bruges' formula
crimper
crippling load
critical —
  c. density of sands
  c. height

critical (*continued*)
    c. hydraulic gradient
    c. path scheduling
    c. point
    c. temperature
    c. velocity
    c. voids ratio of sands
cropper
cross —
    c. bracing
    c. hair
    c. hatching
    c. poling
    c. -section
    c. -sectional area
    c. staff
crosscut —
    c. chisel
    c. file
    c. saw
crossfrogs
crosshead
crossings
crossover —
  scissors c.
crowbar
crowd shovel
crown
crucible steel
crusher —
  gyratory c.
  jaw c.
crushing —
    c. strength
    c. test
crystalline fracture
CSA — cross-sectional area
cube —
    c. strength
    c. test
cu. ft — cubic foot
culmination
culvert —
  box c.
cu. m or m³ — cubic meter
cumec — one cubic meter per second
cumulative errors
cup-and-cone fracture
cuphead
cupola

curb —
  cutting c.
  drum c.
curing —
  accelerated c.
  c. compound
  c. membrane
  c. period
  steam c.
current —
  density c.
  gravity c.
  c. meter
  turbidity c.
curtain —
  grout c.
  c. wall
curve —
  backwater c.
  capacity c.
  compound c.
  deflection c.
  discharge c.
  distribution c.
  duration c.
  easement c.
  elastic c.
  flow c.
  frequency c.
  Gaussian c.
  grading c.
  horizontal c.
  load-extension c.
  mass c.
  mass-haul c.
  normal c.
  railway c's
  c. ranging
  rating c.
  reverse c.
  reversed c.
  simple c.
  S-N (stress-number) c.
  spiral c.
  stress-number c.
  stress-strain c.
  transition c.
  vertical c.
cusec — one cubic foot per second

cushion —
  c. head
  water c.
cut —
  c. -and-cover
  c. and fill
  bastard c.
  center c.
  diversion c.
  draw c.
  c. holes
  lock c.
  c. of a file
  c. -off
  c. -off depth
  c. -off trench
  c. -off wall
  open c.
  pyramid c.
  second c.
  wedge c.
cutout
cutter —
  clay c.
  c. -dredger
  tree c.
cutting —
  concrete c.
  c. curb
  c. list
  c. -out piece
cutwater
cu. yd or **yd³** — cubic yard
cyanide hardening
cyaniding
cycle —
  hydrological c.
  water c.
cyclone
cyclopean
cylinder —
  c. caisson
  foundation c.
  jetty c.
  c. prestressed concrete pipe
  c. test
cylindrical —
  c. slide
  c. -surface method
  c. vault

D

dam —
  arch d.
  box d.
  crib d.
  debris d.
  diversion d.
  earthen d.
  flat-slab buttress d.
  flat-slab deck d.
  framed d.
  gravity d.
  gravity-arch d.
  hollow d.
  hydraulic fill d.
  limpet d.
  movable d.
  multiple-arch d.
  multiple-dome d.
  rock-fill d.
  round-headed buttress d.
  wicket d.
  wing d.
damping
deck —
  d. bolt
  d. bridge
  orthotropic d.
  space d.
damp-proof membrane
Darcy's law
datum —
  Liverpool d.
  Newlyn d.
day joint
DC — direct current
dead —
  d. load
  d. man anchorage
  d. -mild steel
  d. -smooth file
  d. -soft steel
  d. weight
debris dam
deca — a prefix of the decimal system
  meaning ten times
decalescent point
decanting

deci — a prefix of the decimal system
meaning one tenth
decimal system
deck —
bridge d.
d. bridge
decking
declination —
magnetic d.
decompression chamber
dedicated street
deep —
d. blasting
d. compaction
d. foundation
d. manhole
d. -penetration electrodes
d. -penetration test
d. well
d. well pump
deflection —
d. curve
deflectometer
deformation —
plastic d.
deformed bars
deformeter
degree —
d. of a curve
d. of compaction
d. of density
d. of saturation
Dehottay process
de-ionized water
delay-action detonator
delivery
de-mineralized water
de-nitrification
dense concrete
densification
density —
bulk d.
d. current
dry d.
maximum dry d.
d. moisture relationship
relative d.
snow d.
dental — a tooth-like projection on a surface
to deflect the force of flowing water

dentated sill
departure
depressant —
surface-tension d.
derrick —
d. crane
guy d.
guyed d.
oil-well d.
Scotch d.
shears d.
standing d.
stiff-leg d.
three-legged d.
d. tower gantry
derricking —
d. jib crane
de-salination
de-salting
design —
collapse d.
elastic d.
lateral-force d.
limit state d.
d. load
mix d.
plastic d.
seismic d.
structural d.
designer —
d. -detailer
structural d.
de-stressing
detachable bit
detail —
d. drawing
d. paper
detailer —
designer-d.
detonating fuse
detonation
detonator —
delay-action d.
detritus
d. chamber
d. slide
d. tank
Deutsche Industrie Normal
deviation —
standard d.

devil — an iron firegrate used for heating asphalting tools
dewatering
dewpoint
dia. — diameter
diagonal —
  d. brace
  d. eyepiece
  d. tension
Diagrid floor
dial gauge
diamond —
  black d.
  d. drilling
  industrial d.
  d. pyramid hardness test
  d. saw
diaphragm —
  compensating d.
  d. pump
  Stanley compensating d.
  d. wall
die —
  d. -formed strand
Diesel —
  D. engine
  D. hammer
differential —
  d. pulley block
  rectification d.
  d. settlement
diffuser
diffusion —
  Graham's law of d.
digestion — a method of treating sewage sludge when there is no air in closed heated tanks
dike (dyke)
dilatancy
dimensional —
  d. analysis
  d. similarity
  d. stability
DIN — Deutsche Industrie Normal
dip —
  d. compass
  d. needle
dipper dredger
dipping needle

direct —
  d. -acting pump
  d. reading tacheometer
  d. stress
directional drilling
discharge —
  d. coefficient
  d. curve
  d. head
  d. valve
disinfection
dispersing agent
dispersion
displacement —
  d. pile
  d. pump
  silt d.
displacer
disposal —
  sewage d.
  sludge d.
  d. well
distance —
  anchorage d.
  geodetic d.
  d. piece
  sight d.
  tangent d.
  visibility d.
distancing unit
Distomat
distributed load
distribution —
  d. curve
  frequency d.
  moment d.
  particle-size d.
  d. reservoir
  size d.
  d. steel
  d. tile
ditch
ditcher
ditching by explosives
diver
diversion —
  d. cut
  d. dam
  d. requirement

diver's paralysis
divide
dividers
diving —
  d. bell
dock —
  dry d.
  floating d.
  floating dry d.
  graving d.
  self-docking d.
  slip d.
  tidal d.
  wet d.
docking blocks
dog — a square-section spike used to hold heavy timbering
dolly — a block of hardwood placed over a pile helmet to receive the shock of the hammer
dolomite
dolphin —
  Baker bell d.
  bell d.
dome
Doppler shift
dosing —
  d. chamber
  d. siphon
  d. tank
double —
  d. -acting
  d. -cut file
  d. -drum hoist
  d. -headed nail
  d. -layer grid
  d. lock
  d. -rope tramway
  d. -seal manhole cover
  d. sling
  d. -wall cofferdam
down-the-hole drill
dowsing
dozer
Dracone
drafting machine
draftsman —
  estimating d.
  structural designer-d.
  structural d.
  surveyor's d.

draft tube
drag —
  d. shovel
draghead
dragline —
  d. excavator
  d. scraper
  walking d.
drain —
  agricultural d.
  blind d.
  box d.
  buttress d.
  catch d.
  chevron d.
  counter d.
  field d.
  French d.
  garland d.
  herringbone d.
  house d.
  intercepting d.
  land d.
  main d.
  mole d.
  d. pipes
  d. rods
  rubble d.
  sand d.
  spall d.
  stone d.
  subsoil d.
  surface-water d.
  d. tile
  Trammel d.
  trench d.
  vertical sand d.
  well d.
drainage —
  d. area
  d. basin
  land d.
  d. tunnel
drained —
  d. shear test
draw —
  d. cut
  d. -door weir
  d. file
drawbar —
  d. pull

drawbridge
drawdown —
  sudden d.
drawgear
drawing —
  d. board
  cold d.
  d. paper
  scale d.
  wire d.
  working d.
dredge
dredger —
  bucket-ladder d.
  chain d.
  compound d.
  dipper d.
  draghead d.
  dumb d.
  dustpan d.
  elevator d.
  grab d.
  hopper d.
  hydraulic d.
  mechanical d.
  sand pump d.
  stationary d.
  suction d.
  suction-cutter d.
  trailer d.
  trailing d.
  trailing suction-cutter d.
dredging —
  d. well
drift —
  d. barrier
  d. bolt
  littoral d.
  parallel d.
  taper d.
  d. test
drill —
  cable d.
  d. carriage
  churn d.
  core d.
  down-the-hole d.
  electric d.
  d. extractor
  d. feed
  hammer d.
  percussion d.

drill (*continued*)
  pneumatic d.
  rock d.
  d. rods
  sinker d.
  d. steel
  wagon d.
drilling —
  diamond d.
  directional d.
  d. fluid
  jet d.
  line d.
  d. mud
  percussive-rotary d.
  reverse-rotary d.
  rotary d.
  rotative d.
  wet d.
drive —
  d. pipe
driven —
  d. cast-in-place pile
  d. pile
driveway
driving —
  d. bank
  d. cap
  d. helmet
  water-jet d.
drop —
  d. -bottom bucket
  d. hammer
  line d.
  d. on
  d. penetration test
  d. shaft
drowned weir
drum —
  d. curb
  d. gate
  d. screen
dry —
  d. -bulb thermometer
  d. density
  d. -density/moisture-content relationship
  d. dock
  d. galvanizing
  d. joint
  d. pack
  d. weather flow
  d. well
drying shrinkage

Duchemin's formula
duct —
  d. bank
  cable d.
ductile
ductility
Ductube
Duff Abrams' law
dumb —
  d. barge
  d. dredger
dummy joint
dump —
  d. test
  d. truck
dumper —
  pedestrian-controlled d.
dumpling — a mass of ground with
  excavation on two or more sides left
  untouched until the end of the dig
dumpy level
dune
duplex —
  d. engine
  d. -headed nail
  d. track
duralumin
duration curve
dusting
dustpan dredger
Dutch —
  D. deep sounding
  D. mattress
dyeline
dyke (dike) —
  spur d.
dynamic —
  d. consolidation
  d. loading
  d. penetration test
  d. pile formula
  d. similarity
  d. strength
dynamite

E

E — modulus of elasticity
earth —
  e. auger

earth (*continued*)
  e. borer
  e. flow
  fuller's e.
  e. -leakage protection
  e. -moving plant
  e. pressure
  e. pressure at rest
earthen dam
earthquake
earthwork
easement —
  e. curve
easers
easting
ebb channel
eccentric —
  e. load
eccentricity
echo sounder
economic ratio
economizer
eddy —
  e. flow
  e. loss
Eddy's theorem
edge preparation
EDM — electronic distance measurement
effective —
  e. area of an orifice
  e. depth
  e. height of a column
  e. intergranular pressure
  e. length of a strut
  e. pressure
  e. size
  e. span
  e. stress
  e. thickness of a wall
efficiency —
  mechanical e.
  volumetric e.
effluent —
  e. stream
egg-shaped sewer
ejector —
  hydraulic e.
  pneumatic sewer e.
  silt e.
elastic —
  e. constants

elastic (*continued*)
 e. curve
 e. design
 e. limit
 e. moduli
 e. rail spike
 e. strain
elbow — a sharp corner in a pipe or roadway
electric —
 e. -arc welding
 e. drills
 e. eye
 e. motor
 e. shock
 e. traction
 e. welding
electrical —
 e. logging
 e. -resistance strain gauge
 e. strain gauges
electro-chemical hardening
electrode —
 covered e.
electro-dialysis
electrogas
electro-hydraulic lift
electrolysis
electrolyte
electrolytic —
 e. copper
 e. corrosion
 e. lead
 e. zinc
electromagnet
electromagnetic —
 e. cover meter
 e. length measurement
electronic distance measurement
electro-optical length measurement
electro-osmosis
electroplating
electroslag welding
elephant's trunk — a hydraulic ejector
elevated railway
elevating grader
elevation —
 e. head
 sectional e.
elevator —
 bucket e.
 e. dredger
 hydraulic e.

ellipse of stress
elliptical trammel
elongation
elutriation
elutriator
embankment —
 e. wall
emery
empirical formula
emulsifier
emulsion —
 bituminous e.
 e. injection
 tar e.
encastered
encastré
encroachment
end —
 e. -bearing pile
 e. block
 e. contraction
 e. -fixed
 fixed e.
 free e.
 e. span
 stop e.
 stunt e.
 e. thrust
endurance limit
energy —
 electric e.
 kinetic e.
 nuclear e.
 potential e.
 strain e.
engine —
 beam e.
 compound e.
 Diesel e.
 duplex e.
 gas e.
 internal-combustion e.
 multiple-expansion e.
 reciprocating e.
 simple e.
 steam e.
engineer —
 chartered civil e.
 civil e.
 construction e.
 consulting e.
 heating and ventilation e.

engineer (*continued*)
  mechanical e.
  municipal e.
  planning e.
  resident e.
  structural e.
  technician e.
engineering —
  civil e.
  environmental e.
  e. geology
  ground e.
  hydraulic e.
  municipal e.
  traffic e.
  transportation e.
Engineering News formula
Engineers Registration Board
engineer's —
  e. level
  e. transit
enlarged-base pile
enrockment
entrance —
  e. head
  e. lock
  e. loss
environmental engineering
Ephemeris
epoxide
epoxy
equal —
  e. angle
  e. -falling particles
equalization of boundaries
equalizing bed
equilibrium —
  e. moisture content
  e. of floating bodies
equipotential lines
equivalent —
  Joule's e.
  mechanical e. of heat
erecting shop
erector —
  steel e.
erosion —
  subsurface e.
erratic

error —
  accidental e.
  closing e.
  collimation e.
  compensating e.
  cumulative e.
  gross e.
  normal law of e.
  e. of closure
  probable e.
  residual e's
  standard e.
  surveying e.
  systematic e's
  triangle of e.
escape
Escherichia coli
estimating draftsman
ethane
ethoxylene resin
Euler crippling stress
evaporation pan
evapo-transpiration
excavating cableway
excavation —
  hydraulic e.
  slurry e.
excavator —
  bucket-ladder e.
  bucket-wheel e.
  cableway e.
  dragline e.
  multi-bucket e.
  rotary e.
  scraper e.
  slack-line cableway e.
  trench e.
  wheel e.
exciter
exfiltration
expanded —
  e. clay
  e. metal
expanding cement
expansion —
  e. bend
  e. bolt
  e. joint
  e. rollers

expansive —
  e. soils
  e. use of steam
  e. working
expending beach
exploder
exploration —
  geophysical e.
  site e.
explosive compaction
explosives —
  gelatine e.
  high e.
extender
exterior —
  e. panel
  e. vibrator
extrapolate
extruded sections
extrusion
eye bolt

F

fabric
fabrication
Fabridam
face —
  change f.
  free f.
  f. left
  f. piece
  reverse f.
  reversing f.
  f. right
  f. shovel
  f. waling
facing —
  hard f.
  Levy f.
  f. points
  f. wall
factor —
  conversion f.
  global safety f.
  impact f.
  impermeability f.
  load f.

factor (*continued*)
  f. of safety
  reduction f.
  slip f.
faggot —
  bat f.
faggoting
failure —
  compression f.
  foundation f.
fairlead
fall —
  f. block
  f. rope
  f. velocity
falling —
  f. apron
  f. velocity
false leaders
falsework
fan —
  axial-flow f.
  propeller f.
farm —
  f. duty
  sewage f.
fascine
fatigue —
  corrosion f.
  f. test
feathers — steel bars that fit together
feed —
  drill f.
feeder —
  catch f.
feedpump
feedwater
Fellenius's circular-arc method
fence
fender —
  f. pile
  f. post
ferro-concrete
ferro-prussiate paper
fetch
fiber —
  jute f.
  f. -reinforced concrete
  f. rope
Fidler's gear

fiducial —
  f. line
  f. mark
  f. point
field —
  f. book
  f. drain
  f. moisture equivalent
  f. tile
file —
  crosscut f.
  double-cut f.
  draw f.
  float-cut f.
  rat-tail f.
  saw f's
  single-cut f.
  taper f.
fill —
  hydraulic f.
  sand f.
filled bitumen
filler —
  f. concrete slab
  joint f.
  f. -joist floor
  f. rod
fillet weld
filling —
  sand f.
filter —
  f. bed
  biological f.
  f. blocks
  continuous f.
  graded f.
  loaded f.
  f. material
  f. medium
  multi-media f.
  percolating f.
  reversed f.
  sand f.
  toe f.
  trickling f.
  weighted f.
  f. well
filtrate

filtration —
  intermittent f.
final —
  f. grade
  f. setting time
fine —
  f. -adjustment screw
  f. aggregate
  f. cold asphalt
  f. -wire drag
  f. -wire sweep
fineness modulus
fines — small particles
Fink truss
fire —
  f. setting
  f. -tube boiler
  f. welding
firedamp
firing —
  shot f.
firm —
  f. clay
  f. silt
first —
  f. moment
  f. order
fish —
  f. ladder
  f. pass
  f. screen
fished joint
fishing —
  f. tools
fishplate
fishtail —
  f. bit
  f. bolt
fishway
fissured clay
fitchering
fitted bolt
fitter —
  constructional f.
fitting
fit-up
fix — determination of an aircraft's position
  for ground photography

fixed —
f. beam
f. end
f. -end moment
partially f.
f. retaining walls
fixing moment
fixity
flagstone
flame —
f. cutting
oxy-acetylene f.
flange —
blank f.
compression f.
tension f.
flanks
flap —
f. trap
f. valve
flared column head
flash —
f. -butt welding
f. set
f. welding
flashboard
flat —
f. -bottomed rail
f. jack
f. slab
f. -slab buttress dam
f. -slab deck dam
flattened strand rope
flexible —
f. membrane
f. pavement
f. pipe
f. wall
flexural rigidity
flexure
flints
float —
f. -cut file
rod f.
submerged f.
subsurface f.
surface f.
f. switch

floater
floating —
f. boom
f. breakwater
f. crane
f. dock
f. dry dock
f. foundation
f. harbor
f. pipeline
floc
flocculation
flood —
f. channel
f. routing
floor —
f. arch
beam and slab f.
beamless f.
Diagrid f.
filler-joist f.
hollow-block f.
hollow-tile f.
non-skip f.
non-slip f.
orthotropic plate f.
plate f.
pot f.
ribbed f.
f. slab
slab and beam f.
waffle f.
flotation —
f. structure
floury soil
flow —
f. curve
earth f.
eddy f.
free f.
f. index
internal f.
laminar f.
layered f.
f. lines
f. meter
mud f.
multi-phase f.

flow (*continued*)
  f. net
  plastic f.
  sinuous f.
  f. slide
  steady f.
  stratified f.
  streamline f.
  subcritical f.
  subsurface f.
  supercritical f.
  f. -table test
  tortuous f.
  turbulent f.
  viscous f.
flue gas
flume —
  control f.
  Parshall measuring f.
  rating f.
  Venturi f.
fluxes
fly-ash —
  sintered f.
flying buttress
fly-off
foamed concrete
folded-plate
follower
fondu — high-alumina cement
foot —
  acre f.
  f. block
  f. iron
  f. -pound
  pound-f.
  f. screws
  square mile f.
  f. -ton
  f. valve
footing —
  spread f.
  strip f.
footpiece
foot-pound
footway
force —
  centrifugal f.
  moment of a f.
  mooring f's

force (*continued*)
  f. pump
  seepage f.
  shear f.
  tensile f.
  tractive f.
  wind f.
  wracking f's
forced —
  f. drop shaft
  f. vibration
fore —
  f. observation
  f. sight
forebay
forepole
forepoling —
  f. boards
forge —
  f. welding
forging
fork-lift truck
form —
  continuously moving f's
  f. lining
  moving f's
  road f's
  side f's
  sliding f's
  slip f.
  f. stop
  traveling f's
formula —
  Barnes's f.
  bending f.
  Crimp and Bruges' f.
  Duchemin's f.
  dynamic pile f.
  empirical f.
  Engineering News f.
  Hiley's f.
  Lloyd-Davies f.
  Pencoyd f.
  prismoidal f.
  Stevenson's f.
  Stokes's f.
  Wellington f.
formulation —
  f. level

formwork —
  cantilever f.
  climbing f.
Forth —
  F. Bridge
  F. Road Bridge
forward shovel
foul sewer
found
foundation —
  benched f.
  f. bolts
  buoyant f.
  cantilever f.
  f. cylinder
  deep f.
  f. failure
  floating f.
  grillage f.
  pad f.
  f. pier
  piled f.
  raft f.
  refrigerator f's
  shallow f.
  stepped f.
  strip f.
  vibration of f's
  well f.
foundry
four —
  f. -leg sling
  f. -piece set
  f. -stage compression
fpm — feet per minute
fraction
fractional —
  f. -horsepower motor
  f. sampling
fracture —
  brittle f.
  cleavage f.
  crystalline f.
  cup-and-cone f.
  plastic f.
frame —
  A-f.
  ground f.
  guide f.
  hyperstatic f.

frame (*continued*)
  imperfect f.
  isostatic f.
  middling f.
  perfect f.
  pile f.
  plane f.
  poling f.
  portal f.
  redundant f.
  rigid f.
  space f.
  starter f.
  statically-determinate f.
  statically-indeterminate f.
  steel f.
  stiff f.
  top f.
  tucking f.
  unstable f.
  f. weir
  welded f.
framed dam
framework —
  simple f.
Francis turbine
Franki pile
frazil ice
free —
  f. end
  f. face
  f. -falling velocity
  f. flow
  f. haul
  f. -piston compressor
  f. retaining wall
  f. vibration
  f. water
freeboard
freeway
freezing
French —
  F. chalk
  F. drain
  F. truss
frequency —
  f. curve
  f. diagram
  f. distribution
fretting

friction —
    angle of f.
    angle of internal f.
    coefficient of f.
    f. head
    hydraulic f.
    internal f.
    negative skin f.
    f. pile
    skin f.
    wall f.
frictional soil
fringe —
    capillary f.
    f. water
frog —
    f. rammer
front-end equipment
frost —
    f. boil
    f. heave
Froude number
frozen ground
ft — foot or feet
fullering
fuller's earth
full-tide cofferdam
fully —
    f. -divided scale
    f. -fixed
funicular railway
furnace —
    blast f.
fuse —
    blasting f.
    detonating f.
    Primacord f.
    safety f.
fusible plug
fusion welding

G

g — gram or gravity
gabion —
    continuous g.
gad — a pointed steel bar for wedging out
    coal or breaking ore
gage height

gale
gallery
gallium aluminum arsenide
gallon
galvanize
galvanized iron
galvanizing —
    dry g.
    wet g.
gamma radiography
ganat, ghanat
gang —
    g. mold
ganger —
    traveling g.
    walking g.
gantry —
    g. crane
    derrick tower g.
    platform g.
    tower g.
    traveling g.
gap-graded aggregate
garland drain
gas —
    g. carburizing
    g. concrete
    g. engine
    flue g.
    marsh g.
    g. metal-arc
    natural g.
    g. outburst
    sewage g.
    g. -shielded metal-arc welding
    sludge g.
    sludge g.
    g. -tungsten-arc welding
    g. welding
gasket
gate —
    anchor g.
    caterpillar g.
    g. chamber
    crest g.
    drum g.
    head g.
    lift g.
    lock g.
    penning g.

gate (*continued*)
  radial g.
  roller g.
  sector g.
  segmental-sluice g.
  sliding g.
  spillway g.
  tail g.
  Tainter g.
  tilting g.
  g. valve
gathering ground
gauge —
  acoustic strain g.
  American wire g.
  back g.
  Birmingham wire g.
  Bourdon pressure g.
  broad g.
  Brown and Sharp wire g.
  dial g.
  electrical-resistance strain g.
  electrical strain g's
  hook g.
  inclined g.
  g. length
  loading g.
  Maihak strain g.
  micrometer g.
  narrow g.
  point g.
  pressure g.
  rail g.
  rain g.
  recording g.
  resistance strain g.
  slope g.
  staff g.
  standard g.
  Standard Wire G.
  strain g.
  Stub's iron wire g.
  tide g.
  water g.
  g. well
  wheel g.
  wire g.
gauging —
  chemical g.
  g. station

Gaussian curve
gear —
  hard hat diving g.
  helmet diving g.
  masthead g.
  standard diving g.
gelatine explosives
general contractor
generator —
  magneto g.
geodesy
geodetic —
  g. construction
  g. distance
  g. surveying
Geodimeter
geological map
geology —
  engineering g.
geometric similarity
geomorphology
geophone
geophysical —
  g. exploration
  g. prospecting
  g. surveying
geophysics —
  applied g.
geotechnical processes
giant — a nozzle for projecting water at sand or gravel for the purpose of breaking it up and washing it downhill
gin pole
girder —
  bowstring g.
  box g.
  g. bridge
  compound g.
  half-lattice g.
  hollow-web g.
  open-frame g.
  open-web g.
  plate g.
  stiffening g.
  Vierendeel g.
  Warren g.
give-and-take lines
gland —
  g. bolt
glassfiber reinforced concrete

global safety factor
GMA — gas metal-arc
goaf
go-devil
Golden Gate Bridge
Goliath crane
goniometer
go-out
Gow caisson
gpm — gallons per minute
grab —
  g. bucket
  clamshell g.
  g. dredger
  g. sampling
grade —
  final g.
  g. level
  g. separation
  tip g.
graded —
  g. aggregate
  g. filter
  g. sand
grader —
  blade g.
  elevating g.
  motor g.
gradient —
  contour g.
  critical hydraulic g.
  hydraulic g.
  limiting g.
  g. post
  ruling g.
  self-cleansing g.
  g. speed
  temperature g.
gradienter
grading —
  continuous g.
  g. curve
  g. instrument
  size g.
gradiometer
graduation —
  g. of tapes
  sexagesimal g.
grafting tool
Graham's law of diffusion

grain —
  g. -size classification
granite
grano
granolithic
granular stabilization
granulator
graph
grass —
  marram g.
  rice g.
graticule
grating
gravel —
  g. pump
graving dock
gravitational water
gravity —
  g. -arch dam
  center of g.
  g. corrections
  g. current
  g. dam
  g. main
  g. retaining wall
  g. scheme
  specific g.
  g. water
GRC — glassfiber reinforced concrete
grease trap
Greathead shield
green pellets
gribble
grid —
  g. bearing
  double-layer g.
  g. plan
  space g.
  two-way g.
grillage —
  g. foundation
grinding
grip —
  bulldog g.
  g. length
grit —
  g. blasting
  g. chamber
  coated g.

gritter —
  winter g.
gritting —
  g. material
groin — a wall built out from a river bank or seashore; a jetty
grommet
gross —
  g. duty of water
  g. error
  g. loading intensity
  g. ton
ground —
  g. anchor
  g. bashing
  g. beam
  g. control
  g. engineering
  g. frame
  frozen g.
  gathering g.
  g. improvement
  loose g.
  loss of g.
  g. prop
  running g.
  sidelong g.
  water-bearing g.
groundwater —
  g. lowering
grout —
  g. box
  cement g.
  colloidal g.
  g. curtain
  g. pan
grouted —
  g. aggregate
  g. concrete
  g. macadam
  g. machine
  g. method of shaft sinking
grouting —
  claquage g.
  g. machine
  sleeve g.
groutnick
groyne (groin)
grub axe
grubbing
grummet

GTA — gas tungsten arc
  GTA welding
guard —
  g. lock
  g. post
  g. rail
guide —
  g. frame
  g. pile
  g. rail
  g. runner
gullet — a narrow trench
gulley —
  g. sucker
  g. trap
  yard g.
gully (gulley)
guncotton
gunite
gunmetal
Gunter's chain
gusset —
  g. plate
GUTS — guaranteed ultimate tensile strength
gutter
guy —
  g. derrick
  g. rope
guyed —
  g. derrick
  g. -mast
gyratory —
  g. breaker
  g. crusher

H

half —
  h. -hour rating
  h. -joist
  h. -lattice girder
  h. -silvered mirror
  h. -sized aggregate
  h. -socket pipe
  h. -tide cofferdam
  h. -track tractor
Hallinger shield
hammer —
  bush h.
  chipping h.

hammer (*continued*)
Diesel h.
h. drill
drop h.
pile h.
rebound h.
Schmidt rebound h.
sledge h.
water h.
hand —
h. boring
h. distributor
h. finisher
h. lead
h. level
h. rammer
h. sprayer
handling —
h. plant
materials h.
mechanical h.
hanging leaders
harbor —
artificial h.
floating h.
h. models
Mulberry h.
natural h.
h. of refuge
hard —
h. facing
h. hat diving gear
h. solder
h. standing
hardcore
hardenability
hardening —
cyanide h.
electro-chemical h.
nitrogen h.
strain h.
work h.
hardness
hardpan
Hardy Cross method
hatching —
cross h.
haulage —
locomotive h.
h. rope
hauling plant

haunch — a complete half-arch
Hazen's law
head —
h. bay
h. board
discharge h.
elevation h.
entrance h.
friction h.
h. gate
irrigating h.
kinetic h.
loss of h.
lost h.
pan h.
pile h.
position h.
pressure h.
quick-leveling h.
h. race
static h.
suction h.
h. tree
velocity h.
h. wall
weir h.
header
heading —
intake h.
headwater
headway
headworks
heating —
h. and ventilation engineer
h. value
heat treatment
heave —
frost h.
heaving shale
heavy soil
hecto — a prefix denoting one hundred times
heel —
h. post
height —
h. of instrument method
swash h.
held water
helical —
h. conveyor
h. reinforcement
heliograph

helium —
  h. diving bell
helmet —
  h. diving gear
  driving h.
  pile h.
hemp
herringbone drain
high —
  h. -alumina cement
  h. -angle eyepiece
  h. -carbon steel
  h. -early-strength cement
  h. explosives
  h. -pressure steam-curing
  h. -strength friction-grip bolts
  h. -tensile steel
highway
Hiley's formula
hindered settling
hinge —
  plastic h.
histogram
hoe —
  h. scraper
  trench h.
hog — upward bending; the opposite of sag
hogging —
  h. moment
hoist —
  h. controller
  mobile h.
  platform h.
holdfast
holding-down bolt
hole —
  lifter h's
  main h's
  paddle h.
  relief h's
  rib h's
  trial h.
  well h.
hollow —
  h. -block floor
  h. clay tile
  h. dam
  h. quoin
  h. sections
  h. tile

hollow (*continued*)
  h. -tile floor
  h. -web girder
honeycombing
Honigmann method of shaft sinking
Hooghly Bridge
Hooke's law
hook gauge
hoop —
  pile h.
  h. stress
  h. tension
hooping
hopper —
  charging h.
  h. dredger
hoppit
horizon —
  apparent h.
  artificial h.
  h. glass
  sensible h.
  visible h.
horizontal —
  h. circle of a theodolite
  h. control
  h. curve
horsepower —
  h. -hour
hose coupling
hot —
  h. -dip coating
  h. miller
  h. rolling
  h. shortness
  h. working
house drain
Howe truss
Hoyer method of prestressing
Humber Bridge
humidity —
  absolute h.
  h. of air
  relative h.
humus —
  h. tank
hundredweight
hurdle work
hurricane
hydration

hydraulic —
h. cement
h. dredger
h. ejector
h. elements
h. elevator
h. engineering
h. excavation
h. fill
h. fill dam
h. friction
h. grade line
h. gradient
h. jack
h. jump
h. lift
h. main
h. mean depth
h. pile-drivers
h. power
h. press
h. radius
h. ram
h. tensor
h. test
hydraulicking
hydraulics —
loose-boundary h.
Hydrodist
hydrodynamics
hydroelectric —
h. power station
h. scheme
hydrofracture
hydrogeology
hydrograph —
unit h.
hydrographer
hydrographic surveying
hydrography
hydrological cycle
hydrology
hydrometer
hydrometry —
chemical h.
hydrophobic cement
hydrostatic —
h. catenary
h. excess pressure
h. joint
h. press

hydrostatic (*continued*)
h. pressure
h. pressure ratio
h. test
hydrostatics
hydro-stressor
hydroxylated polymers
hygrometer
hygrometry
hygroscopic —
h. coefficient
h. moisture
hypar
hyperbaric chamber
hyperbolic paraboloid roof
hyperstatic frame
hypsometer
hysteresis

I

I — moment of inertia
I-beam
ice —
i. apron
i. breaker
frazil i.
slush i.
idler — a wheel interposed between two others in a gear
igneous intrusion
ignition powder
Imhoff tank
immersed tube
immersion vibrator
impact —
i. factor
i. spanner
i. test
i. wrench
impeller
imperfect frame
impermeability factor
impervious
imposed load
impounding —
i. reservoir
impregnation
improved Venturi flume
impulse turbine

in. — inch
incinerator
incise
incline
inclined —
  i. cableway
  i. gauge
inclinometer
indented —
  i. bars
  i. bolt
indenting roller
index —
  consistency i.
  flow i.
  i. glass
  i. of liquidity
  moisture i.
  i. of plasticity
  i. properties
  remoulding i.
  toughness i.
indicator —
  safe-load i.
  radius-and-safe-load i.
industrial diamond
inertia —
  moment of i.
  polar moment of i.
infiltration —
  i. capacity
inflatables
inflection (inflexion)
influence line
influent stream
infra-red —
  i. distancer
  i. photography
ingot
inherent settlement
initial —
  i. setting time
  i. surface absorption test
injection —
  emulsion i.
  silicate i.
  solution i.
  i. well
inlet —
  street i.
innings — land regained from sea or marsh

insert
in situ —
  i. concrete piles
  i. soil tests
inspection chamber
inspector —
  i. of works
instrument —
  grading i.
  needle i.
  plotting i.
  transit i.
instrumental shaft plumbing
intact clay
intake heading
integrally-stiffened plating
integrating meter
intensity —
  gross loading i.
  net loading i.
  i. of rainfall
  i. of stress
intercept
intercepting —
  i. channel
  i. drain
interception
intercooler
interface strength
interference —
  i. -body bolt
  i. settlement
interflow
intergranular pressure
interheater
interior span
interlock
interlocking piles
intermediate sight
intermittent filtration
internal —
  i. -combustion engine
  i. flow
  i. friction
  i. vibrator
internally-focusing telescope
interpolation
intersection —
  i. angle
  i. point
interstitial water

intrusion
intrusive rock
invar
invert —
   i. level
inverted siphon
inverting eyepiece
ion —
   i. exchange
Irish Bridge
iron —
   angle i.
   benching i.
   branding i.
   cast i.
   channel i.
   chilled cast i.
   i. fighter
   foot i.
   galvanized i.
   malleable cast i.
   i. pan
   i. paving
   pig i.
   smoothing i.
   step i.
   wrought i.
irrigable area
irrigating head
irrigation —
   broad i.
   i. requirement
isochromatic lines
isoclinic lines
isohyet
isolator
isometric projection
isostatic frame
isotherm
isothermal compression
isotropic
Izod test

J

J — joule
jack —
   j. arch
   flat j.

jack (*continued*)
   hydraulic j.
   j. roll
jackblock method
jacked pile
jacket
jaw —
   j. breaker
   j. crusher
jet drilling
jetting
jetty —
   j. cylinder
   open j.
jib —
   j. crane
jig back
jiggle bars
jim crow — a hand-operated rail bender
joggle
joint —
   j. box
   cast-welded rail j.
   construction j.
   contraction j.
   day j.
   dry j.
   dummy j.
   expansion j.
   j. filler
   fished j.
   hydrostatic j.
   lap j.
   movement j's in concrete
   pin j.
   j. -sealing material
   settlement j.
   shrinkage j.
   sliding j.
   slip j.
joist —
   half-j.
   rolled-steel j.
Joosten process
joule
Joule's equivalent
jubilee wagon
jumbo — a drill carriage
jump —
   hydraulic j.
   j. join

jumper
jumping up
junction —
  j. point
  scissors j.
jute fiber

K

kanat
Kaplan turbine
kathode (cathode)
keel blocks
kelly bar
Kennedy's critical velocity
kentledge
kerf
kern
key —
  mechanical k.
  rail k.
kg — kilogram
khanat
kibble
kicker — a concrete plinth
kicking piece
kid — a bundle of brushwood
kidding — faggoting
Kill Van Kull Bridge
kilo — a prefix meaning 1000 times, thus a
  kilogram is 1000 grams
kilowatt —
  k. hour
  k. unit
Kind-Chaudron method
kinematic similarity
kinetic —
  k. energy
  k. head
king —
  k. pile
  k. tower
kip — a kilopound
kJ — kilojoule
km — kilometer
kN — kilonewton
knee brace
kneeler
knife-edge loading

kN/m² — kilonewtons per square meter
kph — kilometers per hour
kWh — kilowatt hour

L

laced column
lacing
ladder —
  fish l.
lagging
laitance
Lake Washington Bridge
Lally column
lamella roof
laminar —
  l. flow
  l. velocity
laminate
lamphole
land —
  l. accretion
  l. chain
  l. drain
  l. drainage
  l. reclamation
  l. surveyor
  l. tie
  l. treatment
landslide
landslip
Lang lay or Lang's lay
lap —
  l. joint
large calorie — a kilogram calorie
laser
lateral —
  l. canal
  l. -force design
  l. support
lath —
  wire l.
latitude
lattice —
  space l.
launching of a bridge
lay —
  l. barge
  l. -by

lay (*continued*)
    Lang l. or Lang's l.
    ordinary l.
layered —
    l. flow
    l. map
laying-and-finishing machine
layout
lb — pound
leach
leachate
lead —
    electrolytic l.
    hand l.
    l. line
    l. sheath
    sounding l.
leader —
    section l.
leaders (or leads) —
    false l's
    hanging l's
least count
leat
LECA — light expanded clay aggregate
ledge —
    l. rock
leech
Leipzig market halls
length —
    gauge l.
    grip l.
    l. measurement
    standardization l.
    transition l.
    transmission l.
letting down
levee
level —
    Abney l.
    altitude l.
    automatic l.
    autoset l.
    batter l.
    l. book
    bubble l.
    circular l.
    dumpy l.
    engineer's l.
    formulation l.

level (*continued*)
    grade l.
    hand l.
    invert l.
    Locke l.
    l. -luffing crane
    l. of control
    quickset l.
    l. recorder
    reduced l.
    reduction of l's
    reflecting l.
    spot l.
    standing-water l.
    striding l.
    tilting l.
    toe l.
    l. trier
    l. tube
leveling —
    precise l.
    reciprocal l.
    l. rod
    l. screw
    l. staff
lever —
    l. arm
Levy facing
Lewis bolt
life linesman
lift —
    canal l.
    electro-hydraulic l.
    l. gate
    hydraulic l.
    l. pump
    l. -slab construction
    static suction l.
lifter —
    core l.
    l. holes
lifting —
    l. block
    l. magnet
    l. tackle
    vacuum l.
light —
    l. alloys
    polarized l.
    l. railway

lighthouse
light weight —
 l. aggregate
 l. concretes
limb — the lower plate of a theodolite
limit —
 consistency l.'s
 elastic l.
 endurance l.
 liquid l.
 l. of liquidity
 l. of plasticity
 l. of proportionality
 plastic l.
 shrinkage l.
 l. state
 l. state design
 sticky l.
 l. switch
limiting —
 l. gradient
 l. span
limits —
 Atterberg l.
 consistency l.
limpet —
 l. dam
line —
 agonic l.
 base l.
 chalk l.
 collimation l.
 contour l.
 l. drilling
 l. drop
 equipotential l.'s
 fiducial l.
 flow l.'s
 give-and-take l.'s
 hydraulic grade l.
 influence l.
 isochromatic l.'s
 isoclinic l.'s
 lead l.
 match l.'s
 neat l.'s
 net l.'s
 l. of least resistance
 l. of thrust
 plumb l.

line (*continued*)
 range l.
 saturation l.
 seepage l.
 sounding l.
 spider l.
 tie l.
 toe l.
liner —
 pipe l.'s
lining —
 form l.
 refractory l.'s
 tunnel l.
link
Linville truss
lip —
 l. block
 l. piece
lipping
liquefaction —
 spontaneous l.
liquid —
 l. limit
 l. -membrane curing compound
 l. nitrogen method of freezing ground
liquidity —
 l. index
 limit of l.
littoral drift
live load
Liverpool datum
Lloyd-Davies formula
load —
 buckling l.
 concentrated l.
 crippling l.
 dead l.
 design l.
 distributed l.
 eccentric l.
 l. -extension curve
 l. factor
 imposed l.
 l. -indicating bolt
 live l.
 moving l.
 point l.
 pre-consolidation l.
 rolling l.

load (*continued*)
  snow l.
  static l.
  sue l.
  superimposed l.
  wind l.
loadbearing wall
loaded filter
loader —
  scraper l.
  wheel l.
loading —
  beam l.
  l. boom
  dynamic l.
  l. gauge
  knife-edge l.
  mechanical l.
  l. shovel
  transverse l.
loam
local attraction — deviation of the magnetic
  needle from the magnetic north
lock —
  air l.
  l. bay
  l. cut
  double l.
  entrance l.
  l. gate
  guard l.
  l. nut
  materials l.
  medical l.
  l. paddle
  l. sill
lockage
locked-coil rope
Locke level
locomotive —
  l. crane
  l. haulage
loess
log —
  calliper l.
  l. chute
  stop l.
logging —
  electrical l.
  resistivity l.
  well l.

logway
London clay
long —
  l. column
  l. dolly
  l. -line method of prestressing
  l. span
  l. ton
longitudinal —
  l. bead test
  l. profile
  l. section
loose —
  l. -boundary hydraulics
  l. core
  l. ground
loss —
  absorption l.
  eddy l.
  l. of ground
  l. of head
  l. of prestress
  seepage l.
Lossier's cement
lost head
low-carbon steel
low-heat cement
low-water valve
lower plate — the limb of a theodolite
luffing —
  l. cableway mast
  l. jib crane
lumping — a method of renewing rail track
lurching allowance
Lytag

M

m — meter
m³ — cubic meter
macadam —
  coated m.
  grouted m.
  m. spreader
  waterbound m.
machine —
  blasting m.
  concrete-finishing m.
  concrete-vibrating m.
  drafting m.

machine (*continued*)
grouted m.
grouting m.
laying-and-finishing m.
milling m.
plotting m.
siding m.
testing m.
m. tools
trenching m.
Magic Mole
magnesite
magnetic —
m. bearing
m. compass
m. declination
m. north pole
m. south pole
m. variation
magneto —
m. generator
magnetometer
MAG welding — metallic active-gas welding
Maihak strain gauge
main —
m. beam
m. canal
m. contractor
m. drain
gravity m.
m. holes
hydraulic m.
m. sewer
m. tie
trunk m.
maintenance —
m. period
malleability
malleable cast iron
mammoth pump
mandrel
mandril
manganese —
m. steel
manhole —
m. cover
deep m.
shallow m.
side-entrance m.
manifold
Manila rope

manipulator
man-lock
manmade fiber rope
manometer
manual metal-arc welding
map —
geological m.
layered m.
solid m.
stereometric m.
margin
marigraph
marine —
m. borers
m. hydrographic surveying
m. surveying
maritime plants
marl
marram grass
marsh gas
masonry —
m. cement
coursed m.
reinforced grouted-brick m.
mass —
m. center
center of m.
m. concrete
m. curve
m. diagram
m. -haul curve
mast —
luffing cableway m.
masthead gear
mastic
m. asphalt
mat — a footing of concrete or steel under a post
match lines
material —
filter m.
m's handling
joint-sealing m.
m's lock
screened m.
silt grade m's
strength of m's
matrix
mattress —
Dutch m.
Reno m.

maturing
maximum —
  m. cement content
  m. dry density
mean —
  m. depth
  m. velocity
measuring —
  m. chain
  m. weir
mechanic —
  rock m's
  soil m's
mechanical —
  m. advantage
  m. analysis
  m. bond
  m. dredger
  m. efficiency
  m. engineer
  m. equivalent of heat
  m. handling
  m. key
  m. loading
  m. rammer
  m. sampler
  m. shovel
median —
  m. strip
medical —
  m. air lock
  m. lock
medium —
  m. carbon steel
  filter m.
meeting post
mega — a prefix meaning one million times
mekometer
member
membrane —
  m. analogy
  curing m.
  damp-proof m.
  flexible m.
  m. processes
  m. theory
  waterproof m.
meniscus
meridian —
  m. of longitude
  m. passage

meridian (*continued*)
  m. plane
  true m.
Merrison committee
mesh
metal —
  anti-friction m.
  m. -arc welding
  expanded m.
  pickling of m.
  white m.
metallic-electrode inert-gas welding
metalling
metallurgical cement
meter —
  cover m.
  current m.
  electromagnetic cover m.
  flow m.
  integrating m.
  moisture m.
  orifice m.
  rotary m.
  sand-grain m.
  ultrasonic flow m.
  Venturi m.
  water m.
metering
methane
method —
  circular-arc m.
  collimation m.
  Fellenius's m.
  Hardy Cross m.
  height of instrument m.
  Honigmann m.
  Hoyer m.
  jackblock m.
  Kind-Chaudron m.
  liquid nitrogen m.
  m. of slices
  pile-placing m's
  sliding-wedge m.
  vacuum m.
metric system
mg — milligram
micro — a prefix meaning one millionth or
  small
micrometer —
  m. gauge
micron

microptic theodolite
microscope —
    optical m.
    petrographic m.
micro-screen
micro-strainer
middle third
middling frame
mid-ordinate
midpoint
midrange
midspan
MIG welding — metallic-electrode inert-gas welding
mil — one thousandth of an inch; a unit used in measuring the thickness of metal coating
mild steel
mill —
    ball m.
    pug m.
    m. scale
    m. tail
milli — a prefix meaning one thousandth
millimeter
millimicron
milling —
    m. machine
miner's dip needle
minimum cement content
minus sight
miser — a large hand auger
mistake
mitre —
    m. post
    m. sill
mix —
    m. design
    m. -in-place
    plant m.
    wet m.
mixed-flow turbine
mixer —
    batch m.
    concrete m.
    non-tilting m.
    pulverizing m.
    soil m.
    tilting m.
    transit m.
    truck m.

mm — millimeter
MMA welding — manual metal-arc welding
mnemonic
MN/m² — meganewtons per square meter
mobile —
    m. crane
    m. hoist
model —
    m. analysis
    harbor m's
modular ratio
modulus —
    bulk m.
    m. of elasticity
    fineness m.
    m. of incompressibility
    plastic m.
    m. of resilience
    m. of rigidity
    m. of rupture
    m. of section
    m. of subgrade reaction
    m. of volume change
    section m.
    shear m.
    Young's m.
Mohr's circle of stress
moil
moisture —
    m. content
    m. index
    m. meter
    m. movement
mold —
    gang m.
    m. oil
moldboard
mole —
    m. drain
    Magic M.
    m. plough
moling
moment —
    bending m.
    m. distribution
    first m.
    fixed-end m.
    hogging m.
    negative m.
    m. of a force
    m. of inertia

moment (*continued*)
  m. of resistance
  polar m. of inertia
  resistance m.
  sagging m.
  static m.
  support m.
momentum
monitor
monkey — a drop hammer
monocable
monolith
monolithic
monorail
monotower crane
monument
mooring forces
mortar —
  pneumatic m.
mosaic
motion study
motor —
  electric m.
  fractional-horsepower m.
  m. grader
  squirrel-cage m.
  m. starter
  universal m.
motorway
mound breakwater
mountain railway
movable —
  m. bridge
  m. dam
movement —
  m. joints in concrete
  moisture m.
moving —
  m. forms
  m. load
mPa — megapascal
muck —
  m. -shifting plant
mucking —
  m. out
mud —
  bentonite m.
  m. flow
  m. flush
  m. jacking

Mulberry harbor
multi —
  m. -bucket excavator
  m. -media filter
  m. -phase flow
  m. -wheel roller
multiple —
  m. -arch dam
  m. -dome dam
  m. -expansion engine
  m. wedge
multiplying constant
municipal —
  m. engineer
  m. engineering
mushroom —
  m. construction
  m. slab

nappe
narrow gauge
natural —
  n. asphalt
  n. frequency of a foundation
  n. gas
  n. harbor
  n. rock asphalt
  n. scale
Nautical Almanac
nautical sextant
Navier's hypothesis
navigation —
  slack-water n.
  still-water n.
navvy —
  steam n.
NDT — non-destructive testing
neat lines
necking
needle —
  compass n.
  dip n.
  dipping n.
  n. instrument
  miner's dip n.
  penetration n.
  Proctor plasticity n.

needle (*continued*)
   n. traverse
   n. valve
   Vicat n.
   n. weir
needling
negative —
   n. moment
   n. skin friction
net —
   n. duty
   flow n.
   n. lines
   n. loading intensity
   n. ton
neutral —
   n. axis
   n. plane
   n. pressure
   n. stress
   n. surface
Newlyn datum
Nicol prism
nip — a wound caused to a diver by a fold in the diving suit
nitrarding
nitriding
nitrocellulose
nitrogen —
   n. hardening
   n. method of freezing ground
nitroglycerin
nitrous fumes
node
nomogram
non-cohesive soil
non-destructive testing
non-metallic minerals
non-return valve
non-skid floor
non-slip floor
non-tilting mixer
normal —
   n. curve
   n. law of error
   n. stress
normalizing
nosing
notch —
   n. effect

notch (*continued*)
   n. plate
   triangular n.
   vee n.
notched —
   n. bar test
   n. weir
notcher
notching
N-truss
number —
   Froude n.
   Reynolds n.

oblique —
   o. aerial photograph
   o. offset
   o. photograph
   o. projection
OBM — Ordnance Bench Mark
OD — Ordnance Datum
oedometer
offset —
   oblique o.
   o. scale
Ohio cofferdam
oil-well —
   o. cement
   o. derrick
on center
open —
   o. caisson
   o. channel
   o. cut
   o. -divided scale
   o. -frame girder
   o. jetty
   o. sheeting
   o. -tank treatment
   o. traverse
   o. -web girder
operation waste
optical —
   o. coincidence bubble
   o. compensation
   o. distance measurement
   o. microscope

optical (*continued*)
  o. plummet
  o. -reading theodolite
  o. square
  o. wedge
optimum moisture content
orange-peel bucket
ordinary —
  o. lay
  o. Portland cement
ordinates
Ordnance —
  O. Bench Mark
  O. Datum
  O. Survey
organic —
  o. clay
  o. silt
oriented-core barrel
orifice meter
origin
orthogonal
orthographic projection
orthophoto
orthophotomat
orthophotoscope
orthoprojector
orthoscan
orthotropic —
  o. deck
  o. plate floor
OS — Ordnance Survey
osmosis —
  reverse o.
osmotic pressure
outburst —
  o. bank
  gas o.
  sudden o.
outcrop
outfall
outrigger
oven-dry soil
overbreak
overbreakage
overburden —
  o. pressure
over-consolidated clay
overfall

overflow —
  bellmouth o.
  o. stand
  storm o.
  stormwater o.
overhaul
overhead —
  o. door
  o. ropeway
  o. traveling crane
overload —
  o. trip
overplanted
overriding brake
overrun brake
oversize
overturning
oxidation ponds
oxy-acetylene flame
ozonizing

P

Pa — pascal
pack —
  dry p.
packer
packing
pad —
  p. foundation
  suction p.
  vacuum p.
paddle —
  p. hole
  lock p.
page — a small wooden wedge used in timbering trenches
pallet — a lifting tray for stacking material with a fork-lift truck
pan —
  evaporation p.
  grout p.
  p. head
  iron p.
panel —
  exterior p.
  p. point
pannier

pantograph
paper —
  building p.
  Whatman p.
parabola
parallel —
  p. drift
  p. -flanged beam
  p. -motion equipment
park-and-ride
parkway
Parramatta Bridge
Parshall measuring flume
partially —
  p. fixed
  p. -separate system
partial prestressing
particle —
  equal-falling p's
  p. -size analysis
  p. -size distribution
parting —
  p. agent
  p. compound
  water p.
Pascal's law
passing place
passive —
  p. earth pressure
  p. resistance
pavement —
  block p.
  flexible p.
  rigid p.
  sheet p.
  storm p.
paver —
  concrete p.
  slip-form p.
paving —
  p. brick
  p. flag
  iron p.
  peg-top p.
  pitcher p.
  radial-sett p.
  stone-block p.
  tar p.
  wood-block p.
peat blasting
pedestrian-controlled dumper

peg —
  quarter p.
  recovery p.
  reference p.
  p. -top paving
pellicular water
Pelton wheel
Pencoyd formula
penetration —
  p. needle
  p. tests
penetrometer
penning —
  p. gate
penstock
peptizing agents
perched water table
percolating filter
percolation
percussion —
  p. drill
  p. tools
percussive —
  p. -rotary drilling
  p. welding
perfect frame
permafrost
permanent —
  p. adjustment
  p. set
  p. shuttering
  p. way
permeability
permeameter
personal equation
Perspex
pervibration
PETN — pentaerythrite tetranitrate
petrographic microscope
PFA — pulverized fuel ash
phosphating
photo —
  p. -elasticity
  p. -electric cell
  p. -electric effect
photogrammetry
photograph —
  oblique p.
  oblique aerial p.
  vertical p.
photomicrograph

phreatic —
  p. surface
  p. water
  p. zone
pick —
  pneumatic p.
picket
pickling of metal
pier —
  baffle p.
  bridge p.
  p. cap
  foundation p.
  standing p.
  p. template
piercing
piezometer tube
piezometric surface
pig — an iron or lead block cast at a smelting
  furnace for remelting
pile —
  anchor p.
  batter p.
  bearing p.
  bored p.
  box p.
  Braithwaite p's
  p. bridge
  p. cap
  cased p.
  concrete p.
  p. core
  displacement p.
  p. drawer
  driven p.
  driven-cast-in-place p.
  p. driver
  end-bearing p.
  enlarged-base p.
  p. extractor
  fender p.
  p. frame
  Franki p.
  friction p.
  p. group
  guide p.
  p. hammer
  p. head
  p. helmet
  p. hoop

pile (*continued*)
  in situ concrete p's
  interlocking p's
  jacked p.
  king p.
  pile-bearing p.
  p. -placing methods
  point-bearing p.
  raking p.
  p. ring
  sand p's
  screw p.
  sheet p's
  p. shoe
  short bored p's
  standard p.
  stay p.
  tension p.
piled foundation
pile-drivers —
  hydraulic p.
  silent p.
  sonic p.
  vibrating p.
pillar
pilot —
  p. circuit
  p. lamp
  p. shaft
  p. tunnel
pin —
  p. joint
  p. jointed
pinchers
pinned
pipe —
  armored p.
  compound p.
  concrete p.
  drain p's
  drive p.
  flexible p.
  half-socket p.
  p. jacking
  p. liners
  prestressed concrete cylinder p.
  p. pushing
  rigid p.
  rubber-lined p.
  sag p.

pipe (*continued*)
  scour p.
  stand p.
  surge p.
  wood-stave p.
piping
pit —
  absorption p.
  p. boards
  borrow p.
  catch p.
  test p.
  trial p.
pitched work
pitcher —
  p. paving
pitching —
  p. ferrules
Pitot tube
pivot bridge
placer —
  concrete p.
placing —
  p. boom
  p. plant
plain concrete
plan —
  grid p.
plane —
  p. frame
  meridian p.
  neutral p.
  p. of rupture
  p. of saturation
  slip p.
  p. surveying
  p. table
  p. -tabling
planer
planimeter
planish
planning engineer
planometric projection
planoscope
plant —
  batching p.
  earth-moving p.
  handling p.
  hauling p.
  maritime p's

plant (*continued*)
  p. mix
  p. -mixed concrete
  muck-shifting p.
  placing p.
  tarmacadam p.
plashing
plastic —
  p. deformation
  p. design
  p. flow
  p. fracture
  p. hinge
  p. limit
  p. modulus
  p. welding
  p. yield
plasticity —
  p. index
  limit of p.
plasticizer
plat
plate —
  anchor p.
  baffle p.
  base p.
  batten p.
  p. bearing test
  bed p.
  checker p.
  checkered p.
  cover p.
  p. floor
  p. girder
  gusset p.
  lower p.
  notch p.
  p. screws
  p. vibrator
  vibrating p.
plated beam
platen
platform —
  p. gantry
  p. hoist
  relieving p.
plot
plotting —
  p. instrument
  p. machine

Plougastel Bridge
plough —
  mole p.
  snow p.
  p. steel
plug —
  p. and feathers
  fusible p.
plum — a large stone dropped into a concrete mass to reduce the volume of concrete
plumb —
  p. bob
  p. line
plumbago
plumbing —
  instrumental shaft p.
  shaft p.
plummet —
  optical p.
plunger
plus sight
pneumatic —
  p. caisson
  p. conveyor
  p. drill
  p. mortar
  p. pick
  p. sewer ejector
  p. shaft sinking
  p. tool
  p. -tired roller
podger —
  p. spanner
podzol
point —
  arrest p.
  balance p.
  p. -bearing pile
  catch p's
  change p.
  control p.
  critical p.
  decalescent p.
  facing p's
  fiducial p.
  p. gauge
  intersection p.
  junction p.
  p. load
  panel p.
  principal p.

point (*continued*)
  recalescent p.
  spring p's
  tangent p.
  trading p's
  trap p's
  turning p.
  yield p.
Poisson's ratio
poker vibrator
polariscope
polarized light
polarizer
polar moment of inertia
polder
pole —
  gin p.
  magnetic north p.
  magnetic south p.
  range p.
poling —
  p. back
  p. boards
  cross p.
  p. frame
polishing
polygonal shell roof
polyhydroxylated polymers
polysulphide sealant
pond —
  oxidation p's
  side p.
pontoon —
  p. bridge
population
pore —
  p. -water pressure
  p. -water-pressure cells
pores
porosity
portable crane
portal —
  p. crane
  p. frame
  p. jib crane
  wind p.
Portland —
  P. blast-furnace cement
  P. cement
  P. -cement concrete
  P. pozzolana cement

position head
post —
  crane p.
  fender p.
  gradient p.
  guard p.
  heel p.
  p. -hole auger
  meeting p.
  mitre p.
  quoin p.
  p. -stressing
  p. -tensioning
pot —
  p. floor
potable water
potential energy
pound —
  foot- p.
  p. -foot
powder —
  ignition p.
  p. spreader
power —
  p. barrow
  p. earth auger
  hydraulic p.
  p. rammer
  p. shovel
  p. take-off
  p. wrench
pozzolana (pozzuolana)
Pratt truss
pre-boring for piles
precast concrete
precipitation —
  chemical p.
precise leveling
precision
pre-coated chippings
pre-consolidation load
pre-formed rope
preliminary treatment
pre-load tank
prepacked concrete
preservatives for timber
press —
  consolidation p.
  hydraulic p.
  hydrostatic p.

pressure —
  active earth p.
  barometric p.
  bearing p.
  capillary p.
  center of p.
  p. creosoting
  earth p.
  effective p.
  p. gauge
  p. head
  hydrostatic p.
  hydrostatic excess p.
  intergranular p.
  neutral p.
  osmotic p.
  overburden p.
  passive earth p.
  pore-water p.
  swelling p.
  p. tank
  total p.
  ultimate bearing p.
  vapor p.
  p. vessel
  wave p.
  p. welding
  wind p.
Pressuremeter
prestressed —
  p. concrete
  p. concrete cylinder pipe
prestressing —
  Hoyer method of p.
  long-line method of p.
  partial p.
pre-tensioning
pretesting
Primacord fuse
primary —
  p. breaker
  p. treatment
  p. triangulation
prime mover
primer
priming
principal —
  p. point
  p. stress

principle —
  p. of Archimedes
  p. of superposition
prism —
  Nicol p.
  p. square
prismatic —
  p. coincidence bubble
  p. compass
  p. telescope
prismoidal formula
probability
probable error
probing
process —
  Dehottay p.
  Joosten p.
  Shell-perm p.
  Trief p.
  wet-sand p.
processes —
  geotechnical p.
  membrane p.
processing
Proctor —
  P. compaction test
  P. plasticity needle
profile —
  longitudinal p.
  p. paper
  soil p.
progression
projection —
  axonometric p.
  azimuthal p.
  cabinet p.
  isometric p.
  oblique p.
  orthographic p.
  planometric p.
  p. welding
proof stress
propeller fan
proportionality —
  limit of p.
proportioning
protective equipment
protection —
  cathodic p.
  sacrificial p.

protection (*continued*)
  scour p.
  shore p.
proving ring
psi — pounds per square inch
pudding stone
puddle —
  clay p.
  p. clay
pug —
  p. mill
pull —
  drawbar p.
  p. -lift
  p. -out test
pulverized —
  p. coal
  p. -fuel ash
pulverizing mixer
pump —
  air p.
  air lift p.
  boojee p.
  borehole p.
  centrifugal p.
  chain p.
  compound p.
  concrete p.
  deep well p.
  diaphragm p.
  direct-acting p.
  displacement p.
  force p.
  gravel p.
  lift p.
  mammoth p.
  ram p.
  reciprocating p.
  rotary p.
  rotodynamic p.
  sand p.
  shell p.
  single-stage p.
  sinking p.
  spout-delivery p.
  submersible p.
  vacuum p.
pun — to drive the air out of wet concrete or
earth with a rod

punch —
 center p.
puncheon
punching —
 p. shear
punner — a wood or metal block used to
 compact earth or paving slabs
pusher tractor
push shovel
puzzolane
pycnometer
pyramid cut
pyrometer

Q

qanat
quadrant
quadrantal bearing
quadrilateral
quarry
quarter
 q. peg
quartering way
quartz
quartzite
Quebec Bridge
queen post truss
quenching
quick-leveling head
quicksand
quickset level
quick test
quoin —
 hollow q.
 q. post

R

race —
 head r.
 tail r.
rack —
 r. railway
 trash r.
racked timbering
racking —
 r. course

radar
radial —
 r. gate
 r. -sett paving
radiation
radiography —
 gamma r.
radiometry
radius —
 r. -and-safe-load indicator
 hydraulic r.
 r. of gyration
radom
raft —
 buoyant r.
 r. foundation
rag bolt
rail —
 r. bender
 bullhead r.
 r. chair
 check r.
 r. fastening
 flat-bottomed r.
 r. gauge
 guard r.
 guide r.
 r. key
 safety r.
 screed r.
 side r.
 sight r.
 slide r.
 stock r.
 r. test
 r. tie
 Vignoles r.
railway —
 cable r.
 r. curves
 elevated r.
 funicular r.
 light r.
 mountain r.
 narrow-gauge r.
 rack r.
 r. transit
 tube r.
 underground r.
 wide-gauge r.

rain —
  r. gauge
rainfall —
  intensity of r.
rainwash
rake
raking —
  r. pile
  r. prop
  r. shore
ram —
  hydraulic r.
  r. pump
rammer —
  frog r.
  hand r.
  mechanical r.
  power r.
ramp —
  slip r.
random sample
range —
  r. line
  r. pole
  r. rod
ranging —
  curve r.
  r. rod
Rankine's theory
rapid —
  r. -hardening cement
  r. -transit system
ratchet-and-pawl mechanism
rate —
  continuous r.
  r. of spread
  spreading r.
rating —
  continuous r.
  r. curve
  r. flume
  half-hour r.
rat-tail file
raveling
Raw bolt
raw water
Raymond standard test
reach — a stretch of water between two locks
reaction turbine
ready-mixed concrete

realignment
ream
reamer
rebound hammer
recalescent point
receiver
recharge —
  artificial r.
reciprocal leveling
reciprocating —
  r. engine
  r. pump
recorder —
  level r.
  rotation r.
  spread r.
recording gauge
recovery peg
rectangular —
  r. coordinates
  r. hollow sections
  r. weir
rectification —
  differential r.
red shortness
reduced —
  r. bearing
  r. level
reduction —
  r. factor
  r. in area
  r. of levels
redundant frame
reed
reeving thimble
reference —
  r. mark
  r. object
  r. peg
reflecting level
reflux valve
refractories
refractory —
  basic r.
  r. clay
  r. linings
refrigerator foundations
refuge —
  street r.
refusal

regime
regimen
reglette
regulating course
reheater
reinforced —
  r. brickwork
  r. concrete
  r. grouted-brick masonry
reinforcement —
  helical r.
  summary of r.
  wire-mesh r.
reiteration
relative —
  r. compaction
  r. density
  r. density of sand
  r. humidity
  r. settlement
relaxation — a loss of prestress
relay
release agent
relief —
  r. holes
  r. well
relieving —
  r. platform
  stress r.
remedial works
remolding —
  r. index
remote control
Reno mattress
repetition
repose —
  angle of r.
representative sample
resection
reservoir —
  clear-water r.
  distribution r.
  impounding r.
  r. roofs
  service r.
  storage r.
resident engineer
residual —
  r. errors
  r. stress

resilience —
  modulus of r.
resistance —
  r. flash welding
  r. losses
  r. moment
  moment of r.
  passive r.
  r. percussive welding
  r. projection welding
  rolling r.
  r. seam welding
  r. spot welding
  r. strain gauge
  tractive r.
  r. welding
resistivity logging
resoiling
resonance
retaining wall
retarder —
  r. of set
  wagon r.
reticle
reticule
retreading roads
return sheave
reverse —
  r. curve
  r. face
  r. osmosis
  r. -rotary drilling
reversed —
  r. curve
  r. filter
reversible tramway
reversing face
revet
revetment
revolver crane
revolving screen
Reynolds —
  R. criterion
  R. critical velocity
  R. number
rib —
  arch r.
  r. center
  r. holes

ribbed —
  r. floor
  r. slab
rice grass
riffle sampler
rift
rig —
  truck-mounted drilling r.
rigger
rigid —
  r. arch
  r. frame
  r. pavement
  r. pipe
rigidity —
  flexural r.
  modulus of r.
ring —
  arch r.
  pile r.
  proving r.
  steel r.
  r. tension
  water r.
riparian
ripper
ripple
rip-rap
rise —
  r. and fall
river purification
rivet —
  tack r.
RO — reverse osmosis
road —
  arterial r.
  r. bed
  r. breaker
  corduroy r.
  r. forms
  r. heater
  r. -making plant
  r. panel
  retreading r's
  r. roller
  service r.
  slip r.
  r. surface

rock —
  r. anchor
  r. bolt
  r. burst
  r. drill
  r. -fill dam
  r. flour
  intrusive r.
  ledge r.
  r. mechanics
  r. noise
rocker —
  r. bearing
  r. shovel
rocket tester
Rockwell hardness test
rod —
  belly r.
  boning r.
  camber r.
  drain r's
  drill r's
  filler r.
  r. float
  leveling r.
  r. man
  range r.
  ranging r.
  stadia r.
  staunching r.
  sway r.
  target r.
  tie r.
  velocity r.
rodding
rolled —
  r. asphalt
  r. -steel joist
  r. -steel section
roller —
  r. bearings
  r. bit
  expansion r's
  r. gate
  indenting r.
  multi-wheel r.
  pneumatic-tired r.
  rubber-tired r.
  sheepsfoot r.
  steam r.

roller (*continued*)
  steel-wheeled r.
  tamping r.
  tandem r.
  three-axle tandem r.
  vibrating r.
  wobble-wheel r.
rolling —
  r. lift bridge
  r. load
  r. resistance
  hot r.
  r. -up curtain weir
rollway
roof —
  r. bolt
  concrete r's
  hyperbolic paraboloid r.
  lamella r.
  polygonal shell r.
  reservoir r's
  shell r.
root — that part of a dam which merges into
  the ground
rooter
Rootes blower
rope —
  cordage r.
  r. diameter
  fall r.
  r. fastenings
  fiber r.
  flattened strand r.
  guy r.
  haulage r.
  locked-coil r.
  Manila r.
  manmade fiber r.
  pre-formed r.
  steel-wire r.
  tail r.
  traction r.
  wire r.
ropeway —
  aerial r.
  bi-cable r.
  continuous r.
  overhead r.
  to-and-fro r.
  twin-cable r.

Rossi-Forel scale
rotary —
  r. blower
  r. drilling
  r. excavator
  r. meter
  r. pump
  r. screen
  r. snowplough
rotational slide
rotation recorder
rotative drilling
rotodynamic pump
roughness
round —
  r. -headed buttress dam
  r. thimble
RPM — revolutions per minute
RSJ — rolled-steel joist
rubber —
  r. -lined pipe
  r. -tired rollers
rubble —
  r. concrete
  r. drain
  r. -mound breakwater
rule —
  Bowditch's r.
  sight r.
  Simpson's r.
  trapezoidal r.
ruling gradient
rumble strip
rummel
runner —
  guide r.
runners
running ground
run-off —
  r. coefficient

S

sacrificial —
  s. anodes
  s. protection
saddle — a steel block over the tower of a
  suspension bridge

safe —
   s. -load indicator
   s. yield
safety —
   s. belt
   factor of s.
   s. fuse
   s. rail
   s. valve
sag —
   s. bar
   s. corrections
   s. pipe
sagging moment
St. Nazaire Bridge
saltation
sample —
   random s.
   representative s.
   snow s.
   soil s.
   s. splitter
   undisturbed s.
sampler —
   bottom s.
   clay s.
   mechanical s.
   riffle s.
   snow s.
   soil s.
sampling —
   fractional s.
   grab s.
   s. spoon
sand —
   s. blast
   s. catcher
   s. drain
   s. fill
   s. filling
   s. filter
   graded s.
   s. -grain meter
   s. piles
   s. pump
   s. pump dredger
   sorted s.
   s. trap
   uniform s.
Sandö Bridge

sandpaper surface
sandstone
sandwich construction
sandwick
sanitary sewer
saturated air
saturation —
   s. line
   plane of s.
   zone of s.
saucer — a flat steel float used for lifting a ship above shallow waters
saw —
   chain s.
   crosscut s.
   diamond s.
   s. files
scabbing
scabbling
scale —
   Armstrong s.
   Beaufort s.
   s. drawing
   fully-divided s.
   mill s.
   natural s.
   offset s.
   open-divided s.
   Rossi-Forel s.
scaling
scappling
scarifier
Schmidt rebound hammer
scissors —
   s. crossover
   s. junction
scleroscope hardness test
scotch block
Scotch derrick
scour —
   s. pipe
   s. protection
scouring sluice
scow
scraper —
   bowl s.
   s. bucket
   dragline s.
   s. evacuator
   hoe s.

scraper (*continued*)
s. loader
slip s.
wheel s.
screed —
s. board
s. rail
screen —
s. analysis
band s.
fish s.
revolving s.
rotary s.
traveling s.
wedge-wire s.
screened material
screening
screenings
screw —
adjusting s.
Archimedean s.
clamping s.
clip s.
clipping s.
coach s's
s. conveyor
fine adjustment s.
foot s's
leveling s.
s. pile
plate s's
set s.
s. shackle
s. spike
tangent s.
screws — Caisson disease
SCUBA — self-contained underwater
breathing apparatus
scumboard
seal
sealant —
polysulphide s.
two-part s.
sea-level corrections
sealing —
s. coat
s. compound
s. drop shafts to rock
s. pneumatic shafts to rock

seam welding
seating — any surface that carries a large
load
seat of settlement
sec. — second
secant modulus of elasticity
second —
s. cut
s. -foot
s. moment of area
s. -order
secondary —
s. beam
s. sedimentation
s. treatment
s. triangulation
section —
angle s.
beaded s.
channel s.
extruded s's
hollow s's
s. leader
longitudinal s.
s. modulus
s. properties
rectangular hollow s's
rolled-steel s.
standard s.
thin s.
trough s's
true s.
tubular s.
sectional —
s. elevation
s. tank
sector —
s. gate
s. regulator
sediment
sedimentation —
secondary s.
seepage —
s. force
s. line
s. loss
segmental sluice gate
segregation
seiche

seismic —
  s. design
  s. prospecting
  s. recording
seismograph
seismology
seismometer
self —
  s. -anchored suspension bridge
  s. -cleansing gradient
  s. -docking dock
  s. -fill
  s. -reading staff
  s. -stressing cement
semi-skilled man
semi-submersible
sensible horizon
sensitive clay
sensitiveness
sensitivity —
  s. ratio
separate system
separator
serrated strip
service —
  s. reservoir
  s. road
set —
  flash s.
  permanent s.
  retarder of s.
  s. screw
  s. square
sett —
  cold s.
setting —
  fire s.
  s. out
  s. up
settlement —
  consolidation s.
  s. crater
  differential s.
  inherent s.
  interference s.
  s. joint
  relative s.
  seat of s.
settling —
  s. basin

settling (*continued*)
  hindered s.
  s. velocity
set-up
Severn Bridge
sewage —
  s. disposal
  s. farm
  s. gas
  s. treatment
sewer —
  egg-shaped s.
  foul s.
  main s.
  s. pill
  sanitary s.
  storm s.
  stormwater s.
  trunk s.
sewerage
sexagesimal —
  s. graduation
  s. measure
sextant —
  box s.
  nautical s.
shackle —
  screw s.
shaft —
  drop s.
  forced drop s.
  pilot s.
  s. plumbing
  s. -plumbing wire
  s. sinking
  working s.
shaking test
shale —
  burnt s.
  heaving s.
shallow —
  s. foundation
  s. manhole
  s. well
shaping
shear —
  s. center
  s. force
  s. legs
  s. modulus

shear (*continued*)
  punching s.
  s. slide
  s. strain
  s. strength
  s. stress
  s. tests
  s. wall
  wind s.
shearing
shear legs
shears —
  s. derrick
sheathing
sheave —
  return s.
sheepsfoot roller
sheet —
  s. pavement
  s. piles
  s. -pile wall
  s. piling
  s. steel
sheeters
sheeting —
  open s.
shelf —
  s. angle
  s. retaining wall
shell —
  thin s.
  s. -and-auger boring
  s. -perm process
  s. pump
  s. roof
shield —
  biological s.
  Greathead s.
  Hallinger s.
shielded —
  s. -arc welding
  s. metal-arc welding
shift —
  Doppler s.
shim
shin — the replaceable edge on a bulldozer
shingle beach
ship caisson
shoe — a steel ring on which a drop shaft is
  erected

shop —
  erecting s.
  s. weld
shore —
  s. protection
  raking s.
short —
  s. bored piles
  s. column
  s. ton
shortness —
  hot s.
  red s.
shot —
  s. blasting
  s. firing
Shotcrete
shovel —
  crowd s.
  drag s.
  face s.
  forward s.
  loading s.
  mechanical s.
  power s.
  push s.
  rocker s.
  steam s.
  tractor s.
shredder —
  soil s.
shrinkage —
  s. joint
  s. limit
shuttering —
  permanent s.
side —
  s. board
  s. -entrance manhole
  s. forms
  s. -jacking test
  s. pond
  s. rail
  s. tree
sidelong ground
sidesway
sidetracking
sidewalk
siding machine
sieve analysis

sight —
s. distance
intermediate s.
minus s.
plus s.
s. rail
s. rule
silent pile-drivers
silica —
s. brick
silicate injection
silicon carbide
sill —
clap s.
dentated s.
lock s.
mitre s.
silo
silt —
s. box
s. displacement
s. ejector
firm s.
s. grade material
organic s.
s. size
siltation
silting
similarity —
dimensional s.
kinematic s.
simple —
s. beam
s. bending
s. curve
s. engine
s. framework
simply-supported beam
Simpson's rule
single —
s. -acting
s. -cut file
s. -pass soil stabilizer
s. -sized aggregate
s. sling
s. -stage compressor
s. -stage pump
sinker —
s. drill
well s.

sinking —
s. bucket
Honigmann method of shaft s.
pneumatic shaft s.
s. pump
shaft s.
sintered —
s. carbides
s. clay
s. fly-ash
sintering
sinuous flow
siphon —
dosing s.
inverted s.
s. spillway
site —
s. exploration
s. investigation
s. weld
size —
s. analysis
s. distribution
s. grading
silt s.
skeleton — 1. a network of survey lines
obtained by triangulation; 2. a building
frame of steel or concrete
sketch
skew bridge
skids
skilled man
skimmer equipment
skimming
skin —
balloon s.
s. friction
skip — a hoisting bucket
slab —
s. -and-beam floor
cored s.
filler concrete s.
flat s.
floor s.
mushroom s.
ribbed s.
s. track
voided s.
slack —
s. -line cableway

slack (*continued*)
  s. -line cableway excavator
  s. -water navigation
slag —
  s. cements
sledge —
  s. hammer
sleeper — a steel, wooden or concrete beam
  passing under the rails of a railway and
  holding them at correct gauge
sleeve —
  bolt s.
  s. grouting
  tension s.
slender beam
slenderness ratio
slewing
sliced blockwork
slickensided clay
slickensides
slide —
  creep s.
  cylindrical s.
  detritus s.
  flow s.
  s. rail
  rotational s.
  s. rule
  shear s.
sliding —
  s. caisson
  s. forms
  s. gate
  s. joint
  s. -panel weir
  s. -wedge method
sling —
  chain s.
  double s.
  four-leg s.
  single s.
  three-leg s.
  two-leg s.
slip —
  s. circle
  s. dock
  s. factor
  s. -form
  s. -form paver
  s. joint

slip (*continued*)
  s. plane
  s. ramp
  s. road
  s. scraper
  s. surface
slipstick — a slide rule
slipway —
  traversing s.
slope —
  s. corrections
  s. gauge
  s. staking
  virtual s.
slough
slow —
  s. bend test
  s. test
sludge —
  s. disposal
  s. gas
sludger
slug — a small quantity of fluid in a pipe that
  does not mix with the main fluid
sluice —
  scouring s.
slump test
slurry —
  s. excavation
  s. trench
slusher
slush ice
SMA — shielded metal-arc
smithing
smith welding
smooth
smoothing iron
snatch block
SN curve — stress-number curve
snow —
  s. course
  s. density
  s. load
  s. plough
  s. sample
  s. sampler
soakaway
soffit
soft —
  s. clay
  s. -suspension theory

soil —
  s. analysis
  s. auger
  s. -cement
  cohesion of s.
  cohesionless s.
  cohesive s.
  s. consolidation
  expansive s's
  floury s.
  frictional s.
  heavy s.
  s. mechanics
  s. mixer
  non-cohesive s.
  oven-dry s.
  s. profile
  s. sample
  s. sampler
  s. shredder
  s. solidification
  s. stabilization
  stabilized s.
  stratified s's
  sulphate-bearing s's
  s. survey
  swelling s's
soiling
soldier —
  s. beam
solenoid
solid —
  s. map
  s. web
soling
solution injection
sonde
sonic pile-driver
Sopwith staff
sorted sand
sounding —
  s. lead
  s. line
southing
space —
  s. deck
  s. grid
  s. frame
  s. lattice
  s. structure

spad
spader
spall —
  s. drain
span —
  clear s.
  effective s.
  end s.
  interior s.
  limiting s.
  long s.
  suspended s.
spandrel wall
spanner —
  impact s.
  podger s.
special —
  s. steel
  s. structural concrete
specific —
  s. adhesion
  s. gravity
  s. retention
  s. speed
  s. surface
  s. yield
specification —
  standard s.
spelter —
  brazing s.
spider —
  s. line
  s. web
spike —
  screw s.
  track s.
spile
spiling
spill
spillway —
  s. gate
  siphon s.
spiral —
  s. curve
splice —
  s. bar
  s. piece
split bubble
spoil
spontaneous liquefaction

spool — a cast-iron separator between timbers
spot —
  s. level
  s. welding
spotting
spout-delivery pump
Sprague and Henwood core barrel
spray —
  s. bar
  s. lance
sprayed concrete
sprayer —
  hand s.
  tank s.
spread —
  s. footing
  rate of s.
  s. recorder
spreader —
  s. beam
  bulk s.
  concrete s.
  macadam s.
  powder s.
spreading —
  s. box
  s. rate
spring —
  s. points
  s. washer
springing
spud —
  anchoring s.
spudding
spur —
  s. dyke
square —
  s. -mile foot
  optical s.
  prism s.
  set s.
  s. thread
squibbing
squirrel-cage motor
stability —
  dimensional s.
stabilization —
  granular s.
  soil s.
stabilized soil

stabilizer —
  single-pass soil s.
stadia —
  s. hairs
  s. rod
  s. work
staff —
  s. gauge
  leveling s.
  s. man
  self-reading s.
  Sopwith s.
  target s.
stage — water level measured from any chosen line of reference
staging
stalk
stanchion (stauncheon)
standard —
  s. deviation
  s. diving dress
  s. diving gear
  s. error
  s. gauge
  s. pile
  s. section
  s. specification
  s. wire gauge
standardization —
  s. corrections
  s. length
  s. temperature
standing —
  s. derrick
  hard s.
  s. pier
  s. -water level
stand pipe
stank — a small wooden cofferdam sealed with clay
Stanley compensating diaphragm
starling — piling driven into a river bed either upstream or downstream of a bridge pier to protect it from floating rubbish or ice
starter —
  s. bar
  s. frame
  motor s.

static —
s. head
s. load
s. moment
s. penetration test
s. suction lift
statically —
s. -determinate frame
s. -indeterminate frame
statics
station —
gauging s.
telecontrolled power s.
trig s.
trigonometrical s.
stationary dredger
statistical uniformity
statistics
stauncheon (stanchion)
staunching —
s. bead
s. piece
s. rod
stay pile
steady flow
steam —
s. boiler
s. curing
s. engine
s. navvy
s. roller
s. shovel
s. turbine
steel —
acid s.
alloy s.
s. band
basic s.
s. bender
carbon s.
cast s.
clad s.
copper-bearing s.
crucible s.
dead-mild s.
dead-soft s.
distribution s.
drill s.
s. erector
s. fixer

steel (*continued*)
s. frame
s. -grit blasting
high-carbon s.
high tensile s.
low-carbon s.
manganese s.
medium-carbon s.
mild s.
plough s.
s. ring
sheet s.
s. sheet piling
special s.
temperature s.
s. tape
weathering s's
s. -wheeled roller
s. -wire rope
steening
steining
Stellite
stem
step —
s. iron
stepped foundation
stereometric map
stereoplotter
stereoscope
stereoscopic —
s. pair
s. vision
Stevenson's formula
stick welding
stiff —
s. clay
s. -fissured c.
s. frame
s. -leg derrick
stiffened suspension bridge
stiffener —
web s.
stiffening girder
stiffness —
center of s.
stilling —
s. pool
s. well
still-water navigation
stimulation

stinger — a pontoon attached to a lay barge to reduce stress on the pipe as it leaves the barge

stirrup

stock rail

Stokes's —
S. law
S. formula

stone —
s. -block paving
border s.
s. drain
pudding s.

stop —
s. end
form s.
s. log
s. plank
s. valve

storm —
s. overflow
s. pavement
s. sewer

stormwater —
s. overflow
s. sewer
s. tanks

straight-run bitumen

strain —
s. aging
elastic s.
s. energy
s. gauge
s. hardening
shear s.

strake

strand

stranded caisson

Stran-steel

strap —
butt s.
cover s.

stratified —
s. flow
s. soils

stratigraphy

streamline flow

street —
adopted s.
dedicated s.

street (*continued*)
s. inlet
s. refuge

strength —
characteristic s.
crushing s.
cube s.
interface s.
s. of materials
shear s.
tensile s.
ultimate s.
ultimate compressive s.
ultimate tensile s.
wet cube s.

stress —
s. analysis
bearing s.
bond s.
breaking s.
s. circle
s. concentration
direct s.
Euler crippling s.
hoop s.
intensity of s.
Mohr's circle of s.
neutral s.
normal s.
s. -number curve
principal s.
proof s.
s. raiser
s. relieving
residual s.
shear s.
s. -strain curve
temperature s.
ultimate tensile s.
unit s.
working s.
yield s.

stressed-skin construction

stretcher

striding level

strike — the horizontal line in the plane of a fault at right angles to the dip

striker — a blacksmith's helper

striking - removing temporary supports from a structure

stringer —
  s. beam
  track s.
strip —
  bi-metal s.
  s. footing
  s. foundation
  median s.
  rumble s.
  serrated s.
  winding s's
stripping
struck capacity
structural —
  s. analysis
  s. design
  s. designer
  s. designer-draftsman
  s. draftsman
  s. engineer
  s. engineering technician
  s. steelwork
structure —
  balloon s's
  flotation s.
  space s.
  suspended s.
  tension s.
  theory of s's
  water-filled s.
strut
Stub's iron wire gauge
stud —
  s. gun
  s. welding
stuffing box
stumper
stunt end
sub-base
subcritical flow
sub-grade
sub-irrigation
submerged —
  s. -arc welding
  s. float
  s. tunnel
  s. weir
submersible —
  s. pump
subsidence

subsoil —
  s. drain
substructure
subsurface —
  s. erosion
  s. float
  s. flow
subtense bar
subway
suction —
  s. -cutter dredger
  s. dredger
  s. head
  s. pad
  s. valve
sudden —
  s. drawdown
  s. outburst
sue load
sulphate —
  s. -bearing soils
  s. -resisting cement
summary of reinforcement
summit canal
sump
  s. pump
sumpers
supercritical flow
superelevation
superficial —
  s. compaction
superimposed load
superintendent
superload
superposition —
  principle of s.
superstructure
supersulphated cement
support —
  lateral s.
  s. moment
suppressed weir
surcharge
surcharged wall
surface —
  s. -active agent
  s. detention
  s. dressing
  s. float
  neutral s.

surface (*continued*)
  phreatic s.
  piezometric s.
  road s.
  sandpaper s.
  slip s.
  specific s.
  Swedish cylindrical s.
  s. tension
  s. -tension depressant
  s. water
  s. -water drain
surfacing —
  thin s.
surfactant
surge —
  s. pipe
  s. tank
  wind s.
survey —
  chain s.
  soil s.
  trigonometrical s.
surveying —
  aerial s.
  borehole s.
  s. error
  geodetic s.
  geophysical s.
  hydrographic s.
  large-scale s.
  marine s.
  marine hydrographic s.
  plane s.
  small-scale s.
  tacheometric s.
  topographical s.
surveyor —
  building s's
  s. draftsman
  land s.
  mining s's
  topographical s.
  s.'s transit
suspended —
  s. -frame weir
  s. span
  s. structure
suspender — a vertical hanger in a
  suspension bridge

suspension —
  s. bridge
  s. cable
  s. -cable anchor
  catenary s.
sustained yield
swamp shooting
swash height
sway —
  s. brace
  s. rod
Swedish cylindrical surface
swelling —
  s. pressure
  s. soils
SWG — Standard Wire Gauge
swing —
  s. bridge
  s. -jib crane
swinger — a pointed bar used for moving
  piles in trench timbering
switch —
  s. blades
  float s.
  limit s.
switchgear
Sydney Harbor Bridge
system —
  combined s.
  metric s.
  partially separate s.
  rapid transit s.
  separate s.
systematic errors

T

table —
  perched water t.
  plane t.
  traverse t's
  water t.
tacheometer —
  direct reading t.
tacheometric —
  t. surveying
tacheometry

tack —
   t. coat
   t. rivet
   t. weld
Tacoma Narrows Bridge
tail —
   t. bay
   t. gate
   mill t.
   t. race
   t. rope
tailwater
Tainter gate
tally
tamp
tamper
tamping roller
tandem —
   t. roller
tangent —
   t. distance
   t. point
   t. screw
tank —
   aeration t.
   break-pressure t.
   detritus t.
   dosing t.
   humus t.
   Imhoff t.
   pre-load t.
   pressure t.
   sectional t.
   t. sprayer
   stormwater t.
   surge t.
tanking
tape —
   t. corrections
   graduation of t's
   steel t.
taper —
   t. drift
   t. file
tapered —
   t. -flange beam
   t. washer
tar —
   t. emulsion
   t. paving

tare
target —
   t. rod
   t. staff
   traverse t.
tarmacadam —
   t. plant
technician —
   t. engineer
   structural engineering t.
tee-beam
tee-iron
tee-section
tee-square
telecontrolled power station
telemeter
telemetry
telescope —
   anallatic t.
   internally-focusing t.
   prismatic t.
telescopic centering
telfer (telpher)
teller — a label marking every meter on a
   surveyor's chain
telltale
Tellurometer
telpher (telfer)
temper
temperature —
   critical t.
   t. correction
   t. gradient
   standardization t.
   t. steel
   t. stress
tempering
temporary adjustment
tenacity
tendon — a prestressing bar, cable, rope, or
   wire
tensile —
   t. force
   t. strength
   t. test
tension —
   t. carriage
   t. correction
   diagonal t.
   t. flange

tension (*continued*)
  hoop t.
  t. pile
  ring t.
  t. sleeve
  t. structure
  surface t.
  vapor t.
tensor —
  hydraulic t.
terminal —
  t. velocity
terotechnology
terracing
tertiary —
  t. treatment
  t. triangulation
Terzaghi
test —
  beam t.
  bearing t.
  bend t.
  box shear t.
  Brinell hardness t.
  California bearing ratio t.
  Charpy t.
  compacting factor t.
  confined compression t.
  crushing t.
  cube t.
  t. cube
  cylinder t.
  deep-penetration t.
  diamond pyramid hardness t.
  drained shear t.
  drift t.
  drop penetration t.
  dump t.
  dynamic penetration t.
  fatigue t.
  flow-table t.
  hydraulic t.
  hydrostatic t.
  impact t.
  initial surface absorption t.
  in situ soil t's
  Izod t.
  longitudinal bead t.
  notched bar t.
  penetration t's

test (*continued*)
  t. piece
  t. pit
  plate bearing t.
  Proctor compaction t.
  pull-out t.
  quick t.
  rail t.
  Raymond standard t.
  Rockwell hardness t.
  scleroscope hardness t.
  shaking t.
  shear t's
  side-jacking t.
  slow t.
  slow bend t.
  slump t.
  static penetration t.
  tensile t.
  triaxial compression t.
  unconfined compression t.
  undrained shear t.
  upending t.
  vane t.
  Vickers hardness t.
  water t.
testing —
  compression t.
  t. machine
  non-destructive t.
  ultrasonic t.
tetrahedron
tetrapod
theodolite —
  microptic t.
  optical-reading t.
theory of structures
thermal —
  t. boring
thermel
thermic —
  t. boring
thermit —
  welding t.
thermite
thermocouple
thermo-osmosis
thimble —
  reeving t.
  round t.

thin —
   t. section
   t. shell
   t. surfacing
third-order
thixotropy
three —
   t. -axle tandem roller
   t. -dimensional vision
   t. -hinged arch
   t. -legged derrick
   t. -leg sling
   t. -pinned arch
   t. -point problem
   t. -tripod traversing
throat — the least thickness of a joint
   between pieces of metal or plastic at faces
   that have been melted
through bridge
thrust —
   t. bearing
   t. borer
   t. boring
   bridge t.
   end t.
tidal —
   t. dock
   t. lag
tide —
   t. gauge
   t. predictor
tie —
   land t.
   t. line
   main t.
   rail t.
   t. rod
tied retaining wall
tight-fitting bolt
TIG welding — tungsten-electrode inert-gas
   shielded-arc w.
till — boulder clay
tillite
tilt — the angle between the vertical and the
   optical axis of a camera
tilting —
   t. gate
   t. level
   t. mixer
timbering —
   racked t.

time and motion study
timekeeper
timing
tine
tip grade
tipping —
   t. lorry
   t. wagon
Titan crane
TNT — trinitrotoluene
to-and-fro ropeway
toe —
   t. filter
   t. level
   t. line
toggle mechanism
ton —
   foot-t.
   gross t.
   long t.
   net t.
   short t.
tool —
   arrissing t.
   fishing t's
   grafting t.
   machine t's
   percussion t's
   pneumatic t.
top frame
topographical —
   t. surveying
   t. surveyor
topping
topsoil
torpedo
torque —
   t. wrench
Torshear bolt
torsion
tortuous flow
total pressure
toughness —
   t. index
tough way
tower —
   anchor t.
   t. crane
   t. gantry
   king t.
   valve t.

township
tracer
tracing —
t. cloth
t. linen
t. paper
track —
t. cable
crawler t.
duplex t.
slab t.
t. spike
t. stringer
tracking
track-laying tractor
traction —
coefficient of t.
electric t.
t. rope
tractive —
t. force
t. resistance
tractor —
half-track t.
pusher t.
t. shovel
track-laying t.
wheeled t.
traffic engineering
trailer dredger
trailing —
t. cable
t. dredger
t. points
training —
t. wall
t. works
trammel —
elliptical t.
Trammel drain
tramway —
reversible t.
Träneberg Bridge
transducer
transfer
transformer
transient
transit —
engineer's t.
t. instrument
t. man

transit (*continued*)
t. mixer
railway t.
surveyor's t.
upper t.
transition —
t. curve
t. length
transmission length
transpiration
transportation engineering
transporter —
t. bridge
cableway t.
t. crane
transverse loading
trap —
flap t.
grease t.
gulley t.
t. points
sand t.
yard t.
trapezoidal rule
trash rack
trass
traveler
traveling —
t. forms
t. ganger
t. gantry
t. screen
travel-mixer
traverse —
closed t.
compass t.
needle t.
open t.
t. tables
t. target
traversing —
t. bridge
t. slipway
three-tripod t.
traxcavator
treamie (trémie)
treatment —
advanced waste water t.
aerobic t.
biological t.
heat t.

treatment (*continued*)
  land t.
  open-tank t.
  preliminary t.
  primary t.
  secondary t.
  sewage t.
  tertiary t.
  water t.
tree —
  t. cutter
  head t.
  side t.
treedozer
treenail (trenail)
trémie (treamie)
trenail (treenail)
trench —
  t. box
  t. compactor
  t. drain
  t. excavator
  t. hoe
  slurry t.
trencher
trenching machine
trepan
trestle —
  t. bridge
trial —
  t. pit
  t. hole
triangle —
  t. of error
  well-conditioned t.
  Weisbach t.
triangular —
  t. notch
  t. weir
triangulation —
  primary t.
  secondary t.
  tertiary t.
triaxial compression test
tribrach
trickling filter
Trief process
trigonometrical —
  t. station
  t. survey

trilateration
trimmers
trimming
trinitrotoluene
trip —
  t. coil
  overload t.
tripod
trommel
troughing
trough sections
truck —
  agitating t.
  dump t.
  fork-lift t.
  t. mixer
  t. -mounted crane
  t. -mounted drilling rig
true —
  t. bearing
  t. meridian
  t. section
  t. -to-scale print
trunk —
  t. main
  t. sewer
trunnion axis
truss —
  Belgian t.
  bridge t.
  Fink t.
  French t.
  Howe t.
  Linville t.
  N-t.
  Pratt t.
  queen post t.
  Whipple-Murphy t.
trussed —
  t. arch
  t. beam
tsunami
tubbing
tube —
  t. à manchette
  bubble t.
  butt welded t.
  chambered-level t.
  draft t.
  immersed t.

tube (*continued*)
    inner t.
    level t.
    piezometer t.
    Pitot t.
    t. railway
    Venturi t.
tubular sections
tucking —
    t. board
    t. frame
tungsten —
    t. carbide
    t. -electrode inert-gas shielded-arc welding
tunnel —
    Channel T.
    drainage t.
    t. lining
    pilot t.
    submerged t.
    t. vault
    wind t.
tunneling speed
tup
turbidity current
turbine —
    Francis t.
    impulse t.
    Kaplan t.
    mixed flow t.
    reaction t.
    steam t.
    water t.
turbo-drill
turbulence
turbulent flow
turfing
turn —
    t. bridge
    t. buckle
turned bolt
turning point
turnout
turntable
twin-cable ropeway
twist
two —
    t. -hinged arch
    t. -leg sling
    t. -part sealant

two (*continued*)
    t. -pinned arch
    t. -stage compression
    t. -way grid

U

ultimate —
    u. bearing capacity of a pile
    u. bearing pressure
    u. compressive strength
    u. strength
    u. tensile strength/stress
ultra-filtration
ultra-high-early-strength cement
ultrasonic —
    u. flow meter
    u. pulse attenuation
    u. testing
unconfined —
    u. compression test
    u. water
underflow
underground railway
underpin
underplanting
under-reaming
undersize
undisturbed sample
undrained shear test
unequal angle
uniform
    u. sand
    u. soil
uniformity —
    u. coefficient
    statistical u.
unit —
    distancing u.
    u. graph
    u. hydrograph
    kilowatt u.
    u. stress
    u. weight
universal —
    u. beam
    u. motor
unstable —
    u. frame

upending test
uplift
upper transit
upsetting

V

vacuum —
  v. concrete
  v. lifting
  v. mat
  v. method
  v. method of testing sands
  v. pad
  v. pump
vadose water
vadose zone
value —
  calorific v.
  heating v.
valve —
  air v.
  anti-flood and tidal v.
  butterfly v.
  check v.
  control v.
  discharge v.
  flap v.
  foot v.
  gate v.
  low-water v.
  needle v.
  non-return v.
  reflux v.
  safety v.
  stop v.
  suction v.
  v. tower
  washout v.
vanadium
vane test
vapor —
  v. barrier
  v. pressure
  v. tension
variance
variation —
  magnetic v.

vault —
  barrel v.
  cylindrical v.
  tunnel v.
  wagon v.
V.-B. consistometer
V-cut
vee notch
vel — a unit of size (velocity in an air elutriator)
velocities in pipes
velocity —
  Belanger's critical v.
  critical v.
  fall v.
  falling v.
  free-falling v.
  v. head
  Kennedy's critical v.
  laminar v.
  mean v.
  v. of approach
  v. of retreat
  v. ratio
  Reynold's critical v.
  v. rod
  settling v.
  terminal v.
vena contracta (Lat) — the narrowest point in the cross-section of a jet beyond the plane of the whole from which it issues
Venturi —
  v. flume
  v. meter
  v. tube
verge
Verrazano Narrows Bridge
vertex
vertical —
  v. alignment
  v. circle
  v. control
  v. curve
  v. interval
  v. photograph
  v. sand drain
viaduct
vial
vibrated concrete

vibrating —
  v. pile-drivers
  v. plate
  v. roller
vibration —
  forced v.
  free v.
  v. of foundations
vibrator —
  exterior v.
  immersion v.
  internal v.
  plate v.
  poker v.
Vibroflot
vibroflotation
vibroreplacement
Vicat needle
Vickers hardness test
Vierendeel girder
Vignoles rail
virtual slope
viscometer
viscosimeter
viscosity
viscous flow
visibility distance
visible horizon
vision —
  three-dimensional v.
  stereoscopic v.
voided slab
void former
voids
  v. ratio
volumetric efficiency
volume yield
volute
vortex shedding
voussoir arch

W

waffle floor
wagon —
  w. drill
  jubilee w.
  w. retarder

wagon (*continued*)
  tipping w.
  w. vault
wake — recurring eddies downstream of an
  obstacle
wale
walking —
  w. dragline
  w. ganger
wall —
  abutment w.
  anchor w.
  cantilever w.
  core w.
  crib w.
  curtain w.
  cut-off w.
  diaphragm w.
  embankment w.
  facing w.
  fixed retaining w's
  flexible w.
  free retaining w.
  w. friction
  gravity retaining w.
  head w.
  loadbearing w.
  retaining w.
  shear w.
  sheet-pile w.
  shelf retaining w.
  spandrel w.
  surcharged w.
  tied retaining w.
  training w.
  wing w.
Warren girder
wash —
  w. boring
  bye w.
washer —
  bevelled w.
  spring w.
  tapered w.
washland
washout valve
waste —
  operation w.
  w. weir

wasteway
water —
  adhesive w.
  w. authority
  w. -bearing ground
  capillary w.
  w. -cement ratio
  circulating w.
  compensation w.
  confined w.
  w. content
  w. cushion
  w. cycle
  de-ionized w.
  de-mineralized w.
  drinking w.
  w. -filled structure
  free w.
  fringe w.
  w. gauge
  gravitational w.
  gravity w.
  w. hammer
  held w.
  interstitial w.
  w. -jet driving
  w. lowering
  w. meter
  w. of capillarity
  w. parting
  pellicular w.
  phreatic w.
  w. pollution control
  potable w.
  raw w.
  w. reducer
  w. -repellent
  w. requirement
  w. ring
  w. supply
  surface w.
  w. table
  w. test
  w. treatment
  w. -tube boiler
  w. turbine
  unconfined w.
  vadose w.
  w. wheel
waterbar
waterbound macadam

waterproofing
waterproof membrane
watershed
waterworks
wattle work
wave pressure
wearing course
weathering steels
weather-resistant
web —
  solid w.
  spider w.
  w. stiffener
wedge —
  w. cut
  multiple w.
  optical w.
  w. theory
  w. -wire screen
weephole
weigh batcher
weighted —
  w. average
  w. filter
weighting
weir —
  Cipolletti w.
  contracted w.
  drowned w.
  frame w.
  w. head
  measuring w.
  needle w.
  notched w.
  rectangular w.
  rolling-up curtain w.
  separation w.
  sliding-panel w.
  submerged w.
  suppressed w.
  suspended-frame w.
  triangular w.
  waste w.
Weisbach triangle
weld —
  butt w.
  fillet w.
  shop w.
  site w.
  tack w.
weldability

welded frame
welding —
  arc w.
  argon-arc w.
  atomic-hydrogen w.
  autogenous w.
  automatic w.
  bronze w.
  carbon-arc w.
  carbon-dioxide w.
  copper w.
  electric w.
  electric-arc w.
  electroslag w.
  fire w.
  flash w.
  flash-butt w.
  forge w.
  fusion w.
  gas w.
  gas-shielded metal-arc w.
  gas-tungsten-arc w.
  GTA w.
  MAG w.
  manual metal-arc w.
  metal-arc w.
  metallic active-gas w.
  metallic-electrode inert-gas w.
  MIG w.
  MMA w.
  percussive w.
  plastic w.
  pressure w.
  projection w.
  resistance w.
  resistance flash w.
  resistance percussive w.
  resistance projection w.
  resistance seam w.
  resistance spot w.
  seam w.
  shielded-arc w.
  shielded metal-arc w.
  smith w.
  spot w.
  stick w.
  stud w.
  submerged-arc w.
  w. thermit
  TIG w.
  tungsten-electrode inert-gas shielded-arc w.
  wet w.

well —
  absorbing w.
  Abyssinian w.
  artesian w.
  w. borer
  Chicago w.
  w. -conditioned triangle
  w. curbing
  deep w.
  disposal w.
  w. drain
  dredging w.
  dry w.
  filter w.
  w. foundation
  gauge w.
  w. hole
  injection w.
  w. logging
  relief w.
  shallow w.
  w. sinker
  stilling w.
  wet w.
Wellington formula
wellpoint
westing
wet —
  w. analysis
  w. cube strength
  w. dock
  w. drilling
  w. galvanizing
  w. mix
  w. -sand process
  w. welding
  w. well
wetted perimeter
wharf
Whatman paper
wheel —
  bull w.
  w. excavator
  w. gauge
  w. loader
  Pelton w.
  w. scraper
  water w.
wheelabrating
wheeled tractor
whip — a short length of wire rope by which loads are fixed to a crane hook

Whipple-Murphy truss
Whirley crane
whiskers — tiny single crystals of much
 greater length than diameter that are 20 to
 50 times stronger than steel
white —
 w. cement
 w. metal
Whitney stress diagram
whole-circle bearing
whole-tide cofferdam
wicket —
 w. dam
wide-gauge railway
wiep
wiepen
wilting coefficient
winch
wind —
 w. beam
 w. force
 w. load
 w. portal
 w. pressure
 w. shear
 w. surge
 w. tunnel
windbrace
winding strips
windmill
windrow
windshield
windy — Scotch term for pneumatic (thus a
 windy drill is a rock drill)
wing —
 w. dam
 w. wall
winter gritter
wire —
 annealed w.
 binding w.
 w. drawing
 w. gauge
 w. lath
 w. -line core barrel
 w. -mesh reinforcement
 w. -rope
 shaft-plumbing w.
wirecut brick
wobble-wheel roller

wood-block paving
wood-stave pipe
work —
 w. -hardening
 hurdle w.
 pitched w.
 remedial w's
 stadia w.
 training w's
 wattle w.
workability
working —
 w. chamber
 w. drawing
 hot w.
 w. shaft
 w. stress
worm conveyor
wracking forces
wrench —
 impact w.
 power w.
wrought —
 w. aluminum alloy
 w. iron

Xylonite — a thermoplastic material for
 making models in photo-elastic analysis
xylophage

yard —
 casting y.
 y. gulley
 y. trap
yield —
 plastic y.
 y. point
 safe y.
 specific y.
 y. stress
 sustained y.
 volume y.

yoke — a stiff beam hanging from a crane hook with ropes or chains attached to it along its length
Young's modulus

Z

Z — modulus of section
zee
zeolite

zinc —
electrolytic z.
zirconia
zone —
z. of aeration
z. of saturation
phreatic z.
vadose z.
zoned construction for dams
zorapteran

Insurance

A

AABD — Aid to the Aged, Blind and Disabled
AAI — Alliance of American Insurers
AB — Aid to the Blind
abandonment
above-normal loss
absolute —
a. assignment
a. beneficiary
a. liability
ACAS — Associate of the Casualty Actuarial Society
accelerated option
accelerative endowment
acceptance —
special a.
accident —
a. and health insurance
a. and sickness insurance
common a.
a. control
a. frequency
inevitable a.
a. insurance
occupational a.
a. prevention
a. severity
a. year experience
accidental —
a. death and dismemberment
a. death benefit
a. death insurance
a. means
accommodation line
account —
a. current
individual retirement a.
a. premium modification plan
a's receivable insurance
separate a.
accumulated —
a. actuarial benefit
a. plan benefit

accumulation —
a. benefits
dividend a.
acquisition cost
act —
a. of God
consumer product safety a.
consumer protection a.
employee retirement income security a.
Fair Credit Reporting A.
Federal Insurance Contributions A.
insurance guarantee a.
Jones A.
Longshoremen's and Harbor Workers' A.
McCarran A.
Occupational Safety and Health A.
Sherman Antitrust A.
active malfunction
actual —
a. cash value
a. total loss
actuarial —
a. asset value
a. equivalence
a. experience gain or loss
a. present value
a. revaluation effect
a. valuation
a. valuation characteristics
a. valuation method
actuary —
AD & D — Accidental Death and Dismemberment
additional —
a. extended coverage
a. insured
a. interest
a. living expense insurance
adjacent
adjoining
adjusted net worth
adjuster —
average a.
independent a.
public a.
adjustment

Adjustment Bureau
administration —
  a. bond
  deposit a.
administrator
admiralty —
  a. court
  a. liability
  a. proceeding
admitted —
  a. assets
  a. company
  a. liability
advance —
  a. payments
  a. premium
adverse selection
advertiser's liability insurance
AFDC — Aid to Families with Dependent
Children
affiliated companies
after charge
age —
  attained a.
  a. change
  life paid up at a.
  a. limits
  misstatement of a.
  a. reduction
agency —
  a. agreement
  apparent a.
  a. contract
  ordinary a.
  a. plant
  power of a.
  a. system
agent —
  a.'s authority
  a.'s balance
  captive a.
  a.'s commission
  debit a.
  exclusive a.
  general a.
  independent a.
  a.'s license
  local a.
  non resident a.
  policywriting a.

agent (*continued*)
  a.'s power
  a.'s qualification laws
  recording a.
aggregate —
  a. excess of loss reinsurance
  a. indemnity
  a. limit
  a. products liability limit
agreed amount clause
agreement —
  buy-sell a.
  hold harmless a.
  insuring a.
  railroad sidetrack a.
  sidetrack a.
  trust a.
A&H — accident and health
AIA — American Insurance Association
ALC — American Life Convention
alcoholic beverage control laws
alcoholic beverage liability insurance
aleatory contract
alienated
alien insurer
Alliance of American Insurers
allocated benefits
allowed assets
all-risks insurance
all states endorsement
ambiguity
American Academy of Actuaries
American agency system
American College
American Council of Life Insurance, Inc.
American Experience Table of Mortality
American Institute for Property and
  Liability Underwriters, Inc.
American Insurance Association
American Life Convention
American Lloyd's
American Risk and Insurance Association
amortized value
amount —
  a. at risk
  face a.
  a. subject
analytic system
ancillary benefits
ANL — above-normal loss

anniversary —
  policy a.
annual —
  a. actuarial value
  a. payment annuity
  a. policy
  a. premium
  a. report
  a. statement
annuitant —
  contingent a.
annuity —
  a. accumulation period
  a. accumulation unit
  a. accumulation value
  annual payment a.
  cash refund a.
  a. certain
  a. commencement date
  contingent a.
  deferred a.
  deferred group a.
  a. due
  fixed a.
  group a.
  immediate a.
  installment refund a.
  joint a.
  joint and survivorship a.
  joint life a.
  joint life and survivorship a.
  life a.
  a. period
  refund a.
  retirement a.
  revisionary a.
  survivorship a.
  tax deferred a.
  tax sheltered a.
  a. unit
  variable a.
  years certain a.
anti-coercion law
anti-selection
app — trade expression for an insurance
  application
apparent agency
application
apportionment

appraisal
approved —
  a. roof
appurtenant structures
APTD — Aid to the Permanently and Totally
  Disabled
"A" rates
arbitration clause
ARIA — American Risk and Insurance
  Association
Armstrong investigation
arson
A&S — accident and sickness
ASA — Associate of the Society of Actuaries
assailing thieves
assessed value
assessment —
  a. company
  a. insurer
  a. society
asset —
  admitted a's
  allowed a's
  a. share value
  net quick a's
  nonadmitted a's
  quick a's
assigned risk
assignee
assignment —
  absolute a.
  collateral a.
Associate Degree in Risk Management
association —
  a. group insurance
  Lloyd's A.
Association of Life Insurance Council
assume
assumed —
  a. liability
  reinsurance a.
assumption —
  a. certificate
  a. of risk
assurance
assured
assurer
Atomic Energy Reinsurance
attachment

attained age
attorney —
   a. -in-fact
   power of a.
attractive nuisance
audit —
   payroll a.
   premium a.
Audit Bureau
auditor
authorization
authorized insurer
automatic —
   a. cover
   a. increase in insurance endorsement
   a. premium loan
   a. premium loan option
   a. reinstatement clause
   a. reinsurance
automobile —
   a. collision insurance
   a. fleet
   a. insurance
   a. insurance plans
   a. liability insurance
average —
   a. adjuster
   a. blanket rate
   a. clause
   a. distribution clause
   free of particular a.
   general a.
   particular a.
   a. rate
   reduced rate a.
   a. weekly benefit
   a. weekly wage
aviation —
   a. accident insurance
   a. hazard
   a. insurance

B

backdating
bail bond
bailee —
   b.'s customer insurance
   b.'s liability coverage
   no benefit to b.

bailment
bailor
balance —
   agent's b.
   b. sheet
bankers blanket bond
bank loan plan
barratry
base premium
basic —
   b. auto policy
   b. limit
   b. limits of liability
   b. premium
   b. rate
bench error
beneficiary —
   absolute b.
   contingent b.
   irrevocable b.
   primary b.
   revocable b.
   secondary b.
   tertiary b.
   third party b.
benefit —
   accidental death b.
   accumulated actuarial b.
   accumulated plan b.
   accumulation b's
   allocated b's
   ancillary b's
   average weekly b.
   coordination of b's
   current service b.
   death b.
   disability b.
   dismemberment b.
   elective b's
   fixed b.
   flat maternity b.
   fringe b's
   graded death b's
   hospital b's
   identification of b's
   loss of income b's
   loss of time b's
   nonduplication of b's
   b's of survivorship
   optional b's
   past service b.

benefit (*continued*)
  payor b.
  permanent disability b's
  proration of b's
  quarantine b.
  surgical insurance b's
  survivorship b's
  temporary disability b's
  title XIX b's
  unallocated b.
betterment
BI — bodily injury liability; business
  interruption insurance
bid bond
binder
binding receipt
birth rate
blanket —
  b. bond
  b. contract
  b. crime policy
  b. fidelity bond
  b. honesty bond
  b. insurance
  b. medical expense
  b. policy
  b. position bond
blasting and explosion exclusion
blighted area
block policy
blowout and cratering
Blue —
  B. Cross
  B. Plan
  B. Shield
bodily —
  b. injury coverage
  b. injury liability
  b. injury liability insurance
boiler and machinery insurance
bond —
  administration b.
  bail b.
  bankers blanket b.
  bid b.
  blanket b.
  blanket fidelity b.
  blanket honesty b.
  blanket position b.
  commercial blanket b.

bond (*continued*)
  completion b.
  construction b.
  contract b.
  court b.
  custom house b's
  depositor's forgery b.
  depository b.
  federal officials b.
  fidelity b.
  fiduciary b.
  financial guarantee b.
  forgery b.
  indemnity b.
  labor and material b.
  license and permit b's
  litigation b.
  lost instrument b.
  maintenance b.
  name position b.
  name schedule b.
  payment b.
  b. penalty
  performance b.
  permit b.
  position schedule b.
  probate b.
  proposal b.
  public official b.
  schedule b.
  surety b.
  warehouse and custom b.
book —
  collection b.
  premium receipt b.
  b. value
booklet —
  b. -certificate
  group b.
bordereau
borderline risk
Boston plan
bottomry
branch —
  b. manager
  b. office
brick —
  b. construction
  b. veneer construction

broad —
  b. form
  b. form all states endorsement
  b. form personal theft policy
  b. form property damage endorsement
  b. form storekeepers insurance
broadened collision coverage
broker —
  excess line b.
  Lloyd's b.
  b. of record
  reinsurance b.
brokerage —
  b. business
  b. department
broker-agent
builder's risk
building code
bullion
bumbershoot policy
bureau —
  Audit B.
  inspection b.
  rating b.
  Stamping B.
burglary —
  b. and theft insurance
  b. insurance
burning —
  b. cost ratio
  b. ratio
business —
  b. auto policy
  brokerage b.
  delivered b.
  examined b.
  in-force b.
  b. insurance
  b. interruption insurance
  issued b.
  line of b.
  b. owners policy
  paid b.
  b. risk exclusion
  submitted b.
  written b.
buy-back deductible
buy-sell agreement

C

calendar year experience
cancellable —
  c. policy
cancellation —
  c. evidence
  flat c.
  pro rata c.
  short rate c.
capacity
capital —
  impairment of c.
  paid-in c.
  c. stock
  c. stock insurance company
  c. stock insurer
  c. sum
  working c.
captive —
  c. agent
  c. insurer
care —
  c., custody and control
  degree of c.
cargo insurance
carpenter cover
carrier —
  common c.
  contract c.
  domestic c.
  insurance c.
  interstate c.
  intrastate c.
  private c.
CAS — Casualty Actuarial Society
cash —
  c. flow program
  c. refund annuity
  c. surrender value
  c. value
Casualty Acturial Society
casualty insurance
catastrophe —
  c. hazard
  c. policy
  c. reinsurance

caveat emptor (Lat) — let the buyer beware
cede
ceding company
cents per cent
certificate —
  assumption c.
  group c.
  c. of authority
  c. of convenience
  c. of insurance
  c. of participation
  c. of reinsurance
  renewal c.
cession —
  c. number
cestui que vie (Lat) — he whose life
  measures the duration of an estate
CGL — comprehensive general liability
charter
Chartered Life Underwriter
Chartered Property and Casualty
  Underwriter
chattel mortgage
Chicago plan
CIET 1961 — Commissioners' Industrial
  Extended Term Mortality Table, 1961
civil commotion
claim —
  c. expense
  c. frequency
  c's made form
  c. report
  c. representative
  c's reserve
  c. severity
  unreported c's
class —
  c. action suit
  protection c.
  c. rate
  rating c.
classification —
  governing c.
classified —
  c. insurance
  not otherwise c.
clause —
  agreed amount c.
  arbitration c.
  automatic reinstatement c.

clause (*continued*)
  average c.
  average distribution c.
  clear space c.
  coinsurance c.
  common disaster c.
  commutation c.
  contestable c.
  contribution c.
  cut-through c.
  debris removal c.
  deductible c.
  delay c.
  delayed payment c.
  demolition c.
  deviation c.
  distribution c.
  divisible contract c.
  dynamo c.
  electrical exemption c.
  entire contract c.
  errors and omissions c.
  evidence c.
  facility-of-payment c.
  fallen building c.
  financial responsibility c.
  fire department service c.
  foundation exclusion c.
  franchise c.
  free-of-capture-and-seizure c.
  full reporting c.
  honesty c.
  "if" c's
  inchmaree c.
  incontestable c.
  insolvency c.
  insuring c.
  iron safe c.
  liberalization c.
  loss c.
  loss payable c.
  lost-or-not-lost c.
  market value c.
  mortgage c.
  mortgagee c.
  noon c.
  omnibus c.
  other insurance c.
  pair and set c.
  pro rata distribution c.

clause (*continued*)
  railroad subrogation waiver c.
  recurring c.
  rehabilitation c.
  retainer c.
  running down c.
  selling price c.
  spendthrift c.
  strike-through c.
  subrogation c.
  sue and labor c.
  three-fourths value c.
  trust and commission c.
  valuation c.
  voyage c.
  war c.
  watchman warranty c.
  water damage c.
  "while" c's
  work and materials c.
clean-up fund
clear space clause
CLU — Chartered Life Underwriter
COB — coordination of benefits
coding
coinsurance —
  c. clause
  waiver of c.
coinsurer
collapse
collateral assignment
collection —
  c. book
  c. commission
  c. fee
College Retirement Equities Fund
collegia
collision —
  convertible c.
  c. insurance
collusion
combination —
  c. business interruption extra expense
    insurance
  c. plan
  c. plan reinsurance
  c. policy
combined —
  c. actuarial value
  c. annuity mortality table
  c. single limit

commercial —
  c. blanket bond
  c. forgery policy
  c. multiple peril policy
  c. policy
  c. property policy
commission —
  agent's c.
  collection c.
  contingent c.
  first year c.
  flat c.
  graded c.
  c. of authority
  overriding c.
  profit c.
  renewal c.
  return c.
  sliding scale c.
commissioners' —
  C. Disability Table
  C. Industrial Extended Term Mortality
    Table, 1961
  C. Standard Industrial Mortality Table,
    1961
  C. Standard Ordinary
  C. Values
commissioners of insurance
common —
  c. accident
  c. carrier
  c. disaster
  c. disaster clause
  c. law
  c. law defenses
  c. law liability
community —
  c. property
  c. rating
commutation —
  c. clause
  c. rights
commute
commuted value
comparative negligence
compensation —
  c. award
  deferred c.
  workers' c.
competency
competitive state fund

completed operations insurance
completion bond
composite rate
composition roof
comprehensive —
  c. crime endorsement
  c. general liability policy
  c. glass insurance policy
  c. major medical insurance
  c. personal liability
  c. policy
  c. "3D" policy
compulsory insurance
concealment
concurrent insurance
conditional —
  c. binding receipt
  c. sales floater
  c. vesting
conditionally renewable
conditions —
  policy c.
confidential risk report
confining
conflagration area
consequential loss
conservator
consideration
consignee
consortium
conspiracy
construction —
  c. bond
  brick c.
  brick veneer c.
  fire resistive c.
  joisted masonry c.
  masonry noncombustible c.
  mill c.
  modified fire-resistive c.
  ordinary c.
  slow-burning c.
constructive —
  c. performance
  c. total loss
consumer —
  c. credit
  c. product safety act
  c. protection act
contents rate

contestable clause
contingency —
  c. reserve
  c. surplus
contingent —
  c. annuitant
  c. annuity
  c. beneficiary
  c. business interruption insurance
  c. commission
  c. fund
  c. liability
  c. vesting
contract —
  agency c.
  aleatory c.
  blanket c.
  c. bond
  c. carrier
  group c.
  individual c.
  land c.
  c. of adhesion
  c. of insurance
  supplemental c.
  unilateral c.
contractual liability insurance
contribution —
  c. clause
contributory —
  c. negligence
control —
  accident c.
  joint c.
  c. provision
controlled insurance
convention —
  c. blank
  c. examination
  c. values
conversion —
  c. privilege
  retroactive c.
convertible —
  c. collision insurance
cooperative insurance
coordination of benefits
co-originator
correction notice
corridor deductible

cost —
 acquisition c.
 guaranteed c.
 interest adjusted c.
 ledger c.
 mortality c.
 c. of insurance
 pure mortality c.
 replacement c.
 towing c's
co-surety
counter man
countersignature —
 c. law
coupon policy
court —
 admiralty c.
 c. bond
cover —
 automatic c.
 discovery c.
 divided c.
 c. note
 open c.
 working c.
coverage —
 additional extended c.
 bailee's liability c.
 bodily injury c.
 broadened collision c.
 continuity of c.
 crash c.
 data processing c.
 dependent c.
 elevator collision c.
 employers liability c.
 extended c.
 full c.
 ground c.
 kidnapping c.
 lay c.
 legislated c's
 limited collision c.
 personal injury c.
 primary c.
 split dollar c.
 underinsured motorists c.
 uninsured motorists c.
 warehouse-to-warehouse c.
 worldwide c.

covered expenses
CPCU — Chartered Property and Casualty Underwriter
CPSA — Consumer Product Safety Act
crash coverage
credit —
 c. card forgery
 c. carried forward
 consumer c.
 c. insurance
 reinsurance c.
 c. report
CREF — College Retirement Equities Fund
crime
criss-cross insurance
criticism
cromie rule
crop insurance
cross purchase
crude death rate
CSI 1961 — Commissioners' Standard Industrial Mortality Table, 1961
CSO — Commissioners' Standard Ordinary
cumulative liability
CUNA — Credit Union National Association
current —
 account c.
 c. disbursement
 c. future service
 c. ratio
 c. service benefit
currently insured status
custom house bonds
cut —
 c. rate
 c. -off
 c. -through clause

D

DA — deposit administration
daily report
damage —
 direct d.
 exemplary d's
 explosion, collapse and underground d.
 indirect d.
 material d.
 physical d.

damage (*continued*)
  punitive d's
  smoke d.
  underground property d.
data processing coverage
date —
  annuity commencement d.
  effective d.
  maturity d.
  d. of issue
  policy d.
D&B — Dun and Bradstreet
DBL — disability benefits law
DDD — dishonesty, disappearance and
  destruction policy
Dean schedule
death —
  d. benefit
  natural d.
  d. rate
debit —
  d. agent
  d. life insurance
  open d.
  d. system
debris removal clause
decedent
declaration
declination
decreasing term
deductible —
  buy-back d.
  d. clause
  corridor d.
  disappearing d.
  flat d.
  franchise d.
defalcation
defendant
deferred —
  d. annuity
  d. compensation
  d. group annuity
  d. premium
  d. premium file
  d. vesting
deficiency reserve
deficit —
  d. carried forward

degree —
  d. of care
  d. of risk
delay clause
delayed payment clause
delivered business
delivery —
  fraudulent d.
demolition —
  d. clause
  d. insurance
dental insurance
dependent —
  d. coverage
dependents
deposit —
  d. administration
  d. premium
deposition
depositor's —
  d. forgery bond
  d. forgery insurance
depository bond
depreciation —
  d. insurance
deviated rate
deviation —
  d. clause
DIC — difference in conditions
direct —
  d. damage
  d. loss
  d. selling system
  d. writer
  d. written premium
directors and officers liability insurance
disability —
  d. benefit
  d. benefits law
  d. income insurance
  intermediate d.
  long-term d.
  partial d.
  d. pension
  permanent partial d.
  permanent total d.
  recurrent d.
  short-term d.
  temporary partial d.
  temporary total d.
  total d.

Disability Insurance Training Council, Inc.
disappearing deductible
discovery —
  d. cover
  d. period
discrimination —
  rate d.
dishonesty, disappearance and destruction
  policy
dismemberment —
  accidental death and d.
  d. benefit
distribution clause
divided cover
dividend —
  d. accumulation
  d. additions
  d. option
  policy d.
  postmortem d.
divisible contract clause
DOC — drive-other-car endorsement
domestic —
  d. carrier
  d. insurer
double —
  d. indemnity
  d. protection
dram —
  d. shop laws
  d. shop liability insurance
"D" ratio
dread disease policy
drive —
  d. -in claim service
  d. -other-car endorsement
druggists liability insurance
dual life stock company
Dun and Bradstreet, Inc.
dwelling —
  d. building and contents form
  d. package policies
dynamo clause

E

earned —
  e. income
  net interest e.
  e. premium

earnings —
  gross e.
  e. insurance
  statutory e.
earthquake insurance
easement
ECE — extended coverage endorsement
educational fund
effective date
elective —
  e. benefits
  e. indemnities
electrical exemption clause
elevator collision coverage
eligibility —
  e. period
  e. requirements
elimination period
embezzlement
emergency fund
emotional distress
employee —
  e. benefit program
  residence e.
  E. Retirement Income Security Act
employers —
  e. liability coverage
  e. nonownership liability insurance
encumbrance
endorsement —
  all states e.
  automatic increase in insurance e.
  broad form all states e.
  broad form property damage e.
  comprehensive crime e.
  drive-other-car e.
  extended coverage e.
  e. extending period of indemnity
  family protection e.
  inflation guard e.
  interstate commerce commission e.
  peak season e.
  scratch e.
  uninsured motorists e.
endowment —
  accelerative e.
  e. insurance
  pure e.
engineer —
  loss prevention e.
entire contract clause

Equifax
equipment —
   e. floater
   mobile e.
equity
ERISA — Employee Retirement Income
   Security Act
ERISA liability
error —
   bench e.
   e's and omissions clause
   e's and omissions insurance
estate —
   e. plan
   e. tax
estimated premium
estoppel
evidence —
   cancellation e.
   e. clause
   e. of insurability
examination —
   convention e.
   medical e.
examined business
examiner —
   insurance e.
   medical e.
excepted period
exception —
   standard e.
excess —
   e. insurance
   e. interest
   e. limit
   e. line broker
   e. loss premium factor
   manual e.
   e. of loss ratio reinsurance
   e. of loss reinsurance
   e. per risk reinsurance
   e. reinsurance
   service e.
excluded period
exclusion —
   e. allowance
   blasting and explosion e.
   business risk e.
   product failure e.
   sisterhood e.
   wear and tear e.

exclusive —
   e. agency system
   e. agent
executor
executrix
exemplary damages
ex gratia payment
exhibitions insurance
expectation of life
expected —
   e. morbidity
   e. mortality
expediting expenses
expense —
   e. allowance
   blanket medical e.
   claim e.
   e. constant
   covered e's
   expediting e's
   general and insurance e.
   general operating e.
   e. incurred
   e. loading
   loss adjustment e.
   loss e.
   management e.
   e. ratio
   e. reimbursement allowance
   e. reserve
   miscellaneous e's
   unallocated claim e.
experience —
   accident year e.
   calendar year e.
   index bureau e.
   e. modification
   policy year e.
   e. rating
   e. refund
experienced —
   e. morbidity
   e. mortality
expiration —
   e. card
   e. date
   e. file
   e. notice
   ownership of e's
expiry

explosion —
    e., collapse and underground damage
    inherent e.
    e. insurance
exports
exposure
extended —
    e. coverage
    e. coverage endorsement
    e. term insurance
    e. wait
extortion insurance
extra —
    e. expense insurance
    e. percentage tables
    e. premium
    e. premium removal

F

face —
    f. amount
facility —
    f. -of-payment clause
    reinsurance f.
Factory Insurance Association
factory mutuals
facultative —
    f. certificate of reinsurance
    f. reinsurance
FAIR — fair access to insurance requirements
Fair Credit Reporting Act
FAIR plan
fallen building clause
family —
    f. automobile policy
    f. expense policy
    f. income policy
    f. maintenance policy
    f. policy
    f. protection endorsement
farmers comprehensive personal liability
farmowners-ranchowners policy
FAS — free along side.
FCAS — Fellow of the Casualty Actuarial Society
FCII — Fellow of the Chartered Insurance Institute
FC&S — free-of-capture-and-seizure

FC&S Bulletins — Fire, Casualty, and Surety Bulletins
FDIC — Federal Deposit Insurance Corporation
Federal —
    F. Crime Insurance Program
    F. Crop Insurance Corporation
    F. Deposit Insurance Corporation
    f. estate tax
    F. Insurance Administration
    F. Insurance Contributions Act
    f. officials bond
    F. Savings and Loan Insurance Corporation
fee —
    collection f.
    nurse f's
    policy f.
    f. simple
FEGLI — Federal Employees Group Life Insurance
Fellow —
    F. of the Casualty Actuarial Society
    F. of the Life Management Institute
    F. of the Society of Actuaries
    f. servant rule
FIA — Factory Insurance Association
FICA — Federal Insurance Contributions Act
fictitious groups
fidelity bond
fiduciary —
    f. bond
field —
    f. force
fieldman
file —
    f. -and-use rating laws
    deferred premium f.
    expiration f.
    suspense f.
    watch f.
financed —
    f. insurance
    f. premium
financial —
    f. guarantee bond
    f. responsibility clause
    f. responsibility law
    f. statement
fine —
    f. arts floater
    f. print

fire —
f. department service clause
friendly f.
hostile f.
f. insurance
f. legal liability
f. maps
f. mark
f. marshal
f. -resistive construction
f. wall
fireproof
fire-resistive
first —
f. loss insurance
f. loss retention
f. party insurance
f. surplus reinsurance
f. surplus treaty
f. year
f. year commission
fixed —
f. annuity
f. base liability
f. benefit
flat —
f. cancellation
f. commission
f. deductible
f. maternity benefit
f. rate
fleet —
automobile f.
f. of companies
f. policy
FLMI — Fellow of the Life Management
Institute
floater —
conditional sales f.
equipment f.
fine arts f.
fur and jewelry f.
installment sales f.
jewelry f.
personal article f.
personal effects f.
personal property f.
f. policy
theatrical f.
wedding present f.

flood —
f. insurance
floor plan insurance
FOB — free on board
following form
forecast approach
foreign insurer
forgery —
f. bond
credit card f.
form —
claims made f.
dwelling building and contents f.
following f.
general cover f.
general property f.
gross earnings f.
motor cargo policy (carrier's f.)
motor cargo policy (owner's f.)
occurrence f.
premium adjustment f.
prior approval rating f's
reporting f.
special building f.
special personal property f.
uniform f's
fortuitous event
foundation exclusion clause
foundering
FPA — free of particular average
fractional premium
franchise —
f. clause
f. deductible
f. insurance
fraternal insurance
fraud —
statute of f.
fraudulent delivery
free —
f. along side
f. -of-capture-and-seizure clause
f. of particular average
f. on board
freight
friendly fire
fringe benefits
fronting
FSA — Fellow of the Society of Actuaries
FSLIC — Federal Savings and Loan
Insurance Corporation

full —
  f. coverage
  f. preliminary term reserve valuation
  f. reporting clause
fully —
  f. insured status
  f. paid policy
funded
fur and jewelry floater
furriers customers insurance

G

GA — general agent
GAAP — generally accepted accounting principles
GAB — General Adjustment Bureau, Inc.
gain and loss exhibit
gambling
GAMC — General Agents and Managers Conference
garage —
  g. keepers legal liability insurance
  g. liability insurance
general —
  g. agency system
  g. agent
  g. agents and managers conference
  g. and insurance expense
  g. average
  g. cover form
  g. liability insurance
  g. operating expense
  g. property form
General Adjustment Bureau, Inc.
generally accepted accounting principles
geographical limitations
gift tax
GI insurance — United States Government Life Insurance issued to members of the armed forces; also called USGLI
glass insurance
good student discount
goodwill
governing classification
grace period
graded —
  g. commission
  g. death benefits

grading schedule for cities and towns
graduated life table
grantee
grantor
gross —
  g. earnings
  g. earnings form
  g. line
  g. negligence
  g. premium
  g. rate
ground coverage
group —
  g. annuity
  g. booklet
  g. certificate
  g. contract
  g. credit insurance
  g. disability insurance
  g. enrollment card
  fictitious g's
  g. health insurance
  g. insurance
  g. life insurance
  g. of companies
  g. permanent life insurance
  g. property and liability insurance
guarantee —
  g. funds
  mortality g.
guaranteed —
  g. continuable
  g. cost
  g. insurability
  g. renewable
guarantor
guardian
Guertin laws
guest law
guiding principles

H

hail insurance
hangarkeepers legal liability insurance
hazard —
  aviation h.
  catastrophe h.
  increased h.
  legal h.

hazard (*continued*)
  moral h.
  morale h.
  occupational h.
  personal h.
  physical h.
head office
health insurance
Health Insurance Association of America
Health Insurance Institute
Health Maintenance Organization
hedging
HEW — Department of Health, Education
  and Welfare
HI — health insurance
HIAA — Health Insurance Association of
  America
highly protected risk
HII — Health Insurance Institute
HIQA — Health Insurance Quality Award
hired car
HMO — Health Maintenance Organization
hold —
  h. harmless agreement
  h. -up
home —
  h. office
  h. service industrial insurance
  h. service life insurance
  h. service ordinary
Home Office Life Underwriters Association
homeowners policy
honesty clause
honorable undertaking
hospital —
  h. benefits
  h. expense insurance
  h. income insurance
hospitalization insurance
hostile fire
house confinement
housekeeping
HPR — highly protected risk
HR-10 Plan — Keogh Act Plan
HUD — Department of Housing and Urban
  Development
**Huebner Foundation for Insurance
  Education**
hull —
  h. policy
  h. syndicates
Hunter disability tables

I

IASA — Insurance Accounting Statistical
  Association
IASS — Insurance Accounting and Statistical
  Society
IBNR — incurred but not reported
ICA — International Claim Association
ICC — Interstate Commerce Commission
ICEDS — Insurance Company Education
  Directors Society
ICPI — Insurance Crime Prevention Institute
identification of benefits
"if" clauses
IHOU — Institute of Home Office
  Underwriters
IIA — Insurance Institute of America, Inc.
IIAA — Independent Insurance Agents of
  America
IIC — Independent Insurance Conference;
  Insurance Institute of Canada
III — Insurance Information Institute
IIS — International Insurance Seminars, Inc.
immediate —
  i. annuity
  i. vesting
impaired risk
impairment of capital
implied —
  i. seaworthiness
  i. warranty
import
improvements and betterments insurance
inchmaree clause
incidents of ownership
income —
  investment i.
  i. policy
  readjustment i.
incompetent
incontestable clause
increased —
  i. cost of construction insurance
  i. hazard
incurred —
  i. but not reported
  i. expense
  i. loss ratio
  i. losses
indemnify
indemnitor

indemnity —
aggregate i.
i. bond
double i.
elective i's
endorsement extending period of i.
multiple i.
quadruple i.
quarantine i.
triple i.
independent —
i. adjuster
i. agency system
i. agent
i. contractor
i. contractors insurance
Independent Insurance Agents of America
index bureau experience
indirect —
i. damage
i. loss
individual —
i. contract
i. life insurance
i. retirement account
i. risk premium modification rating plan
industrial —
i. life insurance
i. risk insurers
inevitable accident
inflation —
i. factor
i. guard endorsement
in-force business
inherent —
i. explosion
i. vice
initial premium
in kind
inland marine insurance
innkeepers legal liability
in-patient
insolvency —
i. clause
i. funds
inspection —
i. bureau
i. report
installment —
i. refund annuity
i. sales floater
i. settlement

Institute of Life Insurance
institutional property
insurability —
evidence of i.
guaranteed i.
insurable —
i. interest
i. risk
insurance —
accident and health i.
accident and sickness i.
accident i.
accidental death i.
accidental death and dismemberment i.
accounts receivable i.
additional living expense i.
advertiser's liability i.
alcoholic beverage liability i.
all-risks i.
association group i.
automobile i.
aviation accident i.
aviation i.
bailees customer i.
blanket i.
bodily injury liability i.
boiler and machinery i.
broad form storekeepers i.
burglary and theft i.
burglary i.
business i.
business interruption i.
cargo i.
i. carrier
casualty i.
certificate of i.
classified i.
collision i.
combination interruption extra expense i.
commissioner of i.
i. company
completed operations i.
comprehensive major medical i.
compulsory i.
concurrent i.
contingent business interruption i.
contract of i.
contractural liability i.
controlled i.
convertible collision i.
cooperative i.
cost of i.

insurance (*continued*)
  credit i.
  criss-cross i.
  crop i.
  debit life i.
  demolition i.
  dental i.
  i. department
  depositor's forgery i.
  depreciation i.
  directors and officers liability i.
  disability income i.
  dram shop liability i.
  druggists liability i.
  earnings i.
  earthquake i.
  employers nonownership liability i.
  endowment i.
  errors and omissions i.
  i. examiner
  excess i.
  exhibitions i.
  explosion i.
  extended term i.
  extortion i.
  extra expense i.
  financial i.
  fire i.
  first loss i.
  first party i.
  flood i.
  floor plan i.
  franchise i.
  fraternal i.
  furriers customer i.
  garage keepers legal liability i.
  garage liability i.
  general liability i.
  GI i.
  glass i.
  group i.
  group credit i.
  group disability i.
  group health i.
  group property and liability i.
  i. guarantee act
  hail i.
  hangarkeepers legal liability i.
  health i.
  home service industrial i.

insurance (*continued*)
  hospital expense i.
  hospital income i.
  hospitalization i.
  improvements and betterments i.
  increased cost of construction i.
  independent contractors i.
  inland marine i.
  jewelers block i.
  joint i.
  juvenile i.
  key man i.
  kidnap-ransom i.
  leasehold interest i.
  legal expense i.
  level premium i.
  level term i.
  liability i.
  libel i.
  life expectancy term i.
  life i.
    generic
    group
    group permanent
    home service
    individual
    industrial
    joint
    narrow
    national service
    ordinary
    permanent
    savings bank
    split
    straight
    trust
    variable
    whole
  liquor liability i.
  livestock i.
  livestock mortality i.
  livestock transit i.
  long-term disability i.
  loss of income i.
  loss of time i.
  loss of use i.
  machinery breakdown i.
  major medical i.
  malpractice i.
  marine i.

insurance (*continued*)
medical expense i.
medical care i.
medical payments i.
mercantile open stock burglary i.
mercantile robbery i.
messenger robbery i.
minimum deposit i.
mortgage i.
mortgage redemption i.
multiple location risks i.
multiple protection i.
national health i.
nationwide definition of marine i.
no-fault automobile i.
nonoccupational i.
nonownership automobile liability i.
ocean marine i.
officers and directors liability i.
old age, survivors, disability and health i.
other i.
outage i.
overage i.
overlapping i.
owners., landlords, and tenants liability i.
package i.
paid-up i.
parcel post i.
participating i.
partnership i.
paymaster robbery i.
payroll deduction i.
physicians and surgeons professional
   liability i.
pluvious i.
i. policy
power interruption i.
power plant i.
premises and operations liability i.
primary i.
product recall i.
products and completed operations i.
professional liability i.
profits and commissions i.
property damage liability i.
property i.
protection and indemnity i.
protective liability i.
public liability i.
quota share i.
radioactive contamination i.

insurance (*continued*)
rain i.
reduced paid-up i.
registered mail i.
rent i.
rental value i.
replacement cost i.
risk premium i.
river marine i.
safe burglary i.
safety deposit box i.
salary savings i.
self-i.
short-term disability i.
sickness i.
sidetrack i.
smoke damage i.
social i.
sole proprietorship i.
specific i.
sprinkler leakage i.
sprinkler leakage liability i.
storekeepers burglary and robbery i.
superintendent of i.
term i.
third party i.
time element i.
title i.
i. to value
transacting i.
transportation i.
travel accident i.
trip transit i.
true group i.
tuition fees i.
turnkey i.
unemployment compensation disability i.
unemployment i.
use and occupancy i.
voluntary compensation i.
war risk i.
water damage legal liability i.
wave damage i.
weekly premium i.
wet marine i.
workmen's compensation i.
wholesale group i.
yacht i.

Insurance Company Education Society
Insurance Hall of Fame

Insurance Information Institute
Insurance Institute of America, Inc.
Insurance Services Office
insured —
  additional i.
  joint i.
  named i.
insurer —
  alien i.
  assessment i.
  authorized i.
  capital stock i.
  captive i.
  domestic i.
  foreign i.
  industrial risk i's
  mixed i.
  mutual i.
  nonadmitted i.
  nonprofit i's
  primary i.
  stock i.
  unauthorized i.
  unlicensed i.
insuring —
  i. agreement
  i. clause
insuror
intentional injury
interest —
  additional i.
  i. adjusted cost
  excess i.
  insurable i.
interinsurance exchange
intermediary
intermediate —
  i. disability
  i. report
International Association of Health
  Underwriters
International Insurance Seminars, Inc.
interstate —
  i. carrier
  i. commerce
  i. commerce commission endorsement
inter-vivos trust
intestate
intrastate —
  i. carrier
  i. commerce

invalidity
investment —
  i. income
  i. reserve
invitee
IRA — Individual Retirement Account
iron safe clause
irrevocable —
  i. beneficiary
  i. trust
ISO — Insurance Services Office
issued business
item

J

jettison
jewelers block insurance
jewelry floater
joint —
  j. and survivorship annuity
  j. and survivorship option
  j. annuity
  j. committee on interpretation and
    complaint
  j. control
  j. insurance
  j. insured
  j. liability
  j. life and survivorship annuity
  j. life annuity
  j. life insurance
  j. tenancy
  j. venture
Joint Underwriting Association
joisted masonry construction
Jones Act
JUA — Joint Underwriting Association
judgment rates
jumping juvenile
juvenile insurance

K

Keeton-O'Connell Plan
Kenney ratio
Keogh Act Plan
key man insurance

kidnapping coverage
kidnap-ransom insurance
Kinne Rule

L

labor and material bond
land contract
landlords protective liability
lapse —
    l. ratio
lapsed policy
larceny
last —
    l. clear chance
    l. in, first out
latent defect
law —
    agent's qualification l's
    alcoholic beverage control l's
    anti-coercion l.
    common l.
    counter signature l.
    disability benefits l.
    dram shop l's
    file-and-use rating l's
    financial responsibility l.
    Guertin l's
    guest l.
    liquor control l's
    multiple line l.
    multiple line underwriting l's
    l. of large numbers
    Poisson's l.
    Public L. 15
    retaliatory l.
    safety responsibility l.
    valued policy l.
lay coverage
Leading Producers Round Table
leasehold —
    l. interest insurance
ledger cost
legal —
    l. expense insurance
    l. hazard
    l. liability
    l. reserve
legal reserve life insurance company

legislated coverages
lessee
lessor
level —
    l. commission system
    l. premium insurance
    l. term insurance
    threshold l.
LIAA — Life Insurance Association of
    America
liabilities
liability —
    absolute l.
    admiralty l.
    admitted l.
    assumed l.
    basic limits of l.
    bodily injury l.
    common law l.
    comprehensive personal l.
    contingent l.
    contractural l.
    cumulative l.
    ERISA l.
    farmers comprehensive personal l.
    fire legal l.
    fixed base l.
    innkeepers legal l.
    l. insurance
    joint l.
    landlords protective l.
    legal l.
    limit of l.
    l. limits
    product l.
    railroad protective l.
    strict l.
    truckmen's l.
    vicarious l.
    warehousemen's legal l.
LIAMA — Life Insurance Agency
    Management Association
libel —
    l. insurance
liberalization clause
license —
    agent's l.
    l. and permit bonds
licensee
lien plan

life —
  l. annuity
  l. conservation
  l. expectancy
  l. expectancy term insurance
  expectation of l.
  l. insurance
    generic
    group
    group permanent
    home service
    individual
    industrial
    joint
    narrow
    national service
    ordinary
    permanent
    savings bank
    split
    straight
    trust
    variable
    whole
  l. paid up at age
  limited payment l.
  term l.
  l. underwriter
**Life Insurance Agency Management
  Association**
Life Insurance Association of America
Life Insurance Conference
**Life Insurance Marketing and Research
  Association**
Life Office Management Association
lifetime policy
**Life Underwriting Political Action
  Committee**
Life Underwriting Training Council
LIFO — last in, first out
limit —
  age l's
  aggregate l.
  aggregate products liability l.
  basic l.
  combined single l.
  excess l.
  liability l's
  l. of liability
  l. of liability rule
  standard l.
  time l's

limitation —
  geographical l.
  loss l.
  statute of l's
  territorial l.
limited —
  l. collision coverage
  l. payment life
  l. policy
LIMRA — Life Insurance Marketing and
  Research Association
line —
  accommodation l.
  l. card
  gross l.
  l. guide
  net l.
  net retained l.
  l. of business
  old l.
  personal insurance l.
  l. sheet
  surplus l's
liquidity
liquor —
  l. control laws
  l. liability insurance
litigant
litigation bond
livery use
livestock —
  l. insurance
  l. mortality insurance
  l. transit insurance
Lloyd's —
  L. Association
  L. broker
  L. of London
  L. syndicate
  L. underwriter
loading —
  expense l.
  loss l.
loan —
  automatic premium l.
  policy l.
  l. value
local agent
LOMA — Life Office Management
  Association
Longshoremen's and Harbor Workers' Act
long-term disability insurance

loss —
    actual total l.
    actuarial experience gain or l.
    l. adjustment expense
    l. clause
    consequential l.
    l. constant
    constructive total l.
    l. control representative
    l. conversion factor
    l. development
    l. development factor
    direct l.
    l. expectancy
    l. expense
    indirect l.
    l. information service
    l. limitation
    l. loading
    maximum foreseeable l.
    maximum possible l.
    maximum probable l.
    l. multiplier
    net l.
    normal foreseeable l.
    l. of income benefits
    l. of income insurance
    l. of market
    l. of time benefits
    l. of time insurance
    l. of use insurance
    partial l.
    l. payable clause
    l. prevention engineer
    l. prevention service
    possible maximum l.
    probable maximum l.
    proof of l.
    l. ratio
    l. report
    l. reserve
    shock l.
    stop l.
    total l.
    ultimate new l.
    underwriting l.
losses —
    incurred l.
    outstanding l.
    paid l.
    statutory l.

lost —
    l. instrument bond
    l. policy release
    l. -or-not-lost clause
LPRT — Leading Producers Round Table
lump sum
LUPAC — Life Underwriting Political Action Committee
LUTC — Life Underwriting Training Council

M

McCarran Act
McClintock Table
machine issuance
machinery breakdown insurance
maintenance —
    m. bond
    m., care and wages
major —
    m. hospitalization policy
    m. medical insurance
malicious mischief
malinger
malingerer
malpractice —
    m. insurance
management —
    m. expense
    risk m.
manager
mandatory valuation reserve
manual —
    m. excess
    occupational m.
    m. rates
manufacturers and contractors liability insurance
manufacturers output policy
manuscript policy
map —
    m. clerk
    fire m's
marine —
    m. definition
    m. insurance
marital reduction
market —
    loss of m.
    residual m.

market (*continued*)
  m. value
  m. value clause
  voluntary m.
marketing representative
masonry noncombustible construction
mass merchandising
master —
  m. policy
  m. -servant rule
material —
  m. damage
  m. fact
mature
maturity —
  m. date
  m. value
maximum —
  m. disability policy
  m. foreseeable loss
  m. loss expectancy
  m. possible loss
  m. probable loss
  m. retrospective premium
MDO — monthly debit ordinary
MDRT — Million Dollar Round Table
Medicaid
medical —
  m. care insurance
  m. examination
  m. examiner
  m. expense insurance
  m. payments insurance
Medical Impairment Bureau
Medicare
mental distress
mercantile —
  m. open stock burglary insurance
  m. risk
  m. robbery insurance
merit rating
messenger robbery insurance
MIB — Medical Impairment Bureau
mill construction
Million Dollar Round Table
minimum —
  m. amount policy
  m. deposit insurance
  m. deposit policy
  m. premium

minimum (*continued*)
  m. rate
  m. retrospective premium
miscellaneous expenses
misrepresentation
misstatement of age
mixed insurer
MLIRB — Multi-Line Insurance Rating
  Bureau
mobile —
  m. equipment
  m. home policy
mode of premium payment
modified —
  m. fire-resistive construction
  m. life policy
money —
  m. and securities broad form policy
  m. purchase plan
monopolistic state fund
monthly —
  m. debit ordinary
  m. debit ordinary status card
moral hazard
morale hazard
morbidity —
  expected m.
  experienced m.
  m. rate
  m. table
mortality —
  m. cost
  expected m.
  experienced m.
  m. guarantee
  m. rate
  m. savings
  m. table
mortgage —
  chattel m.
  m. clause
  m. insurance
  m. redemption insurance
mortgagee —
  m. clause
mortgagor
motor —
  m. cargo policy (carrier's form)
  m. cargo policy (owner's form)
  m. truck cargo policy
MPIC — Multiple Peril Insurance Conference

Multi-Line Insurance Rating Bureau
multi-peril —
m. policy
special m.
multiple —
m. indemnity
m. line law
m. line policy
m. line underwriting
m. line underwriting laws
m. location policy
m. location rating plan
m. location risks insurance
m. protection insurance
Multiple Peril Insurance Conference
mutual —
m. atomic energy reinsurance pool
factory m's
m. fund
m. insurance companies
m. insurer
m. insurer policy
m. investment trust
mutual benefit association
mutualization
MVR's — motor vehicle records
mysterious disappearance

N

NAIA — National Association of Insurance
Agents, Inc.
NAIB — National Association of Insurance
Brokers, Inc.
NAIC — National Association of Insurance
Commissioners
NAII — National Association of Independent
Insurers
NAIW — National Association of Insurance
Women
NALC — National Association of Life
Companies
NALU — National Association of Life
Underwriters
name —
n. position bond
n. schedule bond
named —
n. insured
n. perils

NAMIC — National Association of Mutual
Insurance Companies
NAPIA — National Association of
Professional Insurance Agents
NASD — National Association of Securities
Dealers
National Association of Independent
Insurers
National Association of Insurance Agents,
Inc.
National Association of Insurance Brokers,
Inc.
National Association of Insurance
Commissioners
National Association of Insurance Women
National Association of Life Companies
National Association of Life Underwriters
National Association of Mutual Insurance
Companies
National Association of Securities Dealers
National Auto Theft Bureau
National Convention of Insurance
Commissioners
National Council on Compensation
Insurance
National Fire Protection Association
National Flood Insurance Association
National Fraternal Congress of America
national health insurance
National Insurance Association, Inc.
National Safety Council
National Service Life Insurance
nationwide definition of marine insurance
natural —
n. death
n. premium
negligence —
comparative n.
contributory n.
gross n.
presumed n.
NELIA — Nuclear Energy Liability Insurance
Association
NEPIA — Nuclear Energy Property Insurance
Association
net —
n. amount at risk
n. increase
n. interest earned
n. level premium

net (*continued*)
    n. level premium reserve
    n. line
    n. loss
    n. premium
    n. quick assets
    n. rate
    n. retained line
    n. retention
    n. worth
new for old
newspaper policy
New York standard fire policy
NFIA — National Flood Insurers Association
NFPA — National Fire Protection Association
no benefit to bailee
NOC — not otherwise classified
no-fault automobile insurance
nonadmitted —
    n. assets
    n. insurer
    n. reinsurance
nonassessable policy
nonassignable
noncancellable
nonconfining sickness
noncontributory
noncurrency
nondisabling injury
nonduplication of benefits
nonforfeiture —
    n. options
    n. values
noninsurable risk
noninsurance
nonmedical
nonoccupational insurance
nonownership automobile liability insurance
nonparticipating
nonprofit insurers
nonproportional reinsurance
nonresident agent
nonvalued policy
noon clause
normal —
    n. foreseeable loss
    n. loss expectancy
not —
    n. otherwise classified
    n. taken

notice —
    correction n.
    expiration n.
    premium n.
    n. to company
NPD — no payroll division
NSLI — National Service Life Insurance
nuclear energy contamination
Nuclear Energy Liability Insurance Association
Nuclear Energy Property Insurance Association
nuisance —
    attractive n.
    n. value
numerical rating
nurse fees

OAA — old age assistance
OASDHI — Old Age, Survivors, Disability, and Health Insurance
object
obligatory reinsurance
obligee
obligor
occupancy
occupational —
    o. accident
    o. disease
    o. hazard
    o. manual
Occupational Safety and Health Act
occurrence —
    o. form
ocean marine insurance
odds
offer
offeree
offeror
office —
    branch o.
    o. burglary and robbery policy
    regional o.
    head o.
    home o.
    production o.
    supervisory o.

officers and directors liability insurance
off premises
OL&T — Owners, Landlords, and Tenants
Liability Insurance
**Old Age, Survivors, Disability, and Health
Insurance**
old line
omnibus —
  o. clause
  o. risk
open —
  o. cover
  o. debit
  o. policy
  o. stock burglary policy
option —
  accelerated o.
  automatic premium loan o.
  dividend o.
  joint and survivorship o.
  nonforfeiture o's
  settlement o's
optional —
  o. benefits
  o. modes of settlement
optionally renewable
ordinary —
  o. agency
  Commissioners' Standard O.
  o. construction
  home service o.
  o. life insurance
  o. life policy
  monthly debit o.
  o. payroll
  o. register
OSHA — Occupational Safety and Health Act
other —
  o. insurance
  o. insurance clause
outage insurance
outpatient
outstanding —
  o. losses
  o. premiums
overage insurance
overinsured
overlapping insurance
overline
overriding commission

owners —
  o. and contractors protective liability policy
  o. landlords, and tenants liability insurance
ownership —
  o. of expirations
  incidents of o.
  o. provision

P

package —
  p. insurance
  p. policies
paid —
  p. business
  p. -for
  p. -in capital
  p. -in surplus
  p. losses
  p. -up insurance
  p. -up additions
pair and set clause
P&I — protection and indemnity insurance
par
paramedic
parasol policy
parcel post insurance
parent company
parol —
  p. evidence rule
parole
partial —
  p. disability
  p. loss
participant
participating —
  p. insurance
  p. policies
  p. reinsurance
particular average
partnership —
  p. entity
  p. insurance
party wall
past service benefit
Paul versus Virginia
pay —
  p. -as-you-go
payee

paymaster robbery insurance
payment —
   advance p's
   p. bond
   ex gratia p.
   mode of premium p.
payor benefit
payroll —
   p. audit
   p. deduction insurance
   ordinary p.
PD — physical damage
peak season endorsement
penalty
pend file
per —
   p. capita
   p. diem business interruption
   p. risk excess reinsurance
   p. stirpes
percent subject
percentage participation
performance —
   p. bond
   constructive p.
peril
   multiple p. insurance
perils —
   named p.
   p. of the sea
   specified p.
period —
   annuity accumulation p.
   annuity p.
   discovery p.
   eligibility p.
   elimination p.
   excepted p.
   excluded p.
   grace p.
   policy p.
   probationary p.
   qualifying p.
   waiting p.
permanent —
   p. disability benefits
   p. life insurance
   p. partial disability
   p. total disability
permit bond
persistency

personal —
   p. article floater
   p. auto policy
   p. effects floater
   p. hazard
   p. health statement
   p. injury coverage
   p. injury protection
   p. insurance line
   p. property floater
   p. surety
   p. theft policy
physical —
   p. damage
   p. hazard
physicians and surgeons professional
   liability insurance
PIAA — Professional Insurance Agents
   Association
pilferage
PIP — personal injury protection
piracy
plaintiff
plan —
   account premium modification p.
   automobile insurance p's
   bank loan p.
   Blue P.
   Boston p.
   combination p.
   estate p.
   FAIR p.
   individual risk premium modification
      rating p.
   Keeton-O'Connell P.
   Keogh Act P.
   lien p.
   money purchase p.
   multiple location rating p.
   postdated check p.
   preauthorized check p.
   premium and dispersion credit p.
   prospective rating p.
   qualified p.
   retirement p.
   safe driver p.
   schedule rating p.
   state disability p.
   tabular p.
   trusteed p.
plate glass insurance policy

pluvious insurance
PML — probable maximum loss
Poisson's law
policy —
anniversary p.
annual p.
basic auto p.
blanket p.
blanket crime p.
block p.
broad form personal theft p.
bumbershoot p.
business auto p.
business owners p.
cancellable p.
catastrophe p.
combination p.
commercial p.
commercial forgery p.
commercial multiple peril p.
commercial property p.
comprehensive p.
comprehensive general liability p.
comprehensive glass insurance p.
comprehensive ''3D'' p.
p. conditions
coupon p.
p. date
dishonesty, disappearance and
 destruction p.
p. dividend
dread disease p.
dwelling package p's
family p.
family automobile p.
family expense p.
family income p.
family maintenance p.
farmowners-ranchowners p.
p. fee
fleet p.
floater p.
p's-in-force
fully paid p.
homeowners p.
hull p.
income p.
insurance p.
lapsed p.
lifetime p.
limited p.

policy (*continued*)
p. loan
major hospitalization p.
manufacturers output p.
manuscript p.
master p.
maximum disability p.
minimum amount p.
minimum deposit p.
mobile home p.
modified life p.
money and securities broad form p.
motor truck cargo p.
multi-peril p.
multiple line p.
multiple location p.
mutual insurer p.
New York standard fire p.
newspaper p.
nonassessable p.
nonvalued p.
office burglary and robbery p.
open p.
open-stock burglary p.
ordinary life p.
p. owner
owners and contractors protective
 liability p.
package p's
parasol p.
participating p's
p. period
personal auto p.
personal theft p.
plate glass insurance p.
railroad travel p.
p. register
p. reserve
retirement income p.
schedule p.
short-term p.
single interest p.
single premium p.
special auto p.
specified disease p.
standard p.
standard fire p.
storekeepers liability p.
straight life p.
subscription p.
tenants p.

policy (*continued*)
  p. term
  "3-D" p.
  ticket p.
  tontine p.
  transit p.
  transportation ticket p.
  umbrella liability p.
  underlying p.
  valued p.
  warranty p.
  workers' compensation
    catastrophe p.
  p. year experience
policyholder —
  p.'s surplus
  share to p's
policywriting agent
pool —
  mutual atomic energy reinsurance p.
pooling —
  p. reinsurance
portfolio —
  p. entry
  p. reinsurance
  p. return
  p. runoff
position schedule bond
possible maximum loss
postdated check plan
postmortem dividend
power —
  agent's p.
  p. interruption insurance
  p. of agency
  p. of attorney
  p. plant insurance
preauthorized check plan
preexisting condition
preferred risk
preliminary term
premises —
  p. and operations liability insurance
  off p.
premium —
  advance p.
  p. and dispersion credit plan
  p. adjustment form
  p. audit
  base p.
  basic p.

premium (*continued*)
  deferred p.
  deposit p.
  direct written p.
  p. discount
  earned p.
  estimated p.
  extra p.
  financed p.
  fractional p.
  gross p.
  initial p.
  maximum retrospective p.
  minimum p.
  minimum retrospective p.
  natural p.
  net p.
  net level p.
  p. notice
  outstanding p's
  prepayment of p's
  provisional p.
  pure p.
  p. rate
  p. receipt
  p. receipt book
  p. refund
  reinsurance p.
  restoration p.
  retrospective p.
  return p.
  return of p.
  short rate p.
  standard p.
  subject p.
  underlying p.
  unearned p.
  unearned reinsurance p.
  waiver of p.
  waiver of restoration p.
  whole dollar p.
  written p's
present value
pressure vessel
presumed negligence
prima facie (Lat) — at first sight
primary —
  p. beneficiary
  p. coverage
  p. insurance
  p. insurer

principal —
 p. sum
prior approval rating forms
priority
private carrier
privity
probability —
 simple p.
 theory of p.
probable maximum loss
probate bond
probationary period
proceeds
producer
product —
 p's and completed operations insurance
 p. failure exclusion
 p. liability
 p. recall insurance
 recapture of p's
production office
Professional Insurance Agents Association
professional liability insurance
profit —
 p. commission
 p's and commissions insurance
 underwriting p.
prohibited —
 p. list
 p. risk
proof of loss
property —
 community p.
 p. damage liability insurance
 institutional p.
 p. insurance
 real p.
proposal bond
pro rata —
 p. r. cancellation
 p. r. distribution clause
 p. r. liability rule
 p. r. rate
 p. r. reinsurance
proration of benefits
prospect
prospecting
prospective —
 p. rating
 p. rating plan
 p. reserve

prospectus
protected risk
protection —
 p. and indemnity insurance
 p. class
 double p.
 personal injury p.
 triple p.
protective liability insurance
provisional —
 p. premium
 p. rate
proximate cause
public —
 p. adjuster
 p. assistance
 P. Law 15
 p. liability insurance
 p. official bond
punitive damages
"pup" company — a smaller company
 owned by a large company
pure —
 p. endowment
 p. loss cost ratio
 p. mortality cost
 p. premium
 p. risk
pyramiding

Q

"Q" schedule
quadruple indemnity
qualified plan
qualifying period
quantity discount
quarantine —
 q. benefit
 q. indemnity
quasi-contract
quasi-insurance institutions
quick assets
quid pro quo (Lat) — this for that, or one
 thing for another
quota —
 q. share insurance
 q. share reinsurance

R

radioactive contamination insurance
radius of operation
railroad —
  r. protective liability
  r. sidetrack agreement
  r. subrogation waiver clause
  r. travel policy
rain insurance
rate —
  "A" r's
  average r.
  average blanket r.
  basic r.
  birth r.
  r. card
  class r.
  composite r.
  contents r.
  crude death r.
  cut r.
  death r.
  deviated r.
  r. discrimination
  flat r.
  gross r.
  judgment r's
  manual r's
  minimum r.
  morbidity r.
  mortality r.
  r. of natural decrease
  r. of natural increase
  net r.
  premium r.
  pro rata r.
  provisional r.
  specific r.
  tariff r.
rated —
  r. up
rating —
  r. bureau
  r. class
  community r.
  experience r.
  merit r.
  numerical r.

rating (*continued*)
  prospective r.
  retrospective r.
  schedule r.
  r. territory
ratio —
  burning cost r.
  burning r.
  current r.
  expense r.
  incurred loss r.
  Kenney r.
  lapse r.
  loss r.
  pure loss cost r.
readjustment income
real property
reassured
rebate
rebating
recapture —
  r. of products
receipt —
  binding r.
  conditional binding r.
reciprocal insurance exchange
reciprocity
recision
recording agent
recovery
recruiting
recurrent disability
recurring clause
red-lining
reduced —
  r. paid-up insurance
  r. rate average
reduction —
  age r.
  marital r.
referral risks
refund —
  r. annuity
  experience r.
  premium r.
regional office
register —
  ordinary r.
  policy r.

registered —
r. health underwriter
r. mail insurance
r. representative
r. tonnage
rehabilitation clause
reimbursement
reinstatement
reinsurance —
aggregate excess of loss r.
r. assumed
automatic r.
r. broker
catastrophe r.
r. ceded
certificate of r.
combination plan r.
r. credit
excess r.
excess of loss r.
excess of loss ratio r.
excess per risk r.
r. facility
facultative r.
facultative certificate of r.
first surplus r.
nonadmitted r.
nonproportional r.
obligatory r.
participating r.
pooling r.
portfolio r.
r. premium
pro rata r.
quota share r.
second surplus r.
self-r.
share r.
specific r.
spread loss r.
stop loss r.
surplus r.
ticket r.
treaty r.
reinsurer
rejection
release —
lost policy r.
subrogation r.
surplus r.

remainder
removal —
extra premium r.
renewable —
conditionally r.
guaranteed r.
optionally r.
r. term
renewal —
r. certificate
r. commission
rental value insurance
rent insurance
replacement —
r. cost
r. cost insurance
reporting form
representation
representative —
claim r.
loss control r.
marketing r.
registered r.
sales r.
reserve —
claims r.
contingency r.
deficiency r.
expense r.
investment r.
legal r.
loss r.
mandatory valuation r.
net level premium r.
policy r.
prospective r.
schedule "P" r.
statutory r.
unearned premium r.
valuation r.
voluntary r.
residence employee
resident agent
residual market
res ipsa loquitur (Lat) — the thing speaks for
itself
respondeat superior (Lat) — let the master
answer
restoration —
r. premium
retroactive r.

retail credit company
retainer clause
retaliatory law
retention —
  first loss r.
  net r.
  r. programs
  self-insurance r.
retirement —
  r. annuity
  r. income policy
  r. plan
retroactive —
  r. conversion
  r. extension
  r. restoration
retrocession
retrocessionaire
retrospective —
  r. premium
  r. rating
return —
  r. commission
  r. of cash value
  portfolio r.
  r. of premium
  r. premium
revisionary annuity
revival
revocable beneficiary
RHU — registered health underwriter
rider —
  superseded suretyship r.
riot
risk —
  amount at r.
  r. appraiser
  assigned r.
  assumption of r.
  borderline r.
  builder's r.
  degree of r.
  r. experience program
  highly protected r.
  impaired r.
  insurable r.
  r. management
  mercantile r.
  net amount at r.
  noninsurable r.

risk (*continued*)
  omnibus r.
  preferred r.
  r. premium insurance
  prohibited r.
  protected r.
  pure r.
  referral r's
  seasonal r.
  selection of r.
  speculative r.
  standard r.
  substandard r.
  target r.
river marine insurance
robbery
running down clause
runoff —
  portfolio r.

S

SA — Society of Actuaries
SAA — Surety Association of America
sacrifice
safe —
  s. burglary insurance
  s. driver plan
safety —
  s. consultant
  s. deposit box insurance
  s. responsibility law
salary savings insurance
sales representative
salvage —
  s. crops
SAP — statutory accounting principles
savings —
  s. bank life insurance
  mortality s.
SBA — Small Business Administration
schedule —
  s. bond
  Dean s.
  s. P reserve
  s. policy
  "Q" s.
  s. rating
  s. rating plan
  surgical s.

scratch —
  s. daily report
  s. endorsement
seasonal risk
seaworthiness —
  implied s.
SEC — Securities and Exchange Commission
second beneficiary
second surplus reinsurance
securities
Securities and Exchange Commission
SEGLI — service employees group life
  insurance
selection —
  adverse s.
  s. of risk
self —
  s. -inflicted injury
  s. -insurance
  s. -insurance retention
  s. -reinsurance
selling price clause
separate account
service
  s. employees group life insurance
  s. excess
settlement —
  installment s.
  optional modes of s.
  s. options
SEUA — Southeastern Underwriters
  Association
share —
  s. reinsurance
  surplus s.
Sherman Antitrust Act
shock loss
short —
  s. rate cancellation
  s. rate premium
  s. -term disability insurance
  s. -term policy
sickness —
  s. insurance
  nonconfining s.
sidetrack —
  s. agreement
  s. insurance
simple —
  fee s.
  s. probability

sine qua non rule
single —
  s. interest policy
  s. premium policy
SIR — self-insurance retention
sisterhood exclusion
sliding scale commission
slip — a paper submitted to underwriters at
  Lloyd's of London that identifies syndicates
  accepting the risk of insurance
slow-burning construction
Small Business Administration
smoke damage
smoke damage insurance
SMP — special multi-peril
social —
  s. insurance
Social Security
society —
  assessment s.
Society of Actuaries
Society of Chartered Property and Casualty
  Underwriters
Society of Insurance Research
sole proprietorship insurance
solicitor
sonic boom
sound value
Southeastern Underwriters Association
special —
  s. acceptance
  s. agent
  s. auto policy
  s. building form
  s. multi-peril
  s. personal property form
specific —
  s. insurance
  s. rate
  s. reinsurance
specified —
  s. disease policy
  s. perils
speculative risk
spendthrift clause
split —
  s. dollar coverage
  s. life insurance
spread loss reinsurance
sprinkler —
  s. leakage insurance
  s. leakage legal liability insurance

Stamping Bureau
standard —
  s. exception
  s. fire policy
  s. limit
  s. policy
  s. premium
  s. provisions
  s. risk
state —
  s. agent
  s. disability plan
  s. fund
State Association of Insurance Agents
statement —
  annual s.
  s. blank
  financial s.
  s. of values
statute —
  s. of fraud
  s. of limitations
statutory —
  s. accounting principles
  s. earnings
  s. losses
  s. reserve
stock —
  capital s.
  s. company
  s. insurer
stop —
  s. loss
  s. loss reinsurance
storekeepers —
  s. burglary and robbery insurance
  s. liability policy
straight life policy
stranded
strict liability
strike-through clause
sub-agents
sub-broker
subject —
  amount s.
  percent s.
  s. premium
submitted business
subordination

subrogation —
  s. clause
  s. release
subscription policy
subsidence
substandard risk
sue and labor clause
superintendent of insurance
superseded suretyship rider
supervisory office
supplemental —
  s. actuarial value
  s. contract
surety —
  s. bond
  s. bond guarantee program
  personal s.
Surety Association of America
suretyship
surgical —
  s. insurance benefits
  s. schedule
surplus —
  contingency s.
  s. lines
  paid-in s.
  policy holder's s.
  s. reinsurance
  s. release
  s. share
  s. to policyholders
surrender —
  s. value
survivorship —
  s. annuity
  s. benefits
suspense file
swap maternity
switch maternity
syndicate —
  hull s's
  Lloyd's s.
system —
  agency s.
  American agency s.
  analytic s.
  debit s.
  direct selling s.
  exclusive agency s.

system (*continued*)
  general agency s.
  independent agency s.
  level commission s.
  unlevel commission s.
  universal mercantile s.
  zone s.

T

table —
  combined annuity mortality t.
  Commissioners' Disability T.
  Commissioners' Industrial Extended Term
    Mortality T.
  extra percentage t's
  graduated life t.
  Hunter disability t's
  Leading Producers Round T.
  McClintock T.
  Million Dollar Round T.
  morbidity t.
  mortality t.
  ultimate mortality t.
  Women Leaders Round T.
  X t.
  Z t.
tabular —
  t. cost
  t. plan
target risk
tariff rate
tax —
  t. -and-board
  t. deferred annuity
  estate t.
  t. factor
  federal estate t.
  gift t.
  t. multiplier
  t. sheltered annuity
TDA — tax deferred annuity
TDB — temporary disability benefits
Teachers Insurance and Annuity
  Association
temporary —
  t. disability benefits
  t. partial disability
  t. total disability

tenants policy
term —
  decreasing t.
  t. insurance
  t. life
  policy t.
  preliminary t.
  renewable t.
  t. rule
  yearly renewable t.
termination
territorial limitation
tertiary beneficiary
Thaisoi — an ancient Greek benevolent
  society
theatrical floater
theft
theory of probability
third party —
  t.p. beneficiary
  t.p. insurance
"3-D" policy
three-fourths value clause
threshold level
ticket —
  t. policy
  t. reinsurance
tickler
time —
  t. element insurance
  t. limit on certain defenses
  t. limits
TIRB — Transportation Insurance Rating
  Bureau
title —
  t. insurance
  t. XIX benefits
tontine policy
tort —
  t. feasor
total —
  t. disability
  t. loss
towing costs
transacting insurance
transit policy
transportation —
  t. insurance
  t. ticket policy
Transportation Insurance Rating Bureau

traumatic injury
travel accident insurance
treaty —
   first surplus treaty
   t. reinsurance
trespasser
trip transit insurance
triple —
   t. indemnity
   t. protection
truckmens' liability
true group insurance
trust —
   t. agreement
   t. and commission clause
   t. instrument
   inter-vivos t.
   irrevocable t.
   mutual investment t.
trustee
trusteed plan
TSA — tax sheltered annuity
tuition fees insurance
turnkey insurance
twisting — misrepresentation that induces a
   policyholder to drop an existing policy and
   take another

UAB — Underwriters Adjustment Bureau
UAC — Underwriters Adjusting Company
uberrima fides (Lat) — utmost good faith
UCDI — Unemployment Compensation
   Disability Insurance
UJF — unsatisfied judgment fund
UL — Underwriters Laboratories, Inc.
ultimate —
   u. mortality table
   u. new loss
umbrella liability policy
umpire
unallocated —
   u. benefit
   u. claim expense
unauthorized insurer
underground property damage
underinsurance
underinsured motorists coverage

underlying —
   u. policy
   u. premium
underwriter —
   life u.
   Lloyd's u.
   u's salvage corporation
Underwriters Adjusting Company
Underwriters Adjustment Bureau
Underwriters Laboratories, Inc.
underwriting —
   multiple line u.
   u. loss
   u. profit
unearned —
   u. premium
   u. premium reserve
   u. reinsurance premium
Unemployment Compensation Disability
   Insurance
unemployment insurance
unfunded supplemental actuarial value
uniform —
   u. forms
   u. provisions
unilateral contract
uninsured motorists coverage
United States Aircraft Insurance Group
United States Government Life Insurance
universal mercantile system
unlevel commission system
unlicensed insurer
unoccupied
unprotected
unreported claims
unsatisfied judgment fund
U & O — use and occupancy insurance
USAIG — United States Aircraft Insurance
   Group
use —
   u. and occupancy insurance
   livery u.
USGLI — United States Government Life
   Insurance

vacant
valuable papers and records

valuation —
  actuarial v.
  v. clause
  full preliminary term reserve v.
  v. reserve
value —
  actual cash v.
  actuarial asset v.
  actuarial present v.
  amortized v.
  annual actuarial v.
  annuity accumulation v.
  assessed v.
  asset share v.
  book v.
  cash surrender v.
  cash v.
  combined actuarial v.
  commissioners' v's
  commuted v.
  convention v's
  insurance to v.
  loan v.
  market v.
  maturity v.
  nonforfeiture v's
  nuisance v.
  present v.
  return of cash v.
  sound v.
  statement of v's
  supplemental actuarial v.
  surrender v.
  unfunded supplemental actuarial v.
valued —
  v. policy
  v. policy law
V&MM — vandalism and malicious mischief
variable —
  v. annuity
  v. life insurance
vendee
vendor
vesting —
  conditional v.
  contingent v.
  deferred v.
  immediate v.
vicarious liability
violation

vis major (Lat) — a superior force
void
voidable
voluntary —
  v. compensation insurance
  v. market
  v. reserve
voyage clause

W

waiting period
waiver —
  w. of coinsurance
  w. of premium
  w. of restoration premium
war —
  w. clause
  w. risk insurance
warehouse —
  w. and custom bond
  w. -to-warehouse coverage
warehousemen's legal liability
warranty —
  implied w.
  w. policy
Warsaw Convention
watch file
watchman warranty clause
water —
  w. damage clause
  w. damage legal liability insurance
wave —
  w. damage insurance
  w. wash
WC — workers' compensation
wear and tear exclusion
wedding present floater
weekly premium insurance
welfare
wet marine insurance
"while" clauses
whole —
  w. dollar premium
  w. life insurance
wholesale group insurance
willful injury
will ride
windstorm

Wisconsin life fund
WLRT — Women Leaders Round Table
work —
   w. and materials clause
   w. program
workers' —
   w. compensation
   w. compensation catastrophe policy
working —
   w. capital
   w. cover
workmen's compensation insurance
worldwide coverage
wrap-up
write
written —
   w. business
   w. premiums
wrongful —
   w. death action
   w. extraction

XCU - explosion, collapse and underground
   damage
X table

yacht insurance
yearly renewable term
years certain annuity
York Antwerp Rules
YRT — yearly renewable term

zone system
Z table

Real Estate

A

AAA tenant
abandonment —
  a. of leased premises
abate
abatement —
  a. of rent clause
  a. of taxes
abator
abeyance
"ability to pay" principle
ab initio (Lat) — from the outset
abjure
abnormal sale
abode
abortion — an unsightly structure in poor
  repair
abrogate
abrogation
absentee owner
absolute —
  a. fee
  a. sale
  a. title
abstract company
abstracter
abstract of title
abutting land
accelerated depreciation
acceleration clause
acceptance
accessibility
accession
accessory building
access right
accommodation party
accord and satisfaction
accretion
accrue
accrued —
  a. depreciation
  a. interest
accruing depreciation
acknowledgment
acquisition —
  a. cost

acre —
  a. foot
  forage a.
acreage —
  a. listing form
act —
  a. of bankruptcy
  a. of God
  a. of law
  a. of sale
action —
  a. for commission
  a. on contract
actionable
actual —
  a. age
  a. cash value
  a. eviction
  a. fraud
  a. possession
  a. value
actuary
addendum
addition
address
ademption
ad hoc (Lat) — for a special purpose
adjacent
adjoin
adjudge
adjudication
adjusted —
  a. basis
adjustments
administration of an estate
administrator
  a.'s deed
administratrix
adobe
ad valorem (Lat) — according to the value
  a.v. taxes
advance fee
adverse —
  a. land use
  a. possession
  a. title
aeolian soil
aerial map

aesthetic value
affiant
affidavit —
  a. of title
  a. of value
affiliate broker
affirm
affirmation
affix
afforestation
A-frame construction
after-acquired —
  a. clause in mortgages
  a. title
age-life depreciation
agency —
  a. by estoppel
  a. by necessity
  a. coupled with an interest
  a. form
agent
agrarian
agreement —
  a. for deed
  a. of sale
  a. to sell
  spreading a.
agricultural property
AIA — American Institute of Architects
air —
  a. lot
  a. rights
AIREA — American Institute of Real Estate
  Appraisers
ait
alcove
aleatory contract
alien
alienation
alley
alligator property
allodial system
allonge
alluvion
alluvium
alteration
amenities —
  hidden a.
  visible a.
American Hotel and Motel Association

American Institute of Architects
American Institute of Planners
American Institute of Real Estate
  Appraisers
American Land Development Association
American Land Title Association
American Society of Planning Officials
American Society of Real Estate Counselors
amortization —
  a. table
  a. schedule
amoritize
amortized mortgage
amount realized
anchor —
  a. lease
  a. tenant
ancillary
annex
annexation
annual constant (percentage)
annuitant
annuity
annul
annum (Lat) — year
ante — a prefix meaning before
anticipated value
anticipation
anticipatory —
  a. breach
  a. repudiation
apartment —
  a. hotel
  a. house
  a. house listing form
  a. lease
apparent —
  a. authority
  a. title
appeal
appellant
appellate court
appellee
appointments
apportionment
appraisal —
  a. correlation
  a. report
  summation a.
appraised value

appraisement
appraiser
appreciation —
  a. in value
approaches to value
appropriation —
  a. of water
appurtenances
a priori (Lat) — from what went before
aquatic rights
arbitration
arcade
arch
architect
architecture
arm's length
arpent
arrears
arroyo
arterial street
articles of incorporation
articles of partnership
artificial person
artisan
as is
asking price
ASREC — American Society of Real Estate
  Counselors
assembling land
assessed value
assessment —
  a. roll
assessor
asset
assign
assignability
assignee
assignment —
  a. of chattel mortgage
  a. of contract
  a. of lease
  a. of mortgage
assignor
associate —
  a. broker
Associated General Contractors of America
assume
assuming mortgage

assumpsit (Lat) — action at law to recover
  damages for failure to perform an oral
  contract; or an understanding to perform an
  agreement not in writing
assumption —
  a. agreement
  a. fee
  a. letter
  a. of mortgage
assured
A.T.A. title policy (known also as ALTA) —
  a title insurance policy that expands the
  risks normally insured against in standard
  policies
atoll
at par
atrium
attachment —
  a. of property
attest
attestation
attesting witness
attic
attorney —
  a. -at-law
  a. in fact
  a.'s lien
  a.'s opinion
  power of a.
attractive nuisance doctrine
auction
auditing
authentication
authority of agent
authorization to sell contract
avenue
avigation easement
avulsion
award

B

backfill
backland
backwoods
bad —
  b. faith
  b. title

badlands
bailment
bail-out
balance sheet
balloon —
  b. land
  b. mortgage
  b. payment
Baltimore method
balustrade
bank —
  b. commitment
  b. draft
bankrupt
bankruptcy
bare power
bargain —
  b. and sale deed
bargaining
bargeboard
barony of land
barter
base —
  b. lines
  b. maps
  b. molding
  b. property
  b. shoe
baseboard
basement
basis —
  b. of property
batten
batture land
bay window
beach
beam
beam right agreement
bearer paper
bearing wall
bed rock
bedroom suburb
bench mark
beneficial —
  b. interest
  b. rights
beneficiary
"benefit" principle
bequeath
bequest
berm bank

Bernard rule
best and highest use
betterment
bid
bilateral contract
bi-level house
bill —
  b. of certiorari
  b. of interpleader
  b. of sale
binder
binding
bird dog
black acre and white acre
blacktop
blanket —
  b. insurance
  b. mortgage
blighted area
blind advertising
block —
  b. busting
blue laws
blueprint
blue sky laws
board —
  b. and batten
  b. foot
  b. of appeals
  b. of directors
  b. of equalization
boarding house
bog
boiler-room operation
BOMA — Building Owners and Managers Association
bomb — a derogatory expression for a poorly built structure
bona fide (Lat) — in good faith
bond —
  b. and mortgage
  completion b.
  b. for deed
  performance b.
  statutory b.
bonus
book —
  b. cost
  b. depreciation
  b. value
boom

boondocks

boot — a term in the exchange of realty for the difference in value when the properties traded are not equal

border

boring test

borough

borrower

bote

botel

bottom land

boundary —
  b. rights

bounds

bounty lands

bracing

branch office

breach —
  b. of contract
  b. of trust

breezeway

bridging

brief —
  b. of title

British Thermal Unit

broker —
  b. and salesman contract

brokerage

BTU — British Thermal Unit

budget —
  b. loan
  b. mortgage

buffer zone

buildable area

builder

builder's —
  b. acre
  b. half acre

build for lease

building —
  b. and loan association
  b. area
  b. code
  b. lease
  b. lien
  b. line
  b. loan
  b. maintenance
  b. permit
  b. restrictions
  b. site

Building Owners and Managers Association

build up

built-ins

bulkhead line

bulk zoning

bundle of rights

bungalow

Bureau of Land Management

burn-off

business —
  b. buildings
  b. certificate
  b. chance
  b. district
  b. lease
  b. opportunities
  b. property
  b. property listing form
  b. tax
  b. trust

butterfly roof

butt lot

butts and bonds

buyer

buyers' market

by-bidding

by-laws

C

Canadian Real Estate Association

canal

cancellation clause

canons of ethics

cantilever

cap — the highest point of a building or a block wedged between the props of a roof to better hold it in place

capacity

Cape Cod house

capital —
  c. assets
  c. gains
  c. gain tax
  c. losses
  c. stock

capitalization —
  c. approach
  c. method

capitalization *(continued)*
   c. rate
   c. recapture
capitalize
capitalized value
cap rate — capitalization rate
carport
carrying charges
carryover clause
cartel
casement window
cash —
   c. flow
   c. on the barrel head
   c. on the line
   c. tenant
   c. value
cashier's check
casualty insurance
caveat (Lat) — beware
   c. actor — let whoever acts beware
   c. emptor — let the buyer beware
   c. venditor — let the seller beware
CBS — concrete, block, and stucco
cede
ceiling price
cemetery lot
centering — framing of an arched structure during its erection
central business district
certificate —
   c. lands
   c. of eligibility
   c. of equitable ownership
   c. of estoppel
   c. of no defense
   c. of occupancy
   c. of participation
   c. of reasonable value
   c. of reduction of mortgage
   c. of registration
   c. of release
   c. of sale
   c. of title
certified —
   c. check
   c. public accountant
certify
certiorari (Lat) — proceedings of a higher court or body reviewing actions of a lower one

cession deed
cesspool
cestui que trust (Lat) — the beneficiary of an estate acting as its trustee
chain of title
chalet
chancery
charter
chattel —
   c. interest
   c. mortgage
   c. personal
   c. real
check kiting
chimney cap
chose in action
circuit court
cistern
citation
city —
   c. planning
   c. real estate
civil —
   c. law
   c. rights
   c. wrong
claim —
   c. of lien
   c. of title
claimant
classified property tax
clear —
   c. annual income
   c. market price
   c. market value
   c. record title
   c. title
clearing title
clerestory
clerk of the county court
client
closed-end mortgage
closed mortgage
closing —
   c. costs
   c. date
   c. statement
   c. title
cloud on the title
cloudy title
cloverleaf

cluster developing
C.O. — certificate of occupancy
code of ethics
codicil
co-executor
cognovit note (Lat) — a written authorization
from a debtor to allow entering a judgment
against him
coinsurance
cold canvass
collar beam
collateral —
  c. note
  c. security
collections
collector of decedent's estate
collector street
collusion
colonial house
color of title
column
co-maker
combed plywood
commercial —
  c. acre
  c. bank
  c. law
  c. paper
  c. property
commingle funds
commingling
commission —
  c. agreement
  c. rates
commitment
committee
  c. deed
  c. of incompetent
common —
  c. area
  c. enterprise
  c. law
  c. law trust
  c. passageway
  c. property
  c. stock
  c. wall
community —
  c. property
  c. shopping centers

commutation —
  c. of taxes
compaction
company
comparable value
comparative approach to value
comparison approach
compass points
compensable damages
competency of parties
competent
competition
complainant
completed transaction
completion —
  c. bond
  c. certificate
  c. order
complex
compliance inspection
component —
  c. building
  c. depreciation
composite depreciation
compound —
  c. interest
  c. sum
comprehensive coverage
concession
concurrent authority
condemnation —
  c. appraisal
  c. proceedings
condition —
  c. concurrent
  c. precedent
  c. subsequent
conditional —
  c. commitment
  c. fee
  c. sales contract
condominium —
  c. ownership
conduit
confession of judgment
confidence
confidential relation
confirmation deed
confiscation
conformity

conglomerate
consent
consequential damages
conservation
conservator
consideration
conspiracy
constant
construct
construction —
  c. loan
  c. mortgage
  c. terms
constructive —
  c. eviction
  c. fraud
  c. notice
  c. possession
consummate
consumptive tax
contemporary
contempt
contiguous
contingencies
contingent remainder
continuance
continuous possession
contour map
contract —
  bilateral c.
  c. breach
  c. default
  c. for deed
  c. for exchange
  c. for sale
  naked c.
  nude c.
  c. of adhesion
  c. of benevolence
  c. of record
  oral c.
  parol c.
  c. price
  c. raiding
  reciprocal c.
  c. rent
  rescission of c.
  severable c.
  simple c.
  simulated c.
  verbal c.

contractor
contractual obligation
control
conventional —
  c. loan
  c. mortgage
conversion —
  c. commitment program
  c. factor
convert
conveyance
conveyancing
co-obligor
cooperating brokers or co-brokers
cooperative —
  c. apartment
  c. building
  c. sale
coordinate system
co-owner
copartner
corner —
  c. influence
  c. lot
  c. lot appraisal methods
  c. lot rules
cornerstone
cornice
corporate veil
corporation —
  eleemosynary c.
  foreign c.
  c. not for profit
  c. sole
corporeal —
  c. hereditament
  c. property
correction —
  c. deed
  c. lines
correlation
cost —
  c. approach to value
  c. of living index clause
  c. plus
costipulator
co-tenancy
cottage
counselor
counselor-at-law
counter offer

counterpart
countersign
country
county —
   c. court
   c. deed
   c. judge's court
   c. property
   c. recorder
   c. tax
coupled with interest
course
court
covenant —
   discriminatory c.
   c. for quiet enjoyment
   c's for title
   c. of seisin
   c. of warranty
   restrictive c.
   c. running with the land
coverture
CPA — certified public accountant
crawl —
   c. hole
   c. space
cream-puff — any property easy to sell
creative real estate
creditor
credit report
croft
cropland
crop share rent
cross
crown lands
CRV — certificate of reasonable value
cubage
cubic —
   c. content
   c. foot
   c. foot cost
   c. foot per second
cubing the title
cul-de-sac
curable depreciation
curb —
   c. line
   c. rider
currency
current assets
curtail schedule

curtesy
curtilage
cushion — a financial margin of safety against unforeseen costs or losses
custodial account
custom builder
customer —
   c. record cards
cut-over land
cut-up construction

D

damages
damnum absque injuria (Lat) — an injury or loss without grounds for a legal claim against the person who caused it
dark store clause
data sheet
days of grace
DBA — doing business as
dead-end street
deadline
dead pledge
deal
dealer
debenture
debit
debitum sine brevi (Lat) — debt without a declaration
debt —
   d. instrument
   d. service
debtor
decedent
   d.'s debt lien
deceit
deciduous trees
decision
deck
declaration —
   d. of homestead
   d. of no set-off
   d. of trust
declaratory judgment
declining balance depreciation
decree —
   d. of foreclosure
decrement
dedication

deductible
deductions
deed —
  d. in fee
  d. in lieu of foreclosure
  d. of confirmation
  d. of partition
  d. of release
  d. of surrender
  d. of trust
  d. poll
  d. restrictions
  statutory d.
  support d.
  surrender d.
  voluntary d.
  warranty d.
de facto (Lat) — in actual fact
default judgment
defeasance clause
defeasible fee
defect
defective title
defendant
deferred —
  d. maintenance
  d. payments
deficiency —
  d. decree
  d. judgment
defunct
degree
de jure (Lat) — under authority of the law or
  by right
delinquency
delinquent debt
delivery —
  d. in escrow
  d. of deed
demand note or mortgage
demise
demolition of buildings
density zoning
Department of Housing and Urban
  Development
dependent
depletion
deponent
deposition
deposit receipt

depreciation —
  accelerated d.
  d. base
  component d.
  double declining d.
  physical d.
  straight line d.
depth —
  d. influence
  d. table
dereliction
descent
describe
description of property
detached residence
detainer
deterioration
determinable fee
determine
devaluate
develop
developed land
developer
development
devest; divest
devise
devisee
devisor
devolution
devolve
diluvion
diminishing assets
direct —
  d. property loss
  d. reduction loan
  d. reduction mortgage
  d. sales comparison approach
  d. tax
directional growth
director
disbursements
discharge —
  d. in bankruptcy
disclaimer of estate
disclosed principal
disclosure
discontinuance
discount
discrimination
discriminatory covenants

dispensation
dispossess —
  d. notice
  d. proceedings
disseisin
dissolution
distances
distinct possession
distrain
distraint for rent
distressed property
distress warrant
distributee
district
divest
dividend
divisible contract
division
docketed judgment
dock stamps — documentary stamps
doctrine —
  d. of estates
  d. of tenures
documentary —
  d. evidence
  d. stamps
documents
domain —
  eminent d.
domestic corporation
domicile
dominant estate
dominion
donation lands
donative trust
donee
donor
dormant partner
dormer
dotal property
double —
  d. decking
  d. declining depreciation
  d. dwelling
  d. indemnity
  d. insurance
  d. rent
doubtful title
dower
downey — slang expression for down
  payment

down payment
draft
drainage
driveway
drop-rate
drumlin
dry —
  d. mortgage
  d. rent
  d. trust
  d. wall construction
dual —
  d. contracts
  d. employment
due process of law
dummy — someone who buys property for
  another to conceal the identity of the
  purchaser
duplex
durable lease
duration of lease
duress
Dutch Colonial
dwelling

E

earned increment
earnest —
  e. money
  e. money receipt
earnings approach
earnings-price ratio
easement —
  e. appurtenant
  e. by necessity
  e. by prescription
  dominant estate e.
  express e.
  e. in gross
  e. personal
  servient estate e.
eaves
ecclesiastical property
economic —
  e. approach
  e. depreciation
  e. life
  e. obsolescence

economic *(continued)*
  e. rent
  e. size
  e. value
edifice
effecting —
  e. a sale
  e. loan
effective —
  e. age
  e. date
  e. gross income
  e. procuring cause
effects
efficiency
efficient and procuring cause
egress
eject
ejectment
eleemosynary corporation
elevation
embezzlement
emblements
eminent domain
emphyteutic lease
employ
employment —
  e. contract
  e. of broker
enajenacion (Sp) — transfer of property
enclosed land
encroachment
encumber
encumbrance
endorsement
endow
enfeoff
enhance
enjoin
entail
entirety
entitle
entitlement
entity
entrepreneur
enure
equal —
  e. dignity
  e. opportunity in housing
equalization of assessments

equitable —
  e. lien
  e. title
equiteer
equity —
  e. build-up
  e. kicker
  e. of redemption
  e. participation
  sweat e.
erosion
escalator clause
escape clause
escarpment
escheat
escrow —
  e. account
  e. agent
  e. agreement
  e. analysis
Esq. — Esquire
estate —
  e. at will
  e. by sufferance
  e. by the entirety
  e. entail
  e. for life
  e. for years
  e. from period to period
  e. in fee simple
  e. in land
  e. in remainder
  e. in reversion
  e. in severalty
  e. of freehold
  e. of inheritance
  e. tax
estimate
estop
estoppel —
  e. certificate
  e. letter
estovers
estrepement
et al (Lat) — and others
ethics
et ux — et uxor (and wife)
et uxor (Lat) — and wife
Eurodollar
evaluation

eviction —
  total e.
evidence
examination of title
examiner
exception to title
excess rent
exchange of real estate
excise taxes
exclusive —
  e. agency
  e. authority to lease form
  e. listing
  e. possession
  e. right of sale
exculpate
exculpatory clause
execute
executed contract
execution —
  e. of deed
  e. of judgment
executor
  e.'s deed
executory —
  e. contract
  e. devise
executrix
exempt
exemption
exercise
existing mortgage
ex officio (Lat) — by virtue of holding an office
expansible house
expansion —
  e. attic
  e. joint
expenses
expiration
exposure
express —
  e. agency
  e. authority
  e. contract
  e. easement
expropriate
extended coverage
extension —
  e. agreement
  e. of lease

extension *(continued)*
  e. of mortgage
extinguishment
extortion
extrapolate
extras
exurban
eye appeal

F

fabric —
  f. land
fabricate
facade
face value
facia (fascia)
facsimile
failure —
  f. of consideration
  f. to perform
fair market value
Falcidian law
fall of land
fallow land
false —
  f. advertising
  f. pretense
  f. representation
Fannie Mae — Federal National Mortgage Association
farm —
  f. broker
  f. land
  f. lease
Farm and Land Institute
farmstead
farthing of land
fascia (facia)
fate — a banking term indicating an inquiry concerning the disposition of a specific check
fealty
feasibility study
federal —
  f. estate tax
  f. lands
  f. revenue stamps
  f. stamps

Federal Home Loan Bank
Federal Home Loan Bank Board
Federal Home Loan Bank System
Federal Housing Administration
Federal Land Bank System
Federal National Mortgage Association
Federal Savings and Loan Insurance
  Association
fee —
  f. appraiser
  f. certificate
  f. conditional
  f. determinable
  f. owner
  f. simple
  f. simple absolute
  f. simple determinable
  f. simple limited
  f. simple qualified
  f. tail
  f. upon condition
femme (Fr) — woman
  f. couverte — a married woman
  f. sole — a single woman
fen
feoffare
feoffee
  f. to uses
feoffment
feud — the right to use and occupancy of
  land
feudal system
FHA — Federal Housing Administration
FHLBB — Federal Home Loan Bank Board
fiat (Lat) — a decree
fidelity —
  f. bond
fiducial contract
fiduciary relation
finances
financial statement
finder's fee
fire —
  f. insurance
  f. stop
  f. wall
firm —
  f. contract
  f. commitment
  f. price

first —
  f. deed of trust
  f. devisee
  f. lien
  f. loan
  f. mortgage
  f. mortgage bond
  f. papers
  f. privilege to buy
  f. refusal
  f. right to buy
fiscal year
fixed —
  f. assets
  f. charges
fixture
flashing
flat —
  f. lease
  f. loan
float — a banking term indicating that a
  check had not been cleared for collection
floater policy
floating —
  f. interest rate
  f. zone
floor —
  f. area
  f. plan
flowage right or **easement**
flowing lands
fluid assets
fly-by-night operation
flyspecking
FNMA — Federal National Mortgage
  Association
foot-frontage
footing
forage acre
forced sale
forcible entry and detainer
foreclosure sale
forehand rent
foreign corporation
foreshore land
forest
forfeit
forfeiture
forgery
formal contract

forwarding fee
foundation
4-3-2-1 depth rule
frame construction
framed out
framing
franchise
frankalmoign tenure
frank-tenant
fraud
fraudulent —
  f. concealment
  f. conveyance
  f. representation
free —
  f. and clear
  f. enterprise
  f. entry
  f. tenure
  f. will
freedealer
freehold —
  f. estate
freeholder
freeway
freezing prices
front —
  f. elevation
  f. footage rule
  f. foot value
  f. man
  f. money
frontage
frost line
fructus (Lat) — rights or benefits from the use and enjoyment of property
FSLIC — Federal Savings and Loan Insurance Corporation
full covenant and warranty deed
functional —
  f. depreciation
  f. obsolescence
  f. utility
fundamental risk
funding
furlong
furring
further assurance warranty

future —
  f. acquired property
  f. depreciation
  f. estate
  f. interest

G

gabel
gable —
  g. roof
gain
gambrel roof
gap —
  g. financing
  g. insurance
garden apartment
garnishee
garnishment
garret
general —
  g. agent
  g. benefits
  g. building scheme
  g. contractor
  g. estate
  g. fee conditional
  g. improvement
  g. land office
  g. lien
  g. listing
  g. mortgage
  g. partner
  g. release
  g. warranty deed
General Services Administration
gentlemen's agreement
geodesic dome
geodetic survey
geography
geologic map
geology
Georgian architecture
ghetto
GI — government issue
  GI loan
  GI mortgage

gift —
  g. deed
  g. tax
gingerbread
Ginnie Mae — Government National
  Mortgage Association
girder
give notice
GNMA — Government National Mortgage
  Association
good —
  g. and valuable consideration
  g. faith
  g. faith money
  g. record title
  g. title
  g. will
goods
gore — a small wedge-shaped piece of land
gouging
government —
  g. land
  g. lots
  g. patent
  g. survey
Government National Mortgage Association
grace period
grade —
  g. finish
  g. natural
graded lease
gradient
graduated lease
grain rent
grand incident
grant —
  g. and demise
  g., bargain and sell
  g. deed
grantee
granting clause
grantor
  g. -grantee index
  g.'s lien
grassland
grazing —
  g. licenses
  g. permit
  g. preference on national forest
great ponds

Greensboro plan
grid map
grievance period
gross —
  g. income
  g. income multiplier
  g. lease
  g. receipts
  g. rent multiplier
  g. rent multiplier approach
  g. spendable income
ground —
  g. fee
  g. landlord
  g. lease
  g. rent
  g. water
GSA — General Services Administration
guarantee
guaranteed —
  g. loan
  g. sale
  g. title policy
guarantor
guaranty
guardian
  g. deed
guide meridians

H

habendum clause
habendum et tenendum (Lat) — to have and
  to hold
habitable
half —
  h. bath
  h. section
hand money
handshake deal
hard money
hardpan
hard sell
have and to hold
hazard
head lease
H-beam
heavy industry
hectare

heir
heiress
heirs —
   h. at law
   h. and assigns
hereditament —
   corporeal h.
   incorporeal h.
HHFA — Housing and Home Finance Agency
hiatus — a break in the chain of title or an unclaimed strip of land between property lines
hidden amenities
highest and best use
highland
high ratio financing
high-rise (hi-rise)
highway —
   h. easement
hip roof
Hoffman-Neill rule
Hoffman rule
holder in due course
hold harmless clause
holding —
   h. company
   h. over
holdover tenant
holographic —
   h. instrument
   h. will
home —
   h. building
   h. improvement loan
homeowner —
   h.'s policy
homesite
homestead —
   h. estate
   h. exemption
   h. laws
horizontal property regimes
hostile possession
hotel
house —
   h. consultant
   h. cross section
   h. inspector
   h. lease
   h. listing form

Housing and Home Finance Agency
housing project
HUD — Department of Housing and Urban Development
hundred percent location
husbandry clause
hypothecate

I

I-beam
illegal contract
illuviation
immoral contract
immunity
imperfect title
implied —
   i. agency
   i. authority
   i. contract
   i. easement
   i. listing
imply
impound
improper improvement
improved —
   i. land
   i. value
improvements
impute
Inc. — Incorporated
inchoate —
   i. dower
   i. instruments
   i. interest
incidents of tenure
inclosed land
inclusive rent
income —
   i. approach to value
   i. and expense statement
   i. multiplier
   i. net multiplier
   i. participation
   i. property
   i. tax
incompetent
incorporated
incorporation

incorporeal —
  i. hereditament
  i. property
increment
incubator building
incumbrance
incurable —
  i. depreciation
  i. title
indefeasible
indemnification contract
indemnity lands
indenture deed
independent contractor
index clause
indictment
indirect —
  i. property loss
  i. tax
indorse
indorsement
inducement
industrial —
  i. broker
  i. building
  i. park
  i. property
industrialized building
in fee
infiltration
inflation
information sheet
infringement
ingress
inhabit
inheritance
  i. tax
in invitum (Lat) — something done against
  another's will
  i.i. lien
injunction
inland
in lieu of
in-lot
inn
innocent purchaser
in personam (Lat) — a legal action against a
  specific person
in re (Lat) — in regard to
in rem (Lat) — a legal action against property

inside lot
insolvent
inspection
installation
installment —
  i. land contract
  i. method
  i. note
  i. sales contract
Institute of Real Estate Management
institutional —
  i. lenders
  i. property
instrument
insurable —
  i. interest
  i. risk
  i. title
  i. value
insurance —
  i. agent
  i. broker
  i. of loans
  i. of title
  i. on mortgaged property
insured loan
insurer
intangible —
  i. assets
  i. property
  i. tax
  i. value
integrated
inter alia (Lat) — among other things
interest —
  i. only loan
  i. rate
interim —
  i. financing
  i. loan
interior lot
intermingle funds
International Council of Shopping Centers
International Real Estate Federation
interpleader
interpretation of contracts
interstate commerce
inter-vivos trust (Lat) — a trust created by
  living persons
intestacy

intestate —
  i. laws
intrinsic value
intrusion
inure
invalid
inventory
investment —
  i. property
  i. value
investor
invoice
involuntary —
  i. alienation
  i. lien
in witness thereof
in witness whereof
ipso facto (Lat) — by the fact itself
ipso jure (Lat) — by the law itself
IREM — Institute of Real Estate
  Management
ironclad agreement
irredeemable ground rent
irrevocable
irrigation district
island
islet
istimrar lease

J

jalousie
jamb
jerry-built
jog — an irregularity in a property line
  creating a small pocket of land
John Doe
joint —
  j. adventure
  j. and several liability
  j. annuity
  j. enterprise
  j. estate
  j. executors
  j. liability
  j. note
  j. ownership
  j. tenancy
  j. venture

joists
judgment —
  j. by default
  j. creditor
  j. debtor
  j. D.S.B. (debitum sine brevi)
  j. lien
judicial —
  j. mortgage
  j. sale
judiciary
junior —
  j. financing
  j. lien
  j. mortgage
junker
junk value
jurat
jure (Lat) — by law
jurisdiction
jurisprudence
just —
  j. compensation
  j. title
justice of the peace
justified price

K

kame
key lot
keystone
kick-back
kicker — a slang term for a mortgage
  holder's participation in profits from a
  property in addition to the stated interest
  rate
king post
kiosk
kiting
knock-down construction
knock-down price
know all men

L

laborer's lien
laches

land —
l. certificate
l. claim
l. contract
l. cop
l. court
l. department
l. development
l. districts
l. economics
l. gabel
l. grant
l. improvement
l. office
l. patent
l. planning
l. poor
l. reclamation
l. revenue
seated l.
l. subdivision
l. tax
l, tenements, and heriditaments
l. title and transfer act
l. trust
l. trust certificate
l. usage
virgin l.
l. warrant
landlocked
landlord —
l. and tenant
l.'s distress
l.'s warrant
landmark
landscape —
l. architect
l. gardener
lapse
larceny
last will and testament
late charge
latent
lateral support
lath
latitude
law —
common l.
l. day
Falcidian l.
statutory l.

lawful —
l. age
lawsuit
lawyer
lead — a prospect
lean-to
lease —
l. broker
emphyteutic l.
flat l.
l. insurance
l. interest
l. purchase agreement
l. renewal
step l.
surrender of l.
underlying l.
ungraded l.
virgin l.
leaseback
leased —
l. department
l. fee
l. fee interest
leasehold —
l. appraisal
l. improvements
l. insurance
l. mortgage
l. value
leasing department
leave — to make a gift by will or to consent to take action
legacy
legal —
l. action
l. age
l. aid
l. assets
l. consideration
l. descriptions
l. entity
l. estoppel
l. fraud
l. guardian
l. heirs
l. mortgage
l. notice
l. owner
l. rate of interest
l. representative

legal *(continued)*
   l. residence
   l. rights
   l. tender
   l. title
legality of object
legatee
leisure home
lender participation
lessee —
   l.'s interest
lessor —
   l.'s interest
let — to lease
letter —
   l. of commitment
   l. of credit
   l. of intention
letting
levee
level payment mortgage
leverage
levy
liability —
   l. insurance
   l. loss
liable
liber (Lat) — book or lot book
liberty of contract
license
licensee
licensor
lien —
   l. affidavit
   l. in invitum
   laborer's l.
   l. of commission
   mechanic's l.
   statutory l.
   l. theory states
lienee
lienor
lieu land
life —
   l. estate
   l. insurance for mortgagor
   l. interest
   l. land
   l. rent
   l. tenant
life-hold

lifting clause
light and air easement
light industry
"like kind" property
limitation
limited —
   l. access land
   l. dividend housing
   l. liability
   l. partnership
lineal
line of sight easement
link
lintel
liquid assets
liquidate
liquidated damages
liquidation value
liquidity
lis pendens (Lat) — a pending legal action
lister
listing
litigate
litigation
littoral —
   l. land
   l. property
   l. rights
livability
living trusts
load-bearing wall
loan —
   l. agreement
   l. association
   l. bank
   l. closing
   l. fee
   GI l.
   l. modification provision
   l. policy
   l. relief
   l's on real estate
   l. trust fund
   VA l.
   l. value
   l. value of life insurance
   l. value ratio
lobby
local assessment
location
lock-in

lock, stock and barrel
Locus sigilli (Lat) — under seal or the place
    where a seal is to be affixed
lodging house
loft
long form mortgage clause
longitude
long-term —
    l. capital gain
    l. capital loss
    l. escrow
    l. lease
    l. loan
loophole
lost property
lot —
    l., block and subdivision
    l. book report
    l. line
    l. split
louver
love and affection — the valuable
    consideration used when real estate is
    conveyed between members of a family
    with no exchange of money
low-pressure selling
L.S. — Locus sigilli
LTD. — Limited
lucrative title

M

made land
MAI — Member Appraisal Institute
mail box rule
maintenance reserve
major
majority
make —
    m. a contract
    m. an assignment
maker — a party in a promissory note
mala fides (Lat) — done with bad intent
malfeasance
mall
management agreement
managing agent
mandamus (Lat) — we command; a writ
mansard
manufactured home

margin
marginal land
marina
mark —
    m. down
    m. up
marker
market —
    m. comparison
    m. data approach
    m. price
    m. rent
    m. value
marketable title
marl land
marshalling
marsh land
Maryland ground rent
masonry
Massachusetts trust
mass appraising
master —
    m. lease
    m. plan
Master in Chancery
master's deed
material fact
materialman —
    m.'s lien
maturity value
mead
meadow
meander line
mechanic's —
    m. lien
    m. lien affidavit
median
medium industry
meeting of the minds
megalopolis
megastructure
memorandum of agreement
mercantile law
merchantable title
merged lot
merge line
merger
meridian lines
messuage
meter
metes and bounds

metropolis
metropolitan area
micro-relief
middleman
military —
  m. clause
  m. tenure
mill — one tenth of one cent
millage
mineral —
  m. deed
  m. land
  m. lease
  m. right
minimum —
  m. lot zoning
  m. rental
mining
minor
  m. street
minute — a measurement of degrees of a
  circle
miscellaneous income
misdemeanor
misfeasance
misplaced improvement
misrepresentation
mission architecture
mixed estate — ground rent
mobile home park
model
  m. cities program
modern —
  m. architecture
modernization
modification agreement
module construction
molding
monetary
money market
monitor roof
monopoly
monthly tenancy
month-to-month tenancy
monument
moral —
  m. hazard
  m. obligation
  m. turpitude
moratorium
  mortgage m.

more or less
mortgage —
  amortized m.
  m. assumption
  m. bankers
  m. bond
  m. broker
  m. certificate
  m. clipping
  m. commitment
  m. company
  m. constant
  m. correspondent
  m. debt
  m. deed
  m. discount
  m. equity
  first m.
  m. foreclosure
  GI m.
  m. guaranty insurance
  m. insurance policy
  m. investment company
  junior m.
  leasehold m.
  m. lien
  m. loan insurance
  m. milking
  m. money
  m. moratorium
  m. note
  m. origination fee
  overlying m.
  m. premium
  m. redemption insurance
  m. redlining
  m. reduction certificate
  m. registration tax
  seasoned m.
  second m.
  senior m.
  statutory m.
  sur m.
  tacit m.
  term m.
  third m.
  trust m.
  underlying m.
  VA m.
  m. value
  wrap-around m.

Mortgage Bankers Association of America
mortgagee —
   m. in possession
mortgagor
mortmain
motel
Mother Hubbard clause
motif
motion to quash
movable —
   m. estate
   m. freehold
muck land
multiple —
   m. dwelling
   m. family
   m. listing
   m. nuclei development
   m. transaction
multiplier
multi-story building
municipal —
   m. lien certificate
   m. ordinance
municipality
muniment of title
mutual —
   m. assent
   m. fund
   m. savings bank
   m. water company

naked contract
NAR — National Association of Realtors
NAREB — National Association of Real
Estate Brokers
national —
   n. bank
   n. building code
   n. forest
   n. housing act
National Apartment Association, Inc.
**National Association of Corporate Real
Estate Executives**
National Association of Home Builders
**National Association of Housing and
Redevelopment Officials**

**National Association of Independent Fee
Appraisers**
National Association of Industrial Parks
**National Association of Real Estate
Appraisers**
National Association of Real Estate Brokers
**National Association of Real Estate
Investment Trusts**
National Association of Realtors
**National Institute of Farm and Land
Brokers**
National Institute of Real Estate Brokers
National Society of Fee Appraisers
natural —
   n. affection
   n. financing
   n. person
   n. resource property
necessaries
negative —
   n. easement
   n. leasehold
   n. leverage
negligence
negotiable instrument
negotiate
negotiation
neighborhood —
   n. shopping center
net —
   n. estate
   n. floor area
   n. income
   n. income multiplier
   n. lease
   n. listing
   n. net income
   n. profit
   n. rent
   n. rental
   n. spendable income
   n. worth
New England colonial architecture
NIFLB — National Institute of Farm and
Land Brokers
nihil (Lat) — nothing
NIREB — National Institute of Real Estate
Brokers
no deal, no commission clause
no lien affidavit

nominee
nonbearing wall
nonconforming use
noncontinuous easement
noncupative will
nondisclosure
nonfeasance
non-investment property
non-merchantable title
nonpossessory estate
non-profit corporation
nonrecurring expense
non-resident
nook
normal —
   n. sale
   n. value
notarial
notary public
notice —
   n. of completion
   n. of lis pendens
   n. of sale
   n. of unpaid rent
   n. to quit
notorious possession
novation
NSFA — National Society of Fee Appraisers
nude contract
nuisance value
null and void

O

oath
objection to title
objective value
obligation —
   o. bond
   o. of contract
obligee
obligor
obsolescence —
   economic o.
   functional o.
occasional overflow rights
occupancy —
   o. clause
   o. expense
   o. rate

ocean shore
O-dome construction
offer —
   o. and acceptance
   o. to buy
   o. to sell
offeree
offeror
off-grade lot
office —
   o. building
official
offset statement
offsetting benefits
oil and gas lease
O.L.&T. — owner's, landlord's and tenant's
   public liability insurance
omitted assessment
on demand
one-and-a-half story
onerous
one-third, two-thirds rule
on or about
on or before
open —
   o. and notorious possession
   o. end mortgage
   o. housing
   o. housing law
   o. listing
   o. lot
   o. mortgage
   o. occupancy
   o. possession
operating —
   o. expenses
   o. income
   o. profit
   o. property
   o. ratio
operative —
   o. builder
   o. words
operator
opinion of title
option
optionee
optioner
oral contract
ordinance
organization

orientation
original —
  o. assessment
  o. cost
  o. plat
origination fee
ostensible —
  o. agency
  o. partners
outbuilding
outdoor living space
outlot
overage
overall —
  o. interest rate
  o. property tax limitation
overdue
overflowed lands
overflow right
overhang
overhead
over-improvement
overlying mortgage
override
overt
overzoned
owelty
owner's —
  o. affidavit of no liens
  o. estoppel certificate
  o., landlord's and tenant's public liability
    insurance
ownership

P

package —
  p. deal
  p. mortgage
paper —
  p. profit
  p. street
  p. title
par — the accepted standard of comparison
parallels
paramount title
parapet
parcel
parity clause in mortgage

parking —
  p. lot
  p. ratio
parkway
parol —
  p. evidence rule
  p. gift
parquet floor
partial —
  p. eviction
  p. release clause
partially disclosed principal
partible land
participate
participation certificate
particular —
  p. lien
  p. risk
particulars
parties
partition —
  p. deed
partner
partnership
part performance
party —
  p. driveway
  p. to be charged
  p. wall
passage of title
passing title
patent
patio
pavilion
payee
payer
payment
peaceable possession
pediment
penalty
pendens (Lat) — pending
peninsula
Pennsylvania ground rent
penny — a measure of nail length
pension funds
penthouse
pepper and salt area
per annum (Lat) — by the year
per capita (Lat) — for each person; share and
  share alike

percent
percentage lease
perch — a unit of measure; a rod
percolation test
per diem (Lat) — by day
perfect —
  p. instrument
  p. title
performance —
  p. bond
perimeter heating
periodic tenancy
periphery
permanent financing
permissive waste
permit
perpetual
perpetuity
personal —
  p. easement
  p. insurance
  p. liability
  p. loss
  p. obligation bond
  p. property
personalty — a contraction for personal
  property
per stirpes (Lat) — a method of dividing an
  estate in which the descendants of a
  deceased legatee share as a group in the
  portion to which the deceased would have
  been entitled
pest control clause
petition
physical —
  p. depreciation
  p. deterioration
  p. hazard
  p. life
pick — a narrow strip of land
picture window
piece of the action
pier
pierce the corporate veil
piggy back financing
pilaster
pitch — the incline or rise of a roof
PITI — principal, interest, taxes and
  insurance

place —
  p. lands
  p. of contract
plaintiff
planned unit development
planning commission
plat —
  p. book
plate — a board on or in a wall to support
  girders
platted land
plaza
pledge
pledgee
pledgor
plot
plottage —
  p. increment
  p. value
plotting commission
plow land
PMM — purchase money mortgage
pocket —
  p. license card
  p. listing
points — charge by a bank for taking a
  mortgage
pole structure
poll deed
portability
portico
positive leasehold
possession —
  actual p.
  adverse p.
  constructive p.
  right of p.
possessory —
  p. action
  p. interest
post date
post-dated check
postponement of lien
power —
  p. of appointment
  p. of attorney
  p. of sale
  p. of sale clause
practitioner
precast concrete

preceding estate
pre-closing preparations
precontract
precut
pre-empt
pre-engineered building
prefabricate
preference and priority clause in mortgage
preferred —
   p. debt
   p. stock
preliminary sales agreement
premises
prepaid interest
prepayment —
   p. clause
   p. of mortgage loan
   p. penalty
   p. privilege
   p. yield
prescription — a means of acquiring an
   easement through the open and continuous
   use of real property
presumptive title
preventive maintenance
prima facie (Lat) — at first hand or at first
   glance
primary —
   p. bondsman
   p. members
prime —
   p. location
   p. meridian
   p. rate
principal —
   p. meridian
   p. note
principle
printer's ink statutes
prior —
   p. appropriation
   p. lien
priority of lien
privacy
private —
   p. dwelling
   p. lenders
   p. plat
   p. property
privilege

privity
probate —
   p. court
procedure
proceeding
procuring cause
producing cause
pro facto (Lat) — held as a fact
profile — a sectional elevation of a building
profit
   p. and loss statement
pro forma (Lat) — as a matter of form
progressive tax
progress payments
pro indiviso (Lat) — undivided interest
projected income
project financing
promissory note
promontory
promoter
promulgate
proof
property —
   p. brief
   p. descriptions
   p. insurance
   p. line
   p. loss
   p. management
   p. mortgage
   p. tax
proportional tax
proposal
proposition or purchase agreement
proprietary —
   p. interest
   p. lease
proprietor
pro rata (Lat) — in proportion
prorate
proration of taxes
prospect —
   p. cards
prospectus
protection of title
protective covenants
provisional
proximate cause
proxy

public —
  p. accountant
  p. building
  p. domain land
  p. policy
  p. real estate activities
  p. trustee
PUD — planned unit development
punitive damages
purchase —
  p. and sale agreement
  p. money mortgage
  p. offer
  p. price
purchaser
purlin
pyramid —
  p. roof
  p. zoning

Q

quadrangle
qualified fee
quality of estate
quantity survey
quarry
quarterly
quarter section
quash
quasi (Lat) — as if; almost
  q. -contract
  q. -corporation
  q. -judicial
  q. -official
  q. -possession
queen posts
quick assets
quid pro quo (Lat) — something of value
  given for something else of value
quiet —
  q. enjoyment
  q. title suit
quit —
  q. -claim
  q. -claim deed
  q. rent
quoins
quonset hut

R

race restriction
rack rent
radiant heating
radius
rafter
ranch —
  r. house
range —
  r. lines
ratable property
rate
ratification
ratio
ravine
raw land
ready —
  r. and willing
  r., willing and able
real —
  r. law
  r. property
  r. property laws
  r. property tax
real estate —
  r.e. agent
  r.e. board
  r.e. broker
  r.e. closing
  r.e. dealer
  r.e. investment trust
  r.e. market
  r.e. salesman
  R.E. Settlement Procedures Act
  r.e. tax
realtor
Realtors National Marketing Institute
realty boards
reappraisal —
  r. lease
reasonable value
reassessment
rebate
rebuttable presumption
recapture —
  r. clause
  r. rate
recasting a mortgage

receipt
receiver —
r. clause
receivership
reciprocal contract
reciprocity
recission of contract
reclaim
reclamation
recognized gain
recompense
reconditioning property
reconveyance
record
recorded map or plat
Recorder of Deeds
Recorder's office
recording —
r. of conveyances
r. of deeds
r. of lease
r. of mortgages
recoup
recourse
recover
Rectangular Survey (or Government Survey)
rectification of boundaries
reddendum (Lat) — a reservation
r. clause
redeem
redeemable —
r. rent
r. rights
redemise
redemption
redevelopment
rediscount rate
redlining
reduction of mortgage certificate
re-entry
referee —
r. in bankruptcy
r.'s deed in foreclosure
r.'s deed in partition
reference to plat
referral
refinance
reformation of deed
refund

refunding mortgage
refusal of offer
regional —
r. plan
r. shopping center
register —
r. in bankruptcy
r. of land office
r. of deeds
registered —
r. land
r. title
registration of title
registry of deeds
regression
regressive tax
rehabilitate
rehabilitation
reimbursement
reinforced concrete
reinstate
reinsurance
REIT — real estate investment trust
rejection
release —
r. clause
r. of deed
r. of deposit
r. of dower
r. of lien
r. of mortgage
r. of part of mortgaged premises
re-lease
relet
reliction
relief map
relinquish
remainder estate
remainderman
remaining economic life
remise
remise, release and quit-claim
remit
remittance
remitter
remnant rule
remodeling
removing cloud from title
remuneration

rendering
re-negotiation
renewal of lease
renounce
renovate
renovation
rent —
   r. control
   r. gouging
   r. insurance
   r. roll
rentable area
rentage
rental —
   r. application
   r. department
   r. value
   r. value insurance
renunciation
reorganization
repairs and maintenance
repay
replacement —
   r. cost
   r. cost approach
replevin
report of title
repossess
representation
reproduction —
   r. cost
   r. cost approach
repudiation
reputable
reputed owner
resale
rescind
rescission of contract
reservation
reserved land
reserve fund
reservoir
residence
resident freehold
residential
   r. building rate
   r. listing form
   r. market
   r. property

residual
residuary —
   r. bequest
   r. clause
   r. devisee
   r. estate
   r. legacy
   r. legatee
residue
residuum
resort property
RESPA — Real Estate Settlement Procedures Act
restitution
restoration
restraining order
restraint —
   r. of trade
   r. on alienation
restricted land
restriction
restrictive covenant
retain
retaining wall
retire
retroactive
retrospective assessment
return —
   r. on equity
   r. on investment
revaluation —
   r. lease
revenue —
   r. stamps
reversion
reversionary —
   r. interest
   r. right
reverter
revest
revocable
revocation of agency
rezone
ribbon development
rider — an addition to a document
ridge —
   r. board
ridgepole

right —
  r. of first refusal
  r. of occupancy
  r's of ownership
  r. of possession
  r. of privacy
  r. of property
  r. of redemption
  r. of survivorship
  r. -of-way
  r. patent
  r., title and interest
  r. to action
  r. to redeem
riparian —
  r. doctrine
  r. owner
  r. property
  r. proprietor
  r. rights
  r. water
risk —
  r. capital
  r. insurance
  r. interest rate
  r. prevention
  r. retention
river banks
riverbed
roadside development
rod
rood of land
roof —
  r. inspection clause
  r. joists
roof styles —
  butterfly
  conical
  curb
  double-pitch
  flat
  gable
  gambrel
  hip
  jerkinhead
  lean-to
  M
  mansard
  monitor
  ogee

roof styles *(continued)*
  pyramid
  saw-tooth
  semi-circular
  shed
  single-pitch
root of title
row —
  r. housing
  r. stores
royalties
rule against perpetuities
running —
  r. lease
  r. with the land
  r. with the reversion
rural —
  r. homestead
rurban
rur-urban

S

sale —
  s. and leaseback
  s. in gross
  s. leaseback, buyback
  s. of lease
  s. of leased property
  s. of mortgage
  s. of mortgaged property
saleable
sales —
  s. agreement
  s. approach
  s. contract
  s. deposit receipt
  s. puff
salesman
saline land
salt box — a house of New England Colonial architecture, usually of framed construction
salvage value
sandwich building
sandwich lease
sash
satellite —
  s. community
  s. tenant

satisfaction —
  s. of lien
  s. of mortgage
  s. piece
savings and loan association
scavenger sale
scenic easement
schematic
scilicet (Lat) — to wit
scrap value
scribing — fitting woodwork to an irregular
  surface
scrivener
seal
sea level
sealing
searching the title
seashore
seasoned mortgage
seated land
seawall
second —
  s. deed of trust
  s. home
  s. lien
  s. loan
  s. mortgage
secondary —
  s. building
  s. financing
  s. location
  s. mortgage market
  s. rental
seconds
sectional house
section of land
section, township and range description
securities
security —
  s. agreement
  s. deposit
  s. interest
segregation
seisin
seize
seizen
seizure — taking possession of property by
  legal process
self-supporting wall
sell and lease agreement

seller
seller's —
  s. lien
  s. market
semi-detached dwelling
semi-public property
senior mortgage
sentimental value
separate property
septic tank
sequestration (in equity)
seriatim (Lat) — in succession
service —
  s. charge
  s. property
servicing contract
servient —
  s. estate
  s. tenement
setback line
set-off
settlement
settlor
severable contract
severally
severalty ownership
severance —
  s. damage
  s. tax
sextery lands
shake — a hand-split shingle
sharecropping
share of ownership agreement
sheathing
shed
shell house
shelter
sheriff's —
  s. certificate
  s. deed
  s. sale
shopping center
shore —
  s. lands
  s. line
short —
  s. form
  s. form mortgage clause
  s. lease
  s. rate

shortcut foreclosure
short-term —
  s. capital gain
  s. capital loss
  s. lease
shotgun floorplan
shyster
sidewalk
siding
sight —
  s. draft
  s. line easement
sign —
  s. rights
signatory
signing
silent partner
sill
silo
simple —
  s. contract
  s. interest
  s. listing
simulated contract
single family dwelling
singular title
sinking fund
SIR — Society of Industrial Realtors
site —
  s. plan
siting
situs (Lat) — a site or place
skip payment
sky lease
skyscraper
slab
slander of title
sleeper — a slang expression for property of
  hidden values
slum —
  s. clearance
slumlord
social obsolesence
Society of Industrial Realtors
Society of Real Estate Appraisers
soffit
soft —
  s. dollars
  s. sell

soil —
  s. pipe
  s. rights
Soldiers and Sailors Civil Relief Act
sold notice
sole —
  s. owner
  s. plate
  s. proprietor
solvent
sound investment
southern colonial
span
special —
  s. agent
  s. assessment
  s. benefits
  s. lien
  s. purpose properties
  s. tax assessment
  s. warranty deed
specific —
  s. lien
  s. performance
  s. tax
specifications
speculative —
  s. builder
  s. risk
speculator
spendable income
spinoff
spit — a narrow strip of land extending into
  water
split-level house
split rate
spoil — excavated rock, debris or earth
spot —
  s. builder
  s. zoning
spreading agreement
square —
  s. foot value
squatter
  s.'s rights
SRA — Senior Residential Appraiser
SREA — Senior Real Estate Analyst;
            Society of Real Estate Appraisers
SS — scilicet

standard —
  s. depth
  s. metropolitan area
  s. parallels
stand-by commitment
state —
  s. stamps
statement
statute —
  s. of frauds
  s. of limitations
statutory —
  s. bond
  s. deed
  s. law
  s. lien
  s. mortgage
  s. redemption
steering — directing a prospective buyer away from a certain piece of property
step lease
stepped-up basis
step-up clause
stipulation
stock —
  s. certificate
  s. company
  s. dividend
stockholder
stock-in-trade
store —
  s. lease
storefront
story
straight —
  s. lease
  s. line depreciation
  s. loan
straw man
street —
  s. lot line
  s. rights
string, stringer — a wooden or other support for cross members
strip stores
structure
studding
studio apartment
studs

subagent
sub-chapter S
sub-contract
sub-contractor
subdivide
subdivider
subdivision —
  s. trust
subinfeudation
subjective value
subject to mortgage
sublease
sublessee
sublet
subletting
sub-marginal land
submerged lands
submersible lands
submit
submittal notice
submortgage
subordinated interest
subordination clause
subpoena (Lat) — a legal order directing a person to testify before a court of law
subrogation
subrogee
subscribe
subscribing witness
subsidiary company
subsoil
substantial performance
substitution
subsurface —
  s. easement
  s. right
subtenant
suburban shopping center
suburbia
suburbs
succession —
  s. duty
  s. tax
successor
sufferance
sufficient consideration
summary proceedings
summation appraisal
summons

sum-of-the-years' digits depreciation
sump —
  s. pump
Sunday —
  s. contracts
  s. laws
superficiarius (Lat) — a ground rent tenant
supersede
supplementary proceeding
supply and demand
support deed
surety —
  s. bond
surface rights
sur mortgage
surplus —
  s. land
  s. productivity
surrender —
  s. deed
  s. of lease
  s. of premises
surtax
survey
surveyor
survival clause
survivorship
suspend
swale
swamp lands
sweat equity
syndicate
syndication

T

tacit —
  t. mortgage
tacking
take back a mortgage
takeout commitment
tangible personal property
tax —
  t. abatement
  t. base
  t. book
  t. certificate
  t. clause
  t. consultant

tax *(continued)*
  t. deed
  t. exemption
  t. lease
  t. levy
  t. liability
  t. lien
  t. list
  t. participation clause
  t. receiver
  t. roll
  t. sale
  t. sale certificate
  t. savings
  t. search
  t. shelter
  t. stop
  t. title
taxable —
  t. income
  t. value
taxation
taxpayer
temporary loans
tenancy —
  t. at will
  t. by sufferance
  t. by the entirety
  t. for years
  t. from year to year
  t. in common
  t. in fee
  t. in partnership
  t. in severalty
tenant —
  t. at sufferance
  t. by the curtesy
  t. for life
  t. for years
  t. from year to year
  t. in common
  t. in dower
  t. in fee simple
  t. in severalty
  t. in tail
  t. ownership corporation
tender — an offer, without conditions, to settle a claim
tenement
tenements and hereditaments

tenendum (Lat) — that part of a deed indicating that the grantee is to have and to hold the subject land
tentative map (preliminary plan)
tenure
tenurial ownership
term —
 t. mortgage
 t. of lease
 t. of mortgage
terminate
termination of agency
termite —
 t. clause
 t. shield
terra firma (Lat) — the earth
terre-tenant
territory
testament
testamentary trust
testate
testator
testatrix
testimony clause
thence
third —
 t. loan
 t. mortgage
 t. party
thread of a stream
three-way exchange
threshold
through lot
throw-off
tide —
 t. and overflow lands
 t. land
tidewater lands
tie-in deal
tier
tierce
tillable land
tilt-up walls
"time is of the essence" clause
title —
 t. agencies
 t. by adverse possession
 t. closing
 t. company
 t. deed

title *(continued)*
 t. examination
 t. guarantee
 t. insurance
 t. insurance binder
 t. I loan
 t. II loan
 t. policy
 t. report
 t. search
 singular t.
 slander of t.
 t. theory states
 uninsurable t.
 unmarketable t.
"to have and to hold" clause
tonnage rent
topo — topography
topographic map
topography
topping-off
Torrens —
 T. certificate
 T. title system
tort
total eviction
to wit
town
townhouse
township
tract —
 t. book
 t. house
 t. subdivision
trade
trade-in —
 t. fee
 t. plan
trade name
trader
trailer park
transfer —
 t. books
 t. clause
 t. fee
 t. of title
 t. tax
transported soil
treasurer's sale
trespass

trespasser
tribal lands
tri-level house
trim
triple-A tenant
triplex
true —
    t. bill
    t. value
truss
trust —
    t. account
    t. and confidence
    t. deed
    t. deed mortgage
    t. estate
    t. fund
    t. indenture
    t. in real estate
    t. mortgage
    t. property
trustee —
    t. in bankruptcy
trustee's deed
trustor
turn-key job
turnover
two-family house
two-story

U

UCC — Uniform Commercial Code
ULI — Urban Land Institute
ultimatum
ultra vires (Lat) — beyond its powers
unaccrued
unbalanced improvement
under
    u. and subject
    u. color of title
    u. improvement
    u. lease
underimproved land
underlessee
underlying —
    u. lease
    u. mortgage
undersigned

undertenant
underwrite
underwriter
undisclosed principal
undivided right
undue influence
undulating land
unearned increment
unencumbered property
unenforceable contract
unethical
unfree tenure
ungraded lease
Uniform Building Code
Uniform Commercial Code
unilateral —
    u. contract
    u. listing agreement
unimproved land
uninsurable title
unit
unity
universal —
    u. agent
    u. legacy
unmarketable title
unpaid rent notice
unrecorded —
    u. instrument
    u. plat
unseated land
upland
up-rent potential
upset —
    u. date
    u. price
urban —
    u. homestead
    u. renewal
Urban Land Institute
usable —
    u. floor area
    u. income
use density
U.S. Department of Housing and Urban
    Development
useful life
use value
U.S. Federal Housing Authority
U.S. Government Bureau of Land
    Management

U.S. Government Public Land Description
U.S. Government Survey
usufructuary right
usury
U.S. Veterans Administration
utility —
 u. building
 u. easement
 u. room
uxor (Lat) — wife

VA — Veterans Administration
 VA loan
 VA mortgage
vacancy factor
vacant —
 v. land
 v. lot listing form
vacate
vacated street
vadium (Lat) — a pledge of property as
 security
 v. mortuum (Lat) — a pledge by a
 mortgagor granting a lender the right to
 ownership if there is default of the
 mortgage
valid
valley
valuable —
 v. consideration
 v. improvements
valuation
valuator
value —
 v. in exchange
 v. in use
variable interest rate
variance
vend
vendee —
 v.'s lien
vendible
vendor —
 v.'s lien
vendue
veneer
vent

venture capital
verbal contract
verdict
verification
versus (Lat) — against
vested —
 v. estate
 v. interest
 v. remainder
 v. right
vestibule
vesture of land
Veterans Administration
 VA loan
VHMCP — Voluntary Home Mortgage
 Credit Program
via (Lat) — way or right of way
vicinage
videlicet (Lat) — to wit
virgata
virgin land
virgin lease
visible amenities
visual rights
viz (Lat) — an abbreviation of videlicet
void —
 v. contract
 v. title
voidable —
 v. contract
 v. title
voluntary —
 v. alienation
 v. conveyance
 v. deed
 v. lien
 v. waste
voucher
vs — versus

wainscot
wainscoting
waiver —
 w. of defenses
walk-up
wall bearing
want of consideration

warehouse
warrant
warranties of title
warranty deed
wasteland
wasting property
water —
   w. level
   w. line easement
   w. rights
   w. table
watercourse
waterfront property
waterpower rights
watershed
wear and tear
wetland
wheeler-dealer
white acre
white elephant
wife's equity
wife's separate property
wild land
will
windfall
wire fate
with —
   w. prejudice
   w. right of survivorship
without —
   w. prejudice
   w. recourse
witness —
   w. corner
wood frame construction
woodland
working —
   w. capital
   w. drawing
worth

wrap-around mortgage
writ —
   w. of certiorari
   w. of entry
   w. of execution
   w. of mandamus
written —
   w. contract
   w. instrument

X

x-bracing
xyloid

Y

yard
yearly tenancy
yield
yielding and paying

Z

zangerle curve
zone —
   z. condemnation
zoning —
   z. appeals board
   z. board
   z. commission
   z. map
   z. ordinances
   z. regulations
   z. restrictions
   z. variance

Business Abbreviations

A

AA — author's alterations

aa — average audience

AAA — American Academy of Advertising; American Arbitration Association

AAAA — American Association of Advertising Agencies

AABD — Aid to the Aged, Blind and Disabled

AAF — American Advertising Federation

AAHA — American Academy of Health Administrators

AAI — Alliance of American Insurers

AAIE — American Association of Industrial Editors

AAIM — American Association of Industrial Managers

AANR — American Association of Newspaper Representatives

AASHO — American Association of State Highway Officials

AAW — Advertising Association of the West

AB — Aid to the Blind

ABA — American Bankers Association

ABC — American Broadcasting Company; Audit Bureau of Circulations

ABP — American Business Press; Associated Business Publications

ABWA — American Business Women's Association

ac — alternating current

ACAS — Advisory, Conciliation and Arbitration Service; Associate of the Casualty Actuarial Society

ACB — Advertising Checking Bureau

ACI — American Concrete Institute

ACME — Association of Consulting Management Engineers

ACPA — Association of Computer Programmers and Analysts

ACPI — American City Planning Institute

ad — advertisement

AD — art director; assistant director; associate director

ADB — Asian Development Bank

AD Council — Advertising Council

AD & D — Accidental Death and Dismemberment

ADI — Area of Dominant Influence

ADP — automatic data processing

AEC — Atomic Energy Commission

AFA — Advertising Federation of America

AFDC — Aid to Families with Dependent Children

AFIPS — American Federation of Information Processing Societies

AFL — American Federation of Labor

AFL-CIO — American Federation of Labor and Congress of Industrial Organizations

AFM — American Federation of Musicians

AFTRA — American Federation of Television and Radio Artists

A&H — accident and health

AHA — American Hospital Association

AIA — American Institute of Architects; American Insurance Association; Association of Industrial Advertisers

AID — Agency for International Development

AIDS — American Institute for Decision Sciences

AIM — American Institute of Management

AIMC — Association of Internal Management Consultants

AIP — American Institute of Planners

AIREA — American Institute of Real Estate Appraisers

ALC — American Life Convention

ALGOL — ALGOrithmic Language

all caps — all capital letters

alphanumeric — alphabetic-numeric

ALU — arithmetic and logic unit

AM — amplitude modulation

AMA — American Management Association; American Marketing Association

AMS — Administrative Management Society

AMSO — Association of Market Survey Organizations

ANA — Association of National Advertisers

ANL — above-normal loss

ANPA — American Newspaper Publishers Association

ANSI — American National Standards Institute
A/P — accounts payable
APA — Agricultural Publishers Association
APGA — American Personnel and Guidance Association
APICS — American Production and Inventory Control Society, Inc.
APS — American Purchasing Society
APTD — Aid to the Permanently and Totally Disabled
apx — average page exposure
A/R — accounts receivable
ARB — American Research Bureau
ARC — Acquisition Review Council
ARF — Advertising Research Foundation
ARIA — American Risk and Insurance Association
ARS — Agricultural Research Service
A&S — accident and sickness
ASA — Associate of the Society of Actuaries
ASCAP — American Society of Composers, Authors, and Publishers
ASCE — American Society of Civil Engineers
ASCE MEP — American Society of Civil Engineers Manuals of Engineering Practice
ASCII — American Standard Code for Information Interchange
ASIE — American Society of International Executives
ASIS — American Society for Information Science
ASM — average sample number
ASPA — American Society for Personnel Administration
ASPO — American Society of Planning Officials
ASQC — American Society for Quality Control
ASR — automatic send-receive set
ASREC — American Society of Real Estate Counselors
ASTD — American Society for Training and Development
ASTM — American Society for Testing and Materials
ASTMS — Association of Scientific, Technical and Managerial Staffs

ATA — American Transit Association
a.v. — ad valorem
av. — average
avail — availability
AWE — Association of Women Executives

B

BA — Business Administration
BAI — Bank Administration Institute
balop — balopticon
b and w — black and white
BASIC — Beginner's All-purpose Symbolic Instruction Code
BBA — Bachelor of Business Administration
BBB — Better Business Bureau
BBC — British Broadcasting Corporation
BBM — Bachelor of Business Management
BCD — binary coded decimal
BEA — Bureau of Economic Analysis
BEC — Bureau of Employees' Compensation
BES — Bureau of Employment Security
bf — boldface
BHI — Bureau of Health Insurance
bhp — brake horsepower
BI — bodily injury liability; business interruption insurance
BIAC — Business and Industry Advisory Committee
BIS — Bank for International Settlements
BIT — binary digit
BL — bill of lading
BLS — Bureau of Labor Statistics
BMA — Board of Mediation and Arbitration
BMI — Broadcast Music, Inc.
BOD — bio-chemical oxygen demand
bold — boldface
BOMA — Building Owners and Managers Association
BPA — Business Publications Audit of Circulation, Inc.
BS — British Standard
BSCP — British Standard Code of Practice
BSI — British Standards Institution
BSS — British Standard Specification
BTU — British Thermal Unit
b & w — black and white
BWG — Birmingham wire gauge

C

CA — cost account
CAB — Civil Aeronautics Board
CAC — Central Arbitration Committee
CAI — computer-assisted instruction
CAM — computer-aided management
candid — candid photograph
CAO — Chief Administrative Office(r)
cap rate — capitalization rate
caps — capital letters
CAS — Casualty Actuarial Society
CASA — computer-assisted statistical analysis
CATV — Community Antenna Television
CB, C/B — cost/benefit
CBA — Canadian Bankers' Association
CBC — Canadian Broadcasting Corporation
CBIS — computer-based information system
CBR — California bearing ratio
CBS — Columbia Broadcasting System;
  concrete, block, and stucco
CC — cost control
cc — cubic centimeter
CCAB — Canadian Circulation Audit Bureau
CCC — Commodity Credit Corporation
CD — certificate of deposit; cost differential
CDB — central data bank
CE — cost-effectiveness
CEA — Commodity Exchange Authority;
  Council of Economic Advisers
CED — Committee for Economic
  Development
CEI — cost efficiency index
CEP — continuing education program
cf — compare
CF — cost factor
CFY — current fiscal year
CGL — comprehensive general liability
CHIP — comprehensive health insurance plan
CHR — Commission on Human Resources
CICA — Canadian Institute of Chartered
  Accountants
CIET 1961 — Commissioners' Industrial
  Extended Term Mortality Table, 1961
CIM — Canadian Institute of Management
CIO — Congress of Industrial Organizations
CIS — Congressional Information Service
CISTI — Canadian Institute for Scientific and
  Technical Information

CL — carload
CLU — Chartered Life Underwriter
cm — centimeter
CME — centrifuge moisture equivalent
CMEA — Council for Mutual Economic
  Assistance
CMN — Common Market Nations
CMS — Consumer and Marketing Service
CMX — computer editing
Co. — company
C.O. — certificate of occupancy
COB — coordination of benefits
COBOL — COmmon Business Oriented
  Language
COGP — Commission on Government
  Procurement
COL — cost of living
COM — computer output on microfilm
Comecon — Council for Mutual Economic
  Assistance
comp — comprehensive; complimentary
Comsat — Communications Satellite
  Corporation
co-op — cooperative; cooperative program
COP — career opportunities program
CORAL — a high-level language for real-
  time applications
CP — central procurement
CPA — certified public accountant
CPC — College Placement Council
CPCU — Chartered Property and Casualty
  Underwriter
cpi — characters per inch
CPI — consumer price index
CPM — critical path method; cards per
  minute; cost per thousand
CPS — characters-per-second; cycles-per-
  second
CPSA — Consumer Product Safety Act
CPU — central processing unit
CR — conditioned response
CREF — College Retirement Equities Fund
CRS — Congressional Research Service
CRT — cathode ray tube
CRV — certificate of reasonable value
C/S — cost of sale
CSA — cross-sectional area
CSI 1961 — Commissioners' Standard
  Industrial Mortality Table, 1961

CSIR — Council for Scientific and Industrial Research
CSO — Commissioners' Standard Ordinary
CSPA — Council of Sales Promotion Agencies
CTS — communications technology satellite
CU — close-up
cu. ft. — cubic foot
cu. m or **m³** — cubic meter
cume — cumulative audience
CUNA — Credit Union National Association
cu. yd. or **yd³** — cubic yard
CV — cost variance
CW — calendar week

D

DA — deposit administration
DAC — data analysis computer
D&B — Dun and Bradstreet
DB — delayed broadcast
DBA — Doctor of Business Administration; doing business as usual
DBL — disability benefits law
DBM — data base management
DC — direct current
DC amplifier — directly coupled amplifier; direct current amplifier
DCF — discounted cash flow
DDA — digital differential analyzer
DDD — dishonesty, disappearance and destruction policy
DDL — data description language
demo — demonstration; demonstration recording
DES — data entry system
DFG — diode function generator
DGA — Directors Guild of America
dia. — diameter
DIC — difference in conditions
DIN — Deutsche Industrie Normal
DMA Rating — Designated Market Area Rating
DMAA — Direct Mail Advertising Association
DMMA — Direct Mail Marketing Association
DOC — drive-other-car endorsement
dock stamps — documentary stamps
DOD — Department of Defense; direct outward dialing

DOT — Department of Transportation
DP — data processing
dress — dress rehearsal
DUA — disaster unemployment assistance
dupe — duplicate
DWL — desired work load

E

E — modulus of elasticity
EAC — estimated cost at completion
EAM — electrical accounting machines
EBIT — earnings before interest and taxes
EBR — electron beam recording
ECCS — European Community for Coal and Steel
ECE — extended coverage endorsement
ECU — extreme close-up
ED — experimental design
EDA — Economic Development Administration
EDM — electronic distance measurement
EDP — electronic data processing
EDPM — electronic data processing machine
EDS — exchangeable disk store
EEC — European Economic Community
EEO — equal employment opportunity
EFTA — European Free Trade Association
EHI — employee health insurance
EIB — Export-Import Bank of United States
8 mm — 8 millimeter film
EL — expected loss
EMA — European Management Association
emcee — master of ceremonies
ENG — expected net gain
EOA — Economic Opportunity Act of 1964
EOF — end of file
EOR — end of run
EP — expected payoff
EPA — Environmental Protection Agency
EPS — earnings per share
ERA — Equal Rights Amendment
ERB — Executive Resources Board
ERISA — Employee Retirement Income Security Act
ESOP — Employee Stock Ownership Plan
Esq. — Esquire
ESSA — Environmental Science Services Administration
ET — electrical transcription

et ux — et uxor (and wife)
EURATOM — European Atomic Energy
Community
EV — expected value

F

FAA — Federal Aviation Agency
FAC — Federal Advisory Council
FAF — Financial Analysts Federation
FAIR — fair access to insurance requirements
Fannie Mae — Federal National Mortgage
Association
FAO — Food and Agriculture Organization of
the United Nations
f.a.s. — free alongside ship
fax — complete studio facilities for TV
rehearsal
FBP — Federal Bonding Program
FC — fixed cost
FCA — Farm Credit Administration
FCAS — Fellow of the Casualty Actuarial
Society
FCC — Federal Communications Commission
FCIC — Federal Crop Insurance Corporation
FCII — Fellow of the Chartered Insurance
Institute
FCRC — Federal Contract Research Center
FC&S — free-of-capture-and-seizure
FC&S Bulletins — Fire, Casualty, and
Surety Bulletins
FDA — Food and Drug Administration
FDIC — Federal Deposit Insurance
Corporation
Fed. — Federal Reserve System
FEGLI — Federal Employees Group Life
Insurance
FEI — Financial Executives Institute
FFP — firm fixed price
FHA — Farmers Home Administration;
Federal Housing Administration
FHLBB — Federal Home Loan Bank Board
FIA — Factory Insurance Association
FICA — Federal Insurance Contributions Act
FJIC — Federal Job Information Center
FLMI — Fellow of the Life Management
Institute
FM — frequency modulation
FMA — Financial Management Association
FMC — Federal Maritime Commission

FMCS — Federal Mediation and Conciliation
Service
FNMA — Federal National Mortgage
Association
FOB — free on board
FORTRAN — formula translating system
4A's — American Association of Advertising
Agencies
FP — fixed price
FPA — free of particular average
FPC — Federal Power Commission
fpm — feet per minute
FPR — Federal Procurement Regulations
FRS — Federal Reserve System
FS — feasibility study
FSA — Fellow of the Society of Actuaries
FSLIC — Federal Savings and Loan
Insurance Corporation
ft — foot or feet
FTC — Federal Trade Commission
FUA — Federal Unemployment Account
FUBA — Federal Unemployment Benefit
Allowance
FY — fiscal year

G

g — gram or gravity
GA — general agent
GAAP — generally accepted accounting
principles
GAB — General Adjustment Bureau, Inc.
GAMC — General Agents and Managers
Conference
GAO — General Accounting Office
GATT — General Agreement on Tariffs and
Trade
GAW — guaranteed annual wage
GBL — government bill of lading
GI — government issue
GI insurance — United States Government
Life Insurance
gigo — garbage in, garbage out
Ginnie Mae — Government National
Mortgage Association
GM — general management
GMA — gas metal-arc
GNMA — Government National Mortgage
Association
GNP — gross national product

GO — general obligation
GPD — general purpose data
gpm — gallons per minute
GPO — Government Printing Office
GRA — Governmental Research Association
GRC — glassfiber reinforced concrete
GSA — General Services Administration
GTA — gas tungsten arc
GUTS — guaranteed ultimate tensile strength

H

HE — human engineering
head — headline
HEW — Department of Health, Education and Welfare
HF — human factor
HFMA — Hospital Financial Management Association
HFS — Human Factors Society
HHFA — Housing and Home Finance Agency
HI — health insurance
HIAA — Health Insurance Association of America
hi-fi — high fidelity
HII — Health Insurance Institute
HIQA — Health Insurance Quality Award
HMO — Health Maintenance Organization
HPR — highly protected risk
HRA — Health Resources Administration
HR-10 Plan — Keogh Act Plan
HSA — Health Services Administration
HUD — Department of Housing and Urban Development
HUR — homes using radio
HUT — households using television

I

I — moment of inertia
IAAO — International Association of Assessing Officials
IABP — International Association of Businessmen and Professionals
IAEA — International Atomic Energy Agency
IAL — International Algebraic Language

IAM — Institute of Administrative Management
IAMD — International Association of Managing Directors
IASA — Insurance Accounting Statistical Association
IASS — Insurance Accounting and Statistical Society
IATSE — International Association of Theater and Stage Employees
IBE — information-based evaluation
IBNR — incurred but not reported
IBRD — International Bank for Reconstruction and Development
IC — inventory control
ICA — International Claim Association
ICAO — International Civil Aviation Organization
ICC — Interstate Commerce Commission
ICE — independent cost estimate
ICEDS — Insurance Company Education Directors Society
ICFTU — International Confederation of Free Trade Unions
ICIE — International Council of Industrial Editors
ICJ — International Court of Justice
ICPI — Insurance Crime Prevention Institute
ICPP — Institute of Certified Professional Planners
ICS — inventory control system
ID — identification spot
IDA — International Development Association
IDB — Inter-American Development Bank
IDDC — International Development Data Center
IDI — idea development interview
IDP — integrated data processing
IE — independent evaluation
IFB — invitation for bids
IFC — International Finance Corporation
IFIP — International Federation for Information Processing
IHOU — Institute of Home Office Underwriters
IIA — Insurance Institute of America, Inc.
IIAA — Independent Insurance Agents of America

IIC — Independent Insurance Conference; Insurance Institute of Canada
III — Insurance Information Institute
IIS — International Insurance Seminars, Inc.
IJO — individual job order
ILGA — Institute of Local Government Administrators
ILO — International Labor Organization
IMC — Institute of Management Consultants
IMF — International Monetary Fund
IMI — Industrial Management Institute
IMIS — integrated management information system
IMM — Institute of Marketing Management
IMRA — Industrial Management Research Association
IMS — Industrial Management Society
in. — inch
Inc. — Incorporated
inch — column inch
in sync — in synchronization
Intelsat — International Telecommunications Satellite Consortium
I/O — input/output
IOA — Institute of Outdoor Advertising
IOB — The Institute of Bankers
IP — immediately preemptible
IPMA — International Personnel Management Association
IPOT — inductive potential divider
IPR — Institute of Public Relations
IPS — inches per second
IRA — Individual Retirement Accounts
IR & D — independent research and development
IREM — Institute of Real Estate Management
IRS — Internal Revenue Service
ISAM — index sequential access method
ISM — Institute of Supervisory Management
ISO — Insurance Services Office
IS & R — information storage and retrieval system
ITU — International Telecommunications Union
IWP — International Word Processing Association
IWW — Industrial Workers of the World

J

J — joule
JA — job analysis
JCL — job control language
JON — job order number
JUA — Joint Underwriting Association

K

k — kilo
KCS — a thousand characters per second
kg — kilogram
kine — kinescope
kJ — kilojoule
km — kilometer
kN — kilonewton
kN/m² — kilonewtons per square meter
KP — key personnel
kph — kilometers per hour
kWh — kilowatt hour

L

L and M — layout and manuscript
lb — pound
lc — lowercase
LCL — less than carload
LECA — light expanded clay aggregate
lf — lightface
LIAA — Life Insurance Association of America
LIAMA — Life Insurance Agency Management Association
LIFO — last in, first out
LIMRA — Life Insurance Marketing and Research Association
line — agate line
lip sync — lip synchronization
L & M — layout and manuscript
LMC — Labor-Management Committee
LMSA — Labor-Management Services Administration
logo — logotype
LOMA — Life Office Management Association

LP — linear programming
LPM — lines per minute
LPRT — Leading Producers Round Table
L.S. — Locus Sigilli
LS — long shot
LTD. — Limited
LTM — long-term memory
lucy — camera lucida
LUPAC — Life Underwriting Political Action Committee
LUTC — Life Underwriting Training Council

M

m — meter
M — thousand
m³ — cubic meter
MA — Manpower Administration; Maritime Administration
MAB — Magazine Advertising Bureau
MAC — Management Audit Committee; multi-access computing
M&C — meet and confer
MAD — mean absolute deviation
mag — magazine; magnetic; magtrack
MAG welding — metallic active-gas welding
MAI — Member Appraisal Institute
mat — matrix
matt — mat
matte — mat
MBA — Master in Business Administration
MC — master of ceremonies
MCA — Management Consultants Association
MCEI — Marketing Communications Executives International
MCS — maintenance cost system
MCU — medium close-up
MD — mean deviation
MDB — management data base
MDO — monthly debit ordinary
MDRT — Million Dollar Round Table
MDTA — Manpower Development and Training Act
MET — management engineering team
MF — machine-finish paper
mg — milligram
Mgr. — manager
MIB — Medical Impairment Bureau

MIC — Management Information Center
MICR — magnetic ink character recognition
MICS — Management Information and Control System
MIG welding — metallic-electrode inert-gas welding
MIT — master instruction tape
MLIRB — Multi-Line Insurance Rating Bureau
MM — marketing management
mm — millimeter
MMA welding — manual metal-arc welding
MN/m² — meganewtons per square meter
MO — mail order; money order
modem — modulator/demodulator
mPa — megapascal
MPA — Magazine Publishers Association
MPAA — Motion Picture Association of America
MPIC — Multiple Peril Insurance Conference
MPS — Manpower Placement Service
mr — motivational research
MS — marketing survey; medium shot; motivation survey
mss — manuscript
MTA — motion time analysis
MTBF — mean time between failures
MTTR — mean time to repair
Mutual — Mutual Broadcasting System
MVR's — Motor Vehicle Records
MW — man-week

N

NAA — National Association of Accountants
NAB — National Association of Broadcasters
NAD — National Advertising Division
NAEA — Newspaper Advertising Executives Association
NAIA — National Association of Insurance Agents, Inc.
NAIB — National Association of Insurance Brokers, Inc.
NAIC — National Association of Insurance Commissioners
NAII — National Association of Independent Insurers
NAIW — National Association of Insurance Women

NALC — National Association of Life Companies

NALU — National Association of Life Underwriters

NAM — National Association of Manufacturers

NAMIC — National Association of Mutual Insurance Companies

NAPIA — National Association of Professional Insurance Agents

NAR — National Association of Realtors

NARB — National Advertising Review Board

NAREB — National Association of Real Estate Brokers

NASA — National Aeronautics and Space Administration

NASD — National Association of Securities Dealers

NASPO — National Association of State Purchasing Officials

NATA — National Association of Transportation Advertising

NBC — National Broadcasting Company

NBEA — National Business Education Association

NBP — National Business Publications

NBS — National Bureau of Standards

NBV — net book value

NDT — non-destructive testing

NELIA — Nuclear Energy Liability Insurance Association

NEPIA — Nuclear Energy Property Insurance Association

NFIA — National Flood Insurers Association

NFPA — National Fire Protection Association

NG — no good

NI — net income

NIAA — National Industrial Advertisers Association

NIFLB — National Institute of Farm and Land Brokers

NIH — National Institutes of Health

NIMC — National Institute of Management Counselors

NIREB — National Institute of Real Estate Brokers

NLRB — National Labor Relations Board

NMB — National Mediation Board

NNPA — National Newspaper Promotion Association

NOAB — National Outdoor Advertising Bureau

NOC — not otherwise classified

NOI — net operating income

NORC — National Opinion Research Center

NPD — no payroll division

NPV — net present value

NR — net revenue

NRMA — National Retail Merchants Association

NSC — National Security Council

NSF — National Science Foundation

NSFA — National Society of Fee Appraisers

NSI — Nielsen Station Index

NSLI — National Service Life Insurance

NTI — Nielsen Television Index

NWC — net working capital

O

OAA — Old Age Assistance

OAAA — Outdoor Advertising Association of America, Inc.

OAI — Outdoor Advertising, Inc.

O and M — organization and methods

O and O station — owned and operated station

OAS — Organization of American States

OASDHI — Old Age, Survivors, Disability, and Health Insurance

OBM — Ordnance Bench Mark

OCR — optical character recognition

OD — Ordnance Datum

OECD — Organization for Economic Cooperation and Development

OEEC — Organization for European Economic Cooperation

OEEO & C — Office of Equal Employment Opportunity and Compliance

OEO — Office of Economic Opportunity

OEP — Office of Emergency Planning

OJE — on-the-job experience

OL&T — Owners, Landlords, and Tenants Liability Insurance

OLRT — on-line real time

O.L.&T. — owner's, landlord's and tenant's public liability insurance

OMRD — Office of Manpower Research and Development

O & O station — owned and operated station
op code — operation code
OR — operational research
OS — Ordnance Survey
OSHA — Occupational Safety and Health Act
OT — operating time
OTC — over-the-counter
OTO — one-time-only
OUO — official use only

P

p — page
Pa — pascal
PA — performance analysis
P and W — Pension and Welfare
PCM — punched card machine;
  pulse code modulation
PCV — petty cash voucher
PD — physical damage;
  public domain
PEI — Planning Executives Institute
PERT — Project Evaluation and Review
  Technique
PETN — pentaerythrite tetranitrate
PFA — pulverized fuel ash
PHS — Public Health Service
P&I — Protection and Indemnity Insurance
pi — per inquiry
PI — performance index
PIA — Professional Insurance Agents
PIB — Publishers Information Bureau
pic — picture
PIP — personal injury protection
PITI — principal, interest, taxes and
  insurance
pix — pictures
PL/1 — Programming Language 1
PM — evening paper; preventive maintenance
PML — probable maximum loss
PMM — purchase money mortgage
P.O. — post office
P.O.B. — post office box
POP — point of purchase
POPAI — Point-of-Purchase Advertising
  Institute
postsync — postsynchronize
pp — pages

P&P — procurement and production
PPA — Periodical Publishers Association
PR — performance report; public relations;
  public relations and publicity
PRF — pulse repetition frequency
PROMO — promotional announcement
prop — property
PRR — pulse repetition rate
PRSA — Public Relations Society of America
PS — performance schedule; prime sponsor;
  public service
psi — pounds per square inch
pt — point
PUAA — Public Utilities Advertising
  Association
PUD — planned unit development
Pulse — The Pulse, Inc.
P & W — Pension and Welfare

Q

QC — quality control
QT — qualification test

R

 — registered trademark
RA — random access; regional
  administration; reliability analysis
RAB — Radio Advertising Bureau
RAMPS — resource allocation in
  multi-project scheduling
REA — Rural Electrification Administration
REIT — real estate investment trust
repro — reproduction proof
repro proof — reproduction proof
RESPA — Real Estate Settlement and
  Procedures Act
RFC — Reconstruction Finance Corporation
RFQ — request for quotation
RHU — registered health underwriter
RJE — remote job entry
RO — reverse osmosis
ROA — return on assets
ROE — return on equity
ROP color — run-of-paper color
ROP position — run-of-paper position

ROS — run of schedule; run-of-station
roto — rotogravure
roto comp — rotogravure comprehensive
RP — rear projection; repurchase agreement
RPB — river purification board
RPM — revolutions per minute
RRB — Railroad Retirement Board
RRT — randomized response technique
R & S — research and statistics
RSJ — rolled-steel joist
RT — reaction time; real time
RTDG — Radio and Television Directors Guild

S

SA — Society of Actuaries; supplemental agreement
SAA — Specialty Advertising Association; Surety Association of America
SAG — Screen Actors Guild
SALT — Society for Applied Learning Technology
SAP — statutory accounting principles
SBA — Small Business Administration
sc — small caps
sc. — scilicet
SC — selling cost; single column
SCS — Soil Conservation Service
SCUBA — self-contained underwater breathing apparatus
SDG — Screen Directors Guild
SDR's — special drawing rights
sec. — second
SEC — Securities and Exchange Commission
SEG — Screen Extras Guild
SEGLI — service employees group life insurance
SET — science, engineering and technology
SEUA — Southeastern Underwriters Association
SFX — sound effects
SGA — Screen Actors Guild; Society of Governmental Appraisers
SGSR — Society for General Systems Research
share — share of audience

SIC — Standard Industrial Classification
SID — Society for International Development
SIR — self-insurance retention; Society of Industrial Realtors
SIU — sets in use
16 mm — 16-millimeter film
60 — 60-second commercial
SMA — shielded metal-arc
small caps — small capitals
SMIS — Society for Management Information Systems
SMP — special multi-peril
SMS — state mediation service
SMSA — Standard Metropolitan Statistical Area
SN curve — stress-number curve
SO — service order
SOF — sound-on-film
SOP — standard operating procedure
SP — selling price; standard procedure
space rep — space representative
SPEA — Sales Promotion Executives Association
spec — speculation
SPEC — Systems and Procedures Exchange Center
specs — specifications
spec type — to specify faces and sizes of type
SPMC — Society of Professional Management Consultants
SPT — shortest processing time
SR — systems research
SRA — Senior Residential Appraiser; Station Representatives Association
SR & DS — Standard Rate & Data Service, Inc.
SREA — Senior Real Estate Analyst; Society of Real Estate Appraisers
SRI — Systems Research Institute
SS — same size
SSA — Social Security Administration
SSIE — Smithsonian Science Information Exchange
S & T — science and technology
STAIRS — storage and information retrieval system
stat — photostat
station rep — station representative

stereo — sterotype; stereophonic
stet — leave as originally was; disregard the attempted changes or revisions
STF — special task force
strobe — stroboscope
super — superimposition; super slide
SWG — Screen Writers Guild; Standard Wire Gauge
sync — synchronize

T

t — time
TA — technical analysis; technical assistance; total
TAA — Transit Advertising Association
TAB — Traffic Audit Bureau
TBA — to be announced; Television Bureau of Advertising, Inc.
TC — total cost
TCRB — Television Code Review Board
TD — technical data
TDA — tax deferred annuity
TDB — temporary disability benefits
TDC — total development cost
TDI — temporary disability insurance
TEI — Tax Executives Institute
TF — till forbidden; to fill; to follow
TGI — Target Group Index
35 mm — 35-millimeter film
TIG welding — tungsten-electrode inert-gas shielded-arc welding
TIRB — Transportation Insurance Rating Bureau
TLU — table look-up
TNT — trinitrotoluene
topo — topography
TP — transaction processing
TPM — total program management
TQC — technical quality control
tr. — transpose type as indicated
TS — timesharing
TSA — tax sheltered annuity
TVA — Tennessee Valley Authority
TVR — television recording
20 — 20-second commercial
TWX — teletypewriter exchange
typo — typographical error

U

UAB — Underwriters Adjustment Bureau
UAC — Underwriters Adjusting Company
UC — unemployment compensation
uc — uppercase
UCA — uniform cost accounting
UCC — Uniform Commercial Code
UCDI — Unemployment Compensation Disability Insurance
UEP — unfair employment practices
UHF — ultra high frequency
UI — unemployment insurance
UJF — unsatisfied judgment fund
UL — Underwriters Laboratories, Inc.
ULI — Urban Land Institute
ULP — unfair labor practices
UN — United Nations
UNCTAD — United Nations Conference on Trade and Development
UNESCO — United Nations Educational, Scientific and Cultural Organization
UNIVAC — universal automatic computer
UNRRA — United Nations Relief and Rehabilitation Administration
U & O — use and occupancy insurance
UP — upgrade training (program)
UPU — Universal Postal Union
USAIG — United States Aircraft Insurance Group
USC — United States code
USES — United States Employment Service
USGLI — United States Government Life Insurance
USTC — United States Tariff Commission

V

VA — Veterans Administration
VAC — Verified Audit Circulation Corporation
VAT — value added tax
VDU — visual display unit
vel — velocity in an air elutriator
VHF — very high frequency
VHMCP — Voluntary Home Mortgage Credit Program

VIP — Video Instruction Program
VISTA — Volunteers in Service to America
V&MM — vandalism and malicious mischief
VOC — voice-over-credits
vs — versus
VTR — videotape recording
V & V — verification and validation

W

WBC — World Business Council
WC — Workers' Compensation
wf —wrong font
WFEO — World Federation of Engineering
   Organizations
WFTU — World Federation of Trade Unions
WHO — World Health Organization
WIN — Work Incentive Program
WIP — work-in-process
WL — workload

WLRT — Women Leaders Round Table
WM — working model
WO — work order

X

X — arithmetic mean
XCU — explosion, collapse and underground
   damage

Y

YRT — yearly renewable term

Z

Z — modulus of section
ZBB — zero base budgeting